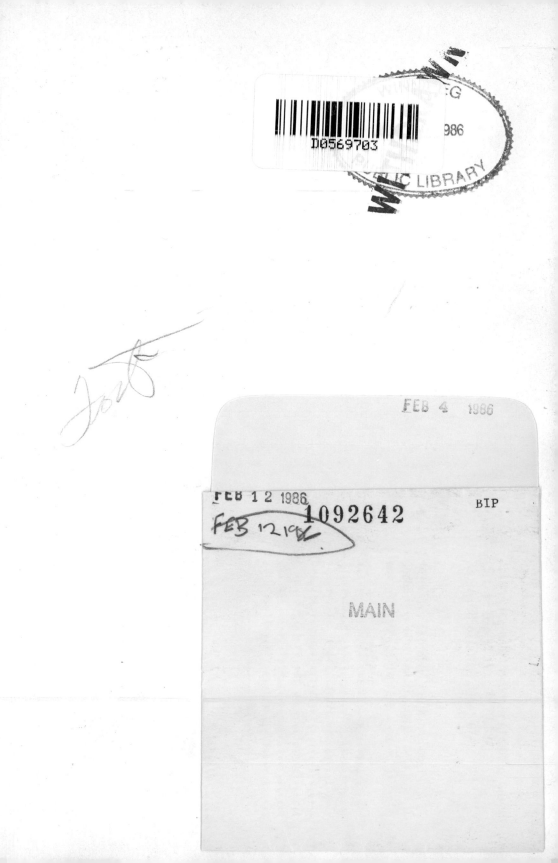

# ANTARCTICA
## AND THE
## ─SOUTH─
## ATLANTIC
Discovery, Development and Dispute

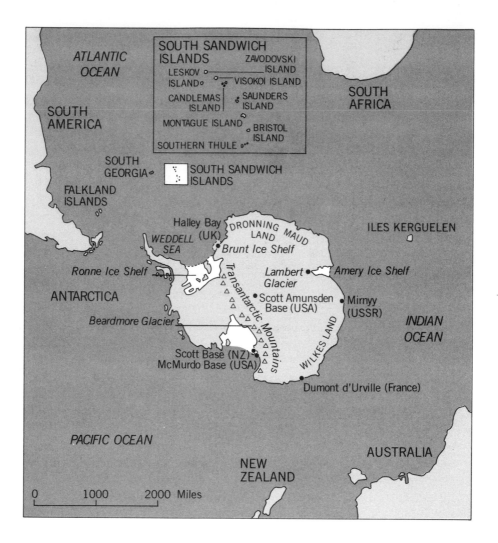

ATLANTIC
OCEAN

SOUTH SANDWICH
ISLANDS
LESKOV ○                    ZAVODOVSKI
ISLAND○        ○⊙          ISLAND
                VISOKOI ISLAND
CANDLEMAS     ⊙ SAUNDERS
ISLAND          ISLAND
MONTAGUE ISLAND
                ○ BRISTOL
                  ISLAND
SOUTHERN THULE ○•

SOUTH
AFRICA

SOUTH
AMERICA

SOUTH
GEORGIA ○      SOUTH SANDWICH
                ISLANDS
FALKLAND
ISLANDS

Halley Bay
WEDDELL (UK)      DRONNING MAUD
SEA              LAND        ILES KERGUELEN
                Brunt Ice Shelf

Ronne Ice Shelf        Lambert •  Amery Ice Shelf
                      Glacier

ANTARCTICA            • Scott Amundsen   • Mirnyy
                       Base (USA)         (USSR)

Beardmore Glacier                              INDIAN
                                               OCEAN

                    Scott Base (NZ)
                    McMurdo Base (USA)

                              Dumont d'Urville (France)

PACIFIC OCEAN

                                        AUSTRALIA

                NEW
                ZEALAND

0    1000    2000  Miles

# ANTARCTICA
## AND THE
# – SOUTH –
# ATLANTIC
## Discovery, Development and Dispute

# Robert Fox

BRITISH BROADCASTING CORPORATION

Published by
the British Broadcasting Corporation
35 Marylebone High Street,
London W1M 4AA

First published 1985

ISBN 0 563 20332 3

© Robert Fox 1985

Typeset by Phoenix Photosetting, Chatham
Printed and bound by Mackays of Chatham Ltd

# Contents

To
The Tradition of Captain James Cook, RN (1728–79)
and
The Memory of George Fox (1911–83).

# Introduction

I first set foot on the Falklands on 21 May 1982 when British troops went ashore to retake the Islands. I returned in December that year. Getting off the plane at RAF Stanley I was surprised at the hint of spring in the air. The mountains to the west seemed very close in the clear evening sky; it was hard to believe it had taken a day's slow march through sleet and slush to reach Stanley from Mount Kent, Longdon and Two Sisters.

In Stanley and the settlements preparations were being made for Christmas, a time to forget about the bloodshed earlier in the year – the worst to touch the Islands since their discovery by Elizabethan sailors four centuries ago – and fears for the future. In December 1982 it was hard to predict the future of the Falklands community, and it is still equally so. In that month three reports and government policy statements were presented to Parliament at Westminster, the least important being the long-winded Defence Committee Report on censorship and press coverage in the campaign. Provisions for the further defence of the Islands were announced: new ships, second-hand Phantom aircraft from America, missiles and equipment for ground troops. Most significant for the Islanders themselves was the announcement by Mr Francis Pym, the Foreign Secretary, that £31 million would be spent on developing the local economy broadly on the lines recommended by Lord Shackleton's *Economic Study* produced earlier in the year. In January 1983 Lord Franks' Committee issued its report on the background to the conflict, a document frustratingly silent on crucial aspects of British South Atlantic policy in the recent past and intelligence appreciations of the intentions of successive regimes in Argentina.

At the end of 1982 I was curious to know exactly where the Falklands story fitted in the wider context of international relations in the South Atlantic. I wanted to clarify or allay the suspicion that there was something more – something very interesting beyond the Falklands themselves, which bore on their destiny.

Almost two years after the campaign I was given the opportunity to climb to the next ridge, as it were, and take a wider look at the South Atlantic. Colin MacGregor, the Captain of HMS *Endurance*, invited me to join his ice patrol ship for one of its work periods in Antarctic waters in early 1984. My employers at BBC Radio News agreed that I could be released for up to six weeks to make radio programmes and reports, and I am grateful to my superiors Larry Hodgson, Bob Kearsley, John Wilson and Alan Protheroe for their support in that enterprise and the production of this book.

In January 1984 I received a letter from Captain MacGregor outlining the programme for the following March and suggesting suitable clothing. He recommended an anorak, woolly hat, polaroid sunglasses and, in an immortal paragraph, suitable evening wear: 'Provided the steam heating keeps going it's always warm inside the ship. In the evenings, the Officers who are not on watch change into "Red Sea rig" [short-sleeved uniform shirt, black trousers, cummerbund]. Our visitors' dress on these occasions depends on personal preference and the extent of their wardrobe! Some wear DJ trousers, evening shirt and cummerbund, others shirt and tie without a jacket. Throughout the time you are with us we will have the JSE [Joint Services Expedition] on board whose evening dress will be hair shirts and the expedition tie! On balance, I think it's probably worth your bringing an evening shirt, cummerbund, etc, with you, for a "Saturday Night at Sea" dinner.' Then in the Captain's handwriting were added the words, 'if the opportunity occurs!'

It was good to learn that the Navy believed in maintaining the highest standards of social dress still, and the generous deployment of exclamation marks. There was to be no 'Saturday Night at Sea', but many other opportunities did arise which I could not have hoped to have experienced otherwise. My thanks go to Colin MacGregor and his ship's company for their help and hospitality, particularly to the helicopter crews and Terry Harding for his assistance in photography. I must also thank Graham Thom of GK Photographic, London and Edgware, and C–Z Scientific for their generous provision of lenses and a wonderful array of filters.

*Endurance* departed Port Stanley on 11 March 1984 for South Georgia, following for part of the way the course of Captain Cook's second southern voyage of discovery in early 1775, possibly the greatest voyage of navigation and discovery in history. First landfall was Bird Island off the north-west of South Georgia, the ship visiting Grytviken later that day and Leith the day after. The next morning the helicopters took us to the king penguin colony at St Andrew's Bay and Royal Bay.

Departing South Georgia the ship sailed through the South Sandwich Islands with a short stop to check the wrecked Argentine base at Southern Thule. A few days later we visited the British Antarctic Survey Base at Signy Island in the South Orkneys and then sailed below latitude 60°S, the boundary of the Antarctic Treaty area. The next task was to finish off some survey work in the Orleans Strait off the Antarctic Peninsula, breaking off to land members of the winter team of the Joint Services Expedition on Brabant Island, 100 miles to the south, and transport back to Stanley the summer team. The survey work off Antarctica was rudely interrupted when *Endurance* grounded on a pinnacle of rock jutting up to within eleven feet of the surface. This necessitated a dash back to the Falklands for a survey of the damage, though we did have time to pay a call

8

on Deception Island in the South Shetlands; the sunken volcano was the most impressive piece of landscape I saw in the whole journey.

My experiences in the South Atlantic and Antarctica triggered a spate of reading on the history and future of the area, once I had returned to England. I must thank members of the British Antarctic Survey (BAS) for all their help in getting to grips with this fascinating and exotic subject, particularly Dr Richard Laws, the Director Dr Ray Adie, his deputy, the department heads, base commanders Dave Rootes and Peter Prince, and Dr Julian Paren. I am particularly grateful to Eleanor Honnywill, the long-time assistant to Sir Vivian Fuchs, for her suggestions on further reading and for her own book, the best introduction to the subject in print in this country. I must also thank Adam Raphael for the care and thought he gave to the two programmes we made for BBC Radio which helped clarify some of the argument in this book.

The thesis of the programmes on BBC Radio in May 1984 was that since the conflict of April–June 1982 British policy, or that of Mrs Thatcher's administration, on Antarctica, islands like South Georgia and the Falklands themselves has become linked. This can be seen in the extension of HMS *Endurance*'s service in the South Atlantic, extra funds for BAS, and policy to regenerate the Falklands' economy. If one part of the Antarctic–South Atlantic policy fails the others are put at risk. Since 1945 Argentina has made one package of her claims in Antarctica, the islands and the Falklands/Malvinas, and this has been reiterated by President Alfonsin in 1984 on visits to Europe and the UN. Territorial claims in Antarctica are set aside, but not cancelled, by the Antarctic Treaty of 1961 which has encouraged the peaceful use of the Antarctic with co-operation in scientific programmes between some thirty member nations. Over the next few years Antarctica is likely to achieve ever greater scientific, strategic and commercial significance. It is feared that the demand for the exploitation of mineral, hydrocarbon and biological resources could strain the Treaty to a point where it breaks or declines into insignificance. If this should occur, the territorial claims become active again, and Anglo-Argentine relations could take another violent and un-predictable twist.

Returning to the Falklands from Antarctica I intended to stay for ten days to look at the development plans for the Islands. The stay was extended because on the morning I was due to leave, 10 April, the King Edward Memorial Hospital in Stanley burnt down, killing eight people, among them a mother and her week-old baby. I feel that the whole saga of the hospital – the spasmodic maintenance, strained relations between civilian and military medical teams, and the desultory pursuit of the declared policy in August 1982 to build a new hospital – illustrates important aspects of the way the Islands have been administered, so that I have devoted a chapter to the episode. By far the biggest chapter in Part II is devoted to development and land reform, on which the future viability of the Falklands community will depend.

The difficulty in writing books like this is not starting them but ending them. Since the main text was finished there have been important developments in the Falklands, and beyond them in the South Atlantic. In 1982 I wrote a short book, *Eyewitness Falklands*, which was my own account of the campaign and what it was like at the time. My perspective on those events is different now, with the gift of hindsight, though one suspects the official records and regimental histories will match the Apocrypha for their strange mixture of myth and fact. This book in some ways is a sequel, more detached perhaps, but still a work of the moment, journalism and not history.

Since August 1983, when the main text was completed, the news has been both good and bad, the mixture as before for the Falklands. After six months' wrangling in Whitehall, principally between the ODA and the Ministry of Defence, with one or two unhelpful comments from elsewhere, it has been decided to build a new military and civilian hospital in Stanley at a cost of £6.4 million, subject to approval from the Falklands government. So far no plans have been finalised for old people's accommodation. The other major development has been the completion of the sale of the San Carlos farm in seven separate parcels, after much debate between Colin Smith, the representative of half the vendor shareholders, the government, and one or two potential purchasers. In very short time the new Development Corporation has produced an effective advisory service and range of grants to the new farmers working their own land. Future housing and immigration prospects are vaguer, and the delays in opening the new wool mill at Fox Bay have been exacerbated by some of the machinery being dispatched from Britain to Pakistan by mistake. In all the development projects there still seem serious doubts about their lack of capital and the need to provide continuing investment for upkeep and improvement in the public sector. The £31 million allocated for improvements along the lines of the Shackleton Report are likely to prove inadequate to cover the five-year span of the project. Despite the fact that parties of MPs are beginning to visit the Islands, it seems there are still grounds for a public assessment by Westminster of the progress of development in the Islands, as the basic data on which Shackleton worked was gathered nearly ten years ago.

While the jury may still be out on the future viability of the internal economy of the Islands themselves, developments beyond the Falklands, and concerning them, have been more ominous. As I write, the counter-claims for their sovereignty are due to be debated once again at the UN, with the roles of Italy and France in the debate likely to prove crucial; there are fears that France may not abstain in the vote. In the latter part of this year, 1984, President Alfonsin's line on sovereignty over the Islands has become harder rather than softer, and one of his Interior Ministers has boasted that the Islands will be Argentine by 1989, the deadline for the next elections in Argentina. Both the Argentina Navy and Air Force have replaced losses sustained in 1982 and are better equipped than before.

The UN, too, is due to look at the special report on Antarctica called for in the 39th Session of the General Assembly, as demands grow from the Non-Aligned Movement to submit the Antarctic to international regulation along the lines of the Law of the Sea. The members of the Antarctic Treaty, including America and Russia, and the rival claimants Argentina, Chile and Britain, seem united as never before against this. Seismic and biological studies proceed apace in the polar region, heralding a new phase in its development, but something of the spirit of Scott and Amundsen persists there. An expedition has set out from *Discovery*'s berth in St Katharine's Dock, London, to trace the route Scott took to the Pole in 1911–12, man-hauling sledges up onto the Beardmore Glacier and across the Plateau, following Scott's precept that this was 'the most noble way' to travel. Why men do such things is one of the great mysteries of Antarctica, and one wonders at the scientific value of such an expedition today, though the members say they will study cold stress in themselves, and hope to raise public awareness of the importance of the Antarctic Treaty, all at a cost £720,000 to the sponsors of Roger Mear and Robert Swan and their fourteen-man team.

By the time Swan and Mear return from the Pole in 1985 the Falklands will have a brand-new constitution and a new eight-man elected council with both a legislative and executive role. The new constitution is due to be presented in the Islands by the end of 1984, and its ratification will automatically bring new elections. Many thought that there should have been elections following the conflict in 1982, as the prospects for the Islands had been changed so radically. Perhaps after the new elections someone else should take up the story and assess whether the community will survive beyond the end of the century.

For my part I would like to thank all the friends and advisers, public and private, who have helped in preparing the book; first those in the Islands, Rex and Mavis Hunt, the Bleaneys, the Chaters, the Bertrands, Eric Goss, Dave Hewitt, Bob and Janet MacLeod, the Forsters, Tim Miller, David Taylor and Alastair and Sukie Cameron at the FIG office in London. John Heap and Andrew Palmer at the Foreign Office have been particularly patient and helpful, so too have successive directors of Army

Public Relations, David Ramsbotham and Mike Hobbs. I would like to thank Major-General David Thorne for a singular kindness in allowing me to travel as observer in a small helicopter delivering mail to fourteen settlements in West Falkland in December 1982. We were entertained royally wherever we stopped and by the end of the day were awash with tea and had eaten our fill of home-made biscuits and cakes, the forte of Falklands cuisine. The views of thousands and millions of albatross, skua, caracara and turkey buzzard fighting the hard wind below the helicopter cockpit were quite breath-taking. As we turned for Stanley across Falkland Sound the isthmus of Darwin and Goose Green unfolded suddenly in the sunlight like a bolt of bright-green cloth as Mount Usborne reared up behind, the most indelible image of the Falklands landscape I possess.

After that visit I made a radio programme in December 1982 called 'The Falklands at Christmas', which prompted a letter from a listener, Mr R. A. Bishop, who farmed at Maldon in Essex. He said he had made rough calculations on the first Shackleton Report of 1976 which suggested that, if its proposals were implemented fully, the cost to the British taxpayer could be in the order of the development costs of the Concorde supersonic airliner. The idea helped trigger several years' work, and Mr Bishop has the dubious privilege of being one of the progenitors of the concluding part of this book.

The other source of inspiration for further investigation was my father, George Fox, who died in April 1983. He quit the City in the thirties to work as land agent and then tenant-farmer in Somerset. In thirty years on his own holding he worked himself to exhaustion with dairy and beef animals, and arable. As businessman and farmer he well understood how farmers on small units, like those he saw round him in Devon and Somerset, could scrape barely more than an existence from their land if their enterprises were undercapitalised and short of funds for improvement and expansion. He told me several times of his worry about grandiose plans for ploughing up and reseeding areas of marginal land such as that in the Falklands, and what misdirected agricultural development schemes there might involve both for the Islanders and the British and Falkland taxpayer. I hope he would have appreciated the manner if not the conclusions of this book.

Finally I must thank those who have helped prepare the pictures and text for publication, Naomi Klein, Philip Lord and Tony Kingsford of the BBC, and Gill Coleridge of Anthony Sheil. Most I have to thank Marianne, Alexander and Emily for their forbearance, for they have now endured one campaign and two books on the Falklands, which is more than enough for anyone in a lifetime.

# Abbreviations

ARC  Agricultural Research Centre
BAS  British Antarctic Survey
BFBS  British Forces Broadcasting Service
BFFI  British Forces Falkland Islands
BIOMASS  Biological Investigations of Marine Antarctic Systems and Stocks
CCAMLR  Convention for the Conservation of Antarctic Marine Living Resources
EOD  Explosives and Ordnance Disposal
FAO  Food and Agriculture Organisation (of the United Nations)
FCO  Foreign and Commonwealth Office
FIARDC  Falkland Islands Agricultural Research and Development Centre
FIBEX  First International BIOMASS Experiment
FIC  Falkland Islands Company
FIDC  Falkland Islands Development Corporation
FIDF  Falkland Islands Defence Force
FIDS  Falkland Islands Dependencies Survey
FIPASS  Falklands Intermediate Port and Storage System
FIPZ  Falkland Islands Protection Zone
FO  Foreign Office

GEU  General Employees' Union (Falkland Islands)
GTU  Grasslands Trials Unit (Falkland Islands)
ICSU  International Council of Scientific Unions
IGC  International Geophysical Co-operation (1959)
IGY  International Geophysical Year (1957–8)
IYQS  International Years of the Quiet Sun (1964–5)
LADE  Líneas Aéreas del Estado (Argentine national airline)
LMA  Laing, Mowlem, Amey Roadstone
MoD  Ministry of Defence
NERC  Natural Environment Research Council
ODA  Overseas Development Administration
OSAS  Overseas Aid Scheme
PSA  Property Services Agency
PWD  Public Works Department (Falkland Islands)
RFA  Royal Fleet Auxiliary
RRS  Royal Research Ship
SCAR  Scientific Committee on Antarctic Research
SOA  Sheep Owners' Association (Falkland Islands)
SWAG  South West Atlantic Group
YPF  Yacimientos Petroliferos Fiscales (Argentine State Petroleum Company)

# PART ONE

# WITH ENDURANCE TO ANTARCTICA

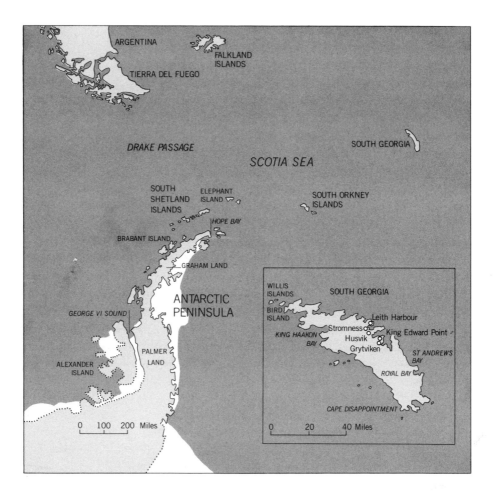

# Chapter 1

# From the Falklands South

The day of HMS *Endurance*'s departure from Port Stanley was exceptionally brilliant. As the ship cleared the outer harbour of Port William, a flotilla of jackass penguins bobbed through the water, their red crests picked out by the sun, in an informal ceremony of farewell. Astern, the dark and ponderous giant petrels wheeled and dived through the wake. Only a week before, at the beginning of March, the Falklands weather had been its precocious worst. The inner harbour was covered by a curtain of rain driven horizontally by the southern gale as tugs battled to save ships dragging their anchors.

That morning of 11 March 1984, *Endurance* was setting out on the third and last work period in the Antarctic of that summer season. This was the first full season the ice patrol ship had served in southern waters since the Falklands conflict of 1982 and the subsequent announcement that her period of service with the Royal Navy was to be extended. In the Defence Review of 1981 she was to have been withdrawn from the South Atlantic and scrapped. It is believed that this proposal more than any other single factor caused the Argentines to think that they could seize the Falklands, and hang onto them, without a fight. Incongruous though it might seem, *Endurance*, a tubby, bright-red freighter bought second-hand from the Danes in 1967, is the symbol of the British presence in the South Atlantic and Antarctic waters. Her duties are to act as the Falklands guardship, to support scientists of the British Antarctic Survey, and to survey uncharted waters for the Navy's Hydrographer. Since 1982 her role as guardship has been taken over by the frigate and destroyer squadron deployed round the Falklands, and *Endurance*'s duties are now almost exclusively in Antarctic waters and South Georgia.

The other main symbol of the British presence in the Antarctic is the British Antarctic Survey. Like *Endurance* the Survey (always known as BAS) has had a change of fortune since the Falklands conflict, in the form of £15 million of extra funds to expand its activities. BAS has its headquarters at Cambridge; of more than 300 staff at least seventy overwinter in the five British bases in the Antarctic. However, British scientific efforts there are dwarfed by those of the United States and Russia. The German and Japanese facilities and equipment are luxurious by comparison with those of BAS ships and bases. But BAS today has a considerable reputation for polar expertise and is still one of the leaders in Antarctic research. Until recently, the Survey was in decline as funds became more limited, but now the revival of its strength and the reprieve of *Endurance* are directly linked to the policies of Margaret Thatcher's Conservative government in the Falklands. So Britain's longer-term prospects in Antarctica as a whole are tied to the narrower perspective of the British stance over the Falklands, known today as the Fortress Falklands policy.

This comes at a time when international interest in Antarctica is increasing. More countries are seeking to join the Antarctic Treaty, which came into existence in 1961. The Treaty bans the use of the continent and waters around it for military purposes and the testing of weapons there, and declares that the fruits of scientific work should be shared internationally. So far it has been a success. The superpowers, Russia and America, co-operate fully, and so do the seven countries who have made claims to territory in Antarctica itself; among them are three with rival claims to the Antarctic Peninsula: Britain, Chile and Argentina.

The Falklands conflict underlined the fragility of the state of international harmony in Antarctica in that two founder-members of the Treaty, Britain and Argentina, had gone to war on the fringes of the Antarctic Ocean over a territorial dispute that extends to parts of Antarctica itself. Another cause for concern about the functioning of the Treaty in the future is that its rules are due to change in 1991, when any single member country can ask for a review and the system of voting changes from consensus, with each nation having a veto, to decision by majority. These theoretical considerations are matched by increased activity in Antarctica itself. Fishing fleets are more numerous and the number of scientists and bases has been going up year by year.

Each of *Endurance*'s work periods takes a different route, and her role includes keeping an eye on the fishing fleets across the Scotia Sea as well as visiting bases in Antarctica. In the last work period of the 1983–4 summer season she was to visit South Georgia first, taking an orni-thologist to winter with the BAS men on Bird Island, and the new garrison commander to Grytviken; after that she was to visit the main island groups of the Scotia Sea, the South Sandwich, South Orkney and South Shetland, all claimed as either Falkland Islands Dependencies or part of the British Antarctic Territory; and finally to replenish the

British expedition on Brabant Island off the coast of the Antarctic Peninsula with stores, take home the summer team and land a new winter party. All of this left little time for the routine task of surveying: 'It's all a bit of a taxi run, I'm afraid,' her captain, Colin MacGregor, said to me apologetically, 'but I hope you see something of Antarctica.'

Technically the Falklands are not part of Antarctica. Geographic pedants like to say the islands are sub-Antarctic, which means they have got a lot of penguins and seals and millions of sea-birds. They also get a fair amount of snow and more than a generous helping of Antarctic gales which produce a wind chill temperature in winter of −20°C and below on exposed ground.

Looking out from *Endurance* as she cleared the Falklands that March Sunday, the human activities on the shore had a curiously impermanent air. The inner harbour at Stanley was cluttered with ships of all shapes and sizes. Floating cranes were busily at work above the pontoons and landing-stages of the new flexible port. Beside them the three huge steel boxes forming the main accommodation blocks for the troops, the coastels, looked like a child's building blocks. It seemed as if they might be whipped away in an instant. On the point, the black-and-white-striped lighthouse gleamed like a liquorice stick. The sandy beaches were deserted except for the occasional group of penguins: humans were fenced out by rows of minefields.

The first day out from Stanley was one of mist, drizzle and heavy skies. In the water schools of dolphins kept pace with the ship, their bodies a gleaming metallic grey. The albatrosses gave ever more spectacular displays as they dived and looped across the wake and over the flight-deck at the stern. The bigger of the wandering and black-browed albatrosses had wingspans of more than ten feet. They would glide past and stand a hundred feet off the side of the ship, casting a leary eye at what was going on on the bridge. But show a camera and they retreated. In the three weeks I spent with *Endurance* I did not once take a successful photograph of one of these graceful birds in flight. It was as if they feared that the Ancient Mariner had traded his crossbow for the steady eye of the telephoto lens.

If the Falklands are not technically part of Antarctica, South Georgia, 800 miles to the south-east, most certainly is. For between the two groups of islands lies the natural barrier called the Antarctic Convergence, where the cold waters flowing up from Antarctica slide under the warmer currents coming south. The Convergence is about twenty-five miles wide and the northern and southern waters differ considerably. The southern oceans are richer in smaller organisms – plankton – food for the larger animals and birds of the Antarctic. They are thought to be the richest reserves in natural protein on earth. Recent attention has focused particularly on krill, a crustacean and the key feature of the food chain of so many of the whales, seals and penguins in Antarctica. Already the Japanese and Russian fishing fleets are probably harvesting more than one million tons of krill a year, though so far preparation of krill products for human diet has had limited success. (Some years ago krill paste flooded the shelves of Moscow supermarkets: it did not get much further, as the babushkas kept their hands on their purses.)

On the eastward journey to South Georgia, *Endurance* crossed the path taken by Captain James Cook on his second voyage to the Southern Ocean, very possibly the greatest voyage of navigation and discovery undertaken by a single commander. By today's standards his achievements were remarkable; by the standards of their own time, just over two centuries ago, they were astonishing.

Born in Yorkshire in 1728, the son of a farm labourer, Cook owed his education to John Walker, a Quaker shipowner who became his lifelong patron. Walker sent the young Cook to sea on his colliers out of Whitby, but in the winter paid for him to study mathematics and navigation. Although he was offered a command by Walker in 1755, Cook joined the Royal Navy as an able seaman and quickly rose to master. It was he who navigated Admiral Saunders' fleet up the St Lawrence river for the capture of Quebec. Cook's real achievements, however, were in times of peace. These began with his three great voyages of discovery from 1768 to his death in 1779.

The first voyage aboard the *Endeavour* was to the South Pacific to witness the transit of Venus, after which Cook sailed in a figure of eight around New Zealand and charted the coasts, going on to make a detailed survey of the east coast of Australia, and arriving back in England in 1771. Cook's skills at chart-making have never been surpassed.

On 13 July 1772 he set sail again with two ships, the *Resolution* and the *Adventure*, to search for the great southern continent (his curiosity about this land, part of marine mythology since classical times, had been roused on the previous voyage). No such continent was found, but the journey saw a great advance in the health of ships' companies on long hauls. On the first southern journey Cook's men had suffered dreadfully from scurvy and on the journey home from Batavia in the East Indies were decimated by malaria and dystentery. Cook ensured that they had plenty of fruit, which was gathered in revictualling stops in New Zealand and the Pacific Islands. The benefits of eating fresh citrus fruits to combat scurvy had long been known, but he was the first to apply this knowledge systematically.

Cook's ships crossed the Antarctic Circle (66°30′S) and on 30 January 1774 *Resolution* reached 71°10′S at longitude 106°54′W. In his journal Cook wrote: 'I will not say it was impossible to get farther to the south; but the attempting it would have been a dangerous and rash enterprise, and what, I believe no man in my situation would have thought of.' Indeed no one got further south than this until James Weddell half a century later.

Off what is now known as Thurston Island, Cook was confronted by a wall of heavy pack ice, and he speculated that it would continue uninterrupted to the South Pole. Again, no one reached as far south in that part of the Antarctic Ocean as he did until two American ice-breakers, the *Staten Island* and the *Glacier,* reached the same point in 1961. During this voyage he revolutionised the use of the chronometer for reckoning positions of latitude.

In the final phase of this journey, *Resolution* rounded the Horn from the Pacific and, avoiding the Falklands, headed towards South Georgia, which was claimed for George III. Cook then sailed east and south, discovering the Candlemas and South Sandwich Islands, and headed home. He was elected a member of the Royal Society and awarded the Copley medal for his work on the prevention of scurvy.

Cook made one more journey: with the *Resolution* and *Adventure* he set out to search for the North-West Passage from the Pacific end. It was on this journey early in 1779 that he was killed in a scuffle at Kealakekua Bay in Hawaii after one of *Discovery*'s boats was stolen by the islanders.

No member of the Royal Navy enjoys such a high reputation internationally as Cook, despite the emphasis in British history texts on martial heroes like Nelson and Drake. He was simply the first, and possibly the greatest, Antarctic navigator and scientist. He was the founder of a tradition of precise observation and measurement in the southern oceans, a tradition inherited by Scott, Shackleton and the BAS. It is a tradition that now might be jeopardised by bureaucratic cheese-paring and the narrow perceptions and policies over the South Atlantic following the Falklands conflict.

Heading towards South Georgia, life aboard *Endurance* settled quickly into the seagoing routine. The helicopter crew maintained their machines and the Royal Marine party trained with small arms. Newcomers like myself were given a quick course in what to do if a helicopter ditched: the waters are so cold that one would stand little chance of surviving in them for more than three minutes, unless one had adequate protective clothing. This usually took the form of an outsize clown's suit called a 'once-only' or, if one was available, an aviator's sealed rubber 'goon suit'. The pilots warned us that it was better to have many layers of thin clothing rather than a few thick items like chunky sweaters. The invention of the multi-layered fabric Gore-Tex has revolutionised the arctic wardrobe: it is very light and allows greater freedom of movement. *Endurance*'s two helicopters have the charming habit of being flown with their rear doors off, which is a wonderful aid to photography but results in temperatures that bring tears to your eyes.

In one respect it seemed that *Endurance* could do with some of Captain Cook's nutritional expertise. Mealtimes occasionally produced some of the most tired-looking vegetables I have seen in my life. Chips, cabbage and sprouts were mounds of dark-brown mush, and the soups, which the stewards' fantasy graced with a rich variety of names, wore the uniform grey-green of Port Stanley harbour on a wet Sunday. Eggs, the constant factor in each nautical breakfast, always had a distinctly sulphurous smell. Not that I am casting any doubts on the culinary ingenuity of the ship's cooks and stewards: *Endurance* has the longest regular deployment out of home waters of any ship in the Navy, and resupply with fresh food is a constant problem for any ship operating in the South Atlantic. She has to carry ten months' stores of food and equipment. However, for many stomachs the end of the ship's deployment is more than adequately summed up by her name. 'By the time you leave this ship you'll think Fawlty Towers is Paradise,' was one of the first greetings I received in the wardroom.

In some respects the ship does resemble a travelling guest-house. A cabin is permanently earmarked on the upper deck for VIPs such as the High Commissioner for the British Antarctic Territory, who is also the Governor or Civil Commissioner for the Falkland Islands (currently Sir Rex Hunt). In the course of the year, members of expeditions, BAS scientists and the occasional journalist also travel with the ship. On reaching South Georgia, the first task was to leave a scientist who was to winter at the base on Bird Island, the smallest of the permanent British bases and the main BAS centre in South Georgia. It is devoted almost exclusively to the life sciences, principally the observation and study of seals, penguins and albatrosses.

The wind was freshening to a small gale when *Endurance* reached the island. In the early morning, the clouds were ragged curtains of vapour over the jagged bluish mountains along the coast. Beneath the peaks, some still covered with snow, was the occasional flash of bright-green vegetation. At first there was some doubt whether the helicopters would be launched – no flying is permitted when the wind reaches speeds of more than forty knots – but eventually it was decided to go ahead despite the conditions.

It was a bumpy ride across the choppy sea. The machines jerked and swung violently as they battled with the wind to cross the central spine of the island. The winds can change direction in an instant and a fierce downward thrust can bash the machines to the ground: one had crashed on South Georgia three seasons before while taking Sir Rex Hunt and his wife ashore.

Looking down from the helicopter the base, 1000 feet below, seemed well camouflaged amongst the tussock grass and mud of the beach. On either side, cliffs and hills were also generously covered with tussock grass and moss, dotted with what looked like large lumps of snow. On later inspection these turned out to be wandering and black-browed albatrosses sitting on their nests.

As the helicopters landed beside the huts, the beach came alive with fur seals and their pups yelping and leaping down to the sea for an early-morning dip. Across parts of the beach, walkways raised on stilts afforded a vantage point to observe them and the albatross nests close to the shore.

I was met outside the huts by the base commander, Peter Prince, the author of one of the standard ornithological works, *The Birds of South Georgia,* and a leading authority in the field. He had a wonderfully dry and casual manner, always referring to penguins as 'pingwings'.

He took me to the living quarters, a new hut with enormous picture windows under which the scientists have their desks; they often take photographs of the seal circus in front of them. The most striking thing about the base was the efficiency and economy with which every space was used. The next thing was the range of decoration: pin-ups, more accessible loves, and pictures of the finest bird and mammal specimens the scientists had photographed themselves around the base. Apart from the pinboards, which marked each man's territory, there were rows and rows of bookcases containing almost every conceivable form of literature. A great deal of care had been taken to insulate the living and sleeping quarters, although Bird Island does not suffer such cold temperatures as bases further south. Entering the porch there is a double door, like an air chamber, and then a corridor to the main room.

Up to ten people work at the base in summer and five or six in winter. Much of the work in the long, dark winter months is devoted to maintaining and repairing the huts and facilities, but otherwise the station's primary commitment is to the Biological Investigations of Marine Antarctic Systems and Stocks (BIOMASS) programme run by the Scientific Committee on Antarctic Research (SCAR), which now has fifteen member nations. BIOMASS concentrates mainly on the potential harvest from krill. According to Peter Prince, the birds and

21

seals of South Georgia eat one and a half million tons of seafood a year. The main scientific project on Bird Island is the study of the wandering and black-browed albatross which, like penguins, breed the year round. Albatrosses are known to feed on twenty-eight different species of squid in the waters round South Georgia.

After eleven seasons on the island Prince spoke of his work in the tones of the dedicated BAS scientist, as enthusiastic about his life there as when he began: 'What excites me most about working here on Bird Island is, obviously, the unique opportunity of working in a wilderness area on animals and birds that lend themselves to scientific research. They're very tame, and obviously we have to be very careful not to breach that privilege. Our greatest concern is for the future. We do see developments taking place in fisheries, and things like that, and we hope the resources are managed in a sensible way that maintains these magnificient populations of birds and seals.'

There are more than 100,000 penguins on Bird Island alone, mostly macaroni penguins; on the neighbouring Willis Islands there are several million pairs. The most accessible area of study is the fur seals, which in a good season increase in population on Bird Island by about four per cent a year; in some years the total fur seal population of South Georgia has gone up by twenty-seven per cent. About 40,000 seal pups are born on Bird Island in a good year – 1500 of them in the little bay around the BAS huts.

But the 1983–4 season was a bad one: fewer than one-third of albatross chicks had been surviving beyond the first few weeks, and the number of seal pups was well down on the year before. Prince explained that little was known about important aspects of the animals' feeding habits and that the migration and swarming pattern of krill was now part of the programme of research carried out by the BAS ship *John Biscoe* around South Georgia. Over the years the seal population had burgeoned in the gap left by dwindling whale stocks. During the summer of 1984, however, no fewer than seven right whales had been sighted thrashing about beyond the kelp beds that fringe the bay. Not that this was an indication of a sudden increase in their numbers – they were more likely to have been searching for the elusive krill.

The kind of work carried out on Bird Island costs so little, Prince said, that it was unlikely to fall victim to the cost-cutting whim of politicians. He was most worried about the related oceanographic studies of krill and other plankton, which require the use of ships and are far more costly than land-based research programmes.

He had arranged for us a tour around the albatross and penguin nesting grounds and to see some of the detailed work being done on seals. But at that point one of the helicopter crew burst into the hut to say that we had to be back on board in twenty minutes as *Endurance* had a rendezvous at Grytviken later that afternoon. Prince's reaction was explosive. Many senior BAS men express similar frustration over *Endurance*'s habits and the uses to which she is sometimes put, such as showing the flag in South American countries. They would like to have guaranteed use of her helicopters for a set number of days each season, but naval officers point out that they are expensive to run and that the scientists do not pay for them; it is also necessary to have some secrecy about plans of operation. 'I suppose they want to get back to the G&T and the cocktail-party circuit. Best news I heard was when John Nott said he was scrapping her,' was Prince's reaction to the cancellation of our expedition.

There was little time to say goodbye to the few seal pups hanging around the entrance to the huts. It was a dark and soupy day, making photography practically impossible. As the helicopter lifted into the wind, I could see, each neatly marked with a stake, the nests of the albatrosses, whose heavy, slightly curved beaks lend such shy and gentle creatures a false impression of menace.

Mountains between St Andrew's Bay and Royal Bay, South Georgia. Much of the high land of the island's interior has not yet been climbed. Ernest Shackleton was the first to cross the central mountains in 1916, a feat not to be repeated for forty years

Whaling sheds and storage tanks at Leith, South Georgia, with the manager's house and dormitory on high ground behind. The tussock grass provides good shelter for elephant seals

Whale flensing sheds at Leith. Note the Japanese characters on the door, a sign of the last inhabitants to work the station

Leith: pipes and metal in pristine condition. Such items brought the Argentine scrap-dealers to South Georgia in March 1982

25

*Endurance*'s crew return to the jetty at Leith after a good run ashore. Note the bulldozer and winches, left by the Argentines

## Chapter 2

# South Georgia

South Georgia is the most attractive of the Antarctic islands in the variety of its landscape and animal and bird life. In late summer the distant mountains and hills radiate a brilliant green, though the peaks are perpetually covered in snow. Many of the highest mountains have still to be climbed, for expeditions to the interior can be ambushed by sudden changes in weather from bright sunshine to ferocious snowstorms.

Legend has it that the island was discovered in 1512 by the Florentine explorer Amerigo Vespucci, who also claimed to have discovered the American continent. An English merchant, Antonio de la Roché, is believed to have sighted it in April 1675, and a bullion ship sailing from Lima to Cadiz, which was blown off course, is supposed to have seen it in June–July 1756. But the first person to survey the northern coast and land was James Cook in January 1775. He appears to have landed in Possession Bay and then sailed to the large inlet with arms stretching east and west, which he named Cumberland Bay. His naturalists and geographer gave detailed accounts of the landscape and animal life.

Tucked below the entrance to Cumberland East Bay are Grytviken, for sixty years the capital of the Norwegian whaling industry in the Antarctic, and King Edward Point, where the magistrate responsible for the Falkland Islands Dependencies has his seat. Anyone wishing to land on South Georgia must seek clearance for immigration from the magistrate, an authority vested in the British troop commander on the island after the Falklands conflict. Before this the base commander of the BAS team at Grytviken assumed the magistrate's mantle.

It was the failure of a party of Argentine scrap-metal dealers to seek his permission to land at Leith in March 1982 that heralded the opening of hostilities between Britain and Argentina. The contract to dispose of scrap at the whaling station there had been won quite legitimately by the firm of Señor Constantino Davidoff of Buenos Aires. He applied to the British embassy and consular authority in Argentina for his men to travel to South Georgia to begin work in early 1982. Once they arrived off the island, they ignored the magistrate at King Edward Point and on 19 March went direct to Leith in Stromness Bay. One of the party raised the Argentine flag there. Towards the end of March the scrap-metal dealers, among whom there were almost certainly military personnel, were reinforced by the tender *Bahia Paraiso*. On the last day of the month *Endurance* landed a party of Royal Marines at Grytviken under the command of Lieutenant Keith Mills. The day after the Falklands fell to the Argentines, the *Bahia Paraiso* appeared off King Edward Point, accompanied by a corvette. The magistrate was asked to surrender. As the corvette rounded the point she was hit by a fusillade of 84-mm Carl Gustav rockets. It was the last thing the Argentines expected. Not only had Keith Mills' ambush taken them completely by surprise but it appeared at the time that they did not know the marines were there at all. A three-hour battle ensued in which two Argentine helicopters were shot down and several Argentine soldiers killed before the British were defeated. The scientists and civilians had hidden in the church in Grytviken. According to the BAS chronicler, Bob Headland, they were given twenty minutes to pack and were then taken aboard the *Bahia Paraiso*. The last to leave were the magistrate, Keith Mills and Headland himself.

Just over three weeks later, on 26 April, British forces retook South Georgia. The operation had a chaotic start when two helicopters trying to land a reconnaissance party of SAS on the Fortuna Glacier, west of Stromness Bay, crashed. Their crews and the SAS men had to be rescued. A patrol setting out in rubber boats fared little better and had to be recovered. Eventually British marines and SAS men were landed, and the helicopters from *Endurance* attacked and damaged the aged Argentine submarine *Santa Fé*, which they found on the surface in open water at the mouth of Cumberland Bay. Hours later 200 Argentine servicemen and civilians surrendered to the captain of HMS *Antrim* and Nick Barker, the then captain of *Endurance*. The Argentine commander, Alfredo Astiz, was wanted by the European Court of Human Rights for his involvement with one of the most notorious torture centres, the marine engineering academy on the outskirts of Buenos Aires, in the so-called 'dirty war' waged by the Argentine military against dissidents and guerrillas from 1976 to 1982. Captain Barker remembered him as a courteous and correct officer, keen to stick to the military formalities. One of his men was less fortunate: he was shot by his British escort who believed he was about to open the sea cocks of the *Santa Fé* and scuttle her. Later Astiz disappeared in Brazil as he and his fellow prisoners were being taken back to Argentina.

It is worth recalling these events because a disproportionate amount of wreckage from the conflict is still strewn along the shore at Grytviken and Leith. Stacks of Argentine ammunition litter the beach at Leith, and there are piles of broken and empty wine bottles around the accommodation quarters there. Captain Barker's men found a cellar of hundreds of full wine bottles, which mysteriously disappeared in subsequent weeks.

Today a red buoy at the mouth of Grytviken harbour marks where the *Santa Fé* eventually sank. Several attempts were made by a British salvage team to recover the submarine, which lay wallowing alongside one of the quays. A salvage tug managed to get the crippled boat under tow but then the submarine broke away. The salvage men had dropped their prize at the critical moment, so the submarine now blocks the harbour as completely as Captain Astiz' men could have desired. Ships like *Endurance* now anchor well out into the bay and take the trip to King Edward Point or Grytviken itself in small boats.

Approaching, Grytviken was a blur of a few buildings and high radio masts, dwarfed by the crags and mountains rising directly above. Below the peaks the vegetation, grass and moss, was a clear emerald green. A dazzling glacier shone off *Endurance*'s port bow as the sun began to appear through the fine rain. The wharf at King Edward Point itself has a curiously northern aspect. The wooden stage with its white rails gives the appearance of a Scandinavian or Scottish fishing village. Beyond the cluster of houses nearest the stage, the harbour-master's and magistrate's houses and post office, a green wooden building called Shackleton House stands on rising ground. This was the BAS base, and the building remains the property of the Survey, though it now temporarily serves as the main accommodation block for the detachment of troops on the island.

In the two-year period following the fighting between the British and Argentines, a company of infantry, with supporting troops of signallers and engineers, has been stationed on South Georgia. The soldiers speak of their deployment on the island with varying degrees of enthusiasm. Their accommodation in Shackleton House is among the best for any of the garrison forces in the Falkland Islands and Dependencies. One officer told me of his enjoyment of the hiking and climbing, fishing and wildlife photography, only to confess in the bar later that evening that most soldiers hated the Falklands assignment, were bored and longed to get home. The same officer revealed that there was a sharp rundown of manpower both on South Georgia and in the Falklands and the contingents sent to South Georgia for the three- to four-month tours were progressively diminishing.

*Endurance* had called at Grytviken to deposit the troop commander of the new garrison company on the island. Major John Rhind of the Royal Scots could boast more offices and titles than the most well-endowed functionary in a Gilbert and Sullivan operetta: troop commander, magistrate, harbour-master, immigration officer, postmaster, customs officer and receiver of wrecks. His two staff sergeants were to be sworn in as special constables. Such pomp and power may seem excessively Ruritanian for the governance of several million penguins, seals and sea birds, but both Major Rhind and his predecessor, Captain Marius Coulon of the Royal Regiment of Fusiliers, have had to exercise their authority as magistrate and customs officer. Captain Coulon had to board a Russian factory ship, which a naval patrol found at anchor in Gold Harbour, well inside territorial waters. 'It was all very amicable really,' he told me. 'I told them they should have asked permission to anchor inside the three-mile limit. They offered us a very good lunch, at which quantities of vodka were consumed, and they sent us off with a dozen or so cases of very good fish.' Factory ships from the whaling fleets often call at Grytviken for fresh water, and the visits are becoming more frequent as the Russian and Polish fleets increase. Recently they have been joined by Bulgarian vessels, and the Spanish and Portuguese are showing interest in catching the squid that form a vital part of the diet of albatrosses and elephant seals.

The first tests of Major Rhind's skill in magistracy were more delicate matters than his predecessor's encounter with the Russians. In recent years quite a number of ocean-going yachts have visited South Georgia and gone on to Antarctica. One, belonging to Jerome and Sally Ponçy, a French-Australian couple, visits the Antarctic each year and their second child was born in southern waters. Jerome has written books and articles about the ecology and conservation of Antarctica and on the proceeds manages the maintenance of both boat and family throughout the austral summer.

In April 1984 three Frenchmen called at South Georgia on their way round the world. Two, Jean-Jacques Argoud and Patrick Cloâtre, had worked previously as assistants in the civilian hospital at Port Stanley where they were well liked. Major Rhind decided to board their yacht as it was said at the time that they were suspected of looting, a rather bizarre charge considering the amount of damage done in the shore stations by sailors from visiting naval destroyers and frigates and from the fishing fleets. Aboard the yacht the soldiers found three firearms, a shotgun, a new rifle and a pistol made in Argentina. One of the Frenchmen said that he had inherited one gun from his grandfather. According to the Frenchmen relations between them and Major Rhind and his party were quite amicable. None the less, a directive came in the name of Sir Rex Hunt that the men were to be declared *personae non gratae* and ordered not to return to South Georgia under any circumstances. The recipients of the ban were naturally aggrieved and thought the action high-handed.

Some of the yachts in the Atlantic Sector of the Antarctic Ocean have visited Argentine ports on their way to and from the Falklands and South Georgia, the only vessels to do so since June 1982. A French yacht, the *Cinq Gars Pour,* had joined Señor Davidoff's scrap men at Leith in late March 1982.

The entertainment of the afternoon was a half-marathon round Grytviken harbour; it was for this fixture that *Endurance* had departed Bird Island so hurriedly. Athletics and football matches against visiting ships are the main means of relieving the monotony of the daily round for the garrison, and the events are often followed by a meal for the ship's company. For hours *Endurance*'s men larded the lean earth of the track round the harbour with their sweat, some of them wearing only boiler suits and running shoes.

Dotted along the shoreline were clumps of gentoo penguins and at the far side snoozing elephant seals, who looked on the parade of human folly with disdain, before dropping off again. In the water there were two or three small steam whale-catchers, their funnels, masts and super-structure almost horizontal in the water. The best preserved, the *Petrel,* lies in the water off one of the big slipways. She has been restored and there have been suggestions that she should be towed back to Britain, but this would be very costly. Ironically, she carries the flag of Argentina because she belonged to the Compañía Argentina de Pesca, the first whaling company to operate a station on South Georgia, which traded at Grytviken from 1906 to 1959. In all, seven stations were established on the island: Grytviken, Leith, Stromness and Husvik operating until the early sixties, Godthul, Ocean Harbour and Prince Olav suffering crises and closure in the twenties and thirties. At the height of the whaling industry about 6000 men, mostly Norwegians and Swedes, worked at the stations and, with the men working on the whale-catchers, factory ships and supply vessels, there could be three times the population when the whaling fleets were at anchor in the harbours.

Today, Grytviken is a sprawl of pipes, chains and hawsers, empty warehouses and sheds, and acres of rusty corrugated iron clanging in the wind. It is a barer, more desolate scene than Leith, and there is not so much machinery and valuable scrap about. The lease for the station now belongs to Christian Salvesen and Company, who acquired it in 1979. After the Compañía Argentina de Pesca sold out, the station was operated by Albion Star and then subleased to a Japanese company, whose failure to make a success of the station marked the end of the onshore whale-processing industry in South Georgia.

Behind the factory buildings stands the manager's house; beyond and to one side, the white wooden Lutheran church with its pointed belfry.

The house and the church look like something from the Norway of Grieg and Ibsen. The church, framed by the jagged granite peak beyond, streaked and crowned with the first snow of winter, resembles a left-over from an amateur production of *The Sound of Music*. It was acquired second-hand from Norway and transported in sections to the present site in 1913. Services were held there regularly until quite recently; shortly after the closure of the whaling stations the church was badly vandalised and now is boarded and locked. The garrison troops have been carrying out a thorough restoration programme. Though some of the white wooden weatherboarding is badly scarred and gashed, the little church must be the most attractive building in Antarctica.

The graveyard is on a hillside flanking the station on the opposite side from the church and manager's house. The headstones and inscriptions chronicle the last hundred years of this part of the island. Some of the dead were little more than boys: Swedes, Scots, Germans and Norwegians of seventeen and eighteen who worked the stations and whalers. There is a cross commemorating the third officer of the *Deutschland,* who disappeared trying to climb the mountains of the interior. He was part of the expedition led by Lieutenant Filchner, who gave his name to the Filchner Ice Shelf in the Weddell Sea.

The most prominent grave with its stone cross is that of Sir Ernest Shackleton who died in Grytviken on 22 January 1922 as he was preparing to set out on his fourth Antarctic expedition. He was struck by heart disease, and his body was shipped to Montevideo for passage home before his widow suggested that it would be more fitting for him to be buried on South Georgia. His companions also erected a memorial cross at Hope Point above King Edward Point, the first landmark on the headland.

Shackleton called South Georgia 'the gateway to Antarctica', though it is not quite clear what he meant precisely. There are few immediate resources that could be developed, and without an airstrip the island is of doubtful logistic value for supporting operations in Antarctica. Shackleton came to South Georgia in 1914 in the first *Endurance* as he was preparing his expedition to cross the Antarctic continent. He was to return to the island from that attempt in circumstances that he could hardly have predicted. After *Endurance* was first beset and then crushed by the pack ice in the Weddell Sea in October and November 1915, the men drifted on ice-floes towards the open sea, eventually landing by ship's boats on Elephant Island in the South Shetlands. Shackleton then sailed over 800 miles to South Georgia in a small ship's boat to get help from the Norwegians in the whaling stations. Unfortunately they landed on the wrong side of the island, and at the first attempt to get ashore were nearly shipwrecked and drowned in the huge breakers. Eventually they managed to land and make safe the boat at King Haakon Bay. They still had to cross nearly thirty miles of mountain and glacier. Shackleton decided to take two companions and to return later for the remaining three who by now were very ill. He set out across the mountains with Frank Worsley, the navigator, and Thomas Crean, the second officer and a veteran of previous expeditions with both Shackleton and Scott. They carried light rations, and at one point ate albatross chicks with their ration stew called 'hoosh'.

Twice they had to turn back as the mountains ahead, part of the Allardyce range forming the central spine of the island, proved quite impassable. At the third attempt they met a deep chasm between the peaks, but there did seem a way down at one end. Frank Worsley's account, *Antarctic Rescue,* tells the story with graphic simplicity. The three men, he said, had decided that time was against them and the weather was closing in, so they had to risk tobogganing down the mountain.

> Each coiling our share of the rope beneath us for chafing gear, I straddled behind Sir Ernest, holding his shoulder. Crean did the same to me, and so, locked together, we let go. I was never more scared in my life than for the first thirty seconds . . . I think we all gasped at that hair-raising shoot into darkness . . . Then, to our joy, the slope curved out, and we shot into a bank of curved snow. We estimated we had shot down a mile in two or three minutes, and had lowered our altitude by two or three thousand feet.

Again they lost their way on the Fortuna Glacier and had to backtrack, but that morning they waited for the whistle calling the whalers to work at Stromness at seven o'clock. 'Right to the minute the steam-whistle came to us, borne clearly on the wind across the intervening miles of rock and snow,' wrote Shackleton in *South*. 'It was the first sound created by outside human agency that had come to our ears since we left Stromness Bay in December 1914.' Before they could get to the settlements they had to lower themselves fifty feet over a waterfall boxed in by rock walls and sheer on either side. That afternoon on the third day of the crossing of the island, they reached Stromness. Two Norwegian boys ran away when they first saw them: their hair and beards were long and matted with soot and grease from eating seal blubber. Eventually they were welcomed into the house of Captain Sølle, manager of the Tonsberg Whaling Company, who at first failed to recognise Shackleton. Later the Norwegians gave him a boat to fetch his men from King Haakon Sound. The story of the crossing is remarkable not only because the men took so few supplies – no tents, no sleeping-bags and very light rations – but because that winter there were only three consecutively fine days, the three days Shackleton chose for his journey.

In the long grass below the cemetery where Shackleton is buried, a family of seals were playing hide-and-seek, snapping and growling behind the tussock clumps like overgrown otters. The fur seals have a sharp bite and will take a nip at humans if they are roused. At the end of the game the pups splashed into the water and glided and bobbed gracefully and with an astonishing turn of speed towards the middle of the harbour.

The fact that there are any seals at all in this part of South Georgia is little short of miraculous. They were killed for their fur and oil over a century before the Norwegian whalers came. Drawn by the careful descriptions by Cook's naturalists, sealers came from Labrador and Patagonia to South Georgia. In 1825 the British sealer James Weddell recorded one of the most quoted statistics in the history of Antarctic life sciences: he calculated that in the fifty years since Cook claimed the island at least 1,200,000 fur seals had been killed there, and over 20,000 tons of blubber oil extracted from the slaughter of elephant seals. If anything, this might have been a conservative estimate because one American sealer boasted of taking 50,000 fur seal skins in a season in 1800. By the beginning of this century the fur seal population on South Georgia was declining rapidly, and by the mid-thirties it is thought that there were fewer than fifty couples along the north coast of the island. The last census, in 1976, put the population at 360,000. Now there are thought to be about a million, and there is even some talk of the need for a cull to prevent the fur seal population upsetting the ecological balance between the different krill-eating species.

In the evening the Fusiliers gave an RPC, military parlance for a 'knees-up', the letters standing for Requests the Pleasure of your Company. The Fusiliers seemed to be pleased that their tour was ending before the bad winter weather came. A military doctor called Nancy told me that she was bored because she had so little to do looking after so many fit young soldiers.

The party was held in Shackleton House, which still had the library and laboratory left by the BAS team. The future of BAS at Shackleton House is uncertain. The scientists are reluctant to move back with so much military activity about, and they would need a regular government contribution of about £250,000 if they were to maintain the position of magistrate there. Even if they did come to an arrangement with the Falklands Dependencies government in the shape of the Commissioner in Port Stanley, the BAS men insist their prime objective in Grytviken would still have to be scientific research. At present they say that a base and laboratory in Cumberland Bay is a low-priority requirement, and the only value of Grytviken at present is to support oceanographic surveys conducted by ships around the coasts of South Georgia. This bureaucratic knot is typical in the tangled story of the Falklands administration. Recently the Falklands Dependencies government has contemplated having a full-time official to serve as magistrate, immigration officer, customs officer and postmaster. Support for him is likely to prove very costly, and there has been a sizeable bill already to bring the Falklands architect by air from London to Stanley and by ship to King Edward Point to look over accommodation there.

Leith gives a clearer impression of a whaling-station at work than Grytviken does. Some of the machinery is still in the sheds; some sits on the main landing-stage where Constantino Davidoff's scrap men dumped it in April 1982. They left behind two tractors and some hauling gear, which they are unlikely to claim as their contract has now lapsed. Leith was operated by the Christian Salvesen Group, who closed operations in the early sixties. For two seasons a Japanese company, Nippon Suisan Ltd of Japan, tried to make the station profitable once more. (There are still hand-painted notices on the doors in Japanese.) But by 1966 the ocean-going factory freezers had destroyed the onshore whale-processing business and in that year Leith, the last of the South Georgia whaling stations, closed. The industry had operated on the island for sixty years.

As the boats were being lowered from *Endurance* while she prepared to make fast to a buoy in Stromness Bay, one of the helicopters took Captain Colin MacGregor and a marine to stalk reindeer in one of the glens at the head of the fjord. Captain MacGregor was a great lover of rural sport and sometimes launched on a line of conversation which seemed to come straight from the country notes of *The Field,* which earned him the nickname of The Squire from the ship's company. The stalking was not a success at first but after two drives the captain shot a mature stag and a hind. They then spent the best part of three afternoons skinning the beasts and preparing the carcasses for cooking or freezing. The meat of the older beast was musky. 'A bit rank,' was Captain MacGregor's summation, 'must have been in rut.' This became a catch-phrase of the marines' commander, a Londoner called George Gelder; whenever he found the Nelson touch and naval lore getting too much for him he said: 'Getting a bit rank, I think – must be in rut.'

The reindeer had been deliberately introduced by the Norwegians to supplement their meat diet. (Rather less deliberately they brought domestic rats to the island as well.) There are now three herds of reindeer, and permission has to be obtained from Sir Rex Hunt in Stanley before they may be stalked and killed. They have been the subject of research by BAS zoologists, who tend to object to them being culled on an ad hoc basis. Farming the herds is perhaps the only prospect of commercial activity on South Georgia at present.

Leith, Husvik and Stromness are the *Marie Celestes* of the old Norwegian whaling industry on South Georgia. It is as if the steamers appeared in the bay one day, the factory whistle blew and everyone packed for home. At Stromness a railway wagon fully loaded with equipment has stopped halfway through the door of the main shed. In one of the accommodation huts a carton of tinned food has been left half opened. Leith is stacked with lengths of iron and piping, never used, and the storage bins are piled with hundreds of plumbing spares, washers, nuts and bolts.

Leith is the worst vandalised of the three stations in Stromness Bay. For nearly ten years the fishing fleets plundered the most valuable navigation instruments from the marine stores. Piles of Argentine wine bottles lie outside one of the dormitory huts. Occasionally British soldiers and sailors have shot the settlements up; it is said that the Lynx helicopter from one of the visiting warships opened fire with machine-guns on the deer herds. *Endurance*'s crew have visited the deserted settlements for years, and the older hands take an almost proprietary attitude to preserving the buildings. Some of these are recent because Salvesen's carried out a programme of renovation and expansion in the fifties, only to close their operation four or five years later. In front of the sheds are broad wooden slipways where the whale carcasses were flensed, the strips of flesh and blubber sliced from them with long knives on poles like the staves of a medieval man-at-arms. At Stromness much of this work was carried out on floating docks and stages out in the water. These are wrecked and beached, though there are hopes of restoring one of them.

Inside the sheds manifests and sheets of the storekeepers' inventories blow across the floor like tumbleweed. One order for the 1955–6 season is for 500 pairs of gloves for Salvesen's men. Another reveals the armoury of the catchers and factory hands: 200 ripping knives, 200 'rippers, long for deep sea fishing', eighteen 'blubber-chopping knives 22″ × 6″, twenty-two meat knives for "rose-down", and twenty-four reversing knives'.

Despite the bloody nature of their job, the Norwegian whalers seem to have been rather a homely community. They are the seamen described in the novels of the early Nobel laureate Knut Hamsun, such as *The Wanderer,* men from poor rural communities who had to go herring fishing or whaling to supplement the living the families were scratching from the bare soil and rock on mountain farms. Cecil Bertrand, a Falkland Islander now in his seventies, worked with the whale factory ships in the mid-thirties. He had been a ranch-hand in Patagonia and from 1953 for twenty-one years farmed Carcass Island in West Falkland with his wife Kitty. He had missed schooling in his boyhood because of an accident when he fell from a child's slide onto the concrete yard at primary school in Tierra del Fuego. When he went to sea with the factory ships he took dictionaries in Norwegian, Spanish and English to improve his knowledge of all three languages.

'The first two seasons I worked on the head-saw,' he recalled, 'sawing off the whales' heads. It was dirty, greasy work rather than bloody. In the second season we circumnavigated the Antarctic continent to see whether we could do better that way. We came back up the Bellingshausen Sea, where, if I remember rightly, the last whale, a small fin whale, was killed on 7 April 1936. We caught mostly fin whales. The biggest was a blue whale ninety-two feet long. We also caught some sperm and humpback whales. In 1936 we predominantly caught smaller whales and we knew that stocks were dwindling, but that year there were forty-eight factory ships operating in the Antarctic.'

Hours were long and arduous – twelve-hour shifts with the watches changing on New Year's Day. The men in the shore stations were used to equally long hours with a lot of overtime at the height of the season. Best paid were the harpoon gunners, up to £2000 a season, a princely sum in those days. They used to buy elegant seaside summer houses on a particular part of the south Norwegian coast. Whether because of the rewards they reaped or because of the arduousness of their work, they tended to retire quite early, mostly in their forties. In the stations themselves the main forms of entertainment were cards, impromptu concerts and renditions by fiddle and accordion bands, and once a week the 'kino', or cinema. Jan Cheek, a Stanley schoolteacher – who grew up on South Georgia where her father was harbour-master at Grytviken – and wife of the legislative councillor John Cheek, also recalls the Norwegians as being a homely community rather than a wild buccaneering crew.

Few official records of the Norwegians remain. Some have been taken to the Scott Polar Research Institute in Cambridge and used for the natural, social and political history Bob Headland has been preparing on South Georgia. The Norwegian library at Leith and the science laboratory have been plundered totally.

Once, whale carcasses floated in the bay off Leith, their blood staining the inshore waters. On the shale beach ribs and bones lay scattered.

Today there are few bones, and these are worn and bleached. Occasionally there is the mummified carcass of a seal. In the tussock grass elephant seal bulls loll with their harems. On the beach itself one bull keeps an eye on an albino elephant pup and flicks sand nonchalantly over his and his wives' backs, grunting the while like a chorus of flatulent tubas.

*Endurance*'s company had been given leave to go ashore if they had nothing better to do, as some important checks had to be made on the ship's wireless and radar equipment. Some of the men walked up to the old four-inch naval gun on the point, erected in 1918 according to the date stamp on the sight – a bit late for one war and rather early for the next, though such guns were manned at both Grytviken and Leith in the Second World War. The sailors teased the elephant seal bulls in time-honoured tradition, throwing pebbles at their long trunk-like noses to make them rear up and roar. Their roar is a long rolling belch, amplified by air pumped into the proboscis. On Anson's voyage around the world in the eighteenth century a sailor put his head inside the mouth of an elephant seal bull to show off to his mates. The seal bit so severely that he nearly took the man's head off altogether, and he died the following day. On the beach a polyglot community of fur seals, gentoos, and the occasional king penguin were setting out for an afternoon swim. Like the fur seals the gentoo penguins move through the water with speed and elegance. The visitors from the ship snapped away with their cameras like a party of day-trippers on Brighton beach.

At the back of the sheds and oil tanks are the accommodation huts, canteen and hospital. 'George M. Hausen Argentina 25/3/82' had been scrawled in black crayon on the wall of one of the dormitories, and beneath it a marine had written, 'Who won, then?' Some of the furniture was still in good condition, though the choice pieces, chests of drawers and armchairs, had already been removed by the souvenir hunters. At the end of the day the last men to go back on board looked as if they had collected several armfuls of prizes at a country fair: small bookcases, a glass retort, a long-tined hand rake, and the odd rusty shovel. A batch of six of these had been commandeered by the team that was to winter on Brabant Island. The most popular souvenirs were the harpoon heads, which lie about in their hundreds. The modern heads have a cavity for an explosive charge; this method was introduced over a hundred years ago, and greatly enhanced the whalers' efficiency.

Most of the harpoon heads were buried in the mud near the oil tanks under the sloping wall of the mountain, which looked like a giant slag heap. In the still air there was the occasional crack and roar as the stones crashed down from the peak. Sudden gusts of wind whipped down from the mountains, scattering debris across the settlement before shooting across the water. The path of the miniature whirlwinds could be seen quite clearly as they flattened then whipped up the sea. These were the katabatics, downward rushing winds from the high ground, which are a menace to helicopters trying to land on the Antarctic islands. The local name for the winds, the williwaws, expresses their action wonderfully.

In the morning the helicopters took off for St Andrew's Bay, east of Cumberland Bay on the island's north coast. There, one of the finest king penguin colonies sits above the bed of an old glacier. We could smell the presence of the birds almost before we could see them, as the stench hit the helicopters while we were still several thousand feet up and more than two miles off. They strolled about the beach like a football crowd who could not be bothered to go home. Higher up on the rocks, where the rookery was sited, there was a steady tide of sound from the cackling birds, with the shrill chirping of the chicks rising above it. The kings are among the most photogenic of Antarctic creatures; they are not quite as big as their cousins, the emperors, who live only on the Antarctic continent, though some have been found marooned on icebergs drifting northwards; they hatch the year round and the males do the sitting. The emperors often sit through much of the Antarctic night and lose about forty-five per cent of their body weight in the process.

Several seasons before, Cindy Buxton and Annie Price studied and filmed the penguins of St Andrew's. They were still studying when the Argentines invaded, but they were rescued by *Endurance*. Today their hut serves as a refuge shelter for anyone stranded on those shores and is kept stocked with emergency rations. Passing ships like *Endurance* regularly check rescue huts to see that the food is still in good condition and that the huts themselves have not been vandalised.

While the hut was being inspected the helicopter crew wandered along the beach and ate lunch in the shadow of their machines. The penguin audience seemed utterly unabashed by the human presence and completely incurious about the weird shapes of blue and red metal that could actually fly.

It was a hot late summer day. Nevertheless, the captain wore a parka and several thick sweaters, and with the hood up he looked like something from *Nanook of the North* or *Scott of the Antarctic*. The kings were totally unconcerned as he sat a foot or two away from their beaks to snap family portraits by the score. They grouped themselves with the nonchalance of professional models. Their orange-red beaks were delicately curved like scimitars, the colour matching the orange and yellow flash at the top of the brilliant white bib of feathers on the chest. From time to time they would throw their heads back and emit the wonderful trumpeting call 'Ah-hah, ha, ha, hah, hah', looking like heralds on a battlement. Across the gushing brook, which was all that remained of the rather tired-looking glacier by the shore, the main rookery was set on a knoll. Between the mature penguins were balls of brown fluff, this year's chicks. The birds sitting still were betrayed by a bulge of white feathers concealing the egg lodged between their feet. Occasionally there was a report as an unfertilised and rotten egg exploded. The penguin would then slash at his neighbours with his beak in a rage of disappointment at being cheated of parenthood after so many weeks of wasted effort.

It is at first difficult to understand why such delightful and harmless beasts should have been prey for humans. After all, they have oily skins and meat, and they hardly make good eating; some of their offal is poisonous. However, it is the oil that attracts the slaughterers. In 1895 Joseph Hatch of Invercargill, New Zealand, opened an industry on Macquarie Island, killing – and boiling their carcasses for oil – over 100,000 king penguins a year for more than twenty years until public outcry forced the authorities to refuse him a licence. Early in this century the captain of a whale-catcher fuelled his ship by burning penguin carcasses, having nothing else left with which to feed the furnaces. And when Shackleton's party landed on Elephant Island in 1916 they slaughtered hundreds of Adélie penguins for both meat and oil. Penguins in Antarctica now have two enemies, the leopard seal, which lives off Adélies and chinstraps from the coastal colonies of the Antarctic continent, and the killer whale. Falkland Islanders frequently eat penguin eggs, slightly larger than goose eggs and with a much greasier yolk.

Penguins are amongst the oldest inhabitants of Antarctica. A fossil of a penguin has been found in the Antarctic Peninsula that dates back sixty million years. It is believed that the beasts were man-sized then, about five and a half feet tall. According to some experts, the bone structure indicates that their predecessors were capable of flight, but today they are more like aquatic birds as their wings are incapable of flexing like those of birds of flight and are used instead as paddles or flippers. In St Andrew's Bay and the neighbouring Royal Bay the king penguins gave wonderfully gymnastic displays diving through the surf and gliding out to sea.

Royal Bay is a long curve, much broader than St Andrew's. Flying across from the kings' colony at St Andrew's we passed some formidable mountains of jagged rock and what looked like crumbling cinder: the range seemed impossible to traverse on foot. On the beach at Royal Bay there was a thinnish crowd of king penguins and a few men who had come ashore from *Endurance* by boat to have a last opportunity to stretch their legs before sailing for Antarctica, and to indulge once again in teasing the slumbering harems of elephant seals. Liveliest of all was the reception from the fur seals who bounced up and down the beach yapping loudly at man and beast. One pup was cuffed sharply round the head by an exasperated king penguin who then beat a judicious retreat. The marines' commander, George Gelder, was snapped at by a particularly noisy family of maturing pups who tried to drive him into the sea before allowing him to photograph them. He decided to bring the family to order with a sharp word of command in his best parade-ground manner, and the pups bolted.

From 1882 to 1883 a survey party stayed at Royal Bay as part of the programme for the First International Polar Year. The German team of eleven was commanded by Dr K. Schrader. They carried out life science studies and prepared maps, including one of this part of South Georgia. Meteorology, geology and magnetometry featured in the programme also. The records of the expedition suggest that they left behind thermometers recording maximum and minimum temperatures. These have never been recovered. Captain MacGregor set off on a steep crag to one side of the bay to see if he could find any trace of the instruments. With two of the helicopter crew, I set off in a more desultory fashion. Unfortunately I was still wearing the seven layers of clothing I had put on that morning for the day's flying. We sweated up the mountain in hot sunshine. The ship was a tiny red dot out at sea in the bay. We could hear the occasional shouts of the men on the beach and then the booming roar of the elephant seals, a steady crescendo of belching sound, the roar of the MGM lion amplified a hundred times by the proboscises of the animals themselves and the echoing mountains. After panting several hundred feet up the loose rock and shale we grasped handfuls of crystalline snow and ate it. From the far side of the bay came a crack like an artillery battery, as small mountains of ice thundered into the sea from the two glaciers.

A couple of hundred feet from the top we gave up the struggle. Captain MacGregor's party had not found the thermometers, but they had found the Germans' flagpole, now rusted through completely, and what might have been the covering for the instruments they left behind. The Polar Year of 1882 was one of the first co-ordinated international research ventures in Antarctica. Most of its projects, in which twelve nations took part, were in the Arctic, and the same happened fifty years later when a Second Polar Year was declared, largely at the instigation of German scientists. The balance of interest between north and south was reversed with the International Geophysical Year (IGY) of 1957–8, the heir to the Polar Year programmes, and this led to the biggest combined scientific assault on Antarctica in modern times. It resulted in, amongst other things, the fulfilment of Shackleton's dream when Sir Vivian Fuchs' Commonwealth Expedition achieved the crossing of the Antarctic continent.

There seems every chance that in the immediate future the main use of South Georgia will be scientific research and little more. In his revised economic study of the Falkland Islands of September 1982, Sir Ernest Shackleton's son, the present Lord Shackleton, expressed the hope that offshore marine resources would be developed from bases on the island. The plunder of the whalers in this century, and the sealers in the last, looks unlikely to be repeated on a large scale. Unfortunately the island does seem likely to remain a pawn in the game of claim and counter-claim for territorial sovereignty between Britain and Argentina.

From the helicopters flying across Royal Bay that evening, South Georgia was at its most tranquil. The sea was flat and calm, the colours of the hills around the bay a light pastel green. The two glaciers, Weddell and Ross, glistened turquoise blue in the evening sun. The penguins and seals were not even dots where the men had teased them in Moltke Bay, named after the ship of the German expedition a hundred years ago. That night *Endurance* followed James Cook's course around the northern coast of South Georgia, which he described as being thirty-one leagues (ninety-three miles) long in 1775. At first he thought it might be part of the southern continent which he had seen shielded by the Great Ice Barrier the year before in the Pacific Sector of the Antarctic Ocean. When he discovered it was not, he named the southernmost tip of the island Cape Disappointment before turning again to the south.

# Chapter 3

# Chess and
# the Scotia Sea

South of Cape Disappointment the seas were murky and grey, the horizons a wall of heavy fog. Icebergs were beginning to appear from the south, though at first they presented no great hazard to navigation. Following the path traced by Cook in 1775, *Endurance* passed the group of islands he called Candlemas, after the festival – 2 February – on which he sighted them. They are part of a chain of islands forming a shallow arc about 290 miles south of South Georgia. So difficult were conditions for surveying in detail that Cook thought many of these islands were one land mass and he named the whole archipelago Sandwich Land after Lord Sandwich, First Lord of the Admiralty.

The islands of the South Sandwich group emerged from the mist as indistinct blurs. It was hard to tell where the icebergs ended and the land began. Rammed up against one side of Bristol Island was a huge tabular iceberg, flat and gleaming like a slab of polystyrene. Beneath the blue mountains, shrouded in snow and mist, glaciers split and tumbled to the sea. It is likely that Cook made his most melancholy judgement on the lands of the Southern Ocean when observing such scenery: 'Thick fogs, snowstorms, intense cold and every other thing that can render navigation dangerous, must be encountered; and these difficulties are greatly heightened by the inexpressibly horrid aspect of the country; a country doomed by nature never once to feel the warmth of the sun's rays, but to lie buried in everlasting snow and ice.' In the next sentence he predicted the fate suffered by the first *Endurance* in the Weddell pack ice in 1915, and countless other whaling and sealing ships: 'The ports which may be on the coast are, in a manner, wholly filled up with frozen snow of vast thickness; but if any should be so far open as to invite a ship into it, she would run a risk of being fixed there for ever, or of coming out in an ice island.'

HMS *Endurance* passed the first island in the chain, Zavodovski, without sighting it in the dark and mist. It was named by Thaddeus von Bellingshausen, commander of the Russian Expedition that circum-navigated Antarctica in 1819–21. Bellingshausen, to judge from his portraits a splendidly heroic figure, in the full dress uniform of Alexander I's Imperial Russian Navy, came from the Baltic and joined the service at the age of ten. He died a full admiral and governor of Kronstadt. In some respects his story is part of the catalogue of heroic failures in the Antarctic, for he was possibly the first to sight the southern continent, though he did not at the time realise what it was. A matter of days later, on 30 January 1820, the British sealing captain Edward Bransfield claimed to have sighted the land of the Antarctic Peninsula.

Though Bellingshausen made no such public claim, he was the first to identify land inside the Antarctic Circle: two islands he named after Peter the Great and Alexander I. Despite his martial appearance he followed closely the serious scientific tradition of Cook and his surveys were both thorough and accurate. He disposed of the suggestion that the South Sandwich Islands were part of a larger land mass, possibly a continent; under his command Lieutenant-Commander Zavodovski, captain of one of his two ships, discovered the volcano on the island named after him. While Bellingshausen himself stayed offshore he climbed halfway up the mountain and found steam shooting from the top. The volcano is reported to be in continuous activity still.

Some place-names in the Antarctic seem to be attractive in inverse proportion to the barrenness and desolation of the locations they are attached to. The South Sandwich group, for example, has some of the most suggestive and alluring, ranging from the mythical to the whimsical to the practical. Others are purely descriptive: the peak Zavodovski climbed and where he was choked with sulphur fumes is called Stench Point, which is not far from Fume Point; and the volcano itself is called Mount Asphyxia. It is a single volcanic cone nine miles in circumference and about 2000 feet high. On Visokoi Island, another volcano, twenty-five miles south-south-east of Zavodovski, are Finger Point and Coffin Rock. A curious mixture of classical mythology and prosaic topographical likeness characterises Candlemas Island: Mounts Andromeda and Perseus rise to 2000 feet; there are Medusa and Gorgon Pool and Chimaera Flats; the all too explicitly named lava ramp of Breakbones Plateau lies next to Lucifer Hill. On neighbouring Vindication Island there is Chinstrap Point, Buddha Rock and Castor and Pollux Rocks, Braces Point (the north-east extremity of the island) and two natural arches in rock, each over 100 feet tall, called Cook Rock and Trousers Rock. Bellingshausen followed Cook's tactful and practical example in acknowledging his patron and the group containing Zavodovski, Leskov and Visokoi are collectively known as the Traversay Islands, after the Marquis de Traverse.

Naming places in Antarctica has now become a tricky business. Since the Antarctic Treaty came into operation in 1961, permission to name new locations has to be obtained from an international committee. Each expedition is usually allowed only two new names.

After Bellingshausen's southern voyage the Russians sent no more expeditions to Antarctica until 1956 when they made a massive contribution to the preparations for the IGY programmes. Now most of their many bases are spread around the coast of the continent itself, and, appropriately enough, that at the tip of the Peninsula is named Bellingshausen.

The list of sealers, whalers and marines who visited the South Sandwich Islands in the century following Bellingshausen reads like an Antarctic 'Who's Who'. In December 1830 an American sealer, Captain James Brown, visited the Traversay Islands, and in the same month John Biscoe, a British sealer, with the brig *Tula* – which only displaced 148 tons – and the cutter *Lively* visited the South Sandwich group. Since he could not land on the islands because of foul weather, Biscoe, a former officer in the Royal Navy, pushed south into the Antarctic ice to discover an area of continental coast, Enderby Land, which bears the name of his employer. The sealers like Biscoe, Bransfield, Weddell and the American Nathaniel Palmer made some of the most important navigational discoveries in Antarctica in the nineteenth century.

At the beginning of this century the Norwegian whaling magnate C.A. Larsen searched the South Sandwich Islands unsuccessfully, with a view to setting up one of his stations there. It was he who brought the Compañía Argentina de Pesca to Grytviken in 1906. Eventually, whaling stations were set up in the islands and they operated sporadically until 1936. In the twentieth century, however, scientists and explorers have been the most distinguished visitors. Lieutenant Filchner's *Deutschland* Expedition took the first photographs in a detailed survey of the islands, and Shackleton made studies on his way south in 1914. In 1922 his second-in-command, Frank Wild, visited Zavodovski. But it has only been possible to make a complete survey of the islands since the advent of helicopters and their use of aerial photography.

The most frequent visitors today are ships of the Royal Navy and the support vessels of BAS, the *John Biscoe* and the *Bransfield*. The group is now on the regular run for *Endurance* in her southern deployment because of the peculiar territorial chess game being played out across the waters of the Scotia Sea by Britain and Argentina. The South Sandwich Islands are regarded by Britain as part of the Falkland Islands Dependencies; island groups in the Scotia Sea south of latitude 60°S, the

Antarctic Treaty's northern boundary, such as the South Orkneys and the South Shetlands, are regarded as part of British Antarctic Territory. All these claims are disputed by Argentina: the sweeping curve from the Falklands through South Georgia, the South Sandwich Islands, South Orkney and Shetland groups are geologically part of the chain formed by the Andes, and this has achieved an almost mystical significance in the claims for Argentine sovereignty in the South Atlantic.

In 1976 the Argentines set up a base on the southernmost island of the South Sandwich group, Southern Thule. On a flat promontory of land at Ferguson Bay they built what they described as a meteorological station. All Argentine bases in Antarctica are manned by military personnel, nearly all air force, whose deployment is allowed by the Antarctic Treaty provided they are used for wholly peaceful purposes and for the logistical support of scientific surveys. Nothing was done to disturb the Argentines, despite the extensive nature of their installations at Ferguson Bay. They had a farm of fuel tanks, raised on stilts to protect them from ground frost and ice, and accommodation blocks, also on stilts, which appeared to have been capable of housing over a hundred men. Intelligence photographs show that the site is dominated by a large aircraft hangar. It is known that the Argentines used the twin-rotored Chinook heavy-lift helicopters to land equipment there; and it was suspected that in an emergency they could have landed Hercules C-130 transport planes on the flat ground beside the buildings. Certainly the photographs show a well-appointed base that could hardly be more military looking, and more than adequately furnished for the observation of the local weather. The establishment of the Southern Thule station was only the second occupation of Falklands and Dependencies territory by the Argentines since HMS *Clio* sent the garrison from Port Louis on the Falklands home to Buenos Aires in 1833. Little action was taken to expel the military meteorologists from Ferguson Bay until the fighting on the Falklands was over in June 1982.

On 20 June of that year a small task group led by HMS *Endurance* with the frigate HMS *Yarmouth* and the tanker RFA *Olmeda,* and a tug in attendance, removed the Argentine personnel. A Royal Marine party was landed and at about the same time *Yarmouth* gave a firepower demonstration, with her main guns dropping a salvo of shells on a bluff near the base. The Argentines surrendered quickly and handed over their personal weapons. I saw them a week later when they were being transferred by tender from the *Yarmouth* to a troop-ship in Stanley harbour. They wore bright-red arctic suits, and had the characteristic smell of tobacco and peat, compounded by the aroma of their standard brew, maté. They looked in better condition than I, and one gestured

46

for me to lift their kitbags aboard the tender. Most of them, if not all, were serving men with the air force.

The station on Southern Thule was left undisturbed, but a visiting British warship discovered six months later that the Union Jack had been taken down and the light blue and white Argentine flag hauled up in its place. Whoever removed the British flag had a delicate touch, because it was found neatly folded under a nearby rock. It is quite likely that a passing fishing vessel had done the deed and not an Argentine naval ship. As a result of the switch of flags, HMS *Apollo* called at the island and a demolition team destroyed the installations with plastic explosive – a rather excessive reaction to this minor tweak to the lion's tail. The promontory at Ferguson Bay is now littered with mangled chunks of metal resembling futuristic sculptures. The only piece of the base still standing is the yard-arm of the flag mast whose concrete plinth still has deep cracks from the demolition operation.

The helicopters from *Endurance* flew towards the spit of land through a soupy sky. The ship moved inshore to carry out a routine sounding of the anchorage which was formed by the sunken cone of a volcano. Whenever she is on passage in southern waters the ship records depths with her echo-sounder: the acrid smell from the carbonised print-out system pervades the chart room and bridge for hours at a time when this task is being undertaken. While the helicopters were flying to the old Argentine base, *Endurance* described a course turning a full 360 degrees, and in the process discovered an astonishing variation in depths across the lagoon. Such findings are forwarded to the Royal Navy's Hydrographer and eventually find their way into one of the navigational bibles, *The Antarctic Pilot*. This is no dry adjunct to the Admiralty charts of the area, but a fund of anecdote and geographical oddity and one of the best sources on the navigational history of Antarctica. The ship's company on the bridge of *Endurance* used to pore over the slim blue volume for hours.

Southern Thule's resident population of gentoo and chinstrap penguins advertised itself to the approaching helicopters even more pungently than did the king penguins at St Andrew's Bay. The flat spit of land by the base was coated in a thick green slime of penguin guano. If an aircraft attempted an emergency landing there now, it would probably skid into the sea. Gentoos, with their grey heads and light orange beaks, waddled and chattered across the old base. The chinstraps had chosen to occupy some of the higher ground beside a sizeable colony of fur seals.

The helicopter crews had come to perform the rite of establishing the British presence by hauling up a flag to the yard-arm. Two previous

Union Jacks had been savaged by the Antarctic gale as brutally as any human agency could devise. While the tatters of the previous flags were cut down, one of the pilots went to the refuge hut beyond the flat ground to check the rations and leave one of a set of Bibles given to *Endurance* by the Scottish Commercial Travellers Christian Union to distribute to such places. The raising of the flag took longer than expected: Gary Hunt, one of the observers, stood on George Gelder's shoulders while he sawed and hacked away at the knots of the old flags, but the halyards were completely destroyed. As a result, the ceremony concluded with a surrealist touch that Luis Buñuel might have envied: because it had to be tied rather than flown, the flag looked as if it were at half-mast.

The episode appears, for the moment at least, to have more to do with the denial of access rather than with utilising the bleak and unpromising lumps of volcanic rock and ash, ice and guano on Southern Thule. In fact, guano, used for fertiliser, is very likely the only commercial resource the island could boast.

Leaving Southern Thule and the South Sandwich Islands, the icebergs became more frequent. Soon the ship would cross the magic line of latitude 60°S. South of this and from longitude 20° to 80°W to the Pole is the wedge of land, sea and ice claimed as British Antarctic Territory, though this claim, along with all others to land on the southern continent, has been set aside under the terms of the Antarctic Treaty. In accordance with this, *Endurance*'s two 20-mm guns were covered with tarpaulins whenever she was in Antarctic waters, and no firing practice was allowed.

Antarctic latitudes are much colder than their equivalents in the Arctic. South Georgia lies at roughly the same distance from the South Pole as Manchester does from the North Pole. Yet the seasonal average temperature is at least 8°C lower in Grytviken than in Manchester. The icebergs were in various states of decay, having travelled north from the Weddell Sea in the mild summer months. Most of them must have been calved from the ice shelf, fed by glaciers moving from the interior of the continent at about half a mile a year. Southern icebergs, tabular bergs, are large slabs of ice, and have none of the angular, jagged edges of Arctic bergs. Some are as big as the smaller islands of the Scotia Sea; a whaler once reported one in the Atlantic Sector of the Antarctic Ocean more than ninety-five miles long, bigger than South Georgia. In 1956 there were reports from the icebreaker USS *Glacier* of an iceberg 335 kilometres (210 miles) by 97 (60 miles) off the Ross Ice Shelf in the Pacific Sector.

Whaling station at Grytviken. The manager's house is to the right, Cumberland Bay beyond

The British Antarctic Survey base on Bird Island

Soldiers of the Grytviken garrison set out on a half-marathon round the harbour

The whale-catcher *Petrel* on the slipway at the whaling station in Grytviken Harbour

The church at Grytviken. It was transferred from Norway and reassembled in
South Georgia in 1913. Services are still held there

51

Whaling sheds at Leith. The station closed in 1964 after the failure of the
Japanese to make it profitable over the previous two seasons

Leith Harbour looking towards the mountains and the Neumayer Glacier,
which Shackleton crossed in 1916

Trying to interview the kings of St Andrew's Bay for radio

*Above and overleaf* The king penguin colony of St Andrew's Bay, South Georgia. This is one of the two big king penguin colonies on the island, with a population of about 20,000 birds

53

A bull elephant seal sounds off as he protects his harem at Leith, South Georgia

*Left* A leopard seal waits for prey on an ice-floe in Orleans Strait, Antarctica. His habitual diet is penguin

*Right* Krill forming, Antarctica. The shrimp-like creatures grow to about two inches long. Krill had just been found forming in chains across the water

Few of the icebergs threaten international shipping routes, though they are a menace to ships in Antarctic waters throughout the year. There is a danger for ships approaching too close of collapse or that an old berg will roll over. Some have underwater rams thrusting thirty or forty feet below the surface, and with smaller bergs barely showing above the water, growlers are particularly hazardous at night. These are small pieces of transparent ice that show the black or green of the sea through them and are less than three feet high. Growlers are difficult for the watchkeeper to spot and can threaten serious damage to the ship's hull or even worse. An even bigger menace in northern waters than in the Antarctic, they are a major hazard to the Labrador fishing fleets and to oil exploration off Newfoundland and Nova Scotia. Occasionally *Endurance* shone her powerful masthead light to pick them out a few hundred feet off the bow.

Further south the icebergs carried a variety of passengers, mostly Adélie penguins and fur seals, who face a long journey home when the ice melts. Penguins make up more than three-quarters of the avian population of Antarctica, if you can label such curious creatures birds. Colonies of more than a quarter of a million Adélies – the most common penguins in Antarctica – have been found on a site of little over fifty acres. There are eleven species of penguin, of which only four are native to the Antarctic continent: Adélie, who have the peculiar circus trick of jumping out of the water as if on springs, chinstrap, emperor and gentoo. Seven species live and breed in the Falklands, and some species have been found as far north as South Africa. One of the most attractive is the chinstrap or ringed, a sociable creature completely unaffected by the presence of humans. At Brabant Island, the British Joint Services Expedition camped in a chinstrap colony and, despite the overpowering stench of the animals and the wild appearance of the men, who had not shaved or cut their hair for months, no one seemed to mind. The most common species on islands like South Georgia is the macaroni, which resembles the rockhopper or jackass of the Falklands, which has tufts of orange hair around the eyes and face, the colour in the case of the macaronis being a much lighter yellow.

The travellers with the greatest stamina were the small birds. At first it was hard for the eye to pick out the snowy petrels against the dazzling white of the icebergs. They and the tiny cape pigeons and Wilson's petrels kept following the ship with quite as much vigour as the larger birds, the albatrosses, petrels and skuas. Laziest of the hitch-hikers on the icebergs were the fur seals who dozed peacefully in the bright sunshine.

Occasionally there would be an announcement over the ship's loud-speakers of a whale sighting. Old hands on *Endurance* reported seeing considerably more whales on the 1984 summer deployment than in previous seasons. Once I made it to the open deck of the bridge wing, camera at the ready, to see the tail of a right whale flick up to the sky, fold back and then slide beneath the waves as the beast made a deep dive. For one glorious moment the tail-fin was a pointed crescent of mammal flesh, silhouetted dramatically against the sea. But I was too slow with my camera and missed that glorious moment, catching instead the instant the tail was horizontal with the surface of the water. The result makes the whale look as if it is some exotic mutation of a water-lily with a thick stem instead of a tail.

Whales divide broadly into two groups: the baleen, who have plates of whalebone to sieve their food, and the toothed, who use their teeth to capture their prey and then swallow it whole.

The baleen's main food source is krill – on a good day a mature blue whale eats up to two tons of the stuff. The principal species are blue, fin, humpback, Bryde's, right and Minke. Of the toothed whales, the sperm is the most famous – thanks to Herman Melville – and orca, the killer whale, the most notorious. Most of this group are fish- and squid-eaters, but the orca lives off seals and penguins, their principal prey in Antarctic waters, and that of the leopard seal.

Pilot whales, slim, shiny black creatures, are not properly whales at all, but a form of dolphin. They frequently encircle ships sailing round South Georgia and the Falklands. In fact, in the late autumn of 1984 the Falkland Islands Company ship *Monseunen* was almost beset by a school of more than fifty, and the master had to heave to while the whales played out their water game. It is not uncommon to see up to a dozen pilot whales beached on the remoter shores of West Falkland.

In the southern oceans, no other species rouses so much emotion from the conservationists as the whales; in the north the debate over whales is matched only by that over the Canadian seal cull. It is thought that over the last 150 years, blue whale stocks have been reduced to five per cent of their former population and humpbacks to three per cent. Factory ships are now going further south to find their prey. In January 1984 the BAS support ship *Bransfield* came across a Russian ship deep in the Bellingshausen Sea close to the ice searching for whales with her sonar and helicopters.

The Japanese and the Russians are now the only nations to hunt whales in Antarctica on a commercial basis. Between them they operate three factory ships of up to 35,000 tons each and thirty to thirty-five whale-catchers, but there are signs that they are now finding whales scarce, and may cease operations altogether. Both countries subscribe to the International Convention for the Regulation of Whaling of 1931 and are members of the International Whaling Commission, set up in 1946. The Commission has moved slowly to establishing quotas, banning, in the 1960s, the hunting of some species, such as blues and humpbacks. However, between the two world wars up to 45,000 whales a year were being slaughtered, and as late as the 1960–1 season over 41,000 were processed by twenty-one factory ships and three land stations. At the 1981 meeting of the Commission an annual catch limit of 8102 Minke whales was set.

Only the Japanese prepare whale meat for human diet – in Japan, where there is a scarcity of other meat sources, it has long been a standard dish. Meat and bone are used otherwise for cattle food and fertiliser; the Russians have at times claimed that only whale oil will suffice for the lubrication of specialised machines in some of their factories. Ambergris, a fatty substance resembling wax, found in the stomach and intestines of the sperm whale, is still prized by the cosmetics industry as a fixative. Sperm whales have been hunted in quantity for spermaceti – the white waxy substance contained in their heads and used for candles and ointments – as well as for meat and oil. The Commission put a limit of 8000 on the annual sperm whale catch for the southern hemisphere. As the larger whales have grown scarce, the whalers have taken smaller species like the Minke, whose meat the Japanese have used, ironically, to feed the animals on mink-farms for their fur trade.

There is some reason to believe that the breeding cycle of many species of whale is becoming shorter, and that this may be related to the depletion of their stocks. Recent ocean surveys by environmental groups such as Greenpeace have suggested a higher rate of pregnancy. But such evidence is almost entirely anecdotal and few modern statistical surveys of stocks are available.

Despite the highly publicised alarm of environmental groups, Dr Richard Laws, director of BAS, and an expert on large mammals, considers that no species are threatened with extinction in the Antarctic today. He initiated the first biological programme at the British base on Signy Island in the South Orkneys in 1948. His studies there were on elephant seals. He subsequently completed three tours in East Africa studying elephants before returning to the British Antarctic Survey.

The South Orkneys lie just over 400 miles south-west of South Georgia and are the most northerly islands of British Antarctic Territory. They were first sighted by sealers in the early nineteenth century. First to arrive was Richard Powell in 1821, accompanied by the American Nathaniel Palmer, who surveyed the two largest islands, Coronation and Laurie. Palmer was a contender, with Bransfield and

Bellingshausen, for the distinction of being the first to discover the Antarctic Peninsula. As a result, the lower part of the peninsula is called Palmer Land. (The northern part is called Graham Land, after the First Lord of the Admiralty in John Biscoe's time, Sir James Graham.) The French explorer Dumont d'Urville called at the South Orkneys before landing on the Antarctic continent.

In the early part of this century, the Scottish National Expedition under Dr William Bruce wintered at Laurie Island and carried out a thorough survey of the anchorage and land. Failing to win financial support for continuing a meteorological centre on Laurie, which he later blamed on Anglo-Saxon prejudice, he handed the station over to the Argentine Meteorological Department in 1904. The Argentines have been there ever since, and their base today is called Orcadas. During the Second World War, when the Navy dispatched a small force to Deception Island as part of Operation 'Tabarin' to prevent German surface ships and submarines sheltering and being resupplied from the Antarctic islands, HMS *Carnarvon* visited the South Orkneys and hoisted a flag on Signy Island, the site of the British scientific base today. The ship's commander, Captain Kitson, visited the Argentines on Laurie at the same time, and the meeting appears to have been friendly, despite fears that the Argentines might have been helping the Germans in other parts of the Southern Ocean. Now, following the Falklands conflict, the British scientists on Signy are counselled by the Foreign and Commonwealth Office not to contact their Argentine neighbours, breaking a tradition of regular chats over the radio that had persisted for decades. It is said that such contacts between British and Argentine scientists at the Antarctic bases went on much as before throughout the first half of 1982.

Signy Island is dominated by the mountains of the larger Coronation Island. The base is tucked behind a bluff which shelters a cove from the blast of onshore wind. In the winter the water around the base is entirely frozen over, and in 1980 conditions were so bad that the ship failed to get in to take away the summer team of scientists, among them the base commander, David Rootes. When I met him, Rootes had just completed seven years working in the Antarctic, five as base commander. He started as a biological assistant and went on to run the station at Signy. Base commanders are usually generalists who are at home handling both men and machinery.

He came aboard *Endurance* with four of the base scientists as the ship's morning routine was beginning. His first job was to stamp the covers for the new issue of British Antarctic Territory stamps. Each base commander acts as postmaster and his signature often gives the first day of issue cover an extra value. Men like Rootes sign hundreds of envelopes a year and the stamps are one of the few income earners in the Antarctic. Once the postal formalities were done with, he accompanied us ashore and gave us a quick guided tour of his domain.

Signy is devoted almost entirely to the life sciences. There are extended studies of shags, the weird cormorants that appear to wear eye make-up, hence the description of one of the principal species, the blue-eyed shags. Adélie and chinstrap penguins and the population of fur seals, which has been going up considerably lately, are studied. Rootes says that so far he has seen no evidence that seals are breeding on Signy, but they are coming south in the summer months to search for krill. As we went by one of the huts he tickled a particularly well-fed specimen, who barked a greeting.

One of the other principal studies is of lichens and mosses growing on the hills of the islands; these are termed the fell field projects. Some of the lichens are hundreds of years old, and the base commanders are concerned that too many people about the settlement at any time can affect these plants permanently. Places like Signy and the Peninsula bases are now on the routes of the tourist cruise ships to the Antarctic and there is some concern that plant life near the camps is at risk.

Another main area of activity is the collection and examination of plant organisms from the freshwater lakes in the mountains. For the morning of our visit *Endurance* sent one of her helicopters to carry a party of scientists to dive beneath the ice of one of the lakes. (Diving continues throughout the winter, as the ice effectively prevents plant life study.) Unfortunately the diaphragm of the breathing apparatus of one of the suits jammed as the dive was getting under way and the diver would have been frozen under the ice had he not been helped out in time. Divers can only work under the ice for a quarter of an hour or so at a time. An expedition to collect specimens involves bringing tents, rations and cooking stoves: for the divers there is a dangerous fall in temperature after coming out of the water, the air often being much colder than the water held by the ice, or the party may be, for some reason, stranded in the hills.

In one of the first huts we visited on the island was a series of tanks full of astonishingly clear water. They contained a host of extravagantly coloured crabs, spiders and fish – orange, yellow and a dreadful, anaemic white. The ice fish – all bulbous head and emaciated body – had a deathly pallor. This is because their haemoglobin is white, unlike that of most fish and animals, and, as Rootes explained, they have comparatively little of it because the waters of their natural habitat are so

61

abundant in oxygen. Underneath their pale bodies were lumps of scaly skin and spindly legs, and they resembled enormous lice. This is exactly what they are, I was told, giant aquatic cousins of the wood louse. Despite their anorexic appearance, the Japanese are beginning to fish them to process as cattle and pig feed.

Many of the huts at Signy are old, some dating back to the early 1950s. The base is in the process of being rebuilt, and the different huts we passed through displayed a strange mixture of the old and very new in Antarctic technology. In one of the working areas there was a visual display unit, part of a small computer; in another there was the long thin Nansen sledge, standard transport for polar explorers for the last hundred years. There were workshops with every conceivable hand-tool, boats in various stages of repair, spare clothing, tents, and stacks of food and cans of beer. The BAS scientists have a strange tradition of buying their own stocks of drink and other stores on the supply ship on the journey south. I asked Rootes how much of a problem chronic drinking and alcoholism were on the bases in the depths of the Antarctic winter. 'Not so much as you might think,' was his most diplomatic reply. 'Generally you try to get the guy with the problem quickly and sort him out. If it's a long-term matter we send him back on the first boat.'

Was boredom the big enemy in winter? 'Again, not as much as you might think. We have superb possibilities for recreation here. The skiing is wonderful on the mountains, and you can take sledges across the sea when it is frozen over. The most spectacular sport is underwater photography. The water is so clear here you can see for many yards in front. Most people become keen photographers here and the results are really breathtaking.'

Skiing and tobogganing have long been organised on a regular basis in Antarctica. South Georgia for years used to have regular winter games for the Norwegians in the whaling stations. But isolation can lead to unpredictable stress. One Christmas recently a man from Grytviken obtained a bottle of Bacardi from one of the Royal Fleet Auxiliary ships supplying the garrison, and died later of alcoholic poisoning. Garrison regulations on drink were tightened up immediately.

The scientists kept telling me how peaceful it was without the steady throb of the generators, the characteristic sound of a base in winter; at Signy they burn about 200 tons of fuel oil a year but much more has to be stored in case there is a delay in the supply ship returning in the summer.

'I suppose you are going to write all that rubbish about scientists going barmy under the ice in the winter,' said a little Scotsman called Dougie Allen, who had been the commander the previous winter of a new base being built in very difficult conditions into the Weddell Ice Shelf at Halley Bay. Allen and Rootes were planning to leave before this winter to go climbing in Peru. Both in their early thirties, they had reached a natural crisis in their lives with BAS. Rootes had decided to seek another job; few scientists and assistants continue working every year in the Antarctic beyond their mid-thirties, whether for reasons of health or family ties.

These two base commanders told me they could see big changes coming in Antarctica soon. Already extra funding for BAS meant building improvements and a revolution in communications using Maritime Satellite links to make direct contact with Cambridge by telephone, telex or facsimile machine. This last meant charts, impossible to describe by voice or in print, could be transmitted in a minute or so. Recently Cambridge had sent a detailed projection of the tides to the Rothera Base on the Argentine Islands, which would have been unthinkable a few years ago.

There was a delightfully informal atmosphere as we chatted over coffee in the kitchen area. Scientists and assistants padded in and out with huge hunks of bread plastered in Marmite. Nearly all wore the uniform of check lumberjack shirt and jeans. As we talked Rootes wondered about the future for science and peaceful scientific co-operation in Antarctica. He said he suspected the commercial exploitation had started already as the fishing fleets round the South Orkneys seemed to be growing year by year. He had seen very little of them lately, but their greater numbers were unmistakable from the sheer volume of radio transmissions they made; quite often this made radio transmission from Signy to Faraday and other bases further south difficult. 'I hope the politicians don't ruin Antarctica by allowing it to be opened up commercially too quickly,' he said. But what of the future of BAS? 'Well, at least there's some expansion after years of cutting back, but it's a pity it took a war to do it.'

A king penguin basks by the tussock grass at Leith

King penguins swimming at Royal Bay

*Above* and *below* Bull elephant seal and one of his harem, South Georgia

Gentoo penguin, Leith

Chinstrap penguin, Leith

*Above* and *below* Fur seal, Brabant Island. Note the ears, a characteristic shared by no other Antarctic or sub-Antarctic species

'Pillars of the community', Royal Bay. King penguins try to outstare a presumptuous young fur seal

Leopard seal, one of the commonest species of seal in Antarctica. It feeds off penguins and crab-eater seals

## Chapter 4

# Ice and Antarctica

A few hours out from Signy Island *Endurance* came to a halt. She lay wallowing in the water like an idle whale for an hour or more, the water banging her sides and rocking the hull quite violently. One of the marine engineers had noticed a knocking sound in the diesel engine and thought the noise should be investigated. A thorough examination failed to reveal the cause, and the engineering officer decided it was safe for the ship to proceed, putting the noise down to yet another symptom of *Endurance*'s creeping senility.

The following morning a thin band of ice appeared on the southern horizon, a string of dots and dashes in blue and white. It was loose pack ice drifting northward from the Weddell Sea, the only sign of the pack we saw on this journey. Usually, in late March pack is more in evidence in the Scotia Sea, and in some years by the beginning of April the sound between Signy and Coronation Island in the South Orkneys is icebound. The austral summer of 1984 had been exceptionally mild. One of the BAS glaciologists working out of the Rothera Base for the summer, Dr Julian Paren, said he had been able to work for ninety-three days out of ninety-six that season, a quite unprecedented record in his own experience; one year he had worked only fifteen. The warm summers seem to follow the pattern of sunspot activity: the greater the number of flares and sunspots the warmer the southern, and northern, polar summer. Flares and sunspots form an important part of the work now carried out by the teams studying atmospheric sciences and climatology in Antarctica. Findings from periods of high sun activity have to be matched with those from the period of lowest activity in the sunspot cycle. One of the first big follow-up programmes to the IGY of 1957–8 was actually called the International Years of the Quiet Sun (IYQS), which involved seventy-one nations using 2000 observing stations in 1964 and 1965. Satellites were used for the first time in a major study of the variation of solar radiation in the X-ray wavelengths.

*Endurance*'s efforts to investigate the band of drifting pack ice, being crudely empirical, could hardly be graced with the mantle of true scientific study. Captain MacGregor had ordered the ship to turn towards the ice to satisfy his curiosity about the thickness of the barrier and how easily the ship could make her way through it. The year before,

*Endurance* had been trapped in the pack off the east coast of the Antarctic Peninsula. The ice house, a rusty metal box with windows at the top of the mast, had been manned by the lookout searching for leads, partings in the ice which could indicate an escape route. Helicopters were sent up to look for leads further out and the paths through the ice were marked by poles with brightly coloured pennants. The 1984 season had been very different, and waters quite far south of the Antarctic Circle had been free of ice. The ship had passed comfortably through the narrow channel between Adelaide Island and the Peninsula, known as the Gullet, in late February.

The line of thick, chunky blue and white ice was much thicker and closer together than had been expected. Rather than go around the barrier again, the captain tried to nose the ship through the weakest part. The ice dipped and rose against the bows and forward part of the hull with the clang and crunch of heavy rock against metal. Some skuas and petrels looked mildly surprised at *Endurance*'s antics, and a sleepy seal even sat up and watched the performance with a disdainful air. Only the snowy petrels seemed unconcerned, and continued to give their bravura display of polar camouflage, their plumage blending with the white floes in the ultimate of 'Now you see me, now you don't' teases.

As the ice crunched and banged round the ship, men hurried forward to the bow and hung over the side snapping photographs. One rushed past me growling, 'Why in the whole wide ocean do we have to head for the biggest bit of ice we can find? What the hell does he [the captain] think we are? A bloody ice-breaker or something?' Indeed *Endurance* carried on as if she were an ice-breaker and pushed and bored her way through the floes, still banging and clanging. One large blue and white floe added a contemporary red slash to its décor, where the ship had left a stripe of her red paint across it.

The characteristics of such ice-floes and bergs are subjects of detailed research by glaciologists. Three seasons previously, the Norwegian glaciologist Monica Kristensen had joined *Endurance* to study icebergs as part of her PhD research on 'Antarctic Tabular Icebergs and Ocean Waves', which she was completing at the Scott Polar Research Institute. The Wasp helicopters would fly her and a colleague to the big bergs, where they would set up strain gauges for a day or so. Apparently, such work is interesting for what it reveals not only about the creation, composition and destruction of icebergs themselves but also about the characteristics and currents of the ocean in which they move.

The weather held fair for *Endurance*'s arrival off the Antarctic Peninsula, where her task was to complete a survey of the Orleans Strait, off Trinity Island. Early that day, Tony Riley, the hydrographer, went off in a helicopter to set up his trisponders at two places on land. These instruments send beams to the ship where the hydrographer's team fixes its position using the intersecting beams. The ship follows a course of parallels, known as tramlines, taking soundings at regular intervals. Position and depth are plotted, then marked by hand on the chart, which when completed looks like a lattice of pencil and ink markings. This work is done on the bridge, the hydrographer yelling 'Fix!' as the position is read from the receivers of the trisponders and the depth recorded from the echo-sounder.

The first of the trisponders was set up on a high bluff of rock flanked by the virgin white of the mountains of Graham Land, their tops scarfed by the thinnest wisp of white cloud. The helicopter could only land at one end of the bluff, so Riley had to haul the heavy batteries and instruments up to the brow of the cliff by hand. Later we flew over and saw a platoon of shags advancing from a concealed position to ambush the men as they assembled the equipment.

From the helicopters we could see up to a hundred miles down the spine of mountains and out to sea. In the sea, chunks of iceberg glistened a deep blue, some embracing lakes of translucent aquamarine where weathering had fashioned holes, whirls and arches worthy of Henry Moore's most majestic achievements in Carrara marble. The mountains themselves reflected a glow of delicate pink as the sun played across them. The glaciers were a forest of blue pinnacles, jagged like rough icing on a cake. The day seemed deceptively mild. After landing more stores for the hydrographers, John Farmar, the flight commander, put the Wasp helicopter into a steady spiralling climb. We swept across the strait to photograph the ship and the islands beyond her.

At 6000 feet we broke through the layer of cloud to see the distant mountain-tops jutting through, points of pure white in the pale-blue sky. By this time my hands were turning shades of bright pink and blue because I had left my gloves behind in order to work the cameras with my fingers; the helicopters were operating with no rear doors as they did habitually in the Antarctic. One of the cameras jammed as the batteries failed in the freezing air. As we flew along the coast and then towards the mountains, enjoyment of the dazzling scene below diminished with the burning pain in my hands suffering temperatures of between $-20°$ and $-25°C$. I had experienced similar agony once before, during the 1976 Icelandic Cod War, when I took a ride across the fishing fleet in a Wasp helicopter without rear doors. I did not have an electrically warmed suit like the pilot and observer were wearing and, after lowering mail to the tugs and trawlers for an hour or so, I returned to the frigate doubled up with cold. It took the rest of the day for me to thaw out properly, and the warming-up process turned out to be even more agonising than the freezing had been.

'That's the stuff we want for our gin and tonics,' said Captain MacGregor, leaning over the bridge wing, 'the absolutely crystal-clear ice.' The chunks of transparent ice had layer after layer laminated together, making it tougher than the strongest steel. Such ice was decades old; some might have even started life one or two hundred years before on the upper reaches of the glaciers. Later, the captain sent one of the ship's boats to collect old ice for the ship's deep-freeze, to be served on Navy days in Portsmouth and at wardroom cocktail parties.

As *Endurance* moved towards the coast on her survey course she would suddenly arrive in a jungle of lumps and rafts of ice – in different shapes and sizes and stages of decay. The older and bigger pieces crashed and thundered against the ship's side and she slipped and shuddered on her course; jagged icicles snapped with loud reports. But she seemed at no risk when she pushed through the waterlogged fragments the seamen describe expressively as slob ice. The forward deflector plates on the hull ensure that a piece of berg does not hit the keel head on. 'But,' said Colin MacGregor, 'it does mean that we have to put more power on than normally to maintain a steady speed through the water. The chunks of iceberg aren't really a danger. In fact there are fewer bits of berg now than when we were here earlier in the season because the temperature has started to drop as the winter approaches. The real problem arises if we have to go astern. While we go ahead, the propeller and rudder are protected because they're in line in the centre of the ship. If we go astern a man has to go down aft and watch the ice. You can damage the rudder badly if it isn't amidships. If it is, then the ice knife behind the propeller can cut through the ice.'

Ice has a vocabulary all of its own. In *The Mariner's Handbook,* a companion volume to *The Antarctic Pilot,* published by the Navy's Hydrographer, there are more than 175 different terms for the various forms and stages of evolution of sea ice. Around the ship as she ploughed her lonely tramline course off Trinity Island we could see a dull film spreading across the open water, the first stage of winter ice, called grease ice. The chunks plopping and cracking in the ship's path were the bergy bits. Some looked like white water-lily leaves with thick curling edges; this is pancake ice. Fast ice is the heavy ice fixed to the continent itself or to the seabed. This can form bays called ice ports where ships can moor. One of the BAS ships moored in an ice port to unload stores for the base at Halley Bay on the Weddell Ice Shelf and stores had to be hoisted and hauled from the ship's decks over ice cliffs more than eighty feet high. Some of the ice vocabulary is self-explanatory while some has an exotic ring: friendly ice is an ice canopy with skylights, thin areas that permit a submarine to surface through them; frazil is fine plates of ice floating in the water; ice breccia are pieces of ice of different ages frozen together; and nilas is an elastic crust of ice which flexes and bends on the surface of the sea. Most threatening are the growlers.

Antarctica is the largest, coldest and highest of the great deserts of the world. In all the superlatives, extraordinary statistics and facts, one set stands out: Antarctica contains in its ice-cap and great ice shelves ninety per cent of all the snow and ice in the world and at least seventy per cent of the planet's freshwater reserves, roughly equivalent to the entire water mass of the Atlantic Ocean. If all the ice melted, the oceans of the world would rise by about 200 feet. Hardly any of the surface of the continent is not covered by ice and snow (about one per cent). The lumps of rock and granite mountain that do jut out of the ice-cap are graced with the Eskimo term nunatak.

The huge reserve of ice makes Antarctica more influential on the world's climate than the Arctic. Satellites show weather systems building up around the continent and being affected by its air stream; they also show the state of sea ice. Thirty years ago, Dr John Heap, now head of the Polar Regions Section, South America Department, at the Foreign and Commonwealth Office, made an exhaustive survey of sea ice in Antarctica for his Cambridge PhD thesis, carrying out months of study round the continent itself. Eight hundred copies of the finished work were printed at the suggestion of the Admiralty. But fewer than twenty have been sold, because within a year of publication satellites with their exact photography had revolutionised the study of sea ice formation and flow. Satellites have also confirmed what geologists had long suspected – a phenomenon known as continental drift. The continents of the earth are not fixed in the oceans but are continuously moving through them: further confirmation was given to this theory by surveys carried out from the space shuttle *Columbia*.

The ice of Antarctica covers eight per cent of the land mass of the southern hemisphere and gives the clearest pointer to what a future ice age might bring. On the land it ranges in thickness from 6000 to 12,000 feet. On 29 January 1968 at Byrd Station in Marie Byrd Land US military scientists drilled through the ice-cap to a depth of 7100 feet and reached the rock beneath. Another method of testing the depth of the ice is one used by oil prospectors: firing a dynamite charge along the surface and listening to the report and echo through special headphones called geophones. On the Commonwealth Trans-Antarctic Expedition of 1957–8 Sir Vivian Fuchs' party fired seismic charges at forty-four different places along their route.

The ice cores extracted from the drilling experiments are remarkable historical records. At the Pole glacier ice forming at about 300 feet is approximately 1000 years old. One to two hundred feet down on the Ross Ice Shelf it is about 200–300 years old and clearly shows the increase in atmospheric pollution from the factories of northern Europe at the beginning of the Industrial Revolution. The Ross Ice Shelf is a sheet of more than 200,000 square miles of ice. The Western Ice Sheet, of which the Ross Ice Shelf is a major part, is much less stable than its bigger eastern counterpart, and the rate at which it accumulates or melts ice is crucial to the world's climate.

The climate of Antarctica is itself full of the unexpected. At the South Pole the average annual snowfall is about two inches, though in the winter on the coasts of the Peninsula more than six feet of snow can fall in a night. *Endurance* was surveying waters off the northernmost part of Antarctica between Trinity Island and the Graham Land Peninsula. The spine of white sugary mountains, the ice, the seals and the birds suggested that this was truly a polar region. Yet we were as far away from the South Pole as that mecca of whalers Nantucket Sound in New England is from the North Pole. Average temperatures are much lower in the Antarctic than they are in the Arctic. This is because Antarctica is a plateau continent covered in ice and snow; the Arctic, on the other hand, is a bowl in which the sea is filled with ice. The average temperature at the South Pole is −50°C and the thermometer never climbs above zero. One of the Russian stations in Greater Antarctica recorded a temperature of −88.3°C.

Over 200 million years ago Antarctica was the centre of a super-continent called Gondwana. Progressively other continents broke away: Africa about 145 million years ago; India about 20 million years later; and finally Australia and New Zealand about 75 million years after that. The name Gondwana derives from the link between Antarctica and the breakaway continents – it means the land of the Gonds, a tribe from one of the mountainous zones of India.

The Antarctic Peninsula is related to the Andean Chain, as are the island groups of the Scotia Sea, from the Falklands sweeping round in a curve through the Sandwich group to the South Orkneys and Shetlands. The continent of Antarctica is today divided into two main areas: Gondwana Province, the shield centred on the South Pole; and the Andean Province, in the west, including the Peninsula. How the Peninsula relates to Gondwana Province is a subject of great debate among geologists and much research. The history of Gondwana and its break-up provides clues to what mineral resources may lie in Antarctica's land mass and continental shelf. All of the continents that broke away from

Gondwana contain valuable minerals and since the composition of the entire supercontinent must have been the same, there is reason enough to believe that there are such deposits in Antarctica itself today.

The oldest rocks are pre-Cambrian – about 4500 to 6000 years old. The oldest fossil was found by Ernest Shackleton on his 1907–9 expedition with the *Nimrod*. In the Beardmore Glacier he discovered a limestone boulder with the fossil of a coral-like organism called an archaeocyathid, which is found elsewhere in rocks from the Cambrian period, and is anything up to 600 million years old. The geology of Antarctica shows that it must have had a warm climate at several different stages in its history. The first recorded ice age was some 250 to 300 million years ago, and this was followed by a warmer time in which parts of the continent were covered with a large fern-like plant called *Glossopetris,* which in the Ohio Range of the Horlick Mountains contributed to coal seams thirteen feet thick. On the return journey from the Pole in 1912, Captain Scott noticed as he crossed the mountains 'coal seams at all heights in the sandstone cliffs and lumps of weathered coal with fossil vegetable. Had a regular field day and got some splendid things in the short time.'

Coal exists in abundance on the continent, but is not considered commercially exploitable. Antarctica also has reserves of cobalt, copper, titanium, iron, nickel, zinc, platinum, uranium, tin and even gold and silver. But it is not known how big they are or if they could be extracted without permanently damaging the environment or at a commercial profit. Oil provides the biggest debate about non-renewable resources. The Japanese and Americans have carried out extensive seismic surveys of both the continent and the continental shelf, but unsurprisingly, government energy departments and commercial oil companies are shy of divulging precise data on their findings and on their predictions of Antarctica's future energy potential. The biggest obstacle to both exploration and exploitation is the ice-cap.

The landscape is made up of glaciers, mountain ranges and deep crevasses. Scott's last expedition had to surmount the barrier of the Beardmore Glacier – at a hundred miles long by twelve wide by no means the biggest in Antarctica – which travels at about a quarter of a mile a year to add fifteen square miles of ice to the Ross Ice Shelf annually. The Eastern and Western Ice Sheets are divided by the Trans-Antarctic Mountain Range, which stretches from Victoria Land, flanking the Ross Sea, to Queen Maud Land in the Atlantic Sector.

The largest of the glaciers, the Lambert, was discovered as recently as 1946–7 by aerial reconnaissance during the American Operation 'Highjump'. The glacier that feeds the Amery Ice Shelf in the Australian Sector was found to be 250 miles long and up to fifty wide, the biggest valley glacier in the world. Overland exploration has been a long and tortuous business and techniques of travel, man-hauling sledges, the use of dog teams and tractors and trains difficult to master. Apart from the shortcomings of man, machine and beast, there was always the dreadful climate and terrain. Winds can reach 120 knots. White-outs are common and blizzards can rage for weeks on end. Apart from crevasses hundreds of feet deep, barriers of glacier ice and mountains, smaller obstacles have blocked the way of the best-prepared expeditions. Sastrugi, dunes of ice from five inches to five feet high, can block the route for tractors and motorsleds. The 1957–8 Commonwealth Trans-Antarctic Expedition had to make detours of several miles to skirt them as they approached the Pole, causing long delays.

The Antarctic continent is roughly the size of Europe, as far as the Urals, and Australia combined, or the United States and Mexico combined. It is the last great wilderness, a playground for animals and birds, for some of the most savage weather known to man, for peaceful scientific endeavour, and for the exercise of the monstrous egos of explorers and navigators. Until very recently more was known to science about the other side of the moon than about much of the ice-cap of the southern continent. As with lunar exploration, satellites have remedied some of the ignorance. They are now used to monitor the weather, observe the state of the ice shelves and map the continent.

Recently the Scott Polar Research Institute in collaboration with American and European universities has produced a Glaciological and Geophysical Folio on Antarctica, the product of a ten-year programme using aircraft radar, aerial photography and echo-sounders. Individual maps show characteristics of the ice sheets, geological make-up and surface temperatures. The complete work, which costs a cool £59 to subscribers, claims to give 'new calculations of the area of Antarctica, mean ice thickness and volume', a mapping achievement that would have enthralled James Cook.

In the wake of the first important land expeditions at the turn of the last century came the first serious claims to territory in Antarctica. The logic of the claims ranges from the eccentric to the surreal, a historical pedant's dream or an international lawyer's nightmare. Since there are no indigenous peoples in Antarctica and no permanent colonies and settlements in the conventional sense, claims are based on first discovery and exploration. Three countries, Australia, Chile and Argentina, adopt a principle enunciated by Paschal Pirier in the Canadian Senate in

February 1907 that countries should be entitled to polar territories bordering them along meridians extended to the poles; a principle that has never been tested in international law. South Africa, although a potential beneficiary of such a theory, has never made a claim to a slice of Antarctic territory.

It is hardly a coincidence that Britain's first important claim to land in Antarctica came in 1908 at the height of what is known as 'the heroic age of exploration'. Letters Patent issued on 21 July 1908 consolidated all territorial claims made in and around Antarctica since 1775, and these now became part of the Falkland Islands Dependencies. In 1917 further Letters Patent clarified the extent of land being claimed in the Antarctic Peninsula itself: the section between longitude 20° and 80°W and named islands. The claims were prompted by commercial considerations as much as by the work of explorers. In 1905 an Anglo-Chilean venture was given a licence by Britain to farm sheep on South Georgia, and the following year the Compañía Argentina de Pesca of Buenos Aires was given a licence by the Falkland Islands government to begin operations at Grytviken. In 1923 a British Order in Council laid claim to the Ross Dependency in the Pacific Sector, later handed over to New Zealand.

The Australian Antarctic Territory claim was made in 1933 by Order in Council and affirmed by an Act of the Canberra Parliament. In 1939 Norway claimed territory between 20°W and 45°E following expeditions from 1929 to 1936 in the area now known as Dronning Maud Land. The Norwegian claim was made partly to forestall the grandiose proclamation by Nazi Germany of a claim to 'Neu-Schwabenland', between 140°W and 20°E. In 1938 the Germans had sent an expedition to Dronning Maud Land; they photographed about 375,000 square miles of Antarctica from the air and dropped metal swastikas at fifteen-mile intervals. After the war no attempt was made to revive the German territorial claim, which had never received outside recognition anyway.

Five countries recognised each other's claims: Britain, Norway, Australia, New Zealand and France, which claimed a narrow strip of Antarctica at Terre Adélie in 1924. The history of France's bid for Antarctic territory is one of the most colourful and strange. It arises from the voyage of discovery made by Jules Sébastien César Dumont d'Urville, a man of extraordinary culture, an expert in botany and entomology and conversant in English, German, Spanish, Italian, Greek and Hebrew. In 1820 during survey work in the Mediterranean he identified the statue of Venus de Milo and persuaded the French consul in Constantinople to secure its preservation; shortly after his promotion to captain in 1829 he was ordered to convey the exiled King Charles X to England.

77

In September 1837 he set out from Toulon with two ships, *Astrolabe* and *Zelée,* and the following January, after surveying the Straits of Magellan, reached the ice pack. He then turned north, stopped in the South Shetlands, sought help for his crew's scurvy in Chile and headed out across the Pacific, stopping at Fiji, Borneo and New Guinea. In 1840 he returned to the ice and discovered a forbidding section of coast – where the gales reached speeds of 200 mph – which he named Terre Adélie after his wife; he landed on small islands, but did not set foot on the mainland. France made her claim to this part of the continent in 1924 but no French expedition landed there until 1949.

Dumont d'Urville was searching for the magnetic pole, and the nearest base to it today bears his name. In 1975 the magnetic pole was fixed at 67°48′S 139°24′E and moving north-west at eight miles a year. Dumont d'Urville returned to France in 1841, only to be killed in a railway accident the following year.

One part of Antarctica has been deemed so hostile – worse than Terre Adélie – that it has never been claimed formally by any country. This is the sector from 90°W to 150°W which embraces Marie Byrd Land. However, three of the national claims are in direct conflict, those of Britain, Argentina and Chile, who all claim the Antarctic Peninsula. Argentina also says the islands of the Scotia Sea and the Malvinas (Falklands) are hers. Chile does not claim South Orkney, South Georgia, or the South Sandwich group, but much of the Bellingshausen Sea, as far west as Peter I Island. This was proclaimed by a presidential decree in 1940, which said it intended 'to fix with accuracy the limits of a sovereignty which has existed since the fifteenth century'. This quaint phraseology is a reference to Pope Alexander VI's decree, enshrined in the Treaty of Tordesillas of 1494, which drew a longitudinal line 370 leagues west of the Cape Verde Islands. Anything to the west of the line was to go to Spain, and to the east to Portugal. Both Chile and Argentina say they are the Hispanic heirs to the treaty.

Argentina began by claiming the South Orkneys in 1925 and the entire Falkland Dependencies in 1927, a claim amplified from 1942 to 1948. In 1942 Argentina left a note rejecting British claims in a sealed canister at Deception Island. The country has contributed quite extensively to the exploration of the islands of the Scotia Sea, and the weather station it inherited from the Scottish Antarctic Expedition of William Speirs Bruce at Orcadas on Laurie Island in the South Orkneys is the longest continually manned base in the entire Antarctic.

Both Russia and America reject Argentine territorial claims and declare their right to work anywhere in Antarctica. In 1949 the Soviet Union declared 'Antarctic Day' in Moscow to celebrate Thaddeus von

Bellingshausen as the first man to discover the continent of Antarctica. In 1956 they embarked on a programme of Antarctic research to support the IGY.

Argentina and Chile reinforce their claim by a strange form of citizenship of their Antarctic territories. In January 1978 Emilio de Palma was born the first national of Argentine Antarctica at Hope Bay at the northernmost point of the Graham Land Peninsula. The families at Hope Bay (Esperanza) change every year. They have a small school, but nearly all the personnel are military, and are said to enjoy some of the best wages in the Argentine armed forces. Chile has been building a more elaborate settlement, Teniente Rodolfo Marsh (formerly Presidente Frei), on Astrolabe Island off the Graham Land Peninsula, where it is hoped to provide accommodation for up to three or four hundred young citizens of Chilean Antarctica. In 1948 the President visited Antarctica, the first head of state to do so, a publicity feat repeated by General Pinochet in January 1977. Four years before, the Argentine cabinet held a four-hour session at Seymour Island in the Weddell Sea to the east of the tip of the Peninsula. The Argentine and Chilean colonies at Esperanza and Marsh require heavy support from the two countries' armed forces and must be very expensive. Britain maintains her presence by altogether cheaper means.

The permanent symbols of the British presence are the BAS scientists and their bases, of which three operate the year round in Antarctica itself. More seasonal and intermittent are publicly sponsored enterprises like the Joint Services Expeditions to Elephant and Brabant Islands. In the summer there are the regular work periods of *Endurance* to survey uncharted waters, support the BAS bases and scientists, in theory at least, and show the flag. The other mark of Britain's presence is the issue of British Antarctic Territory stamps, one of the more attractive aspects of the diplomatic Monopoly game for Antarctic real estate.

The stamps are issued in definitive sets every ten years or so, with special commemorative sets appearing for a few months several times a year. Each base commander has powers as postmaster to frank envelopes at his own base, and the frank can be as valuable as the stamps. Expeditions and military forces set up temporary post offices to issue special covers of stamps, and then the signature of the acting postmaster can be an added attraction. 'Stamps are the bane of my life,' one base commander told me. Most bases receive hundreds of orders for special covers on the first day of issue of a new set of stamps, and the requests come from all over the world. The garrison commander at Grytviken usually signs and franks two to three hundred envelopes in his three or four months there. The whole enterprise is co-ordinated from Stanley, where the head of the Philatelic Bureau at the post office, a former BAS man called Lewis Clifton, is responsible for the issue of new stamps for the British Antarctic Territory, the Falkland Dependencies and the Falklands themselves. The Antarctic stamps yield a profit of about £230,000 a year, which goes to funding BAS, to the scarcely concealed resentment of Sir Rex Hunt.

Many of the BAS men, the crew of *Endurance* and the garrison troops in the Dependencies, become keen philatelists, at least while they are in the south. An added interest for *Endurance*'s collectors is the fact that one of her Wasp helicopters is depicted on the issue commemorating 200 years of manned flight for the Falkland Islands Dependencies. Most avid of the collectors was Wasp 434's pilot, Flight Commander John Farmar, who, in a quest for philatelic one-upmanship, would fly to the most exotic spots to get the helicopter stamp franked. The series celebrates the BAS De Havilland Twin Otters on the five pence stamp, a fact, I should imagine, most of the scientists working in the field find hardly remarkable.

One of the earlier definitive issues was of Antarctic explorers, which posed some delicate diplomatic problems. According to the BAS directors, the plan was to portray as many explorers from the different countries now working under the Antarctic Treaty as possible. Russia, America, Norway, France, Australia, Belgium, were relatively easy to represent, with men like von Bellingshausen, Wilkes and Byrd, Amundsen, Dumont d'Urville, Mawson and de Gerlache, but some of the Latin American countries and newcomers to the field like Japan were hard to reconcile. Also in more anonymous cases, such as the sealer John Biscoe, the likenesses can only have been pretty approximate.

The latest definitive set for the British Antarctic Territory is a far subtler and less diplomatically booby-trapped affair. Ian Loe has prepared some delicate and precise designs of the Antarctic marine ecosystem. It is a highly sophisticated parade of Antarctic creatures great and small, starting, at one penny, with the diatom *Corethron criophilum*. This primitive plant is eaten by herbivores, the most famous of which is our old friend *Euphausia superba*, the krill, which stars on the ten pence issue. The marine heavyweights, such as the crab-eater seal, are on the more expensive stamps and the £3 edition shows the entire food chain from plant through krill to blue whale. The set also shows sponges, jellyfish, such as *Desmonema gaudichaudi,* and squid, such as *Todarodes sagittatus,* plus the isopod *Serolis cornuta,* or giant waterlouse, kinsman to the creature I saw in the tanks at Signy.

The designs are, for me at least, a useful rogues' gallery of the things creeping at the bottom of the Southern Ocean or swimming in it, but they received a thumbs down from *Endurance*'s stewards: 'What have they given us all this lower British pond life for?' a disappointed customer remarked on first seeing the first-day covers. 'I can find more interesting things in the stream at the bottom of my garden back home.'

A recent British Antarctic Territory stamp celebrates one of the successes of international co-operation in Antarctica: the Convention for the Conservation of Seals, agreed in 1972. Looking from the upper decks of *Endurance* as she completed the survey of the Orleans Strait, the seals and the sea birds appeared the true residents of these icebound lands and waters, whatever men might claim with their flags, maps and stamps. Occasionally a floe or bergy bit bearing a sleeping fur seal lay right in the ship's path, the captain ordering a gentle toot on the siren to warn the animal to move in time. Occasionally a broad head would peer above a chunk of ice, and a moment later the slippery black body with a faint mottling on the underside would drop into the water and glide away. This was the leopard seal, who carries an air of quiet menace with its strange bulbous head, rather like that of a giant snake with mumps, and the quick darting movements of its body. The leopard seal is a killer, mainly eating penguins, crab-eater seals and fish.

They have been known to attack humans, too. Shackleton's party were camped on the ice-floes of the Weddell Sea in March 1916, when Orde-Lees, the mechanic, returning to camp one afternoon, found his path blocked by a leopard seal. He shouted to Frank Wild to fetch his rifle, but the animal dived suddenly. Orde-Lees walked to the other side of the floe only to find the creature rearing out of the water snarling at him, showing rows of serrated teeth. It had tracked him by watching his shadow from under the ice. The seal started giving chase when Wild arrived and diverted its attention. Dropping on one knee he had to fire several shots at the advancing beast before he killed it. Later Frank Worsley, another member of the expedition, wrote, 'A man on foot in soft, deep snow and unarmed would not have a chance against such an animal as they almost bound along with a rearing, undulating motion of at least five miles an hour. They attack without provocation, looking on man as a penguin or seal.' The leopard seal shot by Wild was a mature animal, twelve feet long and weighing about 1100 pounds. In its stomach they found balls of hair, the remains of a crab-eater seal it had eaten recently.

On another occasion Shackleton's men were finishing breakfast in the camp on the ice when a leopard seal appeared on a neighbouring floe. Once more Wild grabbed his rifle from his tent and dropped the animal with a single shot. Inside the seal's stomach the men found fifty un-

81

digested fish, which they then prepared for their own meals and found quite edible.

The leopard seals are the most widespread of the Antarctic seals. The rarest is the Ross seal, nicknamed 'the singing seal' for its gentle cooing noise. Like the Weddell seal and the elephant seal, the Ross seal lives largely on squid. The elephant seals are far and away the largest, a mature bull weighing up to four tons, and the Weddell seal is perhaps the hardiest in resisting extreme temperatures. During the winter Weddells spend much of their time in the water under the ice where the temperature is quite a few degrees warmer than the atmosphere on the surface. Weddells stay in the south and do not migrate. Despite their name, crab-eaters live principally off krill, and are found in abundance round the Antarctic Peninsula where they are now being studied closely by life scientists.

Fur seals belong to a different group from the four kinds of Antarctic seal and the elephant seals. They have ears and so are close relatives of the sea-lion. They are migrating in summer towards the Peninsula in greater numbers, very likely following the changing migration of the krill.

The Convention for the Conservation of Antarctic Seals, an instrument arising from the Antarctic Treaty, though not part of it, was agreed in London in February 1972. All hunting of fur, elephant and Ross seals was forbidden and quotas set for other species: a maximum annual catch of 12,000 leopards, 5000 Weddells and 175,000 crab-eaters. Adult Weddell seals are not to be hunted when lying out on fast ice as they are particularly vulnerable to sealers then, and there is to be a closed season for all sealers from the beginning of March to the end of August. Six zones for sealing are designated, and three reserves, where animals may only be hunted after the issue of a permit to cull.

The Convention came into force in 1978, though it has never been actively enforced as there is no sign of a revival of commercial sealing in Antarctic waters at present. About 2500 seals were reported killed from 1964 to 1969, mostly for dog food. The leopard and fur seals on the ice around *Endurance* certainly seemed to think that they might quite safely bask around in the last of the evening sun as it touched the peaks of Trinity Island.

Quality of sunset is a matter for animated debate aboard the ship and is given a rating for photogenic quality on the 'Kodak scale'. As the day's surveying was ending the officer of the watch piped, 'Sunset – Kodak 5.' Kodak 9 is the highest mark given in these waters, but the display the Kodak 5 gave was generous enough. The photographers stood on the upper decks watching as the rays touched the mountains to the west and south – first blue then pink. As it became a ball of orange on the horizon for a few short moments the brash and slob floated in waters of fire. And that was without a lens filter.

In the rarefied air, the mountains of Brabant Island to the south seemed a dozen miles away; they were really about seventy miles off. This was *Endurance*'s next destination, where she would land members of the Joint Services Expedition and make a curious link with the heroic age of Antarctic exploration.

'Flightless bird, birdless flight': king penguins and Wasp helicopter at
St Andrew's Bay

King penguin colony at St Andrew's Bay

Gentle temptation of a party of kings, St Andrew's Bay

*Endurance* and friends, Royal Bay

Unloading stores at Metchnikoff for the winter party of the Joint Services Expedition

François de Gerlache, grandson of Adrien de Gerlache, just before he landed on the island discovered by his grandfather who, in 1898 with the *Belgica* Expedition, was the first to overwinter in Antarctica

# Chapter 5

# Expeditions

When the leaders of the Brabant Island Expedition were laying their plans, they were told not to expect to find too much. Brabant, one of the largest islands to the west of the northern part of the Palmer Peninsula, is a rocky and virtually inaccessible place. No man had spent more than five days there. Glaciers and mountains dominate much of the landscape, the highest peak, Mount Parry, rising to 8250 feet. The coastal rocks and cliffs are largely tillite, and appear fragmented into sharp, jagged pieces.

The Joint Services Expedition of 1983–5, headed by Commander Chris Furse, decided on Brabant as their destination at the suggestion of Sir Vivian Fuchs, former director of BAS. He explained that the island had never been surveyed and was largely unknown to science. The expedition could contribute to a geological survey, collect plant and entomological specimens, and report to BAS on the seals, penguins and sea-birds. After scarcely three months of careful monitoring and collecting Brabant Island had far exceeded expectations and the predictions that they would only find 'a few seals and the odd penguin' were proved almost entirely mistaken.

*Endurance* was the main supply ship for the expedition, which, by the standards of most such enterprises, has been run on modest lines. The ship laid down the first consignment of stores and rations at Palmer, the American base on Anvers Island, the biggest in the Palmer Archipelago, in the first week of March 1982. The expedition had been planned to run consecutively from the austral summer of 1984 through the winter and the austral summer of 1985, with a separate team for each of the three seasonal programmes. Commander Furse and two others decided to stay a full year from January 1984 to January 1985, during which the expedition was to become the first to set out to winter in Antarctica in tents.

The ship arrived off the island on a wild, sunny day in late March. The snowy mountainsides tumbled in small avalanches almost to the sea, and from the coast piles of jagged rock stood up like long, rotten teeth. At Metchnikoff, the main expedition camp, the helicopters had difficulty with the fierce gusts of wind blowing in from the Bellingshausen Sea. They had to fight the gales – which blasted onto the island over thousands of miles of open ocean (2000 miles away to the north-west lies the farthest point from land in the world) – as they made their approach, swirling and dipping around a high bluff of rock and mud that dominated the little cove. The mountains and glaciers were stacked steeply behind. The pilot appeared to indulge in some circus flying as he roared in to the landing zone above the campsite and quickly dropped the machine to earth in a shower of stones, dirt and chips of ice. The main casualty of the landing was one of the tents which Chris Furse had set up the night before as a post office. In the whole day's operation more damage was done to the tents by the helicopters than three months of blizzard, hail, rain, wind and ice showers.

We were welcomed by a group of shaggy men wearing mountaineering clothes of almost every hue. Their faces were a weathered brown framed by long straggly beards and bushy hair. For a group who were seeing the first outsiders for over two months, they were remarkably friendly. Some men have been known to run away from Antarctic bases on the arrival of the first visitors after a long period of isolation. The flight commander, John Farmar, immediately set to work franking the expedition's stamp covers, which should net about £2000 for the team's funds.

As the stamping and countersigning got under way, a tall gangling figure with a long hooked nose and friendly brown face, liberally adorned with thick black beard and hair, loped towards us. His trousers were things of shreds and patches held together with insulating tape, particoloured red and blue after the fashion of contemporary diving and mountaineering gear. This was Commander Furse.

He took me on a tour of his domain accompanied by the photographer, Jed Corbett. While the helicopter crew debated how much flying they could do in the unpredictable and temperamental wind, we slid through the boulders down to the bay. On the way we were eyed by the chin-strap penguins near whose characteristically pungent colony the tents were now pitched. To begin with, the camp had been on the glacier behind, but one night it rained so hard that by morning the tents were left standing on little pedestals of ice several feet high. It was decided to move in with the penguins, a safer prospect but a smellier one. The natives proved friendly, almost too much so, as they regularly walked into the camp on the scrounge at mealtimes. The sheathbills had even less shame and would walk into the tents and attack tins of food and boxes of margarine with their beaks. Sometimes they made night raids into the tents while the men slept, depositing souvenirs of their visits in the boots left at the entrances to the tents.

The penguins shared the bay with several bands of seals. As we climbed along the shore, mature fur seals barked and yapped and played king of the castle on the rocks in the sea. The presence of fur seals had been quite unpredicted, and this must be one of the southernmost colonies ever recorded. More than a thousand have been seen on the island so far and there are high hopes of finding evidence that they are breeding there. The commonest seal round the shores of Brabant is the crab-eater, but between the snapping and growling fur seals lay the dozing, bulbous Weddell seals, soaking up the last summer sun before preparing for winter on and under the ice shelf.

'I'm a great believer in the amateur scientist,' Chris Furse told me as we sheltered from the wind among the rocks of the seals' playground. 'This is a bit of an old-fashioned expedition, with plenty of adventure training for the servicemen, canoeing, mountain-climbing and exploring. This place really is worth exploring, but being so far south we needed plenty of time.'

But why winter in tents in such difficult conditions? 'It wasn't an end in itself. But we really didn't know what support we would get in moving here, and whether we would be able to use *Endurance*. We didn't have the space to bring all the equipment to set up huts. At one point I thought that we might have to hitch a lift on the *Lindblad Explorer,* the tourist ship, so the men would come ashore only with what they could carry in their rucksacks. So it had to be done with tents.'

Furse has been involved in three expeditions to Antarctic islands; two previously have been to Elephant Island in the South Shetlands but the Brabant Island project has been by far the most ambitious of the three. Such enterprises take almost twice as long to organise as they do to execute. Considering private expeditions have been such important vehicles in the past for the discovery and scientific study of Antarctica, it is surprising to observe the disapproval, not to say downright hostility, that they now earn from the scientific establishment operating there. SCAR, the international umbrella organisation set up in 1958 following the IGY, openly states its disapproval of private expeditions. This is because they can consume men and materials of the scientific survey teams – the only organisations in the Antarctic capable of rescuing an expedition in difficulties – that should properly be employed solely in research. BAS might be called on to lend one of its three Twin Otter aircraft to pick up a team stranded on the plateau of the continent, or send one of the ships, the *Bransfield* or the *Biscoe,* to make a rescue by sea. The support given to the Trans-Global Expedition of Sir Ranulph Fiennes, particularly the unexpected request for 100 gallons of fuel from the reserve at Rothera, has become a combination of BAS folk-myth and grievance. Mountaineering and adventure expeditions are now funded privately with very little public input. In December 1983 Chris Bonnington climbed the highest peak on the continent, Mount Vinson, which rises to 16,860 feet in the Lincoln Ellsworth Range. This expedition was backed entirely by his own funds and those of an American benefactor. BAS teams in the Peninsula were told to give the minimum support, and in emergencies only.

In order to qualify for public funds from the Joint Services Trust, the Brabant Island Expedition had to show that it had a serious scientific purpose. The team has collected plant samples and specimens of terrestrial invertebrates ('bugs' as the men called them) for eight universities and scientific laboratories in Britain, and begun a seal and bird census for BAS. Mike Ringe, a geologist from Nottingham University, will complete a year on the island with the winter and second summer party. He is doing a geological survey. 'We're really quite a cheap vehicle for a geologist, all things considered,' said Furse, 'as I doubt if BAS could have afforded to send one man on his own to a place like Brabant.' The botanical finds have turned out as surprising as the zoological: grasses and liverworts have been found on low ground at several spots round the coast.

The Joint Services Committee awarded the team £79,000, which left the members a balance of £71,000 to raise themselves. The Navy gave Avon inflatable rubber boats, and made *Endurance* available for offloading supplies and men. Sponsors donated anything from tents to toothpaste, and quantities of food. A tobacco firm gave 40,000 cigarettes; the most prized item of freight lowered by the helicopter that windy March morning at Metchnikoff Point was a gift of several dozen bottles of Scotch. The expedition was awarded nearly £30,000 by Rolex of Switzerland, but not sample timepieces to test. Commander Furse told me that it would have been all but impossible to mount such a venture without the help of the sponsors, and if the value of their donations is included they bring the total cost of the expedition to about £250,000.

'I don't need an excuse for being here,' Furse replied sharply to a question about the justification for this kind of project. 'There are enough people about who think there are good enough reasons. I'm a very lucky person indeed. Very rarely do you get three chances in your service career to join Antarctic expeditions. I was thirty-four when I went on the first one, and I love the mountains and snow, and the birds and the wild life, and the feeling that you're completely on your own, and that there are no helicopters or mountain rescue to get you if you're in trouble. If you ask me why I do it and how my family feel about my long absences, I suppose I just feel I have to do it, and my wife says I would be unbearable if I didn't.

'The great thing for the blokes who come on these expeditions is that they wouldn't otherwise get the chance to come to Antarctica and they have all the opportunities of mountaineering, canoeing, skiing and boat expeditions as well as the work they do for the scientists. For many it means a complete change of outlook. One member of the first summer team is going back for a mountain leader's course in the services to train other men in climbing techniques. The other thing is the company itself. I came out here in January with people I'd met only once or twice before, and now we're friends for life.'

The friends for life had had more than their ration of excitement and adventure in the summer months. Six men had travelled more than 130 miles in rubber boats from the American base at Palmer to Metchnikoff on Brabant. The Americans were amazed, as they restrict their rubber boats to a radius of two miles from Palmer and the coastguard cutter to ten miles. The boats had to be launched three times, so they could be filmed from several angles; on the third launch they were nearly wrecked as a freak wave threw them inshore towards some jagged rocks. As they moved through the Gerlache Strait, they were flanked by mountains, glaciers and sheer cliffs of rock with no place to land should they encounter trouble. Nearing Brabant they encountered a pair of killer whales, who blasted them with their foul breath as they swam off. The team decided to make a dash for it on the last day as the weather was deteriorating. 'We did it in a nine-hour run,' recalled Corporal Dick Worrall, 'and came surfing into Metchnikoff on a huge wave. We surprised Chris Furse as he was setting out for a spot of bird-watching. It was eleven o'clock in the evening and broad daylight still.'

Later Furse led an expedition to climb Mount Parry, the highest peak on the island. They were within a few hundred feet of the summit and moving along a ridge at much the same height when two of the team started suffering from carbon monoxide poisoning; the attempt had to be aborted. They had been living for a fortnight on three-quarter rations. On another occasion Furse had unroped himself from a party traversing a glacier to look at a plant specimen, only to crash twenty feet down a crevasse, bruising his back and shoulder.

The Sancho Panza to Furse's Don Quixote was the photographer Jed Corbett who had celebrated his twenty-fifth birthday the day he arrived on Brabant. He was a man whose enthusiasm hits you like a punch to the solar plexus, a joking, dancing, spare figure topped with frizzy blond hair and beard. Knives, lenses, pouches of film hung from him like the cutlery and impedimenta of a tramp. To his friends he was 'cosmic Jed', in recognition of his favourite epithet, or 'Jed of the Antarctic'. His verbal patter had the corrosive quality of an Antarctic gale.

'I get really excited here at least three or four times a day. And I think you'd just have to say that everything here is just "cosmic". As you may have gathered, that is my favourite word to describe this place.' This was Jed's opening gambit as we stood watching the seals on the rocks and the chinstrap penguins step through the boulders like old men about to take an early-morning dip. 'These animals own the place and we're just the visitors and we mustn't abuse our privilege.'

Jed, a leading aircraftman and a trained photographer, joined the expedition because it did not seem to require previous experience. The company had been excellent he said and the conditions not really bad. 'We did have a three-foot snowfall in one night, though, and we had to get out of the tents and shovel the snow off them quickly. At least *I* didn't as I had to take the photographs.'

'What do you do when it gets really bad and you're caught in a blizzard?' I enquired. 'Button up. Take on lots of fuel in the food you eat. And when it blows a real hooley, sit there and fester, and hope your tent is still there in the morning.' Jed would enliven such occasions with an attacking style of conversation. He fancied himself as a devil's advocate or Che Guevara of the guerrilla warfare of Brabant small-talk. 'If the talk's about defence, I always take the CND line. It perks things up. One of the lads said you've got to have a dinosaur brain to survive this kind of existence. It can get a bit difficult when you are up in the mountains polking [pulling a sled pack] all day. There you are, the three of you, tied up all day long pulling the 170-pound polk. Everything has to be done by vote, two to one decisions, democracy at work, and you argue. But once you rig your tent at night, you forget it all. You're the best of buddies; what's happened before is all irrelevant.'

Jed's journal was a remarkably graphic document, richly describing everything he observed. High spots were often mealtimes, although the compo army rations offered only half a dozen basic menus. Sometimes the team gorged themselves on sweets: Rolos were Jed's fix. The honesty and wit of Jed's diary make it a wonderful read, though its purpose is as much for therapy as to record for posterity. Journals appear to have been psychological lifelines of many of the great expeditions of the heroic age; Shackleton's men would write up their diaries in even the most trying circumstances during their escape from the Weddell pack, in tents on creaking ice-floes and open boats soaked by rain and snow.

Jed said he derived much of his confidence in difficult moments from the way Chris Furse led the team. 'At first I couldn't have done it without him: he's a remarkable man. The leader has to count for a lot in a thing like this, particularly if you have people like me along. I'm used to sunny holidays in the Isle of Wight.'

Despite his denial of aptitude or experience, Jed seemed to have adapted well to the physical discomfort. On many days it is impossible to wash and in the winter the same clothes will be worn for nine months. 'Quite simple, really,' he explained. 'You get the first three layers on and that's it. You build on that foundation and you build up on the next one until you cannot wear any more. I like big pockets to carry all the bits for the cameras. Change me knicks once a month. I've got twelve pairs. They should last. I might have to start using January's again next January if *Endurance* doesn't come to get us.'

By the time we had wandered back to the camp after watching the seals and penguins, the helicopter had stopped for lunch. The eyes of the expedition members grew round as the pilot produced hard-boiled eggs and apples, two items they could not artificially reproduce despite the culinary variations they could work on the compo menus. Eggs, cheese and fruit were handed over and those of us due to go back to *Endurance* that evening munched Rolos and compo chocolate cake.

The diet and liquid intake of the winter party will be studied carefully as part of the expedition's scientific programme. The one project that more than any other secured the expedition's public funding was the study of the expedition members themselves and how they react to the stress of extreme cold. For a reward of £120 the men of the winter party will have the amount of liquid their bodies are gaining and losing assessed daily and their temperature taken – not always in the most convenient of places – after bouts of exercise.

The cold stress project is the brainchild of a Royal Navy doctor called Howard Oakley, a loquacious and diverting companion with whom I shared a cabin in *Endurance* from Port Stanley. He was a voluble spokesman for the treat-'em-tough school of medicine: a patient should always be told the worst.

While he was not checking and rechecking the stores for the expedition, Oakley explained how his programme had been devised. Two years before, during the Falklands conflict, he had been working at the field hospital at Ajax Bay. As the fighting moved further east he moved to the dressing-station at Teal Inlet and was puzzled by the number of cases of trench foot and frostbite. He had studied cold stress in the dry climate of the Norwegian winter during exercises in Arctic warfare inside the Arctic Circle with the Royal Marines. But he was surprised at how easily trench foot was contracted in the mountains in the Falklands by the British forces and how badly afflicted the Argentines were by frostbite in relatively mild temperatures. At one point, he told me, it was estimated that half the marines on Mount Kent were suffering from trench foot and many could not wear their boots properly. It was thought by the medical profession that all that could be known about this affliction was discovered in the First World War, but there is still a great deal of debate about what it is and how it can be remedied.

Some cold stress experiments, the ones carried out by doctors in Dachau concentration camp for example, have been among the most reprehensible in medical history. Nazi doctors used the prisoners to test reaction to sudden exposure to cold by moving them from warm environments to baths full of ice. The prisoners suffered appallingly and the experiments received universal condemnation. Hypothermia and the effects of exposure in Antarctica have been studied by British doctors for more than thirty years. One of the pioneers was Surgeon Lieutenant-Commander David Dalgliesh who worked for years with the predecessor of BAS, the Falkland Islands Dependencies Survey (FIDS). Under his inspiration, regular grants of about £50,000 a year are made by BAS to the school of medicine at Aberdeen University, which helps organise the medical services for their bases in winter and carries out research into the problems of living at very low temperatures. The interest of such studies is not confined to work in very cold regions. Oakley said he hoped his will be relevant to air-sea rescue work round Britain's coasts, hypothermia in old people, cellular and thermal underwear, and the treatment of cases of mild exposure.

The key to the problems of cold stress, he reckoned, in one of his monologues in the cabin, was not body heat loss so much as fluid loss. Part of the problem may also lie in the surrounding pressure on a body floating in the water. This might explain why so many collapsed and died after rescue from the sea in the Fastnet disaster in 1979. Once the victims were plucked out of the ocean, there was no water pressing on them, and their blood pressure correspondingly dropped as they were taken on board ship or to land. Lifting people from the sea by a strop dangling from a helicopter may become a thing of the past according to Oakley.

'The whole thing is a pretty imprecise science so far,' he told me. 'Cold injury, particularly frostbite, is most likely to occur in someone who is dehydrated. This means the blood becomes thicker and cannot reach out to the fingertips or toes. A skier skis all day and loses moisture through sweat. He tries to replace this by melting snow and drinking it at night, but because he's cold his kidneys are more active and he tends to pass more water. Over a period of three days a man can lose four, five or six pints of water, or even more. If this kind of loss is spread over weeks or months it becomes very serious. You have to limit this by acclimatising, but throughout the winter on Brabant we are all going to need a conscious effort to drink as much as we can.'

The key to acclimatisation is learning to wear as few clothes as possible, and old doctrines about always wearing clean clothes had to go out of the window. 'It doesn't matter really,' was Oakley's view. 'Look at the Eskimos: they wear the same furs all the time. And their furs seem to improve with age. Thermal underwear isn't truly thermal if you compare it with the average thickness of a sweater. We are very interested in finding out just what it does. The best one can say is that it conditions the climate next to the skin, and "wicks" aways the moisture. That's one of the things we hope to find out in our experiments with clothing on Brabant.'

According to Howard Oakley's theories, the difficulties posed to divers in the Antarctic by the extreme cold will limit exploration and extraction of hydrocarbons from the continental shelf. 'There are great limitations on the human side. Working on rigs today poses problems at the limit of what we can do at the moment. An ordinary person loses most of his heat from his skin and clothing. When a diver uses saturated techniques, in other words a highly pressurised helium-oxygen mixture, he moves so much gas through his lungs that this becomes the most important way his heat is lost or gained. In the North Sea it is important to maintain gas temperatures within about half a degree of the right level; half a degree too high he gets hot, half a degree the other way he starts suffering from exposure. When you are talking about diving at greater depths in extremely cold temperatures, you are going to have to regulate the gas temperatures even more closely, and at the moment I really don't think we have the technology to do this. And we don't even have the prospect of the technology to do it. You're talking about getting gas down to a diver at depths of 100 metres or more, and we just don't have the precision required with such an extended system.'

The Brabant Island expedition was not entirely British. The youngest member recruited to the winter party was a twenty-two-year-old Belgian who had just completed his national service with his country's forces deployed with NATO. François de Gerlache is the grandson of Baron Adrien de Gerlache de Gomery, who discovered and named Brabant Island in 1898 when he led what is now generally believed to be the first truly scientific expedition to Antarctica. It was also the first to take tents to the region.

Lieutenant de Gerlache was thirty-five when he commanded the international expedition aboard the *Belgica*. After landing at Brabant and naming Anvers Island, the biggest of the group, the ship drifted south and was beset in the ice for thirteen months at 71°31'S. Thus, the expedition was the first ever to winter in Antarctica. The ordeal was recorded in the account given by the American Dr Frederick Cook in his book *Through the First Antarctic Night*. (Cook later claimed to have been the first to reach the North Pole before Robert Peary.) The crew suffered badly from scurvy, which was alleviated by the ministerings of the mate, a former medical student called Roald Amundsen.

Like so many ventures in Antarctic exploration the *Belgica* Expedition was marked by personal controversy. Many of the team believed that de Gerlache set out deliberately to winter in Antarctica and consciously concealed the navigation record showing that they were heading towards the pack as winter was approaching. The expedition did complete valuable surveys of the Palmer Peninsula coast, particularly the strait that bears its leader's name. Later de Gerlache carried out surveying expeditions to Greenland and the Arctic. In 1914 he helped Ernest Shackleton plan the Imperial Trans-Antarctic Expedition, and sold him his yacht *Polaris* which became the first Antarctic *Endurance,* destined to imitate the *Belgica* by becoming beset in the pack, but not to survive.

The tradition lives on in the de Gerlache family. Baron Gaston de Gerlache, the father of François, paid for his son to become a member of the Brabant Island Expedition. He did so hoping it would encourage Belgium to fund publicly an Antarctic survey so that she could become a full member of the Antarctic Treaty before 1991, when the rules are due to change. In 1957 under the sponsorship of the king, Gaston de Gerlache led Belgium's contribution to the International Geophysical Year programme in Antarctica. Both François' elder brothers have worked in polar regions, one has been to the North Pole five times and assisted missionaries to indigenous peoples in Greenland, and the other has been in Antarctica as part of an international expedition in 1973. One of his sisters, Henri-Anne, has served as a medical assistant to missionaries in the Arctic. François was to help John Spottiswood with the study of crab-eater seals on Brabant.

As he stood on *Endurance*'s flight-deck, waiting to take the helicopter ashore and looking at the unbroken white of the mountains his grandfather discovered eighty-six years ago, he seemed more than a little apprehensive. Maybe it was the thought of the darkness of the Antarctic winter ahead. Possibly it was the weight of the de Gerlache tradition on his shoulders: one of his first duties was to unveil a handsome brass plaque, given by his family to commemorate his grandfather, which was to be fixed to a cairn at Buls Bay. But perhaps his hesitancy had more to do with a simple fear of flying in helicopters after his experiences with NATO forces.

De Gerlache's *Belgica* Expedition of 1897–9 marks the opening of what is now called the 'heroic age of Antarctic exploration' which closes with the death of Shackleton in Grytviken in 1922. The myths of this era are, if anything, more interesting than the achievements – for what they tell us of the social and political attitudes of the nations who backed the ventures, and of the men who took part in them. Three names dominate the story of the heroic era, Scott, Amundsen and Shackleton, and the reputations of all three are still surrounded by controversy. Interesting studies have been written of them as individuals but very little of the ethos of Antarctic exploration as a whole and the weird concoction of fantasy and fact surrounding its heroes. Indeed there is no general study of the history and development of Antarctica currently in print in English.

In the early nineteenth century the tradition of James Cook had been carried on by whalers and sealers, men like Powell, Weddell, Bransfield, Biscoe and Palmer and the whalers of Stonington, Connecticut. They gave detailed accounts of their voyages towards the ice and were motivated by genuine scientific curiosity.

The first man to identify the Antarctic continent was Lieutenant Charles Wilkes of the US Navy. He was sent south with a squadron of five ships to study the possibility of setting up an American whaling industry. In the first season, 1838, he failed to penetrate the Weddell pack and turned north to make repairs and replenish. The following year he cruised round the ice and realised he had sighted the Antarctic continent along a stretch of coast between 150° and 90°E that now bears his name. In doing so he beat Dumont d'Urville by a matter of days. While the French squadron of the *Astrolabe* and the *Zelée* were hove to in the fog during their search for the magnetic pole, they were passed within hailing distance by Wilkes' flagship, the *Porpoise;* characteristically, Wilkes made no attempt to acknowledge the French.

He returned home to face a court martial which upheld complaints of his harsh treatment of the crew. However, his surveying career does not appear to have been hampered: in the American Civil War he commanded the *San Jacinto,* dispatched to find the Confederate commercial destroyer the *Sumter.* In the course of this deployment he stopped and searched a British mail packet, the *Trent.* This caused a serious diplomatic incident because he removed two Confederate commissioners on the passenger list, James Mason and John Slidell. Typically for the career of Wilkes this earned a vote of thanks from the Yankee Congress and public condemnation from President Lincoln; none the less he was promoted rear-admiral on retirement.

The best organised and most successful expedition of that time was led by Sir James Clark Ross, who set out from England in 1839 with two ships, HMS *Erebus* and HMS *Terror.* They were the first to be specially prepared for the southern ice, with double hulls and decks and re-inforced bulkheads. Ross sailed first to Australia and headed south from Tasmania. In January 1841 he sailed through the pack to open water, and went on to discover Victoria Land and the ice shelf that bears his name. Many polar expeditions have set out from the Ross Ice Shelf, including Scott's last and Amundsen's successful bid to reach the Pole first.

Off the southern coast of Victoria Land Ross found two volcanoes: one extinct, which he called Mount Terror; and its twin, which he named Mount Erebus, at 12,450 feet the highest active volcano in Antarctica. Despite failure in his first objective to find the magnetic pole, Ross's expedition completed four consecutive seasons in Antarctic waters carrying out the most detailed and important surveys since James Cook. In 1842 the ships were battered by ice for more than sixty days, had their rudders smashed and were later all but sunk when a gale hurled them against an iceberg. On his return to England Ross published a full account of his southern voyages and in 1848 was elected a Fellow of the Royal Society. That year and the following one, he was in the Arctic searching for Sir John Franklin, who had perished in the discovery of the North-West Passage with, ironically, Ross's former commands, *Terror* and *Erebus*.

From the early 1840s for almost fifty years very little exploration was carried out round Antarctica, and international interest was focused more on the Arctic. In the 1890s enthusiasm for Antarctic discovery returned with a rash of ventures. The Norwegian whalers in search of new harvesting grounds moved further south towards the continent itself, and with them came the explorers. It is an irony of the history of Antarctic exploration that the two men who contributed most to the navigation of the southern oceans and the techniques of travelling across the land, James Cook and Fridtjof Nansen, never saw the continent of Antarctica itself.

Nansen's polymathic achievements are almost unbelievable, even by the standards of the other great explorers in history. In him there was something of the maddening genius of a Leonardo, the great humani-tarianism of a Raoul Wallenberg, the international statesmanship of a Dag Hammarskjöld and the winter athleticism of a Jean-Claude Killy or Ingemar Stenmark. After studying zoology in the Norwegian capital, then called Christiania, his first great interest was Arctic exploration. He set out for Greenland in 1882 and again in 1888. This inspired him with a plan to drift through the Arctic ice by boat, and he laid his project before the government and the Norwegian and Royal Geographical Societies. He told them that he had designed a ship, the *Fram* (meaning forward), with a round bottom so that when the winter ice closed in it would not crush the hull but carry it up on the surface. The ship would then drift on top of the pack. Many thought the scheme crazy and the Norwegian parliament only gave him two-thirds of his requested budget; the king, however, added his name to the list of private subscribers. The *Fram* sailed from Christiania in June 1893; her voyage was a complete success, as everything happened just as Nansen said it would. At one point in March 1895 he thought it safe enough to leave her with the rest of the crew, and with one companion, Hjalmar Johansen, he set out north with dog teams and kayaks. They reached a point (86° 14′N) the furthest north ever achieved and set off back for Spitzbergen. The journey was interrupted by bad ice conditions and the two men were forced to winter in a hut covered with hides, living off polar bear meat and seal blubber. They were carried back to Norway by a British expedition they met on the way led by Frederick Jackson. The *Fram* returned to Christiania in triumph on 9 September 1896.

Nansen was made professor of zoology at Christiania University, but in 1898 he had his title changed to professor of oceanography, a subject that absorbed him for the next twenty years: it led to several scientific voyages in the North Atlantic and the Arctic. He became the inspiration of the great Norwegian explorers in polar regions: Borchgrevink, Amundsen and Shackleton all acknowledged their debt to him. He pioneered and perfected the use of skis and sledges and the proper management of dogs in the polar winter. Skis and sledges bore his name, and the commonest form of transport in the Antarctic is still the long, thin Nansen sledge. He was a great winter athlete and enormously vain about this, cultivating his image with extravagant poses for official portraits in sculpture and paint, and nearly always sporting an enormous broad-brimmed black hat, rather like Henry Raeburn's painting of 'The Skater'. Increasingly he involved himself in politics, championing the dissolution of the union with Sweden, and in 1920 he led the first Norwegian legation to the League of Nations. From this he was asked by the International Red Cross to assist with the repatriation of prisoners of war from the Soviet Union, which did not recognise the League. In September 1921 he told the assembly of the League of Nations in Geneva he had succeeded in repatriating 447,604 prisoners from twenty-six countries. He followed this by raising funds for relieving famine in Russia and later in Greece and Armenia. In 1922 he received the Nobel Peace Prize. He died in 1930.

In 1895 the Sixth International Geographical Congress in London resolved that 'the exploration of the Antarctic regions is the greatest piece of geographical exploration still to be undertaken'. Under this inspiration de Gerlache mounted the *Belgica* enterprise, followed closely by the nominally British venture led by Nansen's friend Carsten Borchgrevink. He was the first man to set foot in Victoria Land on the Antarctic continent with an expedition led by the whaling captain Leonard Kristensen. Borchgrevink's expedition was to be the first to winter there when a camp was established near Cape Adare in Victoria Land in 1899.

The century opened with a flurry of Antarctic expeditions. A Swedish team under Otto Nordenskjöld sledged down the Graham Land Peninsula to 66°S and were later marooned when their ship, the *Antarctic,* was crushed and destroyed by the Weddell pack. Jean-Baptiste Charcot revived France's interest in Antarctica with two ventures, in 1902 and 1908, during which he mapped the Peninsula extensively. In the Pacific Sector a German expedition discovered Wilhelm II Land, at one point fuelling their ship, the *Gauss,* with penguin carcasses. Nearly all the enterprises of the heroic age had a serious goal, but new lands were discovered and named in the image of empire. In keeping with the tradition of the heroic age, the Joint Services team have named a bay after Prince William of Wales.

The era known as the heroic age of Antarctic exploration had opened at the very end of the nineteenth century. It was to last little more than twenty years, in which expeditions national and international, manned by Englishmen, Irishmen, Welshmen and Scotsmen, Norwegians, Swedes and Belgians, Australians and New Zealanders, set about the discovery and scientific exploration of the Antarctic Peninsula and continent. The 'heroic age' is always taken to have opened with de Gerlache's expedition with the *Belgica,* the first to winter in Antarctica, if only by accident, and, for the British at least, the era closes with the death of Ernest Shackleton in Grytviken in 1922.

The belated enthusiasm for Antarctic exploration by nineteenth-century explorers and adventurers appears at first an eccentric historical phenomenon. For most of the nineteenth century much scientific work in Antarctic waters had been sponsored by commercial patrons who sent their ships south to get what harvest they could from seals and fish. Families like City of London oil merchants the Enderbys paid their captains to make meticulous observations of the life of the Antarctic oceans and helped them publish their findings; and the Enderbys subsequently received their reward with the inclusion of their name on the Antarctic map.

Sir George Newnes, the pioneer of popular journalism, subsequently also backed Antarctic discovery. The encouragement of individual patrons was taken up by organisations like the Royal Geographical Society whose Sixth International Geographical Congress in 1895 inspired Baron de Gerlache to organise the *Belgica* Expedition.

As individuals the explorers set out for Antarctica to discover the one completely unknown continent left in the world after the unveiling of the dark continent, Africa, to indulge the craze for amateur geology and biology pioneered by men such as Darwin and Huxley, exercise enormous egos and win fame. For the explorers of the newer nations – Belgium, Norway, Sweden and Australia – there was a chance of enhancing the international reputation of their countries. For men in the services like Scott, it offered the prospect of rapid promotion. For many of the scientists there was a strong artistic and spiritual impulsion to see the glories of natural creation, untouched by the society of men.

In August 1901, the *Discovery,* under the command of Captain Robert Falcon Scott, sailed from Cowes. This expedition marked Scott's greatest achievement in polar exploration, but it led to one of the most pathetic and sordid rivalries in the annals of Antarctica – that between Scott and Shackleton. Controversy over Scott's reputation continues to this day: much writing about it, even in modern school textbooks, amounts to little more than hagiography – criticise him and you risk the charge of disturbing the bones of a saint.

The British Antarctic Expedition, or *Discovery* Expedition as it is generally known today, explored and mapped more of Antarctica than had any previous expedition, and it carried out an extensive biological programme from the ship as she lay in the ice of McMurdo Sound. During the second season, Scott, Ernest Shackleton, who was among the officers, and Edward Wilson, who was later to die with Scott on their return from the Pole in 1912, reached 82° 15'S. In the 1904 season the team surveyed over 1000 miles of land and ice shelf, and new mountains and glaciers. A balloon was used for the first time in the Antarctic, to survey the ice shelf from nearly 1000 feet up.

However, from the beginning, Scott was highly sceptical about the value of dogs for pulling sledges and before setting out he had quarrelled badly with Shackleton, who was invalided home after a severe attack of scurvy in 1903. Scott's criticism of Shackleton in his book *The Voyage of the Discovery,* published the year after his return in 1904, made them enemies for life. They could hardly have been more different. Shackleton was a big, gentle, sentimental, irascible Irishman, always conscious of his role as leader. Scott was an intelligent and dedicated amateur scientist, who seems to have chosen exploration as a path to rapid promotion. His charm and intelligence were greatly admired by his friends and followers in Edwardian society, among them the playwright Sir James Barrie. But in the field his sense of organisation was lamentable, his theories on transport disastrous, and his command curiously indecisive. Scott was the product of the Royal Navy of the Victorian era; Shackleton came from the merchant service.

Scott's second and last expedition to Antarctica, with the *Terra Nova,* is a legend of British Empire, appropriate to the dawn of the era of the popular press. The enterprise was the victim of bad luck from early on. The voyage south from New Zealand in June 1910 was terrible, and three of the Manchurian ponies were lost overboard. Later, as *Terra Nova* lay in McMurdo Sound, one of the three Wolseley motorsleds slipped into the ice and sank as it was being unloaded. Worse still, in February 1911 a northern party commanded by Lieutenant Victor Campbell, which was to explore King Edward VII Land from the east of the Great Ice Barrier of Ross Sea, discovered the Norwegian party led by Roald Amundsen camped at the Bay of Whales, sixty miles nearer the Pole than Scott at McMurdo. The Norwegians approached the *Terra Nova* in a bravura display by driving dog teams across the ice. The meeting confirmed the reports Scott had received earlier that Amundsen intended to race him to the Pole and this appears to have disconcerted his planning and timetable.

The outlines of the story are familiar: the shortage of food because rations for the return journey were consumed on the way out; the failure of the ponies and the superiority of the dog teams; the terrible ordeal of the Beardmore Glacier. On 16 January 1912 Henry Bowers noticed something unusual sticking up in the snow. 'We marched on, found that it was a black flag tied to a sledge bearer,' runs Scott's published journal, 'nearby the remains of a camp; sledge tracks and ski tracks going and coming and the clear trace of dogs' paws – many dogs. This told us the whole story. The Norwegians have forestalled us and are first at the Pole. It is a terrible disappointment, and I am very sorry for my loyal companions.'

The following day Scott and his four companions reached the Pole, exactly a month after the Norwegians. 'Great God! This is an awful place and terrible for us to have laboured to it without the reward of priority,' was Scott's famous verdict delivered for posterity in the journal. Later he raised 'our poor slighted Union Jack, and photographed ourselves – mighty cold work all of it,' and concluded the diary entry for 18 January, 'Well, we have turned our back now on the goal of our ambition and must face our 800 miles of solid dragging – and goodbye to most of the day-dreams!'

Petty Officer Edgar Evans and Captain 'Titus' Oates seemed to suffer most easily from frostbite and were the first to die; Evans's body was left at the foot of the Beardmore Glacier and Oates walked beside the sledge for four days before deliberately sacrificing himself. The party was hit by storms and blizzards. They did manage to pick up the depots laid out earlier, but found that much of the oil had evaporated and the rations were not sufficient. Eleven miles from One Ton Depot Bowers, Wilson and Scott died in their tent. Scott's final written words were: 'Last entry: For God's sake look after our people,' and the legend was born. To the end the team had carried out scientific work: they had dragged thirty-five pounds of rock samples on the sledge to the last camp; they had measured the Pole's height, 9500 feet above sea level, a descent of 1000 feet from 88°S. Amundsen's team did not bother to carry the instruments to make such calculations.

One of the most extraordinary books on the disaster is *The Worst Journey in the World,* by the youngest member of the expedition, Apsley Cherry-Garrard. It was written at the prompting of George Bernard Shaw, a friend of the Cherry-Garrard family, and is a terrible testament to a lifetime's guilt neurosis. Cherry-Garrard had the last realistic chance of finding the polar party on their return journey. In February 1912 he set out with a team of dogs and a sledge loaded with rations, accompanied by Dmetri, a Russian dog-handler. On 4 March he reached One Ton Camp and waited for six days before turning back again, believing the polar party was in no danger. That day Oates was dying, and ten days later the rest of the polar team pitched camp for the last time, eleven miles from where Cherry-Garrard had turned his dogs. He was simply too inexperienced a dog-driver and navigator, and he trusted Scott's timetable for the return from the Pole too blindly. For the rest of his life he was consumed with guilt at his failure to find Scott alive, and he was one of the party who discovered the bodies in their tent on 21 November.

Even Cherry-Garrard's account raises doubts about Scott's planning and execution of his last land journey in Antarctica. Why did he decide on a party of five to make the last part of the run to the Pole from the Great Barrier? The usual practice is to operate in pairs, and a team of four would have been more practical. Like many of his fellow-countrymen versed in polar matters, Scott despised the Scandinavians' use of skis, and most of the expedition had very little experience of them. The use of ponies was an utter failure, particularly without snowshoes when the men accompanying them did use skis. Finally, the laying out and supplying of the depots was questionable.

One of the most readable and critical accounts of the Scott myth is Roland Huntford's *Scott and Amundsen,* which is compiled from myriad original sources, letters, diaries and published works. Huntford questions the myth from beginning to the famous last scene (which was skilfully dramatised for the public by Sir James Barrie). He even questions whether Scott was the last of the trio to die and suggests that they were suffering badly from scurvy through mismanagement of their diet, in contrast to Amundsen's superb organisation of rations. Huntford's book does indeed read sometimes like a polemic against Scott and he sums up the *Terra Nova* venture and its leader as 'one of the most inefficient of Polar expeditions, and one of the worst of Polar explorers'. Much of the exploration establishment has never forgiven Huntford for this, and his use of the extensive archive in the wonderful library of the Scott Polar Research Institute was regarded by some as an abuse. It is still hard to strip the myth from the facts in this tale of disaster, and Scott's champions seem as sensitive as ever more than seventy years after his death.

One of the first intended victims of the myth of the heroic life and death of Captain Scott was Roald Amundsen. It was suggested that he had perpetrated a mean trick by turning the quest for the South Pole into a race, and that he had won by unfair means using dogs instead of man-hauling sledges, 'the most noble form of polar transport', as one of Scott's sponsors put it. Cherry-Garrard writes of 'Amundsen's slick success'. When Amundsen came to give lectures on his journey in England, Lord Curzon, the President of the Royal Geographical Society, refused to meet him. However, the lectures won great public acclaim, his audiences clearly appreciating his serious approach to the subject, though there was precious little time for study and research during the run to the Pole.

After serving as mate with de Gerlache's *Belgica,* Amundsen had spent most of his energies on exploration in the Arctic, and in 1903 made the first successful navigation of the North-West Passage in the forty-seven-ton sloop *Gjoa.* He then planned to drift across the North Pole in Nansen's ship the *Fram.* Despite hearing that Peary had reached the Pole in 1909, he continued to plan an expedition with the *Fram.* By the time she sailed in June 1910 he had planned to attempt to be the first man to the South Pole, which he kept secret, even from the ship's company. A party of scientists waiting to join him for a voyage to the North Pole was left stranded at San Francisco. Fridtjof Nansen was annoyed that Amundsen had not confided in him as he would have helped plan the enterprise, but Amundsen needed little help. A serious student of polar history and navigation, he had made a thorough reading of the published accounts of Borchgrevink, James Clark Ross, Scott's *Discovery* Expedition and Shackleton's *Nimrod* Expedition. He realised that there was land at the Bay of Whales and that he could make a run at the Pole from the eastern side of the Ross Sea. His men were handpicked for this one great adventure, which Borchgrevink likened to a Viking raid in its single purpose. Scott's team included academics, soldiers, navigators, men with previous experience in the Antarctic, and complete novices – like Cherry-Garrard – who paid their own passage.

By starting from the Bay of Whales, Amundsen's party had sixty miles less to run to the Pole than Scott's team. No man has ever again covered such terrain with dogs at such speeds as Amundsen achieved in 1911 and 1912. He, his men, his dogs were dedicated to the race and little else. When they met Victor Campbell's party heading towards King Edward VII Land Amundsen disclaimed any proprietary right to survey first that undiscovered land. Scott, on the other hand, showed just the opposite tendencies about Hut Point and McMurdo, denying the use of his hut there to Shackleton for the *Nimrod* Expedition.

The Norwegian team set out on 20 October 1911 in good conditions, travelling fifteen miles in five or six hours, and on 15 December arrived at the Pole. As they approached, one of the team asked Amundsen to ski to the head of the dog team to urge them; it was a ruse to make sure that their leader was the first man on the South Pole. The men silently shook hands, raised a flag and took photographs. Later, Amundsen wrote:

> I cannot say – even although I know it would have a much greater effect – that I stood at my life's goal. That would be telling stories much too openly. I had better be honest and say right out that I believe no human being stood so diametrically opposed to the goal of his wishes as I did on that occasion. The regions round the North Pole – oh, the Devil take it – the North Pole had attracted me since the days of my childhood, and so I found myself at the South Pole. Can anything more perverse be conceived?

Amundsen clearly marked the Pole with a series of points in a square and then raced to the central point, giving pride of place to Olav Bjaaland, a champion skier from Telemark who had perfected the expedition's skiing technique which, with their use of dogs, was the key to their superiority over Scott's venture.

On 26 January they returned to base at the Bay of Whales. They had been away for little over three months. In that time they had encountered blizzards, white-outs and appalling terrain, particularly the ascent over the Great Barrier at what is called the Devil's Ballroom, which caused them to double back several times.

But Amundsen was to feel his success had been blighted by a number of factors: he was accused of taking little interest in scientific exploration, unlike Scott; he wanted to be the first to the North Pole and had ended up the conqueror of the South Pole – a man of the Arctic trapped in the legend of the Antarctic; the suicide of Hjalmar Johansen, Nansen's sledging companion and his counsellor and companion in the Antarctic, affected him deeply; finally, there was the hagiography of Scott, which concealed the incompetence and shortcomings of the *Discovery* Expedition and implied underhand tactics by the Norwegians. 'I would gladly forgo any honour money, if I could have saved Scott from his terrible death,' was a statement doubtless carefully prepared for the waiting journalists at Madison, Wisconsin, when they asked for his thoughts on the news that Scott had perished, but it contains more than a whiff of Amundsen's characteristic Norse melancholy.

Amundsen returned to the Arctic several times. A sea voyage in 1918 was a failure, and he then tried to fly over the pole with the American Lincoln Ellsworth in 1925, and succeeded the following year in crossing the polar cap by airship with the Italian aeronaut Umberto Nobile. They quarrelled about who should take the credit for the achievement. But in June 1928 when Nobile crashed in the Arctic ice with the dirigible *Italia* Amundsen, in an uncharacteristically foolhardy but generous gesture, set out by seaplane to find him. He was never seen again.

Amundsen's success in reaching the Pole left one great feat of exploration to be completed in Antarctica: the crossing of the continent. This was the aim of Shackleton's expedition, which set out in 1914.

The first such venture under his command, the *Nimrod* Expedition of 1907, had three notable achievements. First, Shackleton himself, with Frank Wild, Lieutenant Adams as meteorologist and Dr Marshall, achieved a Furthest South, setting out from Ross Island on McMurdo Sound and reaching 88°23′S, ninety-seven miles from the Pole. The Manchurian ponies had not been much help and Shackleton realised that if his team went much further they would have difficulty in spinning out the rations at the various depots to complete the return journey. In the end, he and Wild made a dash back to the ship to fetch help for Marshall who was very ill and had to be left behind in a tent under the care of Adams. The team survived, but they were very sick. They had mapped what was to be Scott's route to the Pole, crossing the huge valley glacier which they named, after one of their sponsors, the Beardmore Glacier.

The second achievement was the ascent of Mount Erebus by a six-man party under Professor Edgworth David. It took nearly a week to get to the cone, more than 12,000 feet up, where they were choked by sulphur fumes and saw a column of steam shoot hundreds of feet into the sky. They returned by day, tobogganing down, a technique Shackleton was to improvise crossing the mountains of South Georgia in 1916.

The third triumph was the location of the magnetic pole by a team under Professor David at 72°25′S, 155°25′E at a height of 7260 feet.

Travelling with the party was a young Australian called Douglas Mawson, later to command an expedition of his own. The *Nimrod* sailed for Britain in 1909 with a munificent harvest of scientific data and specimens, over 250 pounds of rock samples alone. More than 1000 miles of new land had been discovered and a team under Brian Armytage had identified five new species of lichen. Mountains and glaciers had been photographed and surveyed. Shackleton was rewarded with a knighthood and received the praise of Amundsen and Scott, who said it was his duty to meet him on his return.

The Imperial Trans-Antarctic Expedition of 1914–16 had no such happy outcome, though it must rank as one of the greatest stories of navigation and survival at sea. Shackleton planned to cross the continent from the Weddell to the Ross Sea. The land party was to set out from Vahsel Bay, and a second group under A.E. Mackintosh was to lay depots out from the Ross Ice Shelf. On 18 January 1915, sixty miles from Vahsel Bay, Shackleton's ship, the *Endurance,* which he had acquired from Adrien de Gerlache, became beset in the Weddell pack, where, as the motor mechanic Orde-Lees so nicely stated in his journal, she was 'frozen like an almond nut in the middle of a chocolate bar'. She drifted north-west until she was abandoned on 27 October; Shackleton had already organised a tent encampment on the ice.

Then the ice under the tents began to crack and the camp had to be shifted at a rush. Wild, Shackleton's friend and the expedition's second-in-command, and the surgeon Dr Alexander Macklin were asked to make a final search of the ship. As they moved through the crew's quarters, beams snapped and shattered with the sound of rifle shots. The ship had been designed by its Norwegian builders to resist only loose ice and not to ride up on dense pack like the *Fram.* Wild and Macklin saw it being gripped by the ice as in a vice, with the heaviest oak bulkheads bulging and buckling. After the final search Dr Macklin wrote, 'I do not think I have had such a horrible sickening sensation of fear as I had whilst in the hold of that breaking ship.' Within an hour of the departure of the two men the ship's side was pierced with barbs of ice and the wheel-house smothered with falling fragments from the floes.

Eventually the men moved in relays across the ice. Food was carefully rationed and seals and penguins were to be killed on the way as the ice-floes in the pack drifted north. There was always the possibility of killing the dog teams for food, a trick learnt from Amundsen, who fed man and beast in the teams with dogs that had become too sick or frail to go on; and on the British base at Rothera today, the only one to maintain dogs, it is still one of the essential practices of dog team economy. The plan, initially, was to head for Paulet Island off the northern tip of Graham

Land where Shackleton hoped for rescue from passing whalers. Progress was painfully slow and for weeks the ship was still in sight.

At five in the afternoon of 21 November, Shackleton yelled, 'She's going, boys!' and the men ran from the tents. They saw the stern of the ship lifted high in the air, her smashed propeller quite visible. Silently she slid into the water and in scarcely a minute the ice had closed over her. In his strangely stiff account of the expedition, *South,* Shackleton does not record his own feelings, but merely gives an entry from the journal of one of his team. By Christmas he had ordered camp struck and for the men to march across the ice, dragging the three ship's boats behind them. Progress was hard and little achieved, so camp, appropriately named Patience, was set again. It was to be base from New Year's Day to 9 April 1916.

The team lived on rations rescued from the ships, the slaughtered dogs, penguins, crab-eater and leopard seals, and the contents of the seals' stomachs where they were edible. They were caught by gales and storms and as they drifted towards the open sea there was the threat of the ice opening beneath them as they slept. During the days of waiting, there were some quarrels and signs of irritation and Shackleton fretted about his authority, never forgetting that he was 'the Boss'. One of the oldest of the party, the carpenter McNeish, refused to pull the boat-sleds further when they were trekking on the ice. Orde-Lees antagonised his fellows by his greed and his habit of hoarding food.

Towards the end of March the floe on which they had drifted for three months in Patience Camp showed signs of cracking. The boats were prepared on 9 April and launched. Then they were tied to a series of icebergs and floes while Shackleton, Wild and Worsley, the captain of the *Endurance,* tried to work out their destination once the boats were sailing in reasonably open water. At night they camped on convenient flat chunks of berg, but the threat of the ice fragmenting was always there. On the night of the 9th a sudden crack cut off one group of men in their tents from the boats. The cry 'Someone's missing' went up and it was Shackleton himself who tore a tent aside to find Leonard Hussey, the meteorologist, drifting away inside his sleeping-bag across the freezing water. He hauled man and soaking sleeping-bag from the sea. The boats were finally launched to head out to the open ocean on 12 April, their destination Elephant Island, 800 miles away in the South Shetlands, a lonely, barren place hardly visited by the whalers.

It was now that Frank Worsley came into his own. His skills as a navigator and helmsman of small boats were astonishing. According to the compilation of many of the journals of the expedition members by the American Alfred Lansing, Worsley had been seen as *Endurance*'s weak and rather fanciful captain before Shackleton joined. His own account of the story, *Antarctic Rescue, Shackleton's Boat Journey,* really begins with the launching of the boats for Elephant Island; the successful landing on 15 April and subsequent voyage to South Georgia were largely due to his excellent abilities as navigator. The landing at Elephant Island was particularly hazardous. 'Squall by squall the wind grew fiercer and the sea heavier,' wrote Worsley later. 'Through a rift in the clouds the moon shone out on the stormy sea and for two minutes revealed the ghostly white uplands and glaciers of the island. Another squall blotted everything out. We heard whales blow right alongside. They may have been killers, but, whatever they were, a push from one of them would have capsized us.'

Camp was soon shifted to a promontory which is now called Cape Wild, where for more than four months they had only a few hundred yards of beach and rock on which to exercise. At the end of April Shackleton set out quickly with the best of the boats, the *James Caird,* a twenty-foot cutter, for South Georgia, leaving Wild in charge of those remaining behind on the island. It says something for his leadership that friction between the men diminished rather than worsened during the long wait. Some were in a sorry state on landing. Perce Blackboro, who had started as a stowaway, had chronic frostbite in his feet. Later, the two doctors amputated the toes, to prevent gangrene spreading, using the last six ounces of chloroform they had in the medicine chest as anaesthetic. Louis Rickenson, the chief engineer, collapsed with a heart attack on the boats' first beaching, but he made a steady recovery. Shackleton and his five companions had to cross some of the worst open water in the world – Drake Passage. Unlike anywhere else on the planet, the winds there roar from west to east across oceans uninterrupted by land. The boat was battered by gales and snowstorms and terrifying waves, between fifty and ninety feet high, known as greybeards. Snow and ice were sometimes a foot thick on the mast and upper decking. If Worsley's navigation was wrong they would miss South Georgia altogether; the nearest land would then be a further 3000 miles away in South Africa. The sun only appeared three times to give Worsley a clear chance of making a fix, but his calculations had pinpoint accuracy. After a fortnight at sea they managed to make a safe beaching in King Haakon Bay on South Georgia.

Camp was made in the upturned boat and after dining on albatrosses and their chicks, Shackleton set out across the mountains with Worsley and Tom Crean, who had accompanied Scott as far as the Beardmore Glacier in 1911. They made the crossing in just under three days, a feat not accomplished again until 1955 and then by a properly equipped team led by Duncan Carse. At Leith the Norwegian skippers asked to meet Sir Ernest and his companions and stood round them shaking their hands in silent admiration and astonishment at their achievement. In a few days Sir Ernest, Worsley and Crean travelled to Haakon Sound to recover the *James Caird* and their three companions. The rescue from Elephant Island was not so easy. Three attempts with three different ships failed. Finally, the Chilean tug *Yelcho*, commanded by Lieutenant Pardo, arrived off the island on 30 August 1916. Not a man had been lost from the entire company that sailed from South America aboard the *Endurance* two years before. However, three did perish with the party that went to the Ross Sea with the Imperial Trans-Antarctic Expedition.

Shackleton was a born leader, but Worsley said at times there was something fussy, over-solicitous, even 'womanish' as he put it, about the way 'the Boss' ran things. Not one to avoid a touch of sentimentality himself, Worsley concludes his short book with a meditation on visiting Shackleton's grave at Grytviken: 'It seemed to me that among all his achievements and triumphs, great as they were, his one failure was the most glorious. By self-sacrifice and throwing his own life into the balance he saved every one of his men – not a life was lost – although at times it had looked unlikely that one could be saved.

'His outstanding characteristics were his care of, and anxiety for the lives and well-being of all his men.'

One of the most outstanding features of the record of Shackleton's expedition with the *Endurance* was the photography of Frank Hurley, who also became an ingenious improviser in the construction of cooking equipment on the ice-floes and at Elephant Island. His photographs of *Endurance* in the ice are among the finest of their kind, particularly the shot of her at night with her yard-arms and mast draped in frost and icicles. He set well over two dozen flares in the snow round the ship and then triggered them simultaneously. His comrades were convinced that he had blown himself up and came running from their tents to look for his body.

Hurley had worked earlier with his fellow countryman Douglas Mawson on the Australian Expedition of 1911–14. On the way south a radio station was set up on Macquarie Island, and for the first time Antarctic exploration established a radio link with the outside world, relaying radio messages regularly from King George V Coast to Australia. On 10 November Mawson with two companions, Lieutenant B.E.S. Ninnis and Dr Xavier Mertz, set out with a pair of dog teams and two and a half months' rations to explore the barren coast from their base at Cape Dennison eastward to Cape Adare. In the first month they covered 300 miles but then suddenly Ninnis and his dog team vanished down a crevasse and were never found. They had taken with them the dog food, the tent and all but a couple of weeks' worth of human rations. Mawson and Mertz then tried to make their way back to base with their six dogs, who became so thin that they carried hardly any flesh on them; the only substantial parts left were their livers. The two men began to suffer from nausea, dizziness, delirium, dysentery, cracked lips and hair loss. Mertz began having fits and one night Mawson had to sit on his chest to quieten him. By the morning Mertz had died. Mawson struggled the last eighty miles alone, resorting even to eating his boots. Eight miles from the Cape Dennison base he was holed up in his makeshift tent by a blizzard which blew for a week. On 8 February he staggered into the base to find the relief ship had just left and only five men were staying the winter. They nursed him back to health in two months. Years later it was discovered that husky liver contains ten times the lethal dose of vitamin A and this had led to Mawson's sickness and the death of Mertz. Hurley had filmed part of Mawson's departure with Ninnis and Mertz, whose names were given to the two biggest glaciers of Adélie Land.

Summarising the qualities of the three men who dominate the story of the heroic age, Sir Raymond Priestley, who was Scott's geologist, wrote: 'As a scientific leader give me Scott; for swift and efficient polar travel, Amundsen; but when things are hopeless and there seems no way out, get down on your knees and pray for Shackleton.'

Shackleton's voyage with *Endurance* and his dramatic rescue mark the end of the heroic era. It is worth dwelling on the deeds of those extraordinary men and the motives that drove them to Antarctica if only because the ethos of that age still pervades – consciously and unconsciously – so many attitudes to polar science and exploration today. Sir Douglas Mawson, along with Sir Raymond Priestley and Sir James Wordie (who sailed with both Scott and Shackleton), embraced the transition from their heroic approach to polar exploration to the more precise, scientific approach which characterises modern national and international polar surveys. After the First World War Mawson collaborated with Admiral Byrd to encourage Australia to set up a publicly funded Antarctic research institute.

Many of the physical achievements of the heroic age were not to be imitated or surpassed until quite recently. No one set foot at the Pole after Scott departed it in January 1912 until Admiral George Dufek, commander of the US operation 'Deep Freeze II', landed there in October 1956, though Byrd flew over it in 1929. Shackleton's dream of crossing the Antarctic continent overland was achieved by Sir Vivian Fuchs and the Commonwealth Trans-Antarctic Expedition of 1957–8, in which he followed very roughly Shackleton's proposed route via the Pole.

Sir Edmund Hillary, leading the party laying out depots from the Ross Sea, quite by chance reached the Pole first.

Amundsen and Scott are still the inspiration for overland expeditions, and at least three are due to follow their routes to the Pole in the closing years of the 1980s. One Anglo-Norwegian team made up of Dr Monica Kristensen and Dr Neil McIntyre (both research graduates of the Scott Polar Research Institute), Bjørn Wold (head of the glaciology department of the Norwegian water board) and Nick Cox (a former BAS station assistant who has been restoring Scott's *Discovery* in St Katharine's Dock, London) will follow much of Amundsen's path. The journey from the Bay of Whales to the South Pole is expected to take eighty-one days from 20 October 1985 to 8 January 1986, four more weeks than it took Amundsen. The training programme for the team will take eighteen months and the budget is £250,000, which the members of the expedition have to raise themselves from academic funds, institutes and private sponsors, in much the same way as Nansen, Amundsen, Scott and Shackleton had to find backing for their ventures.

The expedition plans to use dogs, who will have been broken in and trained for about a year before departure, because they are convinced of their suitability on the ice for small research teams. The main scientific aim of the venture is to examine the flexural bending of the Ross Ice Shelf: why it moves, how it moves and what the implications of this are. The team will also be conducting tests on remote sensing of heat and mass changes in the ice shelf from satellites, and the use of oxygen isotopes in the study of deep ice cores.

The Anglo-Norwegian team will have the comfort of satellite navigation and radio links with potential rescuers. But like Amundsen they will have to make the climb with dogs to the great plateau of Antarctica, where they could face temperatures of −40°C. They could also face white-outs, blizzards, crevasses and sastrugi. In that they will have a common bond with Amundsen and Scott. The twelve men wintering on Brabant Island will have braved the same conditions as Frank Wild and the men of the Imperial Trans-Antarctic Expedition on Elephant Island; gales and squalling williwaws, and long Antarctic nights in which more than six feet of snow can fall in a few hours.

# Chapter 6

# Endurance

'If this ship was my house, it would have been condemned years ago,' groaned Ian Weaver, one of the helicopter observers, on hearing that the essential plumbing of *Endurance* had broken down yet again. She is an old ship by the standards of the Royal Navy and has an air of rundown gentility about her. Much of her electricity supply is on direct current, a distinction she shares with the Royal Yacht *Britannia*. She has one of the biggest, and oldest, diesel engines currently in service in the Navy as her main means of propulsion. For most of her company, the two-year assignment with the ice patrol ship is both a privilege and a test of stamina – *Endurance* by nature and by name. Unusually for most men at sea with the Navy since it came to consist largely of a home waters fleet, anyone serving with *Endurance* can expect two deployments of seven months away from Britain. In that time the ship will show the flag in friendly ports on the way to and from the South Atlantic as well as undertake at least three work periods in the Antarctic itself. While she is away she may carry civilian passengers, BAS personnel, the High Commissioner for the Antarctic Territories, research scientists from British and European universities, and the occasional itinerant journalist. *Endurance*'s prime role is diplomatic; chart-making and help for BAS scientists appear secondary. Along with the BAS scientists, the postage stamps and the occasional publicly sponsored expedition, *Endurance* is a symbol of the British presence in Antarctica; and at times she seems a very odd sort of symbol indeed.

There is little about the present *Endurance* that recalls her famous ancestor which perished in the Weddell pack ice in 1915. Outside the captain's cabin hangs a small sketch of St Paul's Cathedral, which Sir Ernest Shackleton apparently took with him on every one of his major expeditions. I say 'apparently' because several accounts of the abandoning of the old *Endurance* say that Sir Ernest ordered trinkets to be thrown away to lighten the load each man would have to carry or haul across the ice, and he set an example by discarding his personal possessions first. The view of St Paul's is none the less the most prized piece of Shackleton memorabilia in the ship, though there was some dispute in the wardroom on the day the ship ran aground as to whether anyone would have remembered to rescue the sketch had we been told to abandon ship. On

the opposite bulkhead from the picture there is what looks like a piece of dilapidated armchair, which is described as a timber from the ocean tug *Yelcho* with which Lieutenant Pardo of the Chilean Navy and Sir Ernest rescued Frank Wild's party from Elephant Island in August 1916. Dotted about the ship are prints of Hurley's photographs of the old *Endurance* in the ice at night, and the studio photograph of Shackleton himself, his wide face like a broader and more rugged version of the standard silent screen idols of the day.

While her age may not be measured quite in elegance, *Endurance* has a certain comfortable charm. There is far more wood in the panelling and bulkheads, the bridge and chartroom than you would find in most British men-of-war today. The living quarters of most modern frigates and destroyers are an ugly mixture of chrome and plastic. The furnishings of the captain's cabin, the wardroom and the senior ratings' mess have the well-scrubbed respectability and durability of a seaside guest-house of the fifties. The floral patterns of the loose covers of the captain's day cabin are pure Frinton front parlour. The sturdiness of the fittings is matched by the ship's tough construction. 'She's very strong,' Captain Colin MacGregor warned me, 'but she'll roll like a coastal minesweeper.' On the bridge bulkhead a calibrated pendulum measured the angle of the roll from the perpendicular to thirty-five degrees on either side. It was a smaller wood and metal version of the swingometer made famous by the late Professor Bob McKenzie in his British general election forecasts on television. Just as this device used to enliven the dull political patter broadcast at election time, so *Endurance*'s de luxe version of the instrument would light up the conversation in the mess in rough weather. After a heavy roll the enquiry would flash up to the bridge to find out the swingometer reading. The record was achieved crossing Drake Passage when a roll of more than 40° took the swingometer needle off the dial and put the remains of the wardroom breakfast in the laps of a group quietly reading at the starboard end of the room. The long-term victims of such weather were those who had bunks crossways, athwartships, for whom nights were a perpetual and violent ride on a seesaw. Those with bunks the length of the ship tended to be lulled by a gentle roller-coaster motion.

*Endurance*'s history matches her robust construction. She started life in 1956 as the Danish-registered freighter *Anita Dan*. Built in a German yard on the Kiel Canal at Rendsburg, she has a special ice-strengthened hull with steel up to one and a half inches thick in the bows, an ice knife

*Opposite* The first *Endurance* beset in the ice in 1915. This famous photograph by Frank Hurley is displayed in the modern *Endurance*. (©Royal Geographical Society)

immediately behind the propeller for cutting her way out of loose pack if she has to go astern, and ribs and struts built closer together in the forward part of the ship than in normal freighters of this size. She is powered by one Burmeister and Wain diesel, which drives the single shaft and propeller.

She was acquired by the Royal Navy from Denmark in 1967 to replace HMS *Protector,* an old anti-submarine boom defence ship, which had been deployed during the fifties and sixties as the British Ice Patrol Ship in Antarctic Waters. The story of *Endurance*'s selection for the Royal Navy is somewhat unusual: a naval officer spotted her moored to a buoy off Copenhagen. He asked what she was doing and was told that she was for sale as her owners had no further use for an ice-strengthened vessel. Within weeks negotiations to buy her were opened.

*Endurance*'s purchase price was £240,000, but her conversion at Harland and Wolff in Belfast brought the cost up to £1.8 million. A flight-deck was added, extra navigation equipment installed and the hull modified to cope with work in Antarctica. This meant the removal of stabilisers, making her roll in heavy weather more pronounced. She has had several major refits since her acquisition, to add items such as satellite navigation aids and equipment for satellite communication. Today she carries two Wasp helicopters, two of the oldest in service with the Navy, and is armed with two 20-mm guns with mountings for general-purpose machine-guns, added following the Falklands conflict. There is some concern that she and her helicopters would have little in reserve if there is a major mechanical breakdown while she is in the South Atlantic. The Wasps are single-engined machines which work flat out. There is some suggestion that the Wasp's successor in the Navy, the Lynx, should be tried at least for one season. During the conflict the reliable Westland Wessex was put on board for the recapture of South Georgia, though it was an attack from one of the Wasps that crippled the submarine *Santa Fé.*

Since her acquisition *Endurance* has been something of a misfit, epitomised by her red hull and red helicopters, but the 'Red Plum' engenders great affection among most who serve with her. For Captain MacGregor her command is one of the best and most varied jobs in the Royal Navy, not least because south of 60°S, inside the area of the Antarctic Treaty, the captain is his own boss, responsible only to an admiral sitting in the outskirts of London at Northwood.

There is an element of the 'Perils of Pauline' about the saga of *Endurance* because she has been written off and put up for sale or scrap at least three times in her strange career. She was put under the South Atlantic Command, which disappeared with the Defence Review of 1974;

this cut back commitments outside NATO and terminated the agreement to use the South African base at Simonstown. It also cancelled the presence of a frigate as South Atlantic guardship and said that *Endurance* would be paid off. Hasty action by the Argentine Navy secured her reprieve, and not for the last time: in December 1975 an Argentine destroyer fired on the BAS survey ship RRS *Shackleton* as she was carrying out an oceanographic project seventy miles south of the Falklands. Successive Labour defence secretaries, Roy Mason and Fred Mulley, agreed to further deployments of *Endurance* until the 1980-1 Review.

The announcement of her withdrawal at the end of the 1980–1 season – a decision confirmed by Parliament in June 1981 – was to prove a most expensive folly. The Foreign Office had already protested vigorously over the move, with the Foreign Secretary, Lord Carrington, explaining to the Secretary of State for Defence, John Nott, that until the sovereignty dispute with Argentina over the Falklands was resolved, the British presence in the South Atlantic should be maintained at current levels. In the words of the Franks Commission on the Falklands conflict, 'Lord Carrington also pointed out that the hydrographic survey tasks HMS *Endurance* undertook and the operation of her helicopters over a wide area of the British Antarctic Territory were an important aspect of the maintenance of the British claim to sovereignty. Although HMS *Endurance* was nearing the end of her normal working life, it was essential that she should be replaced by a vessel of similar type for Antarctic work.' The Joint Councils of the Falkland Islands protested in similar vein with a message to Lord Carrington on 26 June 1981, which ran in part: 'The people of the Falkland Islands deplore in the strongest terms the decision to withdraw HMS *Endurance* from service. They express extreme concern that Britain appears to be abandoning its defence of British interests in the South Atlantic and Antarctic at a time when other powers are strengthening their position in these areas.' The Argentine press made much of the withdrawal of *Endurance,* but on 9 February 1982, Prime Minister Margaret Thatcher told the House of Commons that despite the difficulty of the decision, 'in view of the competing claims on the defence budget and the defence capability of HMS *Endurance,* the Secretary of State for Defence had decided that other claims on the budget should have greater priority.'

A matter of weeks later John Nott reversed his decision. By that time *Endurance* was in the middle of her most perilous and lengthy deployment with the Navy in a conflict in the South Atlantic she was designed to avert and one in the end she did much to resolve. Her continued service with the Royal Navy was thus assured until 1990, when she will be thirty-four years old.

The ship's isolation and role as lone patrol in southern waters can make her vulnerable, as Captain MacGregor's predecessor, Captain Nick Barker, found out in March 1982. After the Argentine scrap men had raised the flag at Leith, *Endurance* was dispatched to keep the operations in Stromness Bay under surveillance and to land Royal Marines at Grytviken. The Argentine strength off South Georgia that last week in March was impressive. The scrap men had been landed by the *Bahia Buen Suceso,* an Argentine navy support vessel. Later the *Bahia Paraiso,* ostensibly a naval scientific survey vessel, arrived with landing craft and soldiers. (During the conflicts, she was claimed by the Argentines as a hospital ship and appropriately plastered with red crosses, though several eyewitnesses saw tons of ammunition being unloaded from her in Port Stanley.) After the Argentines captured Grytviken, Captain Barker was caught in a strange game of hide-and-seek in the loose ice of the Scotia Sea. Once he tried to conceal his bright-red ship in the lee of an iceberg as an Argentine naval squadron approached. He is convinced that one of the Argentine submarines could have sunk *Endurance,* and only the chivalry of the commander of the Argentine Antarctic Squadron, Captain Trombetta, who knew Barker personally, prevented torpedoes being fired. In view of *Endurance*'s role in the recapture of Grytviken and Leith, Captain Trombetta may have lived to regret his gallantry towards her, if such there was. Following the repossession of South Georgia *Endurance* took command of a Task Group of up to twenty-five ships at a time stationed off the island to replenish the forces attempting to retake the Falklands.

The fact that she had to take part in a conflict at all was almost a symptom of failure of one of her primary roles, as a surveillance vessel. Since the beginning of the year Captain Barker and his crew had noticed signs of increased Argentine activity. *Endurance* had monitored the sharp rise in volume of radio signals between Argentine naval units. The scrap-dealer Señor Davidoff had visited South Georgia aboard the naval ice-breaker *Almirante Irizar,* which later sailed for the Argentine base on Southern Thule. At the end of January *Endurance* paid a visit to the naval port of Ushuaia in Tierra del Fuego where members of the Argentine Navy had been told not to fraternise with the British. Captain Barker passed his information and suspicions of Argentine naval intentions to the British embassy in Buenos Aires. He offered to provide junior members of the embassy with video-cassettes of five programmes made in South Georgia and Antarctica by the BBC Television programme *Pebble Mill at One* which had sent a team aboard *Endurance* the year before. His suggestions received almost as cold a reception from the British diplomats in Buenos Aires as his ship had received from the

Argentine command in Ushuaia. Captain Barker, who went on to study the diplomatic implications of the Falklands conflict at Churchill College, Cambridge, on a Defence Fellowship, says that there is now clear evidence that Admiral Anaya, a member of the junta that came into office on 22 December 1981 and a close political and personal colleague of General Galtieri, had planned the Falklands invasion in November 1981, a proposition flatly denied by the Franks Commission Report, which says that no such plan could have been guessed at by British Intelligence until March 1982.

The 1981–2 deployment was the longest in *Endurance*'s service with the Navy: about eight months, more than 230 days. She returned to a triumphal reception at Chatham but a major refit then curtailed her next season in the South Atlantic. The journey out and back can almost be as long as the deployment itself as *Endurance* shows the flag in three or four ports on the way. In the 1982–3 season she visited Lagos, Nigeria, where her helicopters helped fight a blaze in the main telephone and telegraph exchange (which burnt down in highly suspicious circumstances). For Christmas 1983 she was in Valparaiso, where the ship's company took over a couple of hotels for the festive season; and in April 1982 she called at Rio Grande in Brazil. These last visits were indicative of the close co-operation now being sought by the British with Brazil and Chile in Antarctica. The Brazilians were interested in buying *Endurance* following the announcement of her withdrawal in the 1981 Defence Review. Instead they bought her sister ship, formerly the *Thala Dan,* now christened the *Barao De Teffe.* She is smaller than *Endurance,* displacing 2183 tons to *Endurance*'s 3600. She, too, carries a Wasp helicopter but there is no hangar, only a flight-deck which hangs precariously out from her stern. *Endurance*'s helicopter crews were horrified at the lack of special equipment and training for the Brazilian pilots operating in Antarctica when the two ships met there recently.

The helicopters are *Endurance*'s most valuable asset for research work. They can photograph huge areas of ocean and ice-cap for the map-makers of the hydrography department and the glaciologists and geologists of BAS. On the goodwill visit to the Bahamas at the end of 1983 the helicopter crew carried out a photographic survey of Nassau harbour, but the Chileans refused permission for a similar exercise over the port of Valparaiso. The flight-deck of *Endurance* is the home of a tight-knit team, almost literally so, for every time a camera was waved in their direction they fell into a group photograph pose in a matter of seconds. Because of the added hazard of cold to the air-frames, equipment and aircraft have to be checked constantly. Every month the pilots and observers check that they have sufficient equipment, survival harnesses, boats and tents, to survive in the Antarctic for several weeks if they are forced down by foul weather, blizzards or white-outs. The helicopters are prized by the scientists who work with the ship. Dr Monica Kristensen used them to land on icebergs when she was carrying out stress tests of ice. The Wasps regularly take geologists and glaciologists from the BAS bases onto the Antarctic Plateau, a journey that might take days or weeks with skiddoos and tractors. A BAS geologist calculated that he achieved in two and a half days with helicopters what might have taken him nearly two months otherwise. The main complaint of the BAS scientists is that they cannot work with the helicopters enough.

The helicopter crews tended to be the leaders of the fitness club aboard, and took exercise on the flight-deck and in a stores area nearly every day. The flight commander, John Farmar, relieved training with his passion for stamps, inventing new and more elaborate franks for every location he visited. The second pilot, Dave Issett, looked like an East End 'bovver boy' or a Bay City Roller with his severe crew cut and threatening gait. This was an image he much resented as his intimates took to calling him 'John' with a grunt punctuated by a sharp North London sniff. The image belied his quiet, generous character. An excellent pilot, he was an even more dedicated engineer, and hoped to combine both interests by working as a test pilot for the Navy.

Towards the end of the deployment, most of the company kept themselves to themselves. The lumpy swell and damp days had a soporific effect, and when not working most of the men divided their time between watching videos and sleeping. Video has completely changed the social pattern of life aboard the ships of the Navy. Ten years ago, much thought and energy was expended in mess activities, challenges for a games night to rival messes, chess and card tournaments and quiz competitions. *Endurance*'s company were very much of the television and video generation, and there was only one games night in the three weeks I was with the ship. In a month's deployment with HMS *Scylla*, a 'Leander'-class frigate, in the Cod War of 1976, there were about twenty such events. The video obsession made many of the messes introverted, and some appeared downright resentful that a journalist had been invited for the work period, a surprising reaction for a ship whose role largely depends on public relations. One sea-dog with an enormous black shaggy beard, Leading Seaman George Streams, thought the men should have been consulted first and their families informed. George was on his second two-year posting to the ship, and saw himself rather like the Oldest Member of a London club.

*Opposite* Raising the flag on Southern Thule. The Argentines established a base here in 1976, which was removed by a task force led by HMS *Endurance* in June 1982

The remains of the Argentine base on Southern Thule with *Endurance* sounding Ferguson Bay behind. The station was destroyed by a British naval demolition team after the Argentine flag was raised there again in late 1982

Signy Island, the site of the BAS base, looking towards Coronation Island, South Orkneys

Dave Rootes, base commander at Signy, greets a tame fur seal

The BAS base on Signy Island. Established in 1947 it is now being rebuilt with the extra money BAS has been granted by the government

Deception Island, South Shetlands. The fine natural harbour is formed by the sunken cone of a volcano

Deception Island. *Endurance*'s helicopter beside the rescue hut which had just been used by a Chilean summer party

One of the eighty supply runs by *Endurance*'s helicopters landing stores for the Joint Services Expedition on Brabant Island

Commander Chris Furse (left), leader of the Brabant Expedition 1984, talks to Corporal De Silva before he returns to England with *Endurance*
*Overleaf* Brabant Island. The campsite of the Joint Services Expedition at Metchnikoff, shared with a colony of chinstrap penguins

Antarctica looking south to Brabant Island, more than fifty miles off. Brash ice and bergy bits fill the sea of the foreground

Antarctic sunset, looking south to Brabant

Public relations were in the hands of the instructor officer and meteorologist, a computer expert conscious of upward social mobility, Lieutenant-Commander John Jacob. As a civilian technician he had helped install the computer in the operations room of HMS *Sheffield*, the first major naval casualty of the Falklands conflict. His experience in the construction of the destroyer had made him apply for a postgraduate entry into the Navy. He had inherited a trait of his service from the Falklands conflict, suspicion of the antics of the press. Anxiety about public relations was matched by that about his waistline, which was encouraged by the standard diet and the inhibitions of the weather for exercise on the flight-deck. J.J., as the star wars weather expert liked to call himself, decided on an alternative approach to his weight problem, a diet that consisted of three or four boiled eggs a day. Occasionally he would relieve his egg-bound state with a gymnastic work-out called in *Endurance* argot a 'beasting'.

The king of the beasts was George Gelder, who managed to exercise every day. He, J.J. and a party of marines had undertaken the 'yomp' from San Carlos to Port Stanley with packs and rifles, and accomplished the march as far as Mount Kent in record time. George ran a party of twelve marines, who had to help with seaman duties while they were aboard. They were also responsible for manning the machine-guns and gunnery practice, which can only be done north of the Antarctic Treaty area. On the journey from Port Stanley two mornings of gun drill were organised, but on the second day visibility was so poor that it was difficult to see the target flares fired from the bridge wing. The only thing the gunners were likely to hit that day was a stray flight of wandering albatrosses as they glided down the ship's side.

Because exercise is so difficult to organise aboard ship, every effort is made to organise sports ashore. A football tournament between Port Stanley and *Endurance* is held annually. Recently the Stanley performance has improved dramatically as their team has been infiltrated by the contractors building houses and roads in the town. When the ship called at Rothera in the Argentine Islands off Palmer Land in the Antarctic Peninsula, it was decided to hold the Alternative Winter Olympics, with skiing races and toboggan runs using inflated black polythene rubbish bags for sleds. The petty officer medical assistant told the ship's competitors that no good would come of it and that someone was bound to be injured. The games went off with a swing, with much pawky humour referring to a ski travel company, 'Ski McG', managed by the Captain's wife in London. There *was* one injury after the games had been run. The BAS men and the ship's company were standing round chatting and eating barbecued sausages when some BAS men decided to practise tobogganing and scythed into them, colliding with the Jonah of the winter sports, the petty officer medical assistant. He suffered a compound fracture above the ankle which required immediate surgical attention. After due consultation it was decided to get him back to the Naval Hospital in Plymouth. A BAS Twin Otter plane flew him north to the Chilean base at Rodolfo Marsh where a Russian surgeon from the Bellingshausen base said he could operate. The hospital in Plymouth insisted the man should be returned to Britain with all speed. An RAF Hercules transport plane was dispatched from Port Stanley to Marsh to pick him up so that he could be flown from the Falklands to England via Ascension. The Hercules flight was a round trip of 1000 miles from Port Stanley to the tip of the Antarctic Peninsula. It was the first time a British military aircraft had flown to the Antarctic since the inception of the treaty twenty-three years before. The cost of the medical evacuation of one man must have been somewhere in the region of £20,000 to £30,000. A few months before, the Falkland Islands government had tried unsuccessfully to persuade the Ministry of Defence to spend £50,000 to repair and rewire the King Edward Memorial Hospital in Port Stanley, which burnt down in April 1984.

The hydrographer's department in *Endurance* can actually claim to generate revenue for the Navy. The charts produced by the Naval Hydrographic Department at Taunton earn hundreds of thousands of pounds of foreign exchange each year, and each year *Endurance*'s surveying tasks are drawn up in Taunton. In the 1984 summer season the hydrographic survey was run by an easy-going West Countryman, Tony Riley, who was about to leave the Navy after seventeen years, to help run a taxidermy and thatching business with his two stepsons in North Devon. The charts and instruments are kept in an open work area as well lit as an artist's studio. The lights picked up the alarming colour scheme of Lieutenant-Commander Riley's assistant, Leading Seaman Osborne, who was suffering an attack of hepatitis contracted in Valparaiso; his luminous face shone like a traffic beacon. In each deployment Tony Riley's department does up to 40,000 miles of surveying, partly from *Endurance* herself, and partly from one of the cutters. In February and March 1984, the second-in-command of the ship's hydrographers, Tony Jenks, was asked to survey Port San Carlos in the Falklands using one of the ship's boats, the *James Caird,* predictably nicknamed by the crew the 'James Turd'. The previous season a survey had been made of North Arm settlement at the southern end of East Falkland, which with San Carlos provides one of the best strategic anchorages in the islands away from Port Stanley.

*Endurance* had returned to the Orleans Strait after landing men and stores at Brabant Island, when she struck disaster. The trisponders had been activated the day before, and the ship was due to complete the survey of the waters between Trinity Island and Graham Land before sunset. Shortly after the call for breakfast, or 'shake' in naval parlance, the ship juddered to a halt. 'We must have hit that bloody great iceberg,' someone shouted outside my cabin, and a matter of moments later a marine piped over the tannoy, 'The ship has gone aground.' *Endurance* had been following the course of tramlines while she was surveying, and turning to port at the end of one line of soundings had hit a piece of submerged rock which lay only eleven feet beneath the surface of the water. The obstacle could only have been detected if the ship had been equipped with the very latest side-scanning radar which beams out sideways from the bottom of the hull. The first shocks were followed by attempts to put the ship in reverse which made her yaw heavily. The helicopter crew ran through to the hangar, some with their full flying kit on. Captain MacGregor ordered everyone and everything that could to be moved aft. The day was sunny and serene, not a motion of wind, and a dead calm sea. From the port side a thin wisp of diesel oil drifted across the water; the rock had punctured one of the forward diesel tanks, which fortunately was watertight and could be sealed off from the other forward holds. To lighten the bows the main sea anchors were let go, dropping hundreds of feet of chain into the water, and still *Endurance* lay perched upon the rock. Finally, the captain ordered as many men as could be spared to shift their weight to the aft of the flight-deck for a group photograph. By coincidence it had been arranged to rendezvous with the BAS support ship RRS *Bransfield* that very morning, and the captain informed the ship's company that this was the most likely chance of release.

In the meantime, I asked if I could broadcast to the BBC via Maritime Satellite that the ship was aground. The captain consented, provided the Ministry of Defence was informed first and that the dispatch made it clear that the ship was in no danger and was likely to be towed off the rock within hours. We agreed that nothing should be said that would cause anxiety to the families listening at home. The arrangement worked with no fuss at all, apart from a sermon on the responsibilities of the press from the youngest officer in the ship. It was a novel experience to broadcast from ship aground, aground in Antarctica at that, but the BBC seemed hardly interested. Some papers, reporting second-hand, said that *Endurance* had hit an iceberg. Colin MacGregor's cool and shrewd handling of the press came from his experience as a very successful head of public relations for the Fleet Air Arm. He believed in taking the journalist into his confidence and relying on his discretion, the method adopted by the more imaginative commanders during the land campaign in the Falklands and markedly different from that of many of Admiral Woodward's staff and the Ministry of Defence in London. It was in stark contrast to what was to happen exactly a fortnight later when the joint military-civilian hospital in Port Stanley burnt to the ground.

In the late morning *Bransfield* could be seen hauling over the horizon, a red-and-white speck more than thirty miles off. From one of the cutters, the *Stancomb Wills, Endurance* looked like a beached monster, the line of rust marking her customary waterline three to four feet out of the water at the bow. Lumps of brash ice and bergy bits drifted round the launch; shags and skuas flapped gently overhead eyeing the scene with casual curiosity. From the forward deck of the ship herself the rock could be seen quite clearly, a black shadow, with white specks of quartz twinkling in the middle. It looked like the underbelly of a killer whale amplified and distorted by the clear water. Within minutes of the tow being established with the *Bransfield, Endurance* was pulled clear with a jarring, scraping noise. Some of the ship's company said she was about to float off anyway on the rising tide, but for *Bransfield* and her jovial captain, Stuart Lawrence, it was a moment of triumph. In previous seasons, the *Endurance* had stood by the *Bransfield* after she had gone aground, and had towed the second BAS ship, RRS *John Biscoe,* to Montevideo after her propeller had dropped off.

As soon as the farewells and thanks had been shouted to the *Bransfield* the divers prepared to go over the side to inspect the damage. They were led by my namesake, Surgeon Lieutenant-Commander Mike Fox. A passionate exponent of London hospital rugby when he was at St Thomas's, he exemplified one of the pleasantest traditions of *Endurance* in the way he maintained close contact with the community in the Falklands. During the conflict he had been doctor aboard the supply ship RFA *Blue Rover;* once he was allowed ashore he had visited the hospital and medical staff frequently, and taken particular interest in a number of the older people of Port Stanley. Mike was assisted in the diving operation by Gary Hunt, the senior helicopter observer and one of the ship's action men. He had been the observer of the Lynx helicopter of HMS *Antelope*, which had been deployed to another part of the fleet on 23 May 1982, when *Antelope* blew up and sank in San Carlos Water. Gary said that the morning *Endurance* ran aground he had planned to launch his windsurfer between the ice-floes. Instead he and Mike and four others had to launch themselves from the cutter and *Endurance*'s forward deck. The search of the hull took about an hour as the men inched their way along holding a line to which buoys were attached. The first relay of divers quickly reported a gash about twelve to thirteen feet long and up to seven inches wide under the forward tank, with a smaller split two to three feet long further aft. Captain MacGregor ordered the routine enquiry to be held by the ship's navigator assisted by the instructor officer.

As they worked steadily round the ship some of the divers rested on chunks of ice, using them like surfboards. Mike Fox reported glowingly of the conditions: 'Terrific, ideal, you can see far better than anywhere round the British Isles, and the temperature isn't at all bad, either, only about minus two centigrade.' Just as the men of the team were climbing aboard the *Stancomb Wills* a leopard seal stuck his head between the chunks of brash, watched the divers, then slithered away. Later Tony Riley, the hydrographer, took the launch to attempt to locate and mark the rock that had holed *Endurance*. He searched for more than three hours, a tiny red boat weaving through the ice like an angry fly, a bright point of colour in a scene of green and white. As evening drew in, the boat returned and the elusive rock was never seen again.

Captain MacGregor began looking up the nearest dry docks in South America in the port guide, which resembles an Automobile Association handbook in its listing of facilities at the major repair yards. The plan initially was to sail for the Falklands for a further inspection of the damage by teams from one of the maintenance ships, the *Bar Protector*. These ships have the stores and equipment of a small dockyard and maintain the squadron defending the Falklands. *Endurance* had been lucky on the day she went aground: the weather remained calm (but broke the following day) and purely by chance the *Bransfield*, the first ship *Endurance* had encountered for three weeks since leaving Port Stanley, was in the area.

*Endurance* had gone aground in the Antarctic a few years before, and in the previous season had ripped a hole in the hull on the pack ice. On that occasion her two shipwrights, Stanley Bugg and 'Adge' Cutler, had patched the hull. Between them they have served thirty-seven years in the Navy; their brand of skill is no longer taught as a specialisation in the service. They were responsible for hull maintenance and every aspect of carpentry, joinery and plumbing. On a previous deployment they had to replace twelve feet of the main sanitary piping, as well as make dozens of picture frames and presentation crests for goodwill visits. The head of the department, Lieutenant Kemp Price, had served twenty-seven years and was due to leave after his next deployment in Bermuda. 'Coming from my last appointment with *Illustrious*, the latest of the carriers, to this was like coming from the space age to the stone age,' he told me. 'But I volunteered for this. It's a real challenge. Last year, for example, we had to remove four out of the five pistons and a cylinder lining at Port Stanley.' According to Kemp manufacturers of the main engine have guaranteed that they can provide spares until 1990.

The big question now is what will replace *Endurance* as the Antarctic ice patrol ship or whether she will be replaced at all? It has been suggested that another ship should be purchased second-hand and a list of suitable vessels, including the RRS *Bransfield,* has been drawn up. BAS have said that the *Bransfield* is not for sale, but that they would like to see *Endurance*'s replacement giving their work more support. At present the Survey's senior men are critical of the little use they are allowed of *Endurance*'s helicopters, the one really valuable asset the ship possesses and which their two ships do not. The Navy counter that BAS does not pay for the helicopters, and long periods working with the scientists from the Antarctic bases would affect *Endurance*'s capacity to act as guardship round the Falklands and keep shipping in the South Atlantic under surveillance. None the less the government lists support of BAS as one of the ship's prime roles. At present the ship spends a relatively short summer season in Antarctic waters, about seventy days at the most, and about the same time travelling to and from the British Isles, all at an annual cost of about £4 million, just under half BAS's current total annual budget.

To replace *Endurance* with an equivalent ice-strengthened freighter is likely to prove a poor compromise. Shortly after the purchase and conversion of the *Anita Dan,* plans to build an ice-breaker for the Navy were cancelled. The fact that *Endurance* is not an ice-breaker means she can only work in Antarctica itself from about mid-December to mid-April at the latest. Other countries taking an increased interest in Antarctic resources and territory, including the Argentines, are deploying ice-breakers, which means that they can reach bases along the Graham Land and Palmer Peninsula when British ships cannot. With improved naval repair facilities from ships like the *Bar Protector* in the Falklands there is now an argument for basing the Navy's ice patrol ship in the Falklands and flying in a change of crew once the airfield is open at Mount Pleasant. At present *Endurance* is due to be scrapped the year before the Antarctic Treaty is likely to be altered, and at a time when more countries will be interested in exploiting what Antarctica has to offer. Recently both Chile and Argentina have stated their territorial claim with renewed vigour. The superpowers, Russia and America, have nearly twenty ice-breakers between them, which they can divert from northern polar waters to support their presence in Antarctica.

Both BAS and many of the Naval personnel who have served with *Endurance* would like to see her replaced by a purpose-built ship. It might be possible to have an ice-breaker on which BAS has call for a set number of days or weeks in a deployment, provided there is no more urgent requirement for the ship elsewhere. The ship could be a Royal Fleet Auxiliary with a small naval or marine contingent embarked. *Endurance*'s role as survey ship is carried out more effectively by the custom-built ships like *Hecla, Hecate* and *Hydra,* which have far more modern equipment. The role of *Endurance* is now firmly linked with British policy over Antarctica and in the Falklands. The question of her replacement is a weather-vane of British intentions in the South Atlantic.

*Endurance* in Antarctica off Trinity Island

Heroic image, 1984: Captain Colin MacGregor at St Andrew's Bay, South Georgia

The flight in one of their more 'natural' poses

Mike Fox, the ship's doctor, checks his diving gear before searching *Endurance*'s hull after her grounding

137

Launching the divers to examine the hull

A lumpy crossing of Drake Passage from Antarctica to the Falklands

## Chapter 7

# Exploration into Science

Through the long dark months of the southern winter the British bases in Antarctica and the Scotia Sea are manned by some seventy scientists and technical assistants. Though they contend that their principal purpose is scientific research, in fact for most of the year they constitute the British political presence in the Antarctic. The men are employed by BAS, whose origins lie in a 1943 naval operation to establish bases along the Graham Land Peninsula. The first two were established in 1944 at Deception Island in the South Shetlands and at Port Lockroy, Wiencke Island, in the Palmer Archipelago. Since then British exploration and scientific teams have worked continuously in Antarctica, some of the earlier ones for up to three years on the continent without returning north.

The headquarters of BAS is an almost bleakly anonymous building outside Cambridge, crouching between the university veterinary school and the entrance to the M11 motorway. It is mid-seventies prefab at its plainest and most functional, a purpose-built cloister for science, a monastery made of Lego. The building was opened by the Duke of Edinburgh in May 1976, and the ceremony is commemorated by an inscription on a large chunk of Antarctic rock set into the floor of the entrance-hall. On the walls surrounding the central stairs are photographs of the early leaders of the Survey, the abbots of the order, Sir Raymond Priestley and Sir Vivian Fuchs. Since 1946, BAS, originally FIDS, has had only three directors including the present one, Dr Richard Laws.

The monastic analogy holds particularly well if you follow the long, straight corridors of the main office accommodation. The offices open onto the passage like small cells. Inside the scientists hunch over the benches like brothers over precious manuscripts; instead of pages of delicate illuminated handwriting, sheets of graphs, calculations and computer print-out absorb the brothers' attention. The walls are adorned by photographs of the Antarctic, broad snowscapes with a crystalline clarity or portraits of birds, seals and penguins.

BAS scientists and technicians are known collectively as fids, despite the change of title from Falkland Islands Dependencies Survey to British Antarctic Survey in 1961–2. Fids have their own language and lore born of the long periods of isolation on the southern bases. Fid society is almost entirely male, as no women are allowed to winter in the five permanent stations in Antarctica and the sub-Antarctic. Aboard the support ship *Bransfield,* the main mess area and bar is known simply as the 'fiddery'. Ashore in Port Stanley the fid is easily spotted by his long loping stride, luxuriant beard and deep sun-tan, which contrasts with the raw, red wind-burn of most Falklanders in the summer. There is almost a fid uniform of jeans, sneakers and multicoloured lumberjack shirt. Fids seem either very tall men or short and slight, and few have weight problems. 'You can always tell a fid because he has his hands in pockets,' says Ray Adie who first went south at the age of twenty-one in the first year of FIDS, 1946. 'They need to have their hands in the pockets to keep their trousers up,' he adds with a dash of typical fid humour.

Superficially, the fid ethos appears to be that of the gifted amateur, the true successor of heroic explorers like Scott and Shackleton. Skills with the Nansen sledge and skis are prized by some as much as expertise with satellite communications, computers and sophisticated gadgetry for gauging ice, rock, atmosphere and ocean. However, the image of amateurism is pure bluff. BAS is one of the most efficient and expert of polar exploration and research institutions in history. It covers a wider variety of research programmes and at a lower relative cost than any other major national survey working in Antarctica today. No other national research endeavour studies equally the earth, atmospheric and life sciences. American Antarctic scientists work in the field at five times the average cost of a BAS man, and the American bases are supported by a budget of about $100 million compared to the current £10 million which BAS now devotes to Antarctic science. The Japanese Antarctic research programme has a budget of about £30 million a year, which does not include the cost of the logistical support – ships and aircraft – which it receives from the Japanese defence forces. Salaries for the British scientists are modest and are tied to civil service pay scales for scientific officers. The three Chilean bases in the Antarctic Peninsula are manned by military personnel who are paid six times the normal salary as an inducement to endure the rigours of a southern posting.

Despite the political aspect of their role, BAS men emphasise that they are there 'to do science'. With this attractive piece of modern fid jargon they show themselves as the heirs of Cook and Shackleton, explorers and researchers rather than frontiersmen of empire. The Chileans and the Argentines do little more than maintain a military presence, with the exception of the Argentine weather station at Laurie Island in the South Orkneys which has made observations since 1904, though these have yet to be submitted to a systematic analysis. Members of the Antarctic Treaty regularly report the number of scientists and their published papers for each year. In early 1983 the Chileans reported 201 people on their Antarctic Peninsula stations and two scientific publications, the Argentines 254 and eighteen publications, and the United Kingdom ninety and 181 papers and articles. BAS has been involved in joint projects with the Americans and helped West Germany, India and Brazil establish scientific stations and surveys in Antarctica.

Until recently BAS was the Cinderella of major Antarctic surveys, badly funded and in serious danger of becoming obsolete. Today it is still a David beside the Goliaths of the American and Russian surveys. At the McMurdo base on the Ross Ice Shelf the Americans have more than 700 people working in the summer season, ten times the number of BAS personnel wintering on all five British bases in 1984. Since the Falklands conflict, and largely as a result of it, BAS received an injection of £15 million of extra government funding, to be spread over four years. Even so, for the financial year of 1983–4, this has meant a modest £10.2 million to pay for a staff of 300 men and women, the operation of two support ships and three light aircraft and building improvements to three bases.

In 1967 the budget for the Survey was fixed at £1 million by the Natural Environment Research Council (NERC) which took over supervision of BAS from the old Colonial Office. By 1984 the equivalent of the £1 million awarded in 1967 was taken by the accountants as £6.2 million. Following the Falklands conflict Margaret Thatcher directed that extra funds should be made available for research into natural resources in the Antarctic, and by this stricture excluded the department of atmospheric sciences at BAS, which is involved in some of the most challenging scientific research ever undertaken in Antarctica. Many BAS men I spoke to in early 1984 expressed quite openly their regret that the extra funding had come as a result of the Falklands campaign, and most did not appear to relish a close link between future government policy towards BAS and Antarctica and policy on the future of the Falklands. The additional money does appear to have lifted morale, for throughout the 1970s BAS was faced with cuts in funds and staff redundancies. Since 1982 buildings and equipment in Cambridge have been improved and added to and new staff recruited to work in Britain and Antarctica. The Survey has made available £3.1 million for grants to universities, individual scientists and institutes for Antarctic research and has managed to channel extra funding into the dramatic new projects the atmospheric science department has embarked upon with space agencies in Europe, the United States and Japan.

One of the recipients of the grants was the Scott Polar Research Institute which received £35,000. The Institute was set up as a memorial to Scott by scientists, like Wordie and Priestley, who had worked with him. Today it forms a separate department within Cambridge University, though in the mid-seventies responsibility for Antarctic glaciology research was taken over by BAS. The library is rich in the documents of the early Antarctic expeditions. The sketches and water-colours of Dr Edward Wilson, who died with Scott, are kept there, and a wide range of correspondence about many of the expeditions undertaken at the turn of the century. Original plates of photographs by Frank Hurley and Herbert Ponting and considerable footage of Hurley's film of the Imperial Trans-Antarctic Expedition of 1914–16 are stored there. One sequence shows the *Endurance* moving steadily along a lead to break out of the Weddell pack. It concludes with the prow moving to within inches of the camera lens and the tripod falling over. Hurley became so engrossed with his film that he was knocked off his perch on the ice-floe into the freezing water.

The library itself is not open to the public and permission to use it has to be sought from the director, but the museum on the ground floor of the building can be visited on most afternoons. It is one of the most fascinating small museums in Britain. Some of Wilson's gouaches, watercolours and sketches are displayed on the walls and documents from the first voyages of Cook and Ross are placed in glass cases in the centre of the main room. Most interesting are the examples of early polar skis, such as those pioneered by Nansen, the sledges used by Eskimos and the clothing worn for centuries in the Arctic. Primitive spectacles, wooden slats with narrow holes cut in them, were the first devices used by the explorers and natives against snow-blindness. In those few cool and quiet rooms you quickly appreciate something of the real hardship and rigours endured by the first explorers in the Artic and Antarctic, and really catch something of the spirit of the heroic explorers and the world in which Cook, Ross, Scott and Shackleton lived and worked.

Shortly after the First World War the Discovery Committee began to promote exploration in Antarctica. The committee was established within a few years of the foundation of the Scott Polar Research Institute and together with the Royal Geographical Society set about organising the systematic surveying of the Antarctic continent, the focus of the British claim, the Graham Land Peninsula, in particular. It first met in 1923 to set up a series of projects to map Antarctica and study the marine life of the surrounding oceans, and in 1925 it dispatched a marine biologist, Dr

Neil MacKintosh, to observe the whaling station at Grytviken. During his first year of studying the whale carcasses brought onto the slipway at the station, he was dismayed to discover that between twenty and forty per cent of all whales processed were immature, incapable of reproduction. This was one of the first indications that whale stocks were in danger and whaling faced the same prospect as the nineteenth-century sealing industry.

The Discovery Committee is most noted for the series of voyages it organised for Scott's old flagship, the *Discovery,* after which it is named. A dozen voyages were completed by the *Discovery,* her successor, the *Discovery II,* and the *William Scoresby* between 1925 and 1939 when the programme was stopped by the outbreak of war. *Discovery*'s first voyage of the series lasted two years, and she was used by Sir Douglas Mawson on his British, Australian and New Zealand Expedition, which led to the establishment of Australian and New Zealand claims to Antarctic territory. In 1930–1 the *Discovery II,* which had a cruising range of 10,000 miles without need of revictualling or refuelling, completed a circumnavigation of Antarctica. Surprisingly this was only the fifth time this had been accomplished since James Cook's second southern voyage of discovery.

The *Discovery* voyages marked a change in approach to southern exploration as they shifted the emphasis from the sheer physical feats of travel and exploration to a serious scientific approach to mapping and surveying, recording geological data, and studying marine life systems. The most ambitious British land expedition of the era was the Graham Land Expedition, which was sponsored by the British government and the Royal Geographical Society. The expedition established a base at Marguerite Bay and carried out a comprehensive survey of large areas of the Graham Land Peninsula, and, amongst many other achievements, demolished the myth that there was a deep channel which cut it in two, making it a string of islands linked by ice shelves. Two sledging journeys were made to Alexander I Island from Marguerite Bay and an ice shelf was named after Sir James Wordie, Shackleton's geologist on the *Endurance* Expedition. The Wordie Ice Shelf is a great slab of grounded ice at the neck of the Peninsula where it becomes Palmer Land. There is an apocryphal account that Wordie himself did not believe in the existence of the phenomenon of fast ice ascribed by the Graham Land scientists to the piece of Antarctica that now bears his name. Sir James Wordie was one of the greatest mentors of Antarctic scientists. As a don at St John's College, Cambridge, where he was later master, he encouraged both Sir Vivian Fuchs and Dr Ray Adie in the establishment of FIDS and BAS.

The expeditions of the twenties and thirties differed from those of the heroic age in their systematic scientific approach and in their use of shore bases for more than a single season at a time. Another important technical innovation, however, did have more than a whiff of pioneering heroics about it, and this was the use of aircraft.

The first aviator in the Antarctic was the Australian Sir Hubert Wilkins. In 1928 he took two Lockheed Vega aircraft to Deception Island and began with a number of flights over the South Shetlands and along the Graham Land Peninsula. The venture was backed by Hearst newspapers in the United States and though the publicity was considerable, achievement was limited. An attempt to fly 2000 miles to stake out a southern landing site failed. One of the first flights did succeed in crossing the Peninsula, earning the newspaper magnate the honour of having an island named after him. Wilkins had begun the controversy that the Peninsula was in reality a string of islands; he and his co-pilot claimed to have seen a channel from the Weddell Sea to the waters at the north end of the Bellingshausen Sea, a myth that was to be demolished finally by John Rymill's Graham Land Expedition of 1935. The aircraft were stored at Deception for the winter, but by the next season an American rival, Lincoln Ellsworth, had entered the race to be the first to fly across the Antarctic continent.

Wilkins and Ellsworth flew together in the season of 1933, and two years later Ellsworth set out to cross the continent. On the second attempt to fly south from Dundee Island at the tip of Graham Land they were forced back by blizzards, but a third flight on 23 November 1935 got away in perfect weather. Navigation proved tricky, but Ellsworth and his co-pilot, Herbert Hollick-Kenyon, an Englishman working for Canadian Airways, succeeded in reaching their destination, Little America, the base set up by Richard E. Byrd near the Bay of Whales. Sometime before their forced landing the radio transmitter broke and the two men were feared lost. Wilkins immediately put into action his pre-arranged plan for rescuing the aviators. In reality Ellsworth and Hollick-Kenyon had navigated with almost pinpoint precision and had ditched about a dozen miles from Little America. Their land navigation was not so good as they set out for the huts built by Byrd and his team and they walked several miles past them before arriving at the base on 15 December. Meanwhile *Discovery II* had been diverted to Melbourne to pick up men and machines of the Royal Australian Air Force. On 18 January she launched a Tiger Moth, *Polar Star,* piloted by Flight-Lieutenant Douglas. As the ship pushed through the loose pack, the plane set course for the huts at Little America and just when Douglas made his first pass over the building erected by Byrd, a figure appeared

144

from the door and waved. A day later a party from the ship landed and provided the two aviators with food and fuel for their plane. Ellsworth had a badly poisoned foot and this was tended to before he took off to complete the first crossing of the Antarctic continent by air.

Ellsworth's name is linked with the heroic age of exploration. He worked with Amundsen and Nobile in the crossing of the Arctic in the airship *Norge*. For all the daring and heroics of his flights he was a serious scientist. A graduate of Columbia, Yale, McGill and the London School of Mines, he had directed surveys for the Canadian Pacific Railway in the Rockies. He came to flying in the First World War, and trained both as a combat observer and pilot. In 1924 he surveyed the Amazon basin and the Andes to the shores of Peru, leading an expedition sponsored by Johns Hopkins University. A year later he and Amundsen took two float planes to the Arctic where for more than a month they were given up for lost. The two planes reached 87°44′N before making forced landings. Their radios did not function and one of the planes was abandoned. The crews had to carve a runway from the rough ice before the other plane could take off. Miraculously, it managed to get back to Spitzbergen – grossly overloaded, carrying all six members of the expedition. Subsequently Ellsworth made three private expeditions to the Antarctic, and it was on the third of these that he flew from Dundee Island to the Bay of Whales, completing a remarkable double achievement as the first man to fly over the Arctic and Antarctic. Both Ellsworth and Wilkins showed the aircraft to be an enormous asset to scientific research and to rescue in polar regions. Ellsworth flew over and photographed huge areas of Antarctica, unexplored hitherto, and by 1939 unofficially claimed more than 300,000 square miles of land there for America, naming a broad swathe of mountain and coast south of the Palmer Peninsula James Ellsworth Land, after his father.

Six years before Ellsworth's trans-Antarctic flight, another American, Richard E. Byrd, had become the first man to fly over the South Pole. Byrd is one of the most distinguished Antarctic explorers and the first American to kindle his government's interest in the continent since Charles Wilkes nearly a century before. His career began in the interwar years and it dominates the early phase of development of Antarctica after the Second World War. His achievement embraces the three salient aspects of national and international interest in Antarctica, for he was heroic discoverer, scientist, and military strategist. A figure in the Teddy Roosevelt mould, physically daring, politically astute and very well connected, Byrd's first three expeditions to Antarctica were private ventures, the first backed personally by his friend John D. Rockefeller. His brother, Harry F. Byrd, was a US senator. At the age of twelve he travelled around the world unaccompanied before taking up a career as a professional sailor. By 1912 he was invalided out of the service, crippled by sporting injuries, and it was only his interest in aviation that brought him back into the US Navy. After flying over the North Pole in 1926 he was promoted to commander, and after he repeated the feat over the South Pole on 29 November 1929 he became a rear-admiral. His flight to the Pole and back took over ten hours and as he reached his destination he leaned out of the plane and dropped an American flag attached to a metal pole. Afterwards he remarked, 'Nothing there but the fancy of men. One gets there and that is about all there is for the telling. It is the effort to get there which counts.'

Byrd's own efforts for aviation and polar discovery were prodigious, and the manner in which he established bases and mounted elaborate Antarctic ventures changed the scale and nature of human activity there. In the years from 1928 to 1939 he led five expeditions, the first three privately sponsored, the last two under the auspices of the US government. At the same time he promoted the development of seaplanes and helped Charles Lindbergh prepare the navigation plots for the first solo crossing of the Atlantic. In 1928, at the beginning of his first expedition to Antarctica, he built a base out of packing cases at Little America with the aid of his team of forty-two men. Five different bases were to be built at the Bay of Whales, each bearing the name of Little America, the last from 1956 to 1959, and by that time the nature of the enterprise had altered dramatically. With the logistical support of ice-breakers and heavy transport aircraft it had come to resemble a military operation more than an exercise in scientific research. Not only did Byrd pioneer the use of aircraft in polar study and exploration but he established the use of two-way radio communication to great effect, such great effect that during the 1933 expedition it saved his life. When Douglas Mawson set up a radio link at Macquarie Island to relay messages from his 1911–14 Antarctic expedition, they could be transmitted one way only and he had no possibility of holding a conversation with Australia.

In 1933 Byrd's second expedition arrived at the Bay of Whales to find that the Little America base built in 1929 had been crushed in the ice and was steadily drifting out to sea. Accordingly, Little America II was built before a team headed south to build an advance base for the winter of 1934. On the way the expedition tractor broke down and was abandoned along with a quantity of food, leaving insufficient rations to support the four-man team for the months ahead. Byrd decided that he would winter alone in the prefabricated hut set into the snow at Bolling Advance Base, 123 miles south of Little America II. By May Byrd's health was beginning to deteriorate and he discovered that fumes from his generator engine were leaking into the hut through a crack in the exhaust pipe. Once, during a scheduled radio link-up with Little America II, he collapsed unconscious. Regularly he would communicate in Morse to the northern base, and the men there would reply in voice. Because of the leaking exhaust he would stop the generator during the day, but by mid-June he was suffering severely from carbon monoxide poisoning. None the less he continued to read the meteorological instruments outside the hut. By June the petrol motor generator had broken completely and the radio had to be hand-cranked, a process that exhausted him so much that he had to spend hours in his sleeping-bag recovering after each communication. In June the temperature reached $-62°C$ and when the messages became almost incomprehensible a month later the team at Little America decided to mount a rescue operation. After several attempts they made the journey in the depths of winter using tractors and arrived at Advance Base on 8 August. It took the relief party two months to nurse their leader back to health and in October that year they managed to fly him back to Little America. Despite the fact that he very nearly died in his isolation at Bolling Advance Base, Richard Byrd achieved his aims and a complete meteorological record was achieved from twice-daily readings of instruments at the base from March to October 1934. In the summer work schedule that followed extensive surveys were accomplished by aircraft commanded by Finn Ronne, who was to lead the last of the great private expeditions to Antarctica in 1947–8. Like Scott, Shackleton, Nansen, de Gerlache and Amundsen, Richard Byrd chose men to accompany his expeditions who later became pioneers of scientific work in their own right in the polar regions. With him at Little America II from 1933 to 1935 were Finn Ronne, Richard Black, Richard Cruzen, George Dufek, and Dr Paul Siple, whose names are commemorated today by place-names in the continent and chapters in the annals of the development of Antarctica.

In 1939 President Franklin D. Roosevelt instructed Byrd to establish bases round the Antarctic continent, such was the strategic importance of Antarctica in the estimation of the US administration. The project had hardly started before it was abandoned due to lack of funds and interest by a government increasingly preoccupied by impending hostilities. Byrd himself did return in 1940 to build a third Little America as the head of the US government's Antarctic Service, and a second strategic base was established at Stonington Island only to be abandoned at the end of the summer season. The fledgling Antarctic Service was dismantled shortly afterwards.

American interest revived with a vengeance after the war ended. By 1946 Russia, the former ally, was firmly cast in the role of potential enemy number one by American strategists, and one whose territory stretched to within forty miles of the American back door in the Aleutian Islands off Alaska. In 1946 Operation 'Highjump' was launched in Antarctica under the command of Admiral Byrd for the land bases and under his colleague at Little America II, Admiral Richard Cruzen, for the naval squadron. Thirteen ships and 4700 servicemen were involved. It was the largest single exercise ever mounted in Antarctica and its aims were strategic and political – once more establishing the US claim to Antarctica – as much as scientific. America, like the Soviet Union, claims the right of access to the whole of Antarctica, though neither power has suggested that any part of the continent is its own sovereign territory. Byrd himself did make unofficial claims to sections of the coastline, and named one of the most inhospitable areas of the continent Marie Byrd Land, after his wife. This area is still designated unclaimed territory on most maps, and conditions for work on the land there are so bad as to be hardly worth while.

At the very time the Americans were abandoning their work in 1941 the British were becoming highly alarmed about their strategic vulnerability in the area. The armed cruiser HMS *Queen of Bermuda* sailed into the lagoon at Deception to blow up coal-bunkers and puncture the fuel tanks at the whaling station. Nor was this an act of idle strategic vindictiveness: the Admiralty feared that the Argentines were helping supply and fuel the German commerce-raiders in the Southern Ocean, which that year sank all but three catchers of the Norwegian whaling fleet of the Kerguelen Islands, and possibly U-boats.

In 1942 the Argentines dispatched the *Primero de Mayo* to stake their claim to the Peninsula, leaving bronze plaques and cylinders containing claim documents on the Melchior Islands in the Palmer Archipelago, Winter Island and Deception Island. In 1943 when HMS *Carnarvon* arrived at Deception the crew found the cylinder; it was returned to the Argentine government by the British ambassador in Buenos Aires. *Carnarvon* went on to Signy Island in the South Orkneys, close to the Argentine weather station on Laurie Island. This was the overture to Operation 'Tabarin', which was to establish two British bases – at Deception and Port Lockroy – in 1944.

By the end of 1945 'Tabarin' had become the Falkland Islands Dependencies Survey and by 1947 it had seven bases in Antarctica, including wintering parties at establishments at Hope Bay, Stonington Island, Admiralty Bay on King George Island, the Argentine islands of Cape Geddes and Signy in the South Orkneys.

The wartime operation to set up Antarctic bases had been advised by a special committee of three under Sir Raymond Priestley, which included

Brian Roberts, future head of the Polar Section of the Colonial and Foreign and Commonwealth Office, and Dr Neil MacKintosh, who had studied the whaling stations of South Georgia for the Discovery Committee.

In 1947, the year Chile and Argentina refused the British invitation to take their Antarctic dispute to the International Court of The Hague, the Argentine Navy dispatched a squadron of seven ships to build a base at Deception, but finding two FIDS ships there already, decided to move on. In January the Argentines landed a construction party on Gamma Island in the Melchior Group, and by March had built a base in the Peninsula region, with another base following in January 1948.

Chile, too, opened her first base, Arturo Prat, in the Graham Land region in 1947, at Discovery Bay, Greenwich Island. In January 1948 it was visited by President Gonzalez Videla, the first head of state to land in Antarctica; on 18 February he inaugurated the new base, Bernardo O'Higgins, on the Peninsula itself. Such was the alarm in London at the increasing tempo of the game of claim and counter-claim along the Peninsula that Sir Miles Clifford, the then Governor of the Falkland Islands and the Dependencies, was dispatched to visit all the British Antarctic bases in January 1948 aboard the frigate HMS *Snipe*.

The diplomatic game of cat and mouse over the Antarctic claims has affected the activity of the British bases. Since the International Geophysical Year and the advent of the Antarctic Treaty political disputes between the bases appear to have been mitigated to some degree. Under the Treaty the scientists of all three countries are supposed to work together, but since the Falklands conflict there has been almost no communication at all with the Argentines. While the Treaty still functions the BAS men can prosecute their claim to be in Antarctica for the sake of merely 'doing science'.

In the past ten years the way BAS scientists have worked has changed considerably. 'It's no longer a question of epic journeys by sledge to survey the land. Little time is spent on basic reconnaissance now, as our programmes are designed more and more towards solving particular scientific problems,' is the way the present BAS director, Dr Richard Laws, who succeeded Fuchs in 1973, sums up the change in approach. He regrets that so much of his time today is spent on administration and longs for the prospect of continuing his studies of large animals and the ecology of their herds when he retires from the directorship. Much of his attention is taken by negotiation with the Natural Environment Research Council (NERC) and scientific committees under the Department of Education and Science to ensure BAS receives the funds and the manpower it has been allocated. In the lean years before the Falklands conflict there was a tendency by government to trim the budget during successive years of public expenditure cuts; funds allocated to the BAS budget by NERC would often be taken away to support other public projects.

Of the trinity of BAS departments – earth, atmospheric and life sciences – the most attractive and accessible to the lay observer is the life sciences. Until the postwar years the life science biologists were a poor relation to the respectably established geologists, meteorologists and glaciologists. On the early expeditions animal studies were frequently left to the doctors in their spare moments. On Scott's last expedition Dr Teddy Wilson made a special journey to Cape Crozier to obtain emperor penguin eggs. The party did manage to retrieve six but nearly died in the attempt from blizzards, white-outs and temperatures of −56°C.

The life sciences department at BAS is headed today by Nigel Bonner, whose first experience of research in the Antarctic was at Grytviken in 1951. But it was not until ten years later, he says, that anything approaching a coherent programme of biological research was evolved by the Survey. Bonner is a tall, soft-spoken man, with many of the typical fid characteristics. A quality he shares with his fellow department heads is clarity of expression and economy of language: he outlines the work of his department elegantly and graphically. The department's biggest programme is the study of marine resources, particularly krill. The habits of krill are studied from ships and the potential harvest of the shellfish is also assessed by observing its predators: whales, penguins, seals and sea-birds. In 1981 the Food and Agriculture Organisation of the United Nations reported the annual catch of krill as 450,000 tonnes, though educated opinion suggests that today the Russians and Japanese are taking at least a million tonnes from the southern oceans each year. The BAS scientists on Bird Island and working from the RRS *John Biscoe* are trying to assess the ecological effect of a commercial krill harvest. The 1983–4 summer cruise by the *Biscoe* had some difficulty in tracing the migration patterns of krill and Bonner says there is still a great deal to be learnt about their swarming habits. The large predators, such as the whales, have to seek out swarms otherwise they would expend more energy in looking for the food than they would derive from eating it. A blue whale can swallow several tonnes of krill a day. The decline in krill-dependent species of whale may account for the population expansion of other animals, such as fur seals, for whom it is the staple diet. These studies are continuing on Bird Island, and BAS now have a waiting-list of foreign scientists wishing to work from the base in the summer season.

Major studies of plant life are undertaken at Signy Island in the South Orkneys, one of the few 'nearly pristine natural environments left in the world', according to Bonner. Lichens and mosses give clues about the regeneration of plants following ice ages, and the simplicity of life cycles of plants in the mountain lakes gives information useful to water management in many different parts of the globe. For nine months of the year Signy is a frozen desert and to unravel clues as to how and why freshwater plants and organisms manage to survive in such harsh natural conditions is a remarkable work of detection.

The third principal interest of Bonner's department is conservation in the ocean and on land. The scientists are examining with some urgency the likely impact on the natural environment if minerals are extracted in quantity from Antarctica and its continental shelf. The swelling of human population at the bases and the dramatic increase in the number of fur seals both have had an effect on vegetation, minerals and soil. The population boom of fur seals at Bird Island, for example, has led to the wholesale destruction of tussock grass, leaving ugly expanses of muddy beach of the same colour and consistency as the miles of mud at Weston-super-Mare at low tide. Some tussock plantations are being fenced off to ensure some cover for the nesting albatrosses. Fifty or sixty visitors from an American tourist ship in a morning can destroy lichens hundreds of years old and soil that might take thousands of years to replace.

The life sciences department works closely with the Antarctic Treaty powers in operating the seal protection convention, and Bonner himself is the chairman of the Scientific Committee on Antarctic Research sub-committee on conservation. But he is slightly sceptical about the growing fashion for international scientific and political bodies to hold conferences in the Antarctic islands, as the delegates could do as much damage to the environment as a marauding herd of tourists or colony of playful fur seal pups.

The earth sciences department at BAS is headed by Dr Charles Swithinbank, a rather more austere figure than Bonner, who on first meeting has the forbidding authority of a medieval prior. A graduate of Oxford University, he has made a remarkable career in Antarctic studies. He says he has lived off polar research without a break since graduation, and his facility in five languages has enabled him to work on a number of important international programmes, beginning with the Norwegian-British-Swedish Antarctic Expedition of 1949–52. Later he worked with the Americans at McMurdo and research teams in Canada and the USA. In 1964 the Royal Society arranged for him to spend a year as glaciologist with the Russians at their Mirny Base, and during that year he managed to acquire a working knowledge of the language.

Discussing the work and political future of BAS with Dr Swithinbank I felt like an intruder in the cloister. On our first meeting he had muttered acidly, and with complete accuracy, about 'these journalists who want to write something after only three weeks in Antarctica'. Later he volunteered that he thought one of the best introductions to the subject was *Antarctica* by the former Scott Polar Research Institute librarian Harry King, who had never actually visited the Antarctic continent himself.

In the past fifteen years the image of the earth sciences department has changed almost completely. Sir Vivian Fuchs once said that when he went to the Antarctic as a geologist in the 1940s the main tool was a hammer – to hack out samples from the bare rock. Today the glaciologists and geologists have the use of aircraft, satellite and radar sounding techniques with which they examine fundamentals of the earth's make-up and climate, and a career structure has been established. Glaciologists – applicants with a degree in physics, chemistry, engineering, geology or geography – are trained by BAS itself. Half the graduate entrants are contracted to work with BAS for five years. Within the first year or so the budding glaciologist is sent south, usually to work in a three-man team led by one of the more experienced staff. At the end of his five-year term he may present his research work for a doctorate. Despite the budgetary strictures of the 1970s the BAS earth sciences expanded steadily, assuming responsibility for Antarctic glaciology from the Scott Polar Research Institute in 1976 and Antarctic geology from Birmingham University, where Sir Raymond Priestley once headed the department and eventually became vice-chancellor, in 1974.

Dr Swithinbank is proud of his department's record as the first to produce maps of Antarctica from satellites. But, he adds, the Land Satellite system does not extend below latitude 80°S and the far side of the moon is still better mapped than some parts of Antarctica. Skills in land travel are still highly prized, he insists, reflecting on the heroic origins of BAS. 'Most accidents could be avoided,' he told me on a recent visit to his department, 'provided a skilled operator reads the signs of the weather properly. Really bad weather is usually heralded at least a day in advance.'

The main concerns of the glaciologists of the department are the two ice sheets and the ice-cap for what they can tell us of the world's climate. In the short term, according to Dr Swithinbank, there is little danger of a dramatic change in the earth's climate or of a sudden break-up of the western ice sheet, the more unstable of the two. From the ice-cap glaciologists can discover what happened in past ice ages and project what might happen if they recur.

The BAS geologists are interested in the original formation of the Antarctic continent and how the supercontinent of Gondwana broke up 200 million years ago. Diagrams of Gondwana look like a child's jigsaw with the southern capes and shores of South Africa, India, Australia, New Zealand and South America fitting into the appropriate slots along the coastline of Antarctica as it is today. Research into the rock formations of Antarctica helps understanding of the continents, islands and subcontinents which have broken off. But there is one huge handicap for the BAS geologists: only about one per cent of the Antarctic continent is not covered by ice or snow. Much of their work has to be done by conjecture, inferring what lies under the ice from what is known from the rocks and nunataks above it. They are helped by a battery of new techniques: echo-sounders and magnetometers carried by aircraft, radar scanning of the ice, gravity sounding and the firing of seismic shots. Dr Swithinbank himself experimented with the first airborne echo-sounding devices from the BAS Otter and Pilatus Porter aircraft over the Wordie and Larsen Ice Shelves in the summer of 1967. The airborne magnetometer achieves a response from the magnetic properties of the rocks beneath the ice, thus indicating the depth of the ice-cap and the formation of the rocks. Thickness of the floating part of the ice sheets can be gauged by radar, but assessing the depth of water and the make-up of the seabed beneath is still a problem. In the next few years it is hoped to develop methods of seismic sounding beneath the ice. The Antarctic continental shelf is deeper than most in the world and it extends a much shorter distance from the land mass.

'The real progression in our work is that we have started understanding what we cannot see,' says Dr Swithinbank, 'though there are still a great many problems to be resolved.' The biggest puzzle is the geological jigsaw of Gondwana itself, for though the continental pieces fit quite easily in most cases, there is one part that does not: the Andean chain of South America, the Scotia Sea and the Antarctic Peninsula. The mountains of the Peninsula appear to be the same formation as the Andes but how they related over 100 million years ago is still a mystery. Geologists refer to the Peninsula as 'rotating', and several teams each summer spend their days in a sophisticated geophysical version of the child's game 'pin the tail on the donkey', trying to establish how the spine of the Peninsula relates to the shield of Greater Antarctica. Dr Swithinbank is convinced that the geologists will solve the riddle eventually, but at the moment it causes as much debate, doubt and vehement disagreement as any nice point of theology or canon law did among the brethren of medieval Cluny or Citeaux. One geologist I met in Port Stanley, who had successfully completed his novitiate summer season working from

Rothera, speculated with the boldness of an Abelard or Galileo that the concept of the rotation of the Antarctic Peninsula was merely a hallowed myth.

The earth scientists use the Survey's Twin Otter aircraft more than the members of the other departments. In a good summer season the little planes fly over a triangle equivalent to that between Cambridge, Warsaw and Tunis. In the summer of 1984 the weather was so good that one of the planes could fly to the American base at the South Pole with ease; teams of British earth scientists were able to work within 500 miles of the Pole. The Americans often help by laying out dumps of fuel from their heavier Hercules transports for the British light planes, and American glaciologists and geologists travel and work with their British colleagues in the field. Fuel is exchanged between different national surveys on a barter basis; money never changes hands. Both the Chileans and Argentines have given fuel to BAS regularly, and there have been exchanges of Russian, American and Argentine earth scientists. Dr Swithinbank says that the degree of international co-operation is still excellent, but 'it will stop once accountants and the movement of cash start becoming important down there'.

Not everyone in the southern hemisphere has been cheered by the sight of the bright-orange BAS aircraft, however. On their way south down the coast of South America they were forced down by fighters of the Peruvian air force, and at the beginning of the 1983–4 season sugar was found in their tanks after a refuelling stop in Peru, clearly a result of animosity aroused by the Falklands conflict.

I asked both Dr Swithinbank and Nigel Bonner if they thought international understanding and co-operation were bound to deteriorate in Antarctica over the next few years, particularly as the commercial exploitation of mineral and living resources is increasingly in prospect. Both gave a similar answer, but with an interesting variation of emphasis. Bonner said he thought articles on conservation will have to be written into any convention on mineral resources development under the Antarctic Treaty. 'To that extent there is a sense of a deadline because we must try to get a resources convention soon.' The main difficulty he envisaged was the difference of outlook between the Treaty countries whose main interest in Antarctica is scientific and those whose prime interest is military. 'I think there will be changes,' he concluded, 'but not as bad as many people fear.'

Dr Swithinbank was equally concerned about the prospects of mineral development in the Antarctic, but, he told me, he still thought it would be quite some time before extraction became a commercial proposition. 'We've no doubt that sooner or later something will be found,' he explained, 'but put it in proportion: with a continent ninety-nine per cent covered by ice and seas covered by ice for many months in the year, even if there are good things under the sea – and there may be offshore oil – it is going to be a long time before it is economic. There is still plenty of oil elsewhere in the world. The practical and political problems of working minerals, if and when they are found, do concern us greatly. At the moment we are finding out what's there. Internationally we are working on agreed programmes – we exchange our data – and this is working very smoothly. But I suppose that as soon as you strike something of economic significance you would want to keep people away from it rather than exchange all your findings. That may lie somewhere in the future and that certainly does worry us. We've maintained co-operation for twenty-five years now under the Treaty, but there is apprehension now because of the increasing number of countries coming in and the fact that they may not be as attuned to this kind of collaboration as we are. They may not realise it is in their long-term interest.'

At the end of our interview Dr Swithinbank turned and said, 'All these questions do have to be asked, and we can only give some of the answers at the moment.' In the time and care with which leading BAS scientists answer enquiries about their work and the future of the Survey in Antarctica, they give an impression that at their shoulders are the ghosts of Cook, Ross, the scientists of Scott's and Shackleton's expeditions – the forefathers of the order.

The work of the atmospheric sciences department has a distinctly mystical element to it. To the outsider of limited scientific expertise some of its more esoteric lore is hard to understand, and even more difficult to describe, as much of the programme is related to space technology and the origins and composition of the universe. The head of department is Dr Michael Rycroft, a relative newcomer to BAS, who moved from space research at Southampton University some four years ago. He has had less experience of the training school of the Nansen sledge and its motorised cousin the skiddoo than fellow department chiefs, but he is constantly surprised at the similarity between work and study in space and research in Antarctica. Scientists in space and on the Antarctic bases work in isolation where fuel and food supplies are a major preoccupation and both address the most profound scientific questions of our existence. Dr Rycroft's position might at first glance seem like that of a sorcerer's apprentice because of its sheer range and because it deals with manifestations of pure magic, the celestial fireworks of aurora and corona, which light up the southern winter nights.

Longest established in the department is the study of weather and climate, a tradition that stretches back to the eighteenth century. Cook's naturalist, Johann Reinhold Forster, first named the luminous arcs in the night sky 'aurora australis'; in 1775, nearly sixty years before, the astronomer Edmund Halley gave a detailed account of the northern aurora in a scientific paper. Each of the BAS stations make recordings of the weather every day, but more detailed studies are made at Faraday in the Argentine Islands and Halley on the Brunt Ice Shelf in the Weddell Sea. The Meteorological Office at Bracknell contributes to the work at Halley, though recently it has ceased supporting programmes at Faraday.

Dr Rycroft says the first aim of his department is the understanding of weather and climate in the long term. The second aim, he explained with a seraphic glow lighting up his face, high-domed like one of the boffins in the Dan Dare space stories of the fifties in the *Eagle* boys' comic, is 'front-line international research' into the upper atmosphere and space. With brilliant journalistic shorthand he points out that 'Antarctic science and space really entered the scene together thirty years ago, and they are related. In Antarctica we have the possibility of studying on the ground what is happening in space.'

Since 1981 scientists at Halley Bay have been using the Advanced Ionospheric Sounder to bounce signals off the ionosphere, the electrically charged belt of gas beyond the stratosphere, more than 300 kilometres above the earth. The sounder is linked by satellite to a computer in Cambridge. Halley is particularly suitable for studying the ionosphere in the prolonged periods of darkness in the austral winter and long hours of light in summer. The ionosphere tends to thin out over the two poles and atmospheric conditions in both the Arctic and Antarctic make them ideal for the study of solar flares, sunspots and solar winds in space. The electrical storms generated in the upper atmosphere are important for the study of wireless signals; activity in the ionosphere can suddenly cause a black-out of normal radio communication in the region. An important area of Arctic and Antarctic research is the 'whistler mode signals'. These very low-frequency radio signals originate with lightning flashes in the northern hemisphere and they travel along lines in the earth's magnetic field to emerge from the ionosphere over the southern polar region. As they travel, the lower frequencies are delayed more than the higher ones and this accounts for the characteristic whistling sound they generate. Similar observations are made of the Van Allen belts, layers of highly active electrons and ions that gyrate about the earth's magnetic field, bouncing backwards and forwards between the northern and southern hemispheres, discovered following the IGY of 1957–8.

Beyond the ionosphere and magnetosphere lie the Plasma Pause and space. Antarctica, explains Rycroft, provides one of the few points on earth of access to the study of plasma, the heated gases that form the fourth state of matter. The other three states, solid, liquid and gas, may be more familiar to us in our terrestrial surroundings, but they only constitute one per cent of the universe. The sun is made of plasma, and it alone is one million times the size of the earth.

Dr Rycroft is particularly proud of the position of BAS atmospheric sciences in major international research programmes, though he was disappointed that the terms under which Margaret Thatcher's administration gave extra funding to BAS following the Falklands conflict seem to exclude his department from benefit. However, the management have made arrangements for the atmospheric studies to receive some more money; none the less Dr Rycroft, like his fellow department directors, is distressed at the number of good applications for research funds he has to reject. As a professional space scientist he is particularly proud of the fact that his is the only unit outside North America taking part in the International Terrestrial Physics Programme directed by the American space agency, NASA. His team has links with the NASA Goddard Data Center, and with the European space agency and the Japanese space agency has access to a chain of ten satellites for its programmes.

'We do not know nearly enough about the way the atmosphere works,' was Dr Rycroft's characteristically gentle side-swipe at two of the hoariest myths of Antarctic science, the destruction of the ozone layer by pollution from sprays and aerosols, and the 'greenhouse effect', the heating of the lower atmosphere because of the excessive discharge of carbon dioxide. In the past thirty to forty years the nature of the world's climate has begun to show tangible signs of change due to man's industrial activities. According to Dr Rycroft, research into such phenomena is still at a very early stage. He advocates the use of new instruments, more refined experiments, and the construction of new theoretical models to address the problem. He is convinced that such questions are best examined from Antarctica as the infra-red rays of the sun are more easily observed there. According to the greenhouse theory and the ozone doomsday notion, the earth is more susceptible to the onslaught of the infra-red rays as the local atmosphere is destroyed, particularly the layers that put some filter between the sun and the surface of the planet.

The most southerly BAS base is at Halley Bay on the Brunt Ice Shelf off the Caird Coast in Coats Land, which runs along the south-eastern shore of the Weddell Sea. Halley particularly suits the needs of the atmospheric scientists and meteorologists because it lies in the area of the Antarctic continent furthest away from the magnetic pole. Living conditions at Halley are the most difficult of all the British stations, as the staff have to spend most of their time underground sheltering from the hostile conditions of the Antarctic winter. Depression and withdrawal can be induced by such a lifestyle and this can be oddly contagious in a small wintering party of ten to twelve men. Relief ships can only reach the base once in most summers and often cargo and supplies have to be hauled over massive ice cliffs to the base. In 1982–3 work began on the fourth base at Halley – the first to be built there was part of the Royal Society's programme for the IGY in 1956. That base broke off the ice shelf years ago and is somewhere well out into the Weddell Sea by now. Dr Laws says he expects a base at Halley to last fifteen years at the most; the first BAS base lasted to 1972–3 and its successor was a mile and a half from the edge of the ice shelf when it was abandoned.

The new structure is the product of a modest technical revolution, for instead of heavy metal, flexible plywood is used to form the tubing of the main shell. The two plywood tubes are each over a hundred yards long and ten yards in diameter. They lie in the snow and ice side by side, connected by a corridor, looking very much like a space station. Inside each tube living quarters, laboratories, storage space and generator and machine workshops are laid out on two levels. The skin of the tubes has been designed to resist varying strain from ice and snow as it piles up outside. The foundation was dug six feet into the ice and snow was blown by machine to give covering for the first three years. It took sixty days to build the new base and a team of Royal Engineers had to be enlisted to get it finished in the short time allowed by the summer weather. In keeping with the spirit of the Antarctic Treaty BAS insisted that they worked as civilians and wore no military uniforms. The new design was the invention of a small timber construction firm from Ross-on-Wye called Structaply, who had never attempted anything in polar building and architecture before. The designers paid particular attention to fire prevention and reducing fire risk, one of the biggest hazards facing wintering parties. The new base appears to be a great success and at a cost of £1.5 million was £1 million cheaper than the Germans' base near Halley at Neumayer which used tunnels of heavy steel tubing for the main structure. The Structaply model has been sold to the Indians for their base off Coats Land at Dakshin Gangotri.

Life on the bases follows a ritual reminiscent of the long voyages on grain clippers. At midwinter each member of the community has to produce a gift – a model, a piece of handicraft, a product of his own hands and imagination – which he has worked on for weeks and months. He then draws one item from the pool, and poorly prepared offerings can produce recrimination. To liven up the long evenings impromptu fancy-dress parties are held such as a Wild West or Dracula evening. The regime often has austere values; the directors frown on the use of videos, though for how long they will be able to prevent their import to the bases is uncertain. Judging by their pollutant effect on normal social activity aboard HMS *Endurance* and in the Falklands community, the BAS directors may have a point in discouraging them. Skiing and home-made toboggans provide an invigorating diversion at most of the bases, and at Rothera three teams of dogs are kept, more for recreation and biological study than use for haulage. One evening in Stanley two of the BAS doctors, from Rothera and Halley, gave a slide-show of pictures they had taken at the bases in the previous season. One was particularly proud of his prowess with the team of dogs he adopted at Rothera, and with a display of psychological transference which would have impressed Sigmund Freud, gave an extraordinarily aggressive account of his life and work at Rothera. It was as if he wanted to give a display of machismo to match that of the leader of his dog team, the Admirals. It was an extraordinary performance because his audience was largely fellow members of BAS, plus one or two strangers and visitors. He explained how the dogs were divided into three teams, Picts, Huns, and his beloved Admirals, and described with relish the system adopted by Amundsen and the Norwegians of feeding the carcass of an old and decrepit dog to the rest of the team.

Doctors bear great responsibility among the winter communities; besides medical practitioner, they have to be counsellor and guide and they often conduct important studies of humans and animals. BAS donates a grant each year to the Robert Gordon Centre for Offshore Medicine at Aberdeen University where Dr David Dalgliesh, one of the most illustrious figures in the FIDS and BAS pantheon, has initiated research into cold stress. At the slide-show in Stanley the account given by the doctor from Halley was as gentle as his colleague's was violent. Later I discovered that the doctors and base commanders had had some quite tricky problems of depression to cope with in previous seasons. Despite his months down the tube at Halley, the doctor seemed refreshingly balanced and easy-going.

Complaints about the lack of video and other amenities are usually camouflage for concern about deprivation of the company of women. BAS still does not allow women to winter on their bases, though some have been invited to join specific summer research projects. As we left Signy Base aboard HMS *Endurance*'s cutter, David Rootes yelled, 'When you next see Dick Laws, don't forget to ask him why he doesn't allow women on the bases in winter!' – clearly venting the frustration of seven years as commander on the base.

During the previous season the base cook established contact via the amateur radio link with a wonderful Chilean girl called Maria Isobella. For weeks he talked to her and made plans to visit her. One day he came rushing out of the radio room yelling, 'Anyone want to come with me? She says she's got a sister.' Dave Rootes decided the joke had gone far enough, for *he* was Maria Isobella, speaking from a radio set at the other end of the accommodation building. It took several days to soothe the wrath of the disappointed suitor.

Dr Laws addresses the matter very seriously and has discussed it frequently with the Equal Opportunities Commission. Both he and his predecessor, Sir Vivian Fuchs, say that they are opposed to women on the winter bases as their presence in such a small community of males can be highly disruptive. The Poles, Russians and Americans have all taken women scientists and assistants to Antarctica, though Dr Laws says that the Russians are abandoning the practice. The Americans have the Equal Rights Amendment to contend with. An Australian woman doctor who wintered at the American Scott-Amundsen Base at the South Pole has sued the American government for her treatment there.

The first two women to winter in Antarctica were part of one of the most bizarre expeditions ever and the last major one to be privately sponsored. It was led by Admiral Byrd's old colleague Captain Finn Ronne in 1947–8 and he and his deputy commander, Harry Darlington, were accompanied by their wives, Jackie and Jennie. Jennie Darlington gave a hilarious account of her experiences, published as *My Antarctic Honeymoon* by a journalist called Jane MacIlvaine. Expedition members quarrelled among themselves and with the fids about base facilities at Stonington. Finn Ronne confessed in his account that he did not have time to make a thorough appraisal of his party before setting off and as a result they numbered

a sharp-tongued fellow who sneered at everything, a couple of prima donnas, a jolly kleptomaniac, a modest hard-working member who brooded unhappily, a spoiled youth who flew into tantrums, a brilliant individualist who insisted on doing everything his own way even when it was the wrong way, a lazy cuss who did little besides sit around and talk sex, a politician who demanded a vote on every decision . . . It is not surprising that we had some long-smouldering feuds, quite a few open quarrels and a couple of cases of disciplinary action . . . but from what I have seen of explorers I could have done worse. Compared with some expeditions I have been on, I assure you that our expedition was one big happy family.

I do not know what it says for the state of his marriage but he named one of the biggest ice shelves in Antarctica the Ronne Ice Shelf after his wife. Jennie Darlington returned home to the United States pregnant.

Some of the BAS scientists give ecstatic descriptions of work in the field in good weather conditions. Dr Julian Paren, my cabin-mate aboard *Endurance,* had worked for thirteen weeks out of Rothera. He is a senior member of the permanent staff in the earth sciences department and reckons to work one summer season in two or three in the field. 'This has been one of the best seasons on record,' he enthused. 'We've managed to work round the clock, get a good healthy sun-tan, and logged ninety-three work-days out of ninety-six – really fantastic if you look at the records of sledging journeys in previous years.' He had spent much of the summer studying the interaction of an ice shelf with the sea, drilling holes in the ice for ice cores, sampling sea-water under the ice shelf, measuring currents and salinity and working with trace isotopes. This helped provide data about the movement of the sea under the ice shelf and the rate at which it melts, part of the general survey of the ice and snow balance of Antarctica. Parties of glaciologists from different countries choose to work in sectors of varying sea temperatures, and those most interested in studying the relationship between the ice-cap and the world climate tend to work on the bigger shelves, the Ronne and the Ross Ice Shelves. Paren said that the kind of work he was doing would interest more those studying the possibility of towing icebergs as a freshwater resource for more temperate zones.

Paren said he worked quite easily in good weather with no gloves on for much of the time. 'It's the really bad weather which drains you, the continual noise of the wind on the tent, the drifting snow and the need to dig yourself out all the time.' The glaciologists are based at Rothera on Adelaide Island and fly to the mainland by Twin Otter. After that the workhorse is the skiddoo, a motorised sledge with a ski at the nose and two caterpillar tracks at each side. Powered by a two-stroke engine it travels at eight miles an hour and some scientists have covered 1000 miles in a summer. Every field party is accompanied by a mechanic who can maintain the machines, and he will be paid as much as or more than the novice scientist.

Julian Paren stood in the 1983 parliamentary election as a candidate for the Ecology Party. He considers his work in Antarctica an 'experience of living life to the full, a marvellous antithesis to life in a highly industrialised country like Britain'. Many of the BAS scientists I met at the end of the summer of 1984 appeared to have a similar streak of Henry Thoreau or Jack London in them. In Port Stanley Paren introduced me to Mark Harrison who had just spent his first summer as a

BAS geologist in Antarctica working on the problem of the rotation of the Antarctic Peninsula, amongst other things. 'It's been a tremendous experience, both for the geology and the encounter with Antarctica itself,' was his verdict. 'Some of the rocks in the Antarctic are the most beautiful you could ever see. That's in a geologist's view – other people might think otherwise. It really is the most beautiful part of the world.'

One of the most experienced travellers in Antarctica is the deputy director of BAS, Dr Ray Adie. He spent three summers on the continent of Antarctica from 1946, and in 1948 and 1949 travelled 940 miles by sledge with Vivian Fuchs down King George VI Sound. In his first years in the south, he recalls, he was holed up in a tent for fifteen days at a stretch as the winds and storms raged outside. During that time he read and reread every label on every tin and jar and every scrap of writing in every journal, notebook and instruction manual he could find. When eventually he went to visit his friend Fuchs in Cambridge he said he knew the house to the smallest detail, so carefully and vividly had it been described during their confinement to the tent.

Dr Adie is a kindly man who conveys immediately his enthusiasm for Antarctic science. Between them the directors and their deputies must have more than a couple of hundred years' experience of living in Antarctica. They know that a misfit can disrupt the entire community of a base in winter and seriously affect the work done there. He says he uses none of the orthodox psychological tests to assess the suitability of a potential BAS recruit wintering and working in Antarctica. He and the other directors mingle with the new men during the week-long induction course and interviews are quite informal. Dr Adie says he looks for the calm and well-balanced worker who might on the surface seem rather quiet, even dull. He recalls that during the first two winters he spent at Stonington Island there was only one major row. 'It was about whether you put the milk in the mug before the tea. It went on for four days and raged terribly while it lasted. And then everyone forgot about it completely.'

Complacency can quite often lead to disaster; and a number of scientists and assistants have lost their lives working for FIDS and BAS, often quite mysteriously. A fire in the hut at Hope Bay killed two people. In July 1982 three men from Faraday Base were lost on sea ice near a refuge hut on Petermann Island where they had camped successfully. The Chilean air force helped with reconnaissance aircraft but no trace of the men, a mechanic, a radio operator and a physicist, was found.

Experience in the techniques of Antarctic travel acquired by BAS is recognised internationally. In recent years the survey helped West Germany, India and Brazil prepare to put bases and scientists in

Antarctica, and China has sent representatives to Cambridge to study BAS methods. Dr Adie does not seem unduly anxious about the increasing tempo of activity in Antarctica, though he thinks a minerals regime under the Antarctic Treaty is now a matter of some urgency. His former chief and old friend Sir Vivian Fuchs says that so far there is no published proof of resources in commercial quantity in Antarctica and the continental shelf. Adie disagrees. 'Two hundred and fifty million years ago all the southern continents were united. The mineral resources of South America, Africa, India, Australia are considerable, and it makes one wonder where Antarctica fitted in. That supercontinent of Gondwana was there. Those mineral resources were evenly distributed. The Good Lord didn't leave out Antarctica. So the chances are fairly high that there are resources. But how is one going to get them out?'

Dr Paren regards such a prospect with horror. 'I do understand why the minerals and exploitation side of the Antarctic is crucial for politics but I am sufficiently aware of the limited size of this planet to know that once the world has to fight over the last square miles of Antarctic resources it is almost the end of the planet as far as resources are concerned. I would much rather we realised this in advance and made use of the resources in our own latitudes. But the Antarctic is important for the world, for the world climate and for the subtle interplay between the earth and sun – that does influence conditions in Britain. The Antarctic seems a long way away, and I always hope there will be enough scientists who will go there devoid of politics, dedicated to science, whose work will not be prejudiced by the politicians. I know BAS's funding is partly in response to the Falklands war and the resources the Antarctic has. But ever since men have gone to the Antarctic they have gone as scientists and I hope that this work that has very little commercial return can continue in the spirit of gaining knowledge, just as much as people studying astronomy and astrophysics and space cannot expect financial reward for studying a particular galaxy or why the universe is the way it is.'

The number of countries sending teams to Antarctica has increased rapidly over the past ten years. There are now in the middle of 1984 thirty-one consultative and acceding members of the Antarctic Treaty. Some may be lured by the prospect of commercial gain, political prestige, or strategic advantage. Certainly not all are there merely for the sake of 'doing science'.

## Chapter 8

# Polar Politics

Ernest Shackleton's dream of a land crossing of Antarctica was achieved forty-two years after his rescue from *Endurance,* when the Commonwealth team led by Sir Vivian Fuchs journeyed from Vahsel Bay on the Weddell Sea to McMurdo Sound on the Ross Ice Shelf via the Pole in the summer of 1957–8. The last major goal of the heroic age of exploration had been achieved. Though Sir Vivian and his men had the help of tractors as well as dogs, radios and the occasional use of aircraft, the journey was hazardous enough, and the first few hundred miles were so tough that Sir Vivian freely admits that the whole enterprise was in fact nearly given up.

He had the idea of the journey one day while incarcerated in his tent during one of the marathon sledging journeys down King George VI Sound, and decided that the only way to make it work and worthwhile would be to go all the way across the continent. The logistical effort required to co-ordinate it would be so great that only a Commonwealth Expedition could succeed. But by the time detailed plans were being laid the idea of an International Geophysical Year had been born. The Trans-Antarctic Expedition (TAE) became the most famous symbol of the Antarctic part of the IGY's programme.

Few men alive today have done more to promote understanding of Antarctic exploration than Sir Vivian Fuchs. With his splendidly rugged features he looks as if he might have travelled with Nansen or Shackleton. As the director of FIDS and BAS he led countless expeditions and promoted dozens of research programmes and served on international and national committees by the score. He studied geology at Cambridge where his tutor, Sir James Wordie, brought him direct contact with the heroic age of explorers. Before the Second World War he took part in expeditions to Greenland and Africa, and after war service in South Africa and Normandy became the military governor of Schleswig-Holstein. When he returned from the war he applied for a job as a geologist with FIDS. 'Funnily enough, James Wordie tried to put me off,' Sir Vivian recalls today with a slight smile. 'He thought I'd already started in Africa and Greenland and should continue there.' Sir James, none the less, became a considerable supporter of various Antarctic enterprises devised by his former pupil.

To meet Sir Vivian is a rather awe-inspiring, intimidating experience. His manner of address is short and to the point, but within a matter of minutes his enthusiasm and his ability to encourage novices are apparent. At home in Cambridge he works with youth groups and promotes exploration in his capacity as vice-president and Head of Expeditions of the Royal Geographical Society. He has little of the warm and easy flow of chat of his friend and former sledging companion Ray Adie, but he exhibits two outstanding fid qualities in the clarity and lack of both pomposity and exaggeration in his conversation.

The advance party for the Trans-Antarctic Expedition left London aboard the *Theron* in November 1955. She was to deposit a tractor, Auster aircraft, fuel and twenty-four Greenland huskies at Shackleton Base, Vahsel Bay. It was only the second time a ship had reached so far south in the Weddell Sea since the first *Endurance* was beset and crushed there in 1915. *Theron* herself was beset for a month and the advance party had to build the expedition's base camp in appalling weather conditions. The following year Fuchs' party arrived aboard the *Magga Dan,* sister ship of the present *Endurance,* which was also carrying material for the Royal Society's new base at Halley Bay, 200 miles north-east of Shackleton. The observations made at Halley were to be the Royal Society's principal contribution to the Antarctic programme of IGY.

Sir Vivian's first objective was to establish an advance depot inland, and this turned out to be the toughest part of the entire TAE operation. Three hundred miles south of Shackleton, near the appropriately named Whichaway Mountains, the South Ice staging-post was built. Fuchs himself led the depot-laying party. Time and again they were faced with deep crevasses, and tractors lurched crazily over the cracks. The main mode of transport was the American Sno-Cat tractor towing sledges in tandem. This had four sets of articulated caterpillar tracks beneath the cabin and engine mounting. The expedition members took wonderful photographs: they show the track bogies bent at different angles, like the legs of a drunken giraffe, as they claw over the openings in the ice and snow. Once the party had established South Ice, they returned by aircraft to Shackleton, leaving the four tractors at the advance camp. Meanwhile the first conqueror of Everest, Sir Edmund Hillary, and a team of New Zealanders had begun the process of laying depots towards the Pole from McMurdo Sound using dog teams and two converted Ferguson farm tractors.

Sir Vivian and the main expedition group left Shackleton on 24 November 1957. The journey to South Ice was as bad as ever, with crevasses appearing before them and snow bridges, constructed on the previous journey, suddenly giving way. Several of the team nearly plunged to their deaths in the chasms; on one occasion the second-in-command, Ken Blaiklock, with astonishing presence of mind unclipped himself from his skis only to see them disappear seconds later eighty feet down a crevasse. The route had to be marked carefully with poles carrying brightly coloured flags. Sir Vivian still recalls the choice he had to make as his men tried to reach South Ice: 'At one stage we had to push ninety-three flags into the ice to cover one mile. I remember thinking to myself, "We have to cross this now, or there'll be no expedition".' They reached the advance base on 21 December, spent four days servicing the tractors and on Christmas Day set out on the 550-mile journey to the Pole. Meanwhile Sir Edmund Hillary and the New Zealanders had laid a depot 500 miles north of the Pole in the direction of McMurdo. His group were delighted at the performance of the rubber-tracked Fergusons, long recognised as one of the most superbly engineered tools in the history of modern farming. On a characteristic impulse Sir Edmund's team decided to make a dash across the plateau for the Pole, and on 4 January 1958 drove into the Americans' Scott-Amundsen base aboard a convoy of farm vehicles, the first party to make the Pole overland since Scott and his four companions forty years before.

Sir Vivian's party travelled the last hundreds of miles into the Pole at night – cooler temperatures in the hours of darkness made the snow and ice a little firmer. At one point the vehicles had to navigate a sea of sastrugi (rigid ice dunes). A fortnight before they reached the Pole, the tractor party caught up with the two dog teams which had been scouting the route ahead. On 19 January dogs, men and tractors drove into Scott-Amundsen. Sir Vivian recorded a joyous scene: 'I looked back and thought our convoy a brave sight; the orange "cats" and Weasel, the loaded sledges, bearing many fluttering flags of different colours . . . Our reception here has been a most warm one and we have been invited to sleep and eat in the base instead of our tents.'

The tractors were repaired and serviced at the polar base, and Sir Edmund and the dog teams were flown back to the New Zealand Scott Base at McMurdo. The main expedition's progress was fast to Depot 700, the dump nearest the Pole, laid by the New Zealanders. As they drew near the magnetic pole navigation was incredibly difficult. The compasses behaved erratically and the course had to be plotted by dead reckoning. From time to time white-outs made progress impossible. White-outs occur when the light reflected from overcast sky bounces off the snow and back again obliterating any contrast between sky, snow, mountain and ice; shadows and horizon vanish. If the expedition were delayed unduly, the New Zealand relief ship might become beset in the newly forming winter ice. So Sir Vivian devised a method of navigating by following a line of stakes laid out by the lead vehicle. The navigator and the driver sat back-to-back in each tractor to make sure they were keeping all the stakes aligned, and the last driver and team picked up the stakes for laying out further ahead. As they started to descend to the Ross Sea they were buffeted by the sweeping squalls of the katabatic winds, the 'williwaws'. On 2 March the convoy was accompanied into McMurdo by a flotilla of tractors and tracked vehicles like the heroes of great sea voyages being escorted by small craft on their triumphal return to home port. It had taken Sir Vivian's men ninety-nine days to make the 2158-mile crossing of the continent.

Besides being a marvellous adventure, the expedition had achieved important scientific results. Sir Vivian reckons that it took at least ten years for all the results and conclusions to be compiled, calculated and published. The convoy had set out with half a ton of explosive as well as twenty tons and more of food, tents, fuel and spares. Forty-four seismic shots had been fired along the route: the glaciologists would bore a hole thirty feet deep on the ice plateau and fill it with explosive; all other activity stopped; engines were switched off and even talking ceased as the shot was fired for the echoes from the rocks beneath to be recorded in the cabin of one of the tractors. Studies of rock samples revealed coal in some of the mountains, and fossil plants were found. The geological programme proved conclusively that beneath the ice the continent was one piece of land and not a jumble of islands and lakes. Observations were made of weather and climate, and the men themselves were under scrutiny for reaction to oxygen deprivation and cold stress in a precursor of Howard Oakley's programme of survival medicine on Brabant Island in 1984.

IGY saw bases sprouting like mushrooms all over Antarctica. The Russians arrived in strength for the first time since Bellingshausen's expedition of 1819–21. They ringed coastal Antarctica with bases, placing one, Sovetskaya, at the 'pole of inaccessibility' midway between the Amery Ice Shelf and the South Pole. Huge convoys carried material and supplies inland. Later, when they built the Vostok base near the southern geomagnetic pole, the Soviet scientists laid a railway across the ice and snow from their Mirny Base on the Davis Sea.

The Americans invaded as never before, launching 'Deep Freeze II', which involved ships, aircraft and 5000 men, in 1956. Admiral George Dufek established the Scott-Amundsen base – according to a British contemporary, 'the most political base of all' because it theoretically commands access to the Antarctic interior – at the Pole itself. The base is supplied by air, and for the first few years tanker aircraft would arrive in the austral summer to be dug into the snow for the following winter. The McMurdo base was built into a small town complete with cinema and Chapel of Our Lady of the Snows. The American operation is still the biggest and most sophisticated in Antarctica, and their scientists and directors have acted with great generosity towards their colleagues of the other national surveys. After IGY they handed over a base they abandoned in Wilkes Land to the Australians. McMurdo works closely with its neighbour, the New Zealand station of Scott. Each summer the Americans use Christchurch in New Zealand as a logistical base for their aircraft flying to the Antarctic, and the equivalent of a support regiment is stationed there. The Americans assist the New Zealanders with transport, which is fortunate for the New Zealanders as their research budget is fixed at a nominal NZ$1 million at 1981 rates. Australia increased her Antarctic research budget that year to A$18 million. Both are dwarfed by the US federal expenditure of at least US$100 million on Antarctic activities each year.

Twelve countries set up forty-four new stations in Antarctica for IGY; FIDS was already operating ten stations to which was added the new Royal Society base at Halley. A network of nearly fifty stations reported weather and atmospheric readings daily to the US base Little America V, and international programmes were launched in geology, glaciology, seismology and the study of a range of atmospheric phenomena, especially aurorae, which was where the tradition of such co-operation began; the principal aim of the First International Polar Year of 1982–3 was to study the majestic displays of coronae and aurorae of the south.

IGY was so successful that is was continued for the following year as the year of International Geophysical Co-operation (IGC), and again in 1964–5 for the International Years of the Quiet Sun (IYQS). IGY also had more lasting results: it led to the continuing programme of scientific collaboration in Antarctica through the Scientific Committee on Antarctic Research and to the drawing up of the Antarctic Treaty in 1959, which in 1961 was ratified by the twelve nations participating in the IGY southern programme. It had finally redressed the balance between Arctic and Antarctic research.

SCAR, a committee of the International Council of Scientific Unions, got under way quickly after the close of the IGY and IGC in 1958. It has a secretariat in each of the member countries and working parties for particular disciplines, which meet regularly. Countries must be active in Antarctic research to qualify for membership: others can send observers to the meetings of the working groups and of the committee itself. India, Brazil and Uruguay are the latest countries to announce plans to mount a full Antarctic survey of their own and to become members of SCAR.

Every two years a full meeting of SCAR is held, with a symposium devoted to one subject. It is interesting to note how more attention is now being given to the study of the upper atmosphere. Recently governments have asked SCAR for advice on updating information networks in telecommunications.

Specialist programmes are now studying questions of climate, the environmental impact of possible mineral exploitation and exploration, seals, sea ice and Southern Ocean ecosystems. The oceanic studies have produced the most spectacular exercise of international co-operation, Biological Investigations of Marine Antarctic Systems and Stocks. The project has the backing of several major bodies for international co-operation, among them the Food and Agriculture Organisation of the United Nations. In the miasma of acronyms, initials, subcommittee and diplomatic jargon, the purpose of the BIOMASS programme is beautifully simple. It sets out to study the effect of commercial fishery in the southern oceans, particularly the harvest of krill. Two series of summer exercises have been looking at the migration and swarming patterns of krill and the movement of the ocean currents. The First International BIOMASS Experiment (FIBEX) used thirteen ships from ten nations, covering areas of the Scotia Sea, Drake Passage, and the Indian and Pacific Sectors of the Southern Ocean in 1981. In succeeding summers in 1984 and 1985 seventeen ships from eleven nations have been or will be deployed for a second exercise with the unsurprising acronym of SIBEX. Both operations have become the biggest seaborne experiments ever undertaken. The BAS contribution has been made by the support ship RRS *John Biscoe,* and for the second year of SIBEX the Royal Society's survey support ship *Discovery* has been commissioned.

The RRS *John Biscoe* is an old ship by modern standards: she was launched in the same year as HMS *Endurance,* 1956. She is small, a little over 1500 tonnes, and in 1979 had an extensive refit to construct a suite of laboratories for oceanographic research. Recently, trawl mechanisms and nets have been improved for the capture and detailed examination of krill. Wet laboratories are essential in all marine research, but particularly so with krill, which becomes contaminated by the atmosphere within four hours of being caught. With all the vagaries of the western palate and the difficulties of conserving the shrimp, Nigel Bonner at BAS says he can envisage a good trade in krill products, krill sticks and krill scampi in the next few years. Commercial operators could find krill hunting a frustrating occupation, however, if recent experiences of the *John Biscoe* are anything to go by. In the season of 1983–4 the BAS team aboard her had a hard time and found the swarms very difficult to trace.

For the first weeks of the summer study the twenty-eight scientists aboard the little survey vessel work a rectangular grid in the ocean at intervals of thirty miles. Depth, salinity, temperature and contours of the sea are recorded in detail, and krill density is assessed by netting and use of the echo-sounder. Off the coasts of South Georgia they were examining whether most of the sea-water had flowed up from the Weddell Sea or from the ocean further west, the Bransfield Strait and the Bellingshausen Sea. The second part of the summer exercise was devoted to the continuous fishing of the same area of water, addressing such questions as the depth at which krill swarm, whether they were gathering or dispersing and the distribution of nitrogen around them. The observations of sea-birds, penguins and seals made by biologists on Bird Island are directly linked to the research with the *Biscoe* as consumption by predators and the calorific value of food eaten by the birds and seals can be assessed from them. On the islands and ships television and still cameras are used underwater to observe the swarming krill.

The activities of more than twenty species of fish are also observed; few have any recognisable name to the casual visitor to Billingsgate Market, but there is a real possibility of an expansion in southern fishery. However, there are signs that unless it is monitored properly under the Convention for the Conservation of Antarctic Marine Living Resources (CCAMLR) of the Antarctic Treaty, whole sections of the Southern Ocean could be fished out. Already stocks have been virtually destroyed round the French possession of the Îles Kerguelen in the Indian Ocean Sector. Comprehensive data on the fish of Antarctic waters may take years to appear. According to George Hemmon of the Royal Society, the secretary of the British committee of SCAR, it could take longer to compile the results of BIOMASS than the research exercises themselves. Oceans of calculations are being poured into the World Data System of computers and it could well be the end of the decade before a final conclusion is produced.

Important aspects of the Antarctic Treaty have been equally slow to evolve. The twelve nations taking part in IGY met to discuss the treaty document in 1959 and it was agreed two years later. In 1971 the seal convention was produced by member countries, though it is not part of the Treaty. In 1982 CCAMLR was agreed finally. The Convention aims at the monitoring of all marine stocks with a particular eye to their conservation to avoid a repetition of what happened to seals in the last century and the whales in this. It is far from clear how the Convention will work as more than ninety per cent of commercial fishery is in the hands of the Russians, who are notoriously slow in reporting their results.

The Treaty itself is a unique achievement in modern international relations. It is a peace treaty which involves both superpowers as well as three nations disputing the same piece of territory, the Antarctic Peninsula. The roll of twelve contracting partners in 1959 has now swelled to fifteen consultative members and sixteen acceding countries, thirty-one nations in all by mid-1984. So far the agreement has worked remarkably well, but there are some thorny issues to be resolved and two in particular, the convention on mineral resources and the membership of South Africa, could upset and even wreck the mechanism.

Dr John Heap, the Foreign and Commonwealth Office's genial expert on the Treaty, says he doubts that the agreement achieved in 1959 could be negotiated in the international climate of today. He thinks that the Treaty could reach a crisis over the question of a minerals regime before 1991, the year in which any member state can call for a full review of the whole accord. It is often said that the Treaty will be reviewed in 1991, but the text merely says a review can be called for then, and though the review process should be immediate the ensuing wrangle might go on for years. Since there is so much misunderstanding about what the Treaty really does say, it is perhaps worth giving a summary of the most important articles (direct quotation in italics):

ARTICLE I

*1. Antarctica shall be used for peaceful purposes only. There shall be prohibited,* inter alia, *any measures of a military nature, such as the establishment of military bases and fortifications, the carrying out of military manoeuvres, as well as the testing of any type of weapons.*
*2. The present Treaty shall not prevent the use of military personnel or equipment for scientific research or for any other peaceful purpose.*

ARTICLE II

*Freedom of scientific investigation in Antarctica and co-operation toward that end, as applied during IGY, shall continue, subject to the provisions of the present Treaty.*

ARTICLE III encourages the exchange of information and staff, the notification of scientific programmes and co-operation with UN specialist agencies.

ARTICLE IV

*1. Nothing contained in the present Treaty shall be interpreted as:*
  *(a) a renunciation by any contracting party of previously asserted rights of or claims to territorial sovereignty in Antarctica;*
  *(b) a renunciation or diminution by any contracting party of any basis of claim to territorial sovereignty in Antarctica which it may have whether as a result of its activities or those of its nationals in Antarctica, or otherwise;*

171

*(c) prejudicing the position of any contracting party as regards its recognition or non-recognition of any other state's right of or claim to territorial sovereignty in Antarctica.*

*2. No acts or activities taking place while the present Treaty is in force shall constitute a basis for asserting, supporting or denying a claim to territorial sovereignty in Antarctica or create any rights of sovereignty in Antarctica. No new claim, or enlargement of an existing claim, to territorial sovereignty in Antarctica shall be asserted while the present Treaty is in force.*

ARTICLE V prohibits nuclear explosions and the disposal of nuclear waste, unless this is changed by consensus.

ARTICLE VI states the Treaty applies to below latitude 60°S.

ARTICLE VII lays out provisions for observers and their right of complete access to stations of member countries, their ships and equipment, and provides for aerial observation, all on the condition that the places to be visited have been notified.

ARTICLE VIII lays down rules for consultation between partners if there is a dispute over jurisdiction.

ARTICLE IX lays out procedures for ratification and the appointment of observers.

ARTICLE X enjoins members to fulfil obligations under the UN Charter.

ARTICLE XI states that disputes shall be settled by consultation and in the last resort by the International Court at The Hague.

ARTICLE XII *1.* states that the Treaty can be altered by full agreement between all parties, and any member can withdraw.

*2.* deals with the crucial question of review. It states:

*(a) if, after the expiration of thirty years from the date of entry into force of the present Treaty, any of the contracting parties whose representatives are entitled to participate in the meetings provided for under Article IX so requests by a communication addressed to the depository Government, a conference of all contracting parties shall be held as soon as practicable to review the operation of the Treaty;*

*(b) that the conclusions of such a Conference shall be agreed by majority of those entitled to participate and will take immediate effect;*

*(c) that a dissenting member could then withdraw from the Treaty, provided due notification is given.*

ARTICLE XIII states that ratification should be carried out according to the constitutional practice of member countries and lays down procedures for new members wishing to accede to the Treaty.

ARTICLE XIV states that the Treaty document in English, Russian, French and Spanish shall be deposited in the archive of the US government which must distribute copies to all member countries.

To sum up: the Treaty declares that Antarctica shall be used only for peaceful purposes, and testing of weapons nuclear and conventional is banned there. Military personnel may only be used to help service the scientific projects. Research is to be shared and member countries have the right of access to the work and installations of Treaty partners. After thirty years the mechanism can be reviewed at a conference of all members and then the method of regulation will change from consensus to majority vote. Territorial claims by member countries are frozen while the Treaty functions. Scientific work under the Treaty is to accord with the regulations of certain UN specialist agencies and certain international bodies like the International Council of Scientific Unions (ICSU) and SCAR.

There are two important things that the original Treaty document does not do: provide for a regime for the commercial development of living and mineral resources, and cancel the claims to Antarctic territory by member states. Once the Treaty fails, these claims become active again. It took twenty-one years before CCAMLR was ratified and brought into effect. It is likely to be an even harder task to establish a regime for the exploitation of mineral resources, so much so that some involved with negotiations over the proposal think it will be impossible to achieve with the consensus of all thirty-one nations now acceding to the Antarctic Treaty.

Scientists and legal experts involved in the deliberations over the regulation of Antarctic development have noticed a sharpening commercial interest in the area at all levels – individual, corporate and national. BAS is inundated with applications and enquiries for work and study on their bases, from the 'banana belt' – as the warmer sub-Antarctic climes of South Georgia and its islands are known by BAS men – to the southern continental bases. Dr Adie says that he has noticed that quite a number of the applicants nowadays are interested in personal glory and financial gain, judging from the prompt questioning he gets about salaries and allowances. Wistfully he recalls that he was paid an annual salary of £200 plus an extra £50 danger money when he set out for

Antarctica in 1946 for three seasons of polar adventure and what he calls 'doing science'.

The increasingly commercial aspect of Antarctic research is strongly in evidence in the approach of countries – like West Germany and Japan – that have stepped up their projects there in the past few years. West Germany has a new base on the continent at Neumayer on the Princess Martha Coast in Dronning Maud Land and a new support ship, the RV *Polarstern*. She is leased on a commercial basis and the prospectus is like a high-class travel brochure. The 4000-ton ship was commissioned in December 1982, a research vessel with facilities for sixty-five 'passengers' and forty-five crew and equipment for biological studies, a meteorological station, sea beam equipment for spatial recording of the sea bottom beyond 500 metres of water depth, machinery for geologists, lab containers on deck which can augment the 'several types of laboratories' on the main work-deck. The sales pitch on 'the ship and its purpose' enthuses that 'the special design of *Polarstern* as ice-breaker, supply vessel, and helicopter carrier is reflected in her bulky shape and her large dimensions. This results in a draught of approx. 10.5 metres. On the other hand, the ship is comfortable even at long cruises. It allows 40 scientists and technicians to work on board, and it has additional room for 25 scientists and technicians to reach the polar stations, all this besides a permanent crew of 41.' All of which costs, at a conservative estimate according to BAS, at least £4.5 million a year at 1983 prices to run. Her ice-breaking capabilities are likely to be needed for only a few days a year, and it will probably be difficult to get sixty-five 'passengers' to subscribe. BAS directors like Nigel Bonner say a small ship like the *Biscoe* can be an advantage if you have to work within strict budgetary limits. In 1984–5 BAS is due to operate three ships, three aircraft, five bases and nearly 320 staff at just over double the cost of running *Polarstern*.

*Polarstern* will be working with *Biscoe* and the *Discovery* in the SIBEX survey, but the programmes undertaken by the Germans' land base of Neumayer are heavily weighted towards the earth sciences. A German geologist told Nick Barker, the former captain of HMS *Endurance*, that it was quite clear why his country was taking such interest in Antarctic research. It was to give some chance of direct access to strategic reserves of hydrocarbons in the next century. Japan, another country with few natural energy resources, has been searching vigorously for oil round Antarctica.

So far there has been no published report of a major oil find and some Antarctic experts doubt if there are any hydrocarbon and mineral deposits that can be exploited commercially. Sir Vivian Fuchs says that the ice-cap is the major obstacle, and recalls finding 'quite a bit of low-grade coal seams and a tiny lead sample, so small you could stuff it in your pocket' on the Trans-Antarctic Expedition. But men like Sir Vivian and the BAS directors today consider it essential to have a minerals regime against the day when commercially viable deposits may be found. The Whaling Commission began to operate only at the point where whale stocks had been all but destroyed, and it is the example of the destruction of the whale populations that spurs many of the Treaty powers to look for a minerals convention.

The deliberations over such a convention have taken a long and winding path. The issue was first aired at a meeting of Treaty powers in Tokyo in 1970, and in June 1982 the gathering of representatives in Wellington, New Zealand, addressed themselves specifically to it. Ironically the meeting was held on 14 June 1982, the day General Menendez surrendered his forces at Port Stanley, and both Argentine and British delegates were present and on speaking terms. In all, there have been five meetings devoted to mineral resources from 1982 to mid-1984, when the fifth such discussion took place in Tokyo, but very little progress has been made beyond a polite taking note of different positions held by Treaty members.

The argument centres on two questions: the conservation of the environment if minerals and petroleum are extracted eventually, and who should benefit from their commercial exploitation. It is widely acknowledged that the Antarctic environment is particularly vulnerable to oil spillage, the erosion of rocks and soil and the destruction of vegetation. For the Treaty countries the most difficult question is how exploration and development should be managed. In this there is a sharp division between claimant and non-claimant powers, many of the former saying what they find in their sector of the continent and offshore deposits is theirs alone. Some would like to see the cost of investment in exploration and the profits shared between all Treaty members. Some of these take the view that there should be no development of mineral resources at all, and Antarctica should be a world natural park, as was proposed by the New Zealand foreign minister in 1975. Some Treaty powers would like a complex mechanism whereby some of the rewards for exploitation would go to the country backing the exploration and extraction and a royalty would have to go to a UN agency to be held as an international heritage fund.

Some British experts involved in the discussions believe that if the present impasse is not broken the Treaty itself is in jeopardy and will cease to function long before a member calls for review in 1991. The whole debate on the development of mineral and petroleum resources in

175

Antarctica is coloured by two arguments. The first states that so far there have been no published reports of big finds of oil and minerals in Antarctica. Those who support this view, like Sir Vivian Fuchs, say there is still nothing to suggest that Antarctica will become a major strategic reserve of valuable minerals and continental and offshore oil. The second line of argument says that it is only a matter of time before the full economic potential of Antarctica will be revealed. Supporters of this view say that it is more than likely that there are giant or supergiant oilfields (70 million tons or 700 million tons, 5 billion barrels of oil) beneath the Ross and Weddell Ice Shelves. Opinion of scientists, diplomatic experts, and financiers I have consulted over the past year divides evenly between these two schools of thought. In looking at the problems of developing the Antarctic Treaty and devising a minerals regime, two publications are invaluable: *The Handbook of Measures in Furtherance of the Principles and Objectives of the Antarctic Treaty,* published by the Treaty Organisation itself, and *Antarctic Resources Policy,* edited by the Chilean ambassador to Britain, Francisco Orrego Vicuna. This book, a collection of papers by an international panel of experts, gives the state of the art of current public knowledge about oil and mineral resources. A paper by the head of the Norwegian polar research institute, Tore Gjelsvik, sums up the problem neatly:

> Another perspective exists for the petroleum potential of the continental shelf of Antarctica, although it should be understood that no discovery has yet been made, and very little information on the potential accumulation of petroleum exists. The interest in the petroleum potential of the Antarctic shelf stems from different considerations. Petroleum deposits have been located off the southern coast of Australia and in Argentine waters . . . If sedimentary sections of adequate thickness and extent exist on the Antarctic shelf, accumulations of hydrocarbons could be present.

Gjelsvik says that much aeromagnetic surveying has been done by the Russians over the Amery Ice Shelf and in the Weddell Sea and by the Americans in the Ross Sea.

More than one million square kilometres of the Weddell Sea and Filchner Ice Shelf have been surveyed according to the paper by Oscar Gonzalez-Ferran, professor of geology at the University of Chile. He calculates that a hundred times the sums devoted to the search for Antarctic oil ten years ago are now being spent, but that only giant fields (yielding 0.5 billion barrels), or supergiant fields (5 billion barrels) would be viable. In 1975 the American seismic survey ship *Glomar Challenger* surveyed the Ross Sea, and she has been on station in

Antarctic waters again in the mid-1980s. Professor Gonzalez-Ferran lists a number of similar surveys by the Japan National Oil Corporation, the Australian Antarctic Survey Organisation with the research ship *Nella Dan,* and seismic study in progress in 1983 by the Chilean National Service of Geology and Mines. He concludes his article with the exhortation:

> It would seem that we have passed beyond the threshold of the stage of commercial exploration and exploitation of Antarctica's natural resources, the process having been accelerated by man in his efforts to meet his food and energy needs. The need for such a regime is therefore urgent; we can no longer afford to put the problem off by arguing that studies on Antarctic environmental protection are lacking or that appropriate technology does not exist. One must consider the facts, which indicate that everything is on the move and that these problems will soon be resolved; but a political decision is urgently needed before that happens. Avoiding the decision works in favour of greater internationalization and the dissolution of the Treaty.

The quickening tempo of mineral and hydrocarbon exploration is the subject of a chapter of the lively and colourful history of Antarctic development, *Antarctica: Wilderness at Risk* by Barney Brewster and Friends of the Earth. This elegant and racy book suggests that mineral resources exist in fair abundance on the continent, as do interested parties waiting to find and develop them. The resolution of the problem is very different from that of the Chilean geology professor, and the book states firmly that the risk to the world's climate is so great that it is simply not worth developing oilfields that might be able to supply the West's needs for a few years. The book suggests that gold, silver, cobalt, chromium, copper, iron, manganese, nickel, lead, platinum, titanium, tin, uranium and zinc have been found in the Peninsula, round the coast of the East Antarctic Shield and in the Trans-Antarctic Mountain Range. Texaco and Gulf Oil have been planning to carry out extended studies at huge expense, according to Friends of the Earth, as has the Japan National Oil Corporation. BP has been taking more than passing interest in the prospect of Antarctic oil and have recruited a series of geologists at the end of their contracts with BAS. The big corporations, however, have said little or nothing of their work in the southern oceans; such secrecy often appears among the least attractive attributes of modern multinational industry.

Much of Friends of the Earth's concern arises from fears of a serious accidental oil spillage. Experience in the Beaufort Sea and High Arctic indicates that it could threaten thousands of square miles of sea and coast because of the nature of marine life in polar regions and the slow rhythm of reproductive cycles. A workshop of Treaty and SCAR delegates at Bellagio in Italy in 1979 met to discuss just such possibilities and suggested that icebergs and pack ice would be a major hazard to the transport of oil and gas by ship and that it could be managed only for a very short season in the austral summer.

Quite apart from the political rows, the Siberian gas pipeline has presented a number of snags caused by low temperature and the Russians appear well behind Canada and the United States in Arctic pipeline technology. Some suspect that this has made them reluctant to join in a minerals regime under the Treaty which might give free rein to the wealthier and better-equipped nations. The Russians are cautious in producing their findings from seismic surveys, particularly those of some of the more promising mineral-bearing areas. However, most observers say they stick by the letter of the Treaty and conventions and agreements under it and SCAR. They are prepared to exchange personnel and publish data. 'The trouble is that their methods are entirely different from ours,' a senior BAS scientist commented about some recent Russian papers he had seen. 'You get the conclusions all right, but they never write up the methods they used, which is so important in a field like geology in the Antarctic.'

The evidence on whether there are large resources in Antarctica is still circumstantial, at best. Sir Vivian Fuchs and other leading British Antarctic experts point out that so far there has been no published report of a major oil strike in Antarctica; but, on the other hand, why are so many large oil corporations and national surveys interested in putting so much money into continuing study of mineral resources? Last year the Gulf Corporation of Canada invested three-quarters of a billion US dollars in a new drill ship for the Beaufort Sea and the High Arctic. Prospects there have not turned out as good as previously forecast. I asked Jim Feicke, secretary of the Canadian Petroleum Association, what would happen to the investment in the new exploration ship if the programme continued to be weak in the Beaufort Sea. Without hesitation he said, 'They say they can take the ship to the Antarctic, which might well happen within a couple of seasons.'

While the Treaty powers debate whether or how a minerals convention should be devised, pressure for the conservation of the Antarctic environment and rights of access for the poor nations of the Third World is being orchestrated by an increasing array of environmental groups. In Australia, New Zealand, America and Europe, at least 200 such bodies are now linked, Friends of the Earth, Greenpeace, the Ecology Party, the Greens in Germany being merely the flag-bearing vanguard. Sophisticated and well-produced news-sheets are published and distributed several times in the year. As the Treaty powers want to avert a repetition of the experience of the whaling industry, where controls were produced after the damage had been thoroughly done, so the environmentalists want to avoid in Antarctica an ecological disaster like the destruction of the Amazonian rain forests.

An acerbic view of the issue is put forward in *Frozen Stakes,* a little book published by the International Institute for Environment and Development. It is an extended version of a paper prepared by the author, Dr Barbara Mitchell, for the US Environmental Protection Agency. In her conclusion she gives three principal solutions in her analysis: leave things as they are, as a world national park; share Antarctica between all or some of the Treaty powers; or make it a global asset like the ocean seabed under the International Law of the Sea. The last of the scenarios is what Dr Mitchell terms 'jurisdictional ambiguity', in other words leaving things in their present confusion, and the three precedents are the Antarctic Treaty, the CCAMLR and the US-Brazilian shrimp agreement.

The signs are that the Third World and the non-aligned countries are beginning to take greater interest in what happens in Antarctica. India, a leader in the Non-Aligned Movement, has just launched a programme of Antarctic research from her new base near Halley. The late Mrs Gandhi told the Indian legislature that the country needed a station in Antarctica to help study the origins of the monsoons. At the Delhi conference of the non-aligned nations the final communiqué made reference to the 'question of Antarctica', at the insistence of Malaysia. A strange alliance of Malaysia and Antigua raised the matter further at the UN, contending that the Treaty was a rich man's club and that Antarctica was a global resource for all mankind. At a plenary session on 15 December 1983 the General Assembly of the UN adopted a resolution that requested the Secretary-General 'to prepare a comprehensive, factual and objective study on all aspects of Antarctica, taking fully into account the Antarctic Treaty system and other relevant factors'; that the Treaty powers, scientific agencies and other members of the UN assist in the study; and that the Secretary-General report to the General Assembly in the thirty-ninth session in which the 'question of Antarctica' is placed on the agenda.

Friends of the Earth, Greenpeace and ecological Antarctic travellers like Jerome and Sally Ponçy on their yacht are becoming increasingly worried about pollution in Antarctica. A small urban settlement like the US base at McMurdo and Palmer leaves refuse that takes decades to

179

clear. The worst problems are the dozens of rusty fuel drums that litter most Antarctic bases. Polythene bags of rubbish, like the 'gash' bags ditched at sea by HMS *Endurance*, take years to decompose, and the problem of effluent has been resolved only in recent times by the use of chemical toilets. One US scientist at McMurdo predicted that instead of the rich marine life there now, the floor of the Sound will be covered by 'a veritable rug of litter'. In 1962 the US Navy installed a portable nuclear power plant, Nukey Poo, at the top of a hill overlooking McMurdo, but after a decade of breakdowns and suspected radiation leaks it was shut down.

Tourism also comes in for severe criticism from the ecologists, though the bloom of this bizarre form of package holiday is already fading. The Antarctic cruise really is a fat cat's game. Two operators have organised cruises to Antarctica, the bases of the Peninsula and McMurdo and Scott on the Ross Sea at the height of the austral summer. The voyages of the *World Discoverer* are organised by Society Expeditions, Cruises Inc. of Seattle. In a two-week round-trip from Port Stanley via South Georgia to the Peninsula and back to the Falklands, the cruise members used to get a taste of Antarctica, with lectures and entertainment thrown in, for about US$3000. The *World Discoverer* is due to continue her career as a floating gambling den in the South China Sea. Since 1965 Lindblad Tours of New York have sent the *Lindblad Explorer* south. BAS scientists and their colleagues have been impressed by the briefings and lectures the Lindblad tourists have been given, though they admit to finding the billings and cooings of the denizens of Ohio, Oregon and Ontario over penguin and fid in his summer plumage a little disconcerting. Damage from a party of thirty to forty visitors can be considerable to rock, soil and plant, even if unintentional. The Treaty handbook is explicit in its recommendations on tourism and private expeditions. In both cases qualified guides should be used and scientific bodies working in the area should be notified months ahead.

Tourism occasioned the worst human disaster in Antarctic history when in November 1979 an Air New Zealand DC 10 crashed on Mount Erebus killing all 257 people aboard. Flights over Antarctica began in 1968 with an excursion organised by Richard E. Byrd from Boston. Qantas followed Air New Zealand's example in the 1970s. The Mount Erebus crash meant such flights virtually ceased. Only two months before a conference of Treaty powers in Washington had warned of the dangers of such flights – not only would it be difficult to mount rescue missions if they hit trouble but they were at the mercy of freak radio conditions and ferocious swirling winds round the high ground. Radio signals might be blacked out altogether and the katabatic winds could beat a low-flying aircraft mercilessly; and it appears that it was a freak wind that brought down the New Zealand jet.

To conclude, then, it appears that we have arrived at the period of great change in the history of human activity in Antarctica. Following the ages of heroic exploration and international scientific co-operation, we are now on the threshold of an era of commercial development. Some seasoned Antarctic scientists are now worried about the number of newcomers to the continent. They fear a long and difficult wrangle over living and mineral resources if the UN really does try to get its hands on the 'question of Antarctica'. There is already some challenging of South Africa's membership of the Treaty, which ostensibly operates under the Charter of the UN, from which she is banned. Some British Antarctic hands suggest that if the same procedure is adopted as with the International Law of the Sea, no coherent management will be established, as Antarctica needs careful handling by those who have invested in expertise in polar science and exploration over the years.

'So far co-operation under the Treaty has been very successful indeed,' Nigel Bonner of BAS sums up, 'particularly in view of the fact that logistics are so much worse there than anywhere else in the world.' Dr Charles Swithinbank rejects the charge that the Treaty Organisation is an exclusive club because the Treaty powers make no claims to exclude others from Antarctica. 'It has worked extraordinarily well because most countries have realised that problems are too big in the Antarctic to solve alone, and only by collaboration can we get answers in reasonable time and at reasonable cost.'

Nigel Bonner thinks that changes will come in the next few years, 'but not as big as some people think'. But with the internal tangle over the minerals regime among Treaty powers, rumours that a fifty-billion-barrel supergiant oilfield lies under the Ross Sea, and the Third World and non-aligned nations demanding a bigger part of the Antarctic action through the UN, the Antarctic Treaty is likely to meet its biggest test well before the review year of 1991. So far it has worked well. It has established peace between the superpowers and the three rival claimants to the Peninsula, though two of these have gone to war on the fringes of Antarctica, and it has spurred international co-operation in 'doing science' to an almost unprecedented degree. Few treaties and agreements in modern times can claim such a record.

# Chapter 9

# Deception

The day after *Endurance* had grounded in the Orleans Strait was damp and blustery, a complete contrast to the brilliant sunshine and flat calm of its predecessor. As the ship headed north for the South Shetland Islands and the bumpy ride across Drake Passage and the Burdwood Bank to the Falklands, the sea was rising into a choppy, short swell. For an hour or so there was some doubt whether the helicopter could be launched for a last mission in the 'Red Plum's' Antarctic deployment for the summer. In the early afternoon the helicopter did manage to haul away from the pitching flight-deck and into the teeth of what promised to be a miniature gale. Gaining height, the machine turned towards a small island, a ring of rock draped in cloud, which blew across our path as if a gigantic warship had been laying a smoke-screen.

The island was Deception, a sunken volcano which provides one of the best natural harbours in the southern hemisphere. Its crater is submerged and provides a lagoon and anchorage stretching for several miles. The entrance is a narrow gap – known as Neptune's Bellows from the trumpeting of the west wind through it – between jagged pinnacles, deep purple and blue as the sun lights them. With the wind head-on it can be a delicate manoeuvre for a ship to enter the lagoon, and ancient mariners' folklore says sailors on watch would put their hand out and touch the sides of the gully as the ships edged their way into the anchorage. It was a tricky enough operation for the helicopter as it nosed through the dank wisps of cloud, sudden thuds of wind pushing it down towards the ridgeline round the rim of the volcano, dark purple rocks veined with lines of the first snow of winter. Sweeping down to the lagoon itself the machine circled a desolate huddle of huts and rows of rusting oil drums. Stacked neatly along the most sheltered side of one of the huts lay the fading orange fuselage of a BAS Twin Otter aircraft. The wooden slats of the huts looked ragged and bleached and the settlement had the deserted air of a camp abandoned by disappointed Klondike gold prospectors.

From the beach the eye struggled with the contrast of the darkness and gloom of the foreshore round the huts and the dazzling light opposite as the sun struck the rocks and sea in the distance picking out the bands of green vegetation; the purple and brown rock on the vertical cliffs in the distance and the flashes of snow breaking through the scurrying clouds. The beach before the huts was a thick funeral rug of volcanic ash and rock.

Deception is one of the most active volcanoes in Antarctica. For more than a century, mariners and explorers have marvelled at its hot springs and spouting geysers. One whaler reported the water of the lagoon so hot that the paint peeled from the ship's sides. In 1829 HMS *Chanticleer* landed a party to explore the island. Dr Webster reported temperatures in one of the inland pools as high as 88°C, 'hot enough to cook an egg'. On the shoreline temperatures of up to 50°C were recorded over the next century. For a time Deception became the centre of a South Shetlands whaling industry and from 1910 a British magistrate was in residence for the summer season until 1931 when the shore station, started by Chileans and continued by Norwegians, closed. After the Second World War the British, Chileans and Argentines have had bases there.

In the late austral summer of 1967 a number of tremors were noticed by the FIDS team based on the island. In November they were repeated and on the morning of 4 December the British scientists noticed a column of ash and dust rising from behind the Chilean base. In his book *Of Ice and Men,* Sir Vivian Fuchs quotes from the Base Report, which bears astonishing similarities to Pliny's account of the eruption of Vesuvius:

> Our first actions were quick and decisive. As a man we raced to the base hut, grabbed our cameras and rushed out again to take pictures. Having done the most important thing, we set about the secondary things like saving our skins – and our films! . . . We changed into our warmest clothing, collected goggles and silk scarves as protection against falling ash, and went out to launch two rowing boats. These were launched firstly with the idea of going to the aid of the Chileans, secondly with a view to saving ourselves should this be necessary. Since the eruption we had tried to contact the Chileans without success. . . . We had just completed preparations when the ash started to fall. This was black and like coarse sand, and fell for some minutes while we took shelter in a small hut. Walking became difficult because the snow was melting from below from the warmth of the ground, and because the ash and the hail had fallen on top to a depth of some inches. All the time it was getting darker, even though in summer the night was normally never more than twilight.

> When the storm broke we made a dash for the base unit amid continuous thunder and lightning crashing round the hills. There were little flashes of fork lightning in the air at eye level and about

three feet in length, looking for all the world like tinsel from a Christmas tree in mid air. About this time I saw a chinstrap penguin stagger from the sea with his 'shirt-front' grubby and looking slightly dazed; he was the image of an evening-suited reveller on the morning after the night before.

This wonderful description continues with the story of the rescue by Chilean, British and Argentine ships, and of the Chileans staggering into the British base, filthy with ash and soot. The scientists thought the eruption a minor and isolated event and landed a research team the following year, but in February 1969 there was another explosion. With great skill and courage Chilean pilots flew helicopters through storms of ash and snow to rescue the scientists trapped in the bases. Deception was abandoned and in 1970 passing ships reported falls of ash as they passed the island.

Summer parties continue to work from the huts on the island. A green building on stilts had 'Chile Skua' daubed across the porch, a clear sign of a recent visit. Colin MacGregor found the door open, and stepped inside to leave a Bible from the Scottish Commercial Travellers Bible Society. Inside he found the Chileans' visiting cards – scraps of food and greasy, unwashed cooking utensils.

Deception has been on occasion the epicentre of the diplomatic tussle between Britain, Argentina and, to a lesser extent, Chile over claims to the Antarctic Peninsula and the Falklands and their Dependencies. I have already described some of the incidents on Deception in Chapter 7 but the dispute between Britain and Argentina over territory in the South Atlantic is long and tangled. In 1833 a naval party from HMS *Clio* removed the garrison of the Republic of Buenos Aires from Port Louis in the Falklands and sent them home and in the following year the Buenos Aires government protested that the British occupation of the Islands was illegal. They claimed the Islands on three counts, which remain much the basis of the Argentine claim today: because they lay off the coast of the Republic of Buenos Aires; because the British had seized them by force; and because the Republic of Buenos Aires was the heir of the old Spanish title to those lands. Little further was done about the matter. In 1890 the Argentines planned to put a navigation lighthouse on the South Shetlands but were dissuaded, and in 1904 they took over the weather station on Laurie Island in the South Orkneys from the Scottish National Expedition of William Speirs Bruce.

Relations were soured by the British claims consolidated in the Letters Patent of 1908 and 1917, which were based on discovery, a formal declaration of possession and continuing exploration. The declarations of possession by the Crown by Cook, Bransfield and Ross are constantly referred to in this context. The Argentines have countered that discovery and exploration have often only been partial and ships of many other nations sailed to outlying islands of the Scotia Sea and Antarctica where no one had been before. In 1925 the Argentines completely ignored an invitation to join a major survey by the *Discovery*, and in 1927 built a radio transmitter on Laurie without a licence from the British magistrate in the area.

Throughout the early part of the century the Argentines extended the scope of their claim to South Atlantic lands, and in 1945 consolidated them in one document, as the British had done earlier in Letters Patent. Not only were they spurred to this by British activities with Operation 'Tabarin' but also by the renewed vigour of the Chilean claims. On 6 November 1940 decree no. 1747, issued in Santiago, stated: 'All lands, islets, reefs of rocks, glaciers, already known or to be discovered, and their respective territorial waters in the sector between longitudes 43° and 90° West, constitute the Chilean Antarctic or Chilean Antarctic Territory.' Eight years later Argentina had three, Chile two and Britain seven Antarctic bases.

In 1952 the story took another twist at Hope Bay in the Trinity Peninsula where Argentina had established a base uncomfortably close to the British FIDS station. As a British party of scientists was landing supplies for the summer season they were greeted by a hail of small arms fire from the Argentines. Diplomatic protests flew between London and Buenos Aires and the Falklands Governor, Sir Miles Clifford, sailed to Antarctica from Port Stanley. The incident was smoothed over quickly; but it was not an entirely isolated occurrence. In 1948 an Argentine warship had ordered a Norwegian whaling research ship, the *Brategg,* to heave to and hand over her papers. The Norwegian captain was informed formally that he was trespassing in Argentine waters.

Much the same happened in February 1976 seventy miles south of the Falklands when an Argentine destroyer fired on the support ship RRS *Shackleton* and tried to arrest her for operating in Argentine waters. According to the Franks report the operation had been planned for nearly two months previously. The incident led to the first reprieve of HMS *Endurance,* a strengthening of the small Royal Marine party on the Falklands and little besides. This is surprising because later in 1976 the Argentines established their weather station and military logistical base on Southern Thule. In view of the Argentine claim to Laurie Island and the Argentine charge that Britain's discovery and settlement of large parts of the South Atlantic and Antarctic territories was only partial, it was surprising that so little was done about Southern Thule by the

British authorities. Care was taken to give the Argentine presence in the South Sandwich Islands as little publicity as possible. The latest supplement to the *Antarctic Pilot* is less than straightforward about the matter. The 1974 edition simply states that an Argentine team had worked there from 1956 to 1957, and the supplement published in 1983 merely says, 'Ferguson Bay, Thule Island. 1955 Occupied 1980–82. Evacuated 1982. Inspected 1982. Food, fuel and accommodation for 40.' Paragraph 52 of the Franks Report says, 'On December 20th 1976 a helicopter from HMS *Endurance* discovered the existence of an Argentine military presence on Southern Thule in the South Sandwich Islands.' It was thought the Argentine party had established themselves at Ferguson Bay the previous month.

A senior Foreign Office official, replying to my demand about why so little heed was taken of the Argentines on Southern Thule from 1976, said, 'I suspect you are reading the danger signs backwards from the capture of South Georgia and the Falklands in 1982. But what was there to go on? Was this something new? Or was it a continuation of the regular exchange of diplomatic notes in the years between 1947 and 1955 when we were always protesting formally but getting along quite well for most of the time?'

Sir Vivian Fuchs records the strange twists and turns of relations with the Argentines in *Of Ice and Men*. After the shooting at Hope Bay, the scientists there found the Argentine commander particularly helpful, both socially and professionally. The course of the relationship seems to have run the gamut of a child's emotions at a pantomime, and diplomats and observers in Whitehall appear to have been quite unprepared for a sudden qualitative change in the Argentine policy, working from diplomatic precedent rather than a careful assessment of present events.

Sir Vivian thinks it a vindication of the Treaty that hostilities between Britain and Argentina in 1982 did not spill over into the Treaty area. But the outlook for the future is far from reassuring, particularly for BAS, which he helped found. BAS states firmly that it works for science, yet it is seen as a political presence. In maintaining a strong national identity in its work, following in the tradition of Captain Cook, it has done as much as any organisation in Antarctica to promote international co-operation. But once the framework for such understanding, the Treaty, is seen to be under attack and in danger of collapse, all the claims to pieces of Antarctica burst into life again. As the debate over resources continues, more countries make demands for Antarctic rights through the UN and Argentina reiterates her nineteenth-century nationalist stance on the South Atlantic, the future looks as unpredictable as the temperamental volcano of Deception itself.

After a trudge through the pumice and soot of the beach at Deception and a glance at the pastel red of the rock stacks – the brick kilns, as Captain Parsons of HMS *Chanticleer* called them – I clambered aboard the helicopter. We took off, struggling above Neptune's Bellows back to the ship. In the wardroom that afternoon the men of the Joint Services Expedition threw a Tom Collins cocktail party. The 'Red Plum' headed out towards the lumpy seas of the Drake Passage for the Falklands with several cracked ribs in the bows and a four-metre gash under her forward hold. Behind her the clouds closed in round Deception, perhaps the most impressive and suggestive sight of my short visit to the Antarctic Peninsula.

It was perhaps appropriate that Port Stanley was to be the next port of call for *Endurance*. Extra funding for BAS, the extension of *Endurance*'s service with the Navy and the policies on the defence and development of the Falklands are linked, at least in the perspective in which Mrs Thatcher's administration is working. BAS took some measures to reduce the tie with the Falklands when a few years ago it withdrew its twenty-two-man logistical staff from Port Stanley, leaving only a part-time assistant for the summer season.

But if many of the Thatcher government see a link between the Falklands and Britain in the Antarctic, so too does President Alfonsin of Argentina. On his visit to Spain in June 1984 he said that both Spain in Gibraltar and Argentina in the Falklands were victims of British colonialism, and he reiterated his country's claim not only to the Falklands, South Georgia and the islands of the Scotia Sea but to the Antarctic Peninsula as well. So much for the spirit if not the letter of the Antarctic Treaty.

# PART TWO

# THE FALKLANDS DIMENSION

# Chapter 10
# Falklands Revisited

'Have you noticed much change since you were last here?' is the customary greeting for a visitor returning to Port Stanley. Whatever pleasantry the traveller can muster after fourteen hours in a Hercules Transport from Ascension or a bumpy ride across Drake Passage is met with the rejoinder, 'Well, I bet you find things different in Stanley,' uttered with a mixture of apprehension and defiance.

For anyone whose first view of Port Stanley was smouldering peat fires and the debris of a retreating army it is hard to gauge how greatly the little town has been changed by the Argentine conflict. That week in June 1982 the streets were awash with mud, the footpaths crowded with weary soldiers, their olive-green jackets turning a sooty black soaked with the steady rain and occasional snow flurries. Some of the houses were damaged, the residence of the Catholic priest, Monsignor Spraggon, had the roof torn open as if by a giant can-opener, a spectacular piece of wild shooting by British forces from across the harbour. Most of the Argentine troops were quiet and well-behaved, almost unexpectedly so in view of the violent change of fortune that had befallen them. Equally quiet were the people of Stanley who had remained in the town. Little public account has been given of their numbing experience as British guns bombarded from the sea and the field artillery pieces closed in from the mountains. Argentine artillery discharged with a deafening report from among the houses. Dr Alison Bleaney, the senior civilian doctor, recalls Islanders behaving quite irrationally, wandering into the streets to see what was happening as the shelling reached a crescendo.

Returning to Stanley in December 1982, I found that such experiences had taken their toll. People I had got to know quite well in the latter part of June that year seemed weary. Mercifully they did not want to talk about 'the war' as it had come to be termed but craved for rest, a time to switch off, as they put it, and prepare for Christmas. The streets and houses had been tidied and new boards, verandahs and roofing had been put up. The roads were much worse, and nearly every street in the little port had been pounded by military traffic and lorries taking sections of the new houses to the building-site at the western edge of the town. The ring of craggy hills to the west seemed astonishingly close in the thin air of an early summer evening. One marvelled that it could have taken a

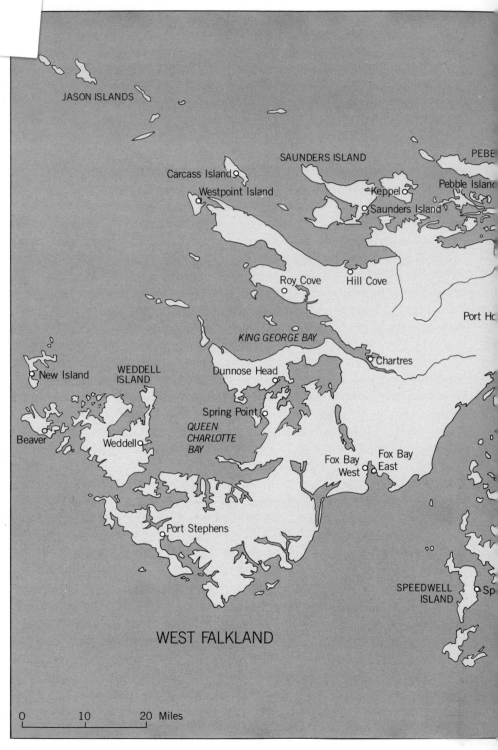

JASON ISLANDS

SAUNDERS ISLAND

PEBE

Carcass Island

Westpoint Island

Keppel

Pebble Island

Saunders Island

Roy Cove

Hill Cove

Port Ho

KING GEORGE BAY

New Island

WEDDELL
ISLAND

Dunnose Head

Chartres

Spring Point

QUEEN
CHARLOTTE
BAY

Beaver

Weddell

Fox Bay
West

Fox Bay
East

Port Stephens

SPEEDWELL
ISLAND

Sp

WEST FALKLAND

0       10       20  Miles

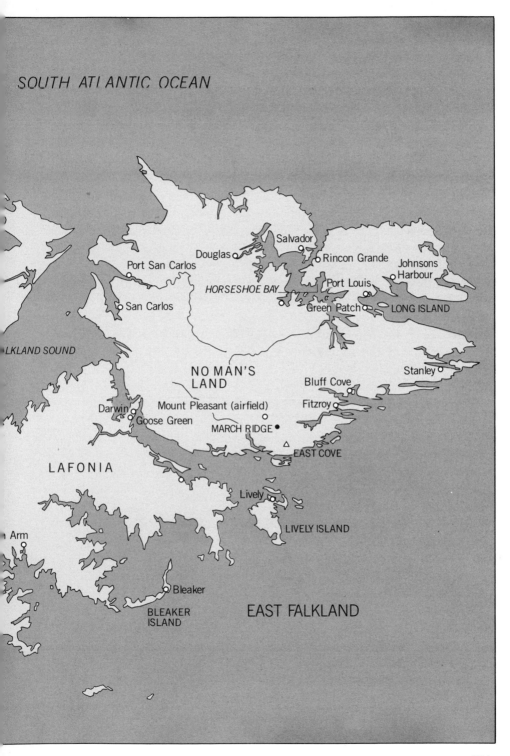

SOUTH ATLANTIC OCEAN

Douglas
Salvador
Rincon Grande
Johnsons
Harbour
Port San Carlos
HORSESHOE BAY
Port Louis
San Carlos
Green Patch
LONG ISLAND
LKLAND SOUND
NO MAN'S
LAND
Stanley
Bluff Cove
Darwin
Mount Pleasant (airfield)
Fitzroy
Goose Green
MARCH RIDGE
LAFONIA
EAST COVE
Lively
LIVELY ISLAND
Arm
Bleaker
BLEAKER
ISLAND
EAST FALKLAND

column of marines nearly six hours to walk in from the tallest of the southerly peaks, Two Sisters. Admittedly some of the delay had been caused by the new snow concealing the mines laid across the track.

That early summer Darwin Hill was a stripe of brilliant yellow from the distance as the line of gorse marking the boundary between Darwin and Goose Green burst into full flower. Closer inspection revealed gashes of burnt scrub like ugly scars where we had cowered that late afternoon in May. Along the shore the peat was churned up and pocked still from the mortar and artillery bombardment of the Argentines from the sheepyards in Goose Green itself. Along one side of the gorse hedge ammunition left by the Argentines had been stacked in dozens of boxes; some, ironically supplied by Britain before the conflict, was to be sold on the open market with a price tag of about £750,000. One December afternoon I was taken to a pit by the northern beach of the isthmus to see the last consignment of rockets, mortars, mines and unstable ammunition blown 100 feet into the sky, sending the sheep and horses stampeding down the paddocks. On that beach an army doctor of a peculiarly ornithological disposition had found the body of a young wandering albatross which had become fouled with oil miles out to sea. The fierce lines of the creature's beak contrasted strangely with the gentleness of its eye.

The community of Goose Green was subdued, taking stock from their month-long confinement in the community centre the previous May. Several had left for England for medical treatment and rest. It was shearing time, 100,000 sheep to be clipped in six weeks, one of the biggest drives of sheep in the world. The manager, Eric Goss, was all bustle and good humour, looking forward to the Boxing Day races at North Arm, though whether for the riding, the betting or the feasting was hard to decide. One of the shearing gang snagged his shears on a fragment of mortar bomb in a fleece and drove the knives into his forearm. Adrian Gilbert, a hand nearing the end of the two-year contract which brought him from Britain, swore he would never dream of working in such conditions again – the spartan facilities of the bunkhouse, the endless meals of cold mutton and the pay – £200 a month; laments have been heard from the contract worker for more than a century. The mood before Christmas that December of 1982 was of quiet introspection and anticipation. What was to be done to repair and revive the economy of the Islands, now that Whitehall and what remained of the Imperial title of the Parliament at Westminster had been forced so abruptly to pay them attention?

*Opposite* The cutter *Stancomb Wills* searches for the submerged rock on which *Endurance* had gone aground

Gunnery practice with one of the 20 mm Oerlikons. In the Antarctic Treaty area the guns are covered

Surveying in the Orleans Strait. Tony Riley (right) watches the setting up of the receivers for the trisponder transmitters already ashore

*Endurance* at sea. One of her two Wasp helicopters is on the point of landing on the flight-deck

Still waters may not run deep . . . View from the deck of the stranded *Endurance*.
*Overleaf Endurance* aground in the Orleans Strait, Antarctic Peninsula

RRS *Bransfield* preparing to tow *Endurance* (left) off the rock on which she had been grounded in the Orleans Strait

The Graham Land Peninsula, looking south towards the Palmer Peninsula and the Antarctic Plateau, viewed from the helicopter at about 7000 feet above sea level

198

Royal Bay, South Georgia: one of the two large glaciers with icebergs about to be calved

Iceberg in the Orleans Strait, seen from above. The ram beneath the sea surface shows up in light blue. *Overleaf* Sunset in the Orleans Strait. In the foreground the new winter ice, grease ice, is forming

Returning to the Islands some fourteen months later, at the end of February 1984, it was possible to see something of what had been achieved by the plans for immediate rehabilitation following the fighting. Soon after my previous visit, there had been an event of enormous political and psychological significance for many Islanders, the almost miraculous apparition of Mrs Thatcher in Port Stanley in January 1983. It confirmed her position as their champion, and her speeches and progress through the Islands cast the same glow as the descriptions of Queen Bess reviewing her troops at Tilbury. She promised the people of Port Stanley that the Islands' sovereignty would never be given away, and in an emotion-charged meeting in the community hall at Goose Green, the families practically refused to let her leave. The regard many Islanders have for Mrs Thatcher is very like that for a late medieval or Tudor monarch, for her touch can have the potency to dispel the evils that beset them. The problems from London, as they see it, often arise from the factious councillors who hedge her about, and in this context the chief villain is the Foreign Office. Mrs Thatcher's austral triumph was followed by the celebrations of the 150th anniversary of the colony, with the Minister for Overseas Development, Mr Timothy Raison, representing Mrs Thatcher's government; royalty, to the chagrin of the Islanders, were absent.

By early 1983 the funding of development in the Islands had been settled. £31 million was to be spent on a development programme broadly in accord with the revised report produced by Lord Shackleton's team in late 1982; this was in addition to the £15 million already allocated for immediate rehabilitation, and the £3 million for compensation for war damage. A road from Port Stanley to Darwin was to be completed and funded under a separate project. The new airport at Mount Pleasant also was to be funded separately under provisions for the defence of the Islands at an initial cost of about £215 million. By March 1984 most of the funds for rehabilitation had been allocated and spent, but the Development Corporation, a central part of the Shackleton proposals, was barely out of the egg.

The main aims of the rehabilitation programme were to provide much-needed housing and to repair the roads which had appeared in such sorry case by the end of 1982. Ironically a large part of the damage to the roads in Port Stanley itself was caused by the lorries carrying the prefabricated houses purchased with rehabilitation funds and which have become the symbols of the most monumental folly of the administration of the Falklands since the conflict. It had been decided after consultations between the FO and the Overseas Development Administration (ODA) in London to purchase fifty-four prefabricated timber houses built by the firm of James Brewster and based on a Swedish design. They were to be adorned with double-glazed picture-windows, specially designed furniture and fittings, all to a degree hitherto unheard of in the Falklands.

The Brewster house saga came to be one that Sir Rex Hunt has referred to as 'that strange combination of Murphy's Law and the Falklands factor', for the final bill for fifty-two came to £7.2 million. Two houses had been ordered to replace dwellings wrecked by artillery and were paid for out of compensation funds.

The Brewster houses were high-quality products, built to a specification agreed by Whitehall, and the basic units were by no means overpriced. The additional cost accrued in the confusion over administration, the accidents of loading, shipping and dispatch of the kits, and their discharge and eventual construction in Port Stanley. The shipping and assembly of the Brewster houses had been dogged by bad luck from the first. The freighter from England broke down and the cargo had to be transferred, thus incurring demurrage charges. The sections of the houses had been loaded in the wrong order, delaying the construction programme in Stanley itself. After they had been built, the town was still short of twenty to thirty dwellings for families already in the Islands. The presence of the modern homes led to unseemly wrangles over who should be given them. The military command demanded their share, and most of the remaining ones were distributed to public servants, nearly all on Overseas Aid Scheme (OSAS) supplements because few living and working on local wages could afford the rent. By June 1984 some of the houses along one side of the new Sir Jeremy Moore Avenue could not be inhabited as the rock underneath the foundations made it unexpectedly difficult to lay drainage and water services.

Housing is a critical issue for the Falklands today, for only with additional accommodation in place can there be any hope of bringing immigrants to the Islands. The need to bring in fresh blood – to redress the decades of neglect by London – was clear after the conflict in 1982. In the two years following the surrender of the Argentines in June 1982 the number of immigrants who have settled permanently in the Islands has been pathetically small. Rather than being a gesture of confidence in the future of their community and economy, the Brewster houses have become expensive status symbols, causing resentment among many native-born Islanders.

The story of the roads has hardly inspired more optimism. The contractors, Faircloughs, were hired to repair roads in Port Stanley and to the old airport. In March 1984 Falkland Islands councillors were informed that the road programme had cost £6.9 million which would be paid from the rehabilitation fund of £15 million with a sizeable contribution from the Ministry of Defence. The new Chief Executive, David Taylor, said that the funding had been inadequate as more money was needed to complete the programme. Resurfacing the schoolyard, which had been broken by trucks used by army units when they first entered the town, was to cost £31,000, of which £26,000 had been for labour costs and £4500 for materials. Taylor explained to me that the labour costs were often high because of the complex method of dealing with tenders for public projects of this nature: 'It often has to involve the ODA, and quite often both the Crown Agents and the Property Services Agency [PSA], and be scrutinised carefully by each, as we don't want to repeat the mistakes made in the past.' After the first snows of the winter the road to the airport, according to several reports, was beginning to break up.

New commercial ventures have started in the Islands over the past two years. Most conspicuous are the five cafés and takeaway food emporia which have flourished and faded with varying degrees of success. Rather more picturesque are the stories of the bank and the brewery, which both began life amid much trumpeting.

The first independent commercial bank to open in Port Stanley belongs to Standard Chartered who have a venerable history in Britain's colonial outposts. The gesture of opening a branch is thought to be not unconnected to the fact that the chairman of the group is Lord Barber, who served as Chancellor of the Exchequer in Edward Heath's Conservative administration of 1970–4. The bank occupies a spare but tidy building along the main shore road in the town. Business coming through the doors can hardly be called brisk. The bank took over a certain amount of business from the Falkland Islands Treasury, in particular the handling of deposit accounts of small savers, some of whom have complained that they were given little or no notice that their funds were being switched from the Treasury to the bank. In some respects the bank has hindered rather than helped the flow of cash in the Falklands economy because initially it could not cash cheques from two out of the four major British clearing banks. Standard Chartered staff were deeply apologetic but said the two big banks in Britain simply would not play ball. I found it easier to cash a British cheque in Sicily than in Port Stanley, where I had to resort to a subterfuge of handing a cheque to one of the consultants from London auditing the Falklands government accounts. Several times I was caught outside the grey box of the secretariat building, staring guiltily into the middle distance while waiting for my money. The local Cable and Wireless office, one of the few commercial organisations in Stanley that will handle cheques backed by banker's cards, decided to bypass the local bank in Stanley altogether. Ian Stewart, the manager, said the Stanley bank wanted to charge between fifty and ninety pence for handling each cheque. In the end he found it much cheaper to bundle all the cheques received into a registered envelope which would be deposited at the bank branch nearest head office in Holborn; and that bank was not a branch of Standard Chartered.

The new brewery has hardly enjoyed much luck either. Backed by Everard's Brewery of Burton-on-Trent, a small-scale local plant, using the latest machinery, started producing a nutty-flavoured brew called Penguin Ale. Sales did not leap away from the starting blocks, as the brewmaster, 'Firkin Phil' Middleton, freely admitted. Firkin Phil is one of Stanley's natural philosophers. He can be recognised from the end of the shore road by his loping gait and gentle, cheery salute, his military dress forage cap crammed over his shaggy hair, and his face suitably concealed by a straggly black beard. The first snag in his sales campaign was his failure to attract the armed services because the price of canned beer in the NAAFI was several pence cheaper. Stanley's besetting problem of low water-pressure upset the brewery machinery and it seemed that the whole project was doomed. Towards the end of the second year of trading the prospects suddenly brightened, however, as the price of canned beer rose. The NAAFI became more interested and Everard's promised to support the venture, though the point at which it might start returning a profit still appears a long way off.

Any journalist returning to the Islands after some months should not turn to the officials of the Falkland Islands government or omnipresent MoD information officers if he or she really wants to know the mood of Islanders in Stanley and in the settlements outside in the countryside, or camp, as it is always called. For this, visits to Eileen Vidal, who operates the radio links with camp, and Don Bonner, the driver, butler and general aide-de-camp to the Civil Commissioner at Government House, are essential. Don and his wife, Vera, know everything that is or is not worth knowing about the contemporary social history, real or imaginary, in Port Stanley.

Eileen maintained the radio links with camp for medical consultations throughout the conflict. She has an almost uncanny ability of knowing where you are going before you know yourself, arranging for planes to the outlying settlements to be met and divining what parcels and mail have to be delivered where. Sitting in the wireless shack she converses easily, while listening to the 'music of the Islands' – the bursts of chatter over the radio – hardly missing a word of it. She has an easy, gentle delivery in her speech, which is punctuated by a slow, mischievous smile. When I first saw her again in December 1982 she was very subdued. Her son, who had just gained his merchant service master's ticket, had been killed the previous month in a motor-cycle accident in Denmark. But in 1984 she seemed as calm and philosophical as ever. I asked how she saw the future for the Islands. 'Things are pretty quiet, now,' she said. 'They are all right for now, but I really don't know what is going to happen in the future. I really don't and in the long term the uncertainty is going to become pretty worrying.' A typical piece of Falkland Islands understatement, if you like.

The Islanders are concerned about the future for two reasons. Though not as vociferously expressed as the grumbles of the growing expatriate community, the fears of the Kelpers run deep. They stem from the way they see the Falklands colony being run now and from what they consider the record of perfidy and neglect by successive administrations in London for decades past. Most understand fully the raw statistics of their social predicament. They are a small community of about 1815 people, of whom between 850 and 1000 live in Stanley; this figure fluctuates as people move between the capital and camp and leave the Islands on holiday or for training. The economy is based on one product, sheep wool, and the market for this has seen better years. The population as a whole is ageing, and in Stanley there is a disproportionately high number of old people, who have come in from camp to retire. And there is a disproportionately low number of young single women; the Shackleton Report of 1982 says that in 1980 there were only twenty-six between the ages of twenty and thirty in the entire Islands. In 1980 the Gross National Product was recorded as £4,374,800 and the average annual income £2319. Unrevised figures for the financial year July 1983–June 1984 gave government receipts as £3,290,000. For years the Falklands government has endeavoured to live within its budget, to balance the books, for fear of becoming the remittance man of the ODA or the FCO in London in the way that Newfoundland was hocked to Whitehall because of its bankruptcy in the thirties. Working with such a tiny budget gives little room for big capital projects for improving public utilities and services, as the eccentric behaviour of the water and electricity supply in Port Stanley has proved for years.

The present development programme is designed to reverse the trends of the past fifty years, to bring people into the Islands, improve services and encourage investment and diversification of the wool industry. Compared with the massive military budget (by mid-1984 well over £2.5 billion) the sums being spent on development appear paltry: a mere £49 million on the Island community itself, and this figure includes compensation and rehabilitation grants. The £31 million for development under the Shackleton Report proposals, according to its calculations, will mean an expenditure of about £3250 to £3750 per Falklander per year for five years, whereas the equivalent expenditure per head on St Helena, a South Atlantic colony with 6000 inhabitants, was £615 in 1980–1. Grants per head of population for the Highlands and Islands of Scotland in a similar period amounted to £644 a year. One can drink the heady draught of Falklands investment and budgetary statistics almost endlessly but comparisons with St Helena and the Scottish Isles are valuable as they are the ones most often used by those now managing the Falklands development programme. The funding of that programme is modest by modern standards; none the less there are several aspects of the plans that are raising doubts in the minds of a number of Falkland Islanders.

Since the conflict two years ago, sharp divisions have appeared in Falklands society. As the Argentines went away, the better-heeled in Port Stanley joined the video and wine-box society. The town's biggest grocery, the West Store, owned by the Falkland Islands Company (FIC), has now assumed the pretensions of a suburban supermarket. On the extensive drink shelves pride of place goes to the wine-box. With it go the various accoutrements, stuffed olives in jars and the like, for the cocktail parties with which the new proconsuls and nabobs of the Falklands entertain each other.

The purchasing power of garrison troops and the tribe of advisers sent from Britain turned a trickle into a steady flow of luxury goods in the two or three stores of Port Stanley. Cameras, watches and video-recorders were particularly popular – there are now probably more video-recorders per family in the Falklands than almost anywhere else in the southern hemisphere. Gifts and sales at heavy discounts of televisions and recorders to go with them were part of the Argentines' 'hearts and minds' programme to win over the Kelpers and persuade them to learn Spanish and taste the delights of Argentine television. Some Islanders were inclined to take the video bait but forget about the Spanish. The officer in charge of General Menendez' educational programme, a cultivated Anglo-Argentine, Captain Melbourn Hussey, now promoted Rear-Admiral, told one Kelper, 'If I had to suffer Argentine television programmes every day, I'd want to remain British too.' One of the few residents to have bought his own video-recorder before the conflict, Jack Abott, consoled his hours of loneliness during the heavy bombardment of the last few nights of Argentine occupation by watching over and again the BBC's video-recording of the Royal Wedding. The video far more than the Land-Rover is the true status symbol in Stanley today.

In the Falklands Sancho Panza's dictum that the world is divided into the haves and the have-nots has to be adjusted slightly into the division between those who have overseas living allowances and tax-free OSAS subsidies and those who do not. If you watch people shopping the difference becomes apparent in a few minutes. In April 1984 a salaries commissioner, sent from London to assess wages for employees of the Falkland Islands government, stood in the West Store for two hours to observe what Islanders could afford. Despite more than thirty-five years of such work in colonies across the world, from Montserrat to Hong Kong, and West Africa to Borneo, the commissioner said he was horrified at the contrast between the carefree spending of the families on aid schemes and overseas living allowances and the careful shopping of the local people.

Resentment can run deep between the native Kelper and the sub-sidised expatriate. The expatriate can afford the rent of one of the new Brewster houses, but even senior local employees cannot. By a bizarre twist, the Islands' council actually raised the rent at which they were to be let to £10 a month above that originally recommended. One public servant with two growing daughters to support was in genuine emotional distress when he explained to me that he had just heard that his rent was to go up from £24 to well over £30 a month, a leap of about thirty per cent. Salaries and wages have always been low in the Falklands, partly because of the tied-cottage system on the land and the provision of food and bunkhouse shelter for the single hands and shepherds. Today wages are negotiated on behalf of the Islands' workers by the General Employees' Union (GEU), whose office is a glorified hut next to the Public Works Department. The Union must be the only one in the British community across the world that can boast a signed photograph of Mrs Thatcher, or would want to.

Terry Betts is the chairman of the GEU. He is also the general manager of the FIC's Stanley office and does not hide the fact that some-times he finds the two roles hard to reconcile. He is a stocky, amply proportioned man in his thirties. Fair-haired, he is ruddy of complexion, the result of the Falklands climate and diet – wind and mutton. For years he was a stalwart of the local soccer team and is Port Stanley's most ardent supporter of Tottenham Hotspur. He aims, he says, to give the GEU a thorough overhaul and make it work like a modern union; for this he has sought and received help from the Trades Union Congress in London who are preparing a three-month training course for him when he can get to Britain again. Terry, one of the most dynamic of the younger Islanders, is quite forthright about his views on the Islands' future. He is worried that time may be running short for a development programme along the lines proposed by the Shackleton Report to succeed in bringing new forms of employment and new people to the Islands.

In 1983 negotiations he led on wages and cost-of-living allowances awarded to local employees were protracted and difficult and nearly led to a strike throughout the Islands. All seemed well, said Terry, until a new set of wage proposals were sent to Coalite, the FIC's parent company. Surprisingly, the FIC had taken over the role of negotiator for the employers from the Sheep Owners' Association (SOA), who represent the big independent landowners and farmers. Negotiations on behalf of the Islanders proved particularly tough when locals realised how much contractors from Britain, hired to repair the roads in and round Stanley and to build the airport at Mount Pleasant, were paying their men. At the new airport site a bulldozer operator would earn an annual wage of £12,500 plus a bonus of fifteen per cent if he finished his contract. The contractors were discouraged from hiring local labour as it was feared that no one would be left to work the farms or run the public services in Stanley. For all the army of advisers in the Falklands since the conflict, there are still more jobs than people because of the declining native population and traditionally low local wage. The salary commissioner sent from London found nearly a quarter of local administration jobs were vacant, an unusually high level, he said. In most small colonies an eight- to ten-per-cent vacancy rate in public posts was the norm.

The GEU celebrated its fortieth anniversary in October 1983, marking the occasion by issuing a short history of its activities, some thirty pages of typescript reproduced on the office stencilling machine. For its size it is the most valuable published document on the social history of the Falklands, both Shackleton Reports included. It tells a story of low wages, tough working conditions, and the stranglehold of the paternalist employers, the individual landowners of the SOA, or 'the sheepocracy' as they are sometimes known, and the omnipresent FIC. Notes from the Union archive reveal that a general farm labourer earned £6 per month in 1938, which by 1949 was supplemented with a £1. 12s. 6d. cost-of-living bonus. By 1969, the monthly wage rose to £37. 8s. 0d. with a £5 cost-of-living bonus. On 1 October 1983 a new scale of wages and allowances came into force, after the wrangle over cost-of-living allowances had gone to arbitration. A farm labourer was to receive a minimum monthly wage of £219.60, a foreman £283.56, and boys and girls of fifteen to eighteen from £201.18 to £212.59. Long-service awards range from £1 a month after three years' service to £20 a month after twenty-five; a host of allowances and bonuses range from extra money for handling dirty loads to bonus rates for shearing (£0.76 an hour for those shearing between 150 and 180 fleeces a day) to payments for servicing tractors and breaking colts.

Minutes taken from one of the first meetings held between union negotiators from the fledgling Falkland Islands Labour Federation (as the Union was first named) and the SOA in August 1944 to discuss conditions of the shepherds and labourers in camp are revealing. The second topic on the agenda was the question of wages and conditions for boys of fifteen.

*Mr Goddard (SOA)*: The custom in the Falkland Islands Co. Ltd is, if a boy is doing a man's work then he receives a man's pay. Of course there are boys who will never be able to do a man's work. There are cases where even into manhood he would not be entitled to this, but if a boy is considered willing he would receive £5 or £6 per month.

*Mr Barnes (Labour Federation)*: I do not consider that a boy of sixteen years should be asked to do a man's work, if it means breaking him up. What would he be like as a man?

*Mr Goddard*: I do not believe a boy of this age, looking after himself, I mean no smoking or liquor, could do himself any harm. I quote myself; I started work at fifteen, damn hard work and today I am fifty-five years old. Do I look broken down?

*Mr Barnes*: What would happen to a boy, then, who asked for a rise of pay if still on a low rate?

*Mr Goddard*: He would be told to look for another job if this did not suit him as it would be considered that he was not satisfactory.

This exchange has a contemporary ring, as the GEU is still trying to achieve proper redundancy legislation for the Islands. The lack of it annoys Terry Betts and the Union's secretary, Neville Bennett. The annals of the Union are full of arguments about pay for cooks, conditions in the bunkhouses for the single men: in 1944 there was a regulation that lights should be out by 10.30 p.m. and some owners debated whether they could really afford improving bunkhouse furniture by purchasing army beds.

Today the Union is faced with the continuing contrast of the standard of living of locally employed men and those on OSAS salaries. Often OSAS men and locals will work side by side doing the same job. This occurs most often in the Public Works Department where a local tradesman knows he may be doing the same job as an expatriate earning twice as much.

OSAS is operated by the ODA, headed by the Minister for Overseas Development, who generally, but not always, has a seat in the cabinet. It is an agency, hiring skilled staff for colonies unlikely to be able to provide such key workers themselves; it advertises for carpenters and consultants, solicitors and surveyors, plumbers and teachers. In name it also has a training role. Under the original OSAS prescription those hired by the agency were to attempt to train local people to replace them, stay in the colony for a few years only (one or two tours) and not invest in the colony by purchasing property. For the transience of the posting and the difficult physical conditions the OSAS worker often faced, he or she would be paid a local salary, taxed locally, plus a tax-free supplement which might often double the basic wage. In addition there would be allowances for houses, education of the children, and passages home to the United Kingdom. However, in the Falklands the OSAS system has in many cases become distorted. Because of the tiny indigenous population, there has been little or no training of local staff. One person on a high salary, even by OSAS standards, is on a third tour, has virtually become a settler and bought a house. There has been frequent muddle, particularly in the Public Works Department (PWD). In the southern autumn of 1983 one of the surveyors returned from sick leave in England to find he had been replaced. So Port Stanley had two surveyors doing the job of one at a total cost to the British and Falklands taxpayer of about £40,000 a year.

In Port Stanley many OSAS workers are resented for another reason, a scar of recent history. During the Argentine occupation of the Islands in April and May 1982 OSAS employees, such as the technical officers at the agricultural Grasslands Trials Unit (GTU) and the schoolteachers, were allowed to go back to the United Kingdom. They were flown out by the Argentines at the end of April that year. With them went the family of the most prosperous landowner on West Falkland, Bill Luxton, who were forced into exile at gunpoint by the Argentine police chief, Major Patricio Dowling. The Islanders in Stanley then tried to arrange for the children and old people to be taken out, fearing heavy street fighting and bombardment as the British prepared to land. Their fears were well founded as it appears that the Argentine regular infantry stationed to the east of the town did want to counter-attack through Stanley on the day General Menendez surrendered. The request for an agreement to remove the families was refused. From England Rex Hunt broadcast that this would mean abandoning the town and, by implication, the cause for which Britain was fighting.

Sometimes the differences in conditions and pay between local employees and those on OSAS salary supplements and allowances have led to difficulties where they have to work together. Three locally paid teachers said that in the secondary school common-room there was palpable tension between those on OSAS salaries and locally paid staff, who were either native Kelpers or settlers in the Islands.

One of the local teachers freely admits to feeling guilty about the fighting for the Islands and the fact that so many men died for such a small population. She says most Islanders are grateful for the attempt to repair the years of neglect by Britain leading up to the fighting with Argentina, but it is the manner of the repair operation that causes them most concern. It is now almost a case of too much too late. Local councillors are bewildered by the sheer numbers of advisers descending on the Islands and the increase in civil servants from England now running the local administration. At Government House Sir Rex Hunt has had the staff of a small embassy. He has two assistants of first secretary rank, for a short period one of second secretary status, a personal assistant and two typists. His predecessor but one, Sir Neville French, had the occasional assistance of the government's Chief Executive and one typist. In the words of Mrs Betty Miller, one of the first ladies of the sheep-owning set, 'Never have so few been governed by so many.'

In the year and a half since Mrs Thatcher's triumphal progress through the Islands only three of her ministers, one of cabinet rank, have visited the Falklands. The month after her tour the Overseas Development Minister, Timothy Raison, attended the 150th anniversary celebrations of the colony. The OSAS workers took the opportunity to tell him of their plight at a specially convened meeting. He went away muttering about doing something 'for those poor OSAS workers'. The something he achieved was a fresh set of allowances announced in a memorandum issued on 30 May 1983 following a visit by OSAS consultants the previous month. Leave to Britain was now to be granted annually instead of once every two years. Cars were to be shipped to the Islands free, and fuel bills paid by the British government, and the Falkland Islands government 'should produce a priority list for the allocation of houses'.

The OSAS scheme began to operate in the Falklands at the beginning of the 1970s, at which point suspicion about Britain's long-term intentions over the Islands became seriously aroused. Throughout the 1960s there had been some indication that the Labour government of Harold Wilson was prepared to do a deal with Argentina. In March 1968 the foreign secretary, Michael Stewart, told the House of Commons that talks about the Falklands had been going on in Buenos Aires. By August 1968 it appears that agreement had been reached in principle about the transfer of sovereignty over the Islands at a future date which would be determined as soon as Her Majesty's Government was satisfied that the Islanders' well-being would be taken into consideration by the Argentine government. Following these announcements efforts were made to reassure the Islanders, but it became clear that an agreement with Argentina had been discussed in detail, down to such matters as the Islanders' exemption from Argentine military service and their need to carry special identity documents when travelling in Argentina. The British government insisted that some understanding with Argentina was vital to ensure communications for passengers and freight. In 1969 the FIC had announced the withdrawal of the steamship *Darwin* which plied between Stanley and Montevideo with passengers and freight. Eventually a temporary airstrip was built at Cape Pembroke, a spit of land west of Port Stanley, with a contingent of Argentines in the labour force, and an air link with Comodoro Rivadavia was opened by the civilian branch of the Argentine air force, LADE, in November 1972. Two years later it was agreed that the Argentine state petroleum firm Yacimientos Petroliferos Fiscales (YPF) was to build a tank farm outside Port Stanley and be the principal supplier of fuel oil to the Islands. In 1976 the *Shackleton* incident in which an Argentine destroyer fired on the survey vessel hardly reassured the Islanders, nor did the rumours of a new Argentine base being built on Southern Thule in the South Sandwich Islands towards the end of the year. On 1 May 1977 a more permanent airstrip at Cape Pembroke was opened by Sir Vivian Fuchs and LADE announced an improvement to the service between Comodoro and Stanley as they would now use the Fokker F28 jet airliner.

The change of government in Britain hardly improved matters. In November 1980 Nicholas Ridley, Permanent Under-Secretary at the Foreign Office, arrived in the Islands and at a public meeting in Stanley Town Hall offered the Islanders three alternatives for the constitutional future of the Falklands: a condominium or sharing of rule with Argentina; a freeze in the sovereignty dispute for a set period after which the matter would be discussed fully; or ceding sovereignty to Buenos Aires with a lease-back to Britain in order to continue running the Islands as before. The reception to such ideas was hostile, and continued throughout his brief visit. In the House of Commons the same proposals received a drubbing.

However, it made many Islanders realise that Britain would not back them for ever and that some sort of deal would be put forward again soon. This accounts for the suspicion aroused by the meeting at the UN at the end of February 1982 between a team led by Richard Luce,

Nicholas Ridley's successor at the Foreign Office, and an Argentine team led by Señor Enrique Ros, the Deputy Foreign Minister. Two Island councillors, John Cheek and Tim Blake, were present as observers. Cheek says the talks convinced him that the Argentines were prepared to use force if their timetable for the transfer of sovereignty was brushed aside again; but he had no inkling that they were preparing to use force so soon. The Falklands community in March 1982 was far more apprehensive over its future than official accounts, such as the Franks Report might seem to indicate. Several Islanders wondered whether it would not be wiser to make a deal with Buenos Aires on the best possible terms, given what they considered the track record of British, and particularly FCO, perfidy since the early 1960s. The night the Argentines invaded, in the words of one prominent West Falkland farmer, 'there was a hell of a row' as farmers, owners and managers argued on the two-metre band radio about whether the Argentines should be resisted at all costs or the inevitable – that they would inherit the Islands one day anyway – be accepted.

The Foreign Office is still seen as the villain of the piece. Despite the outpouring of development money, the huge sums spent on the defence of the Islands, and the arrival of cohorts of advisers and administrators, there is still strong local suspicion that 'they', always meaning the Foreign Office, want to 'get rid of the Islands anyway'. Locals find the discrepancy between their standard of living and that of the expatriate workers and the servicemen irksome in any event, particularly as they suspect that the expatriates' paymasters in London do not want to keep the Islands British. This complex of resentment has had an ugly little symptom. A grenade was found attached between two vehicles belonging to the family of a technical officer working for the FIARDC. Fortunately the home-made bomb was found in time, but the culprit was never caught. It may have been the work of a deranged soldier, an Islander or an expatriate, but the incident was particularly disturbing in such a small and highly-strung community as Stanley.

There are surprisingly few obvious reminders of the fighting round Port Stanley now. Islanders do not refer to the episode constantly, though their memories of it are not far away. Stanley now has its own war memorial, built at a cost of £59,000, largely raised by a public appeal in which Sir Rex Hunt played a prominent role. Some regret that so much money was spent on hardly the most tasteful example of funerary monumental art in the southern hemisphere and would have preferred the money to have gone towards something that would bring comfort and pleasure to young and old in the Falklands – a home for old people in the town, which has been needed for years past, or a swimming pool. An appeal fund for a swimming pool was opened years ago but prospects for its construction are slim. The garrison forces have allowed school parties to use the small swimming pool in their floating hotel accommodation, and have provided swimming instructors but the coastels, the aquatic barracks, are due to move when the garrison buildings at the new airport at Mount Pleasant are completed in 1986.

Port Stanley now has three war memorials, to the battle of the Falklands in 1914, to the dead of both World Wars at the cemetery, and to the conflict of 1982. Islanders gave their time for nothing to build the new monument. It consists of a series of heavy bronze plaques bearing the names of those who died in the campaign and the units involved, a comprehensive but incomplete list, as one or two army air corps units were left out by mistake. In front of the plaques a bronze figure graces a tall plinth. In true Falklands style, according to accounts of its construction, the mythical figurehead at first lurched to one side as if buffeted by a South Atlantic gale. Behind the plinth a bronze relief portrays a scene Roy Lichtenstein would have admired, making his pop art paintings of American fighter planes pictures of aerial tranquillity in comparison. Harrier planes zoom above aircraft carriers, and marine paratroopers storm onto the beaches and guns, men, planes, ships, helicopters and submarines attack the observer from all sides. Particularly unsuited to the medium is the heavy style of lettering, similar to that adorning so many Italian public buildings of the thirties – heavy, square and with vague classical pretensions. For all the good intentions behind the project, the product seems oddly out of place and obtrusive. One disgruntled Kelper remarked, 'It's the style of military monument you might find in any town in Argentina.'

Below the farms at San Carlos settlement a neat circle of sandstone encloses what might at first be taken as a small sheep corral. The enclosure looks towards an inlet of San Carlos Water. Standing by the farms the walls are concealed in shadows from the high clouds and the knoll behind covered by gorse bushes. This is the cemetery designed by the Commonwealth War Graves Commission for those who wanted their dead to be left buried in the Falklands. It is as discreet a memorial as you could hope to find anywhere. If you want to find it and visit it, it is there; if you do not want to be reminded of it, it looks like part of the more permanent buildings of the farm where the first British troops landed on 21 May 1982. The layout of the graves and the arrangement of the memorial tablet behind is as restrained as the external effect of the enclosure. The graves are tended regularly by Pat and Isobel Short who were managing the farm in 1982. With little advertisement they weed the small plots round the graves and renew the flowers and plants left by mourners. Curiously, the garish orange of the marigolds suits the scene on a wild sunny day in autumn; they have been the most successful of all the new flowers. It is a place of fitting tranquillity for the marines, paratroopers, air corps men and signallers buried there.

Flying from Stanley to Goose Green the plane crosses some bare close-cropped ground several miles before the Darwin isthmus. The green and brown downland rolls with a gentle swell for miles, with hardly a landmark in sight. On one of the open hillsides a small paddock is marked with white posts and rails in a severe geometric pattern. The enclosure is marked with dozens of white dots, the wooden crosses of the graves of Argentine soldiers who fell at Goose Green and in some of the fighting for Stanley. The isolation of the site and the abstract pattern of the railings and crosses make it seem remote and impermanent, as if waiting for the day when the crosses can be removed and the remains of the fallen taken home.

Goose Green itself has changed dramatically since the conflict. At the end of May 1982 the settlement was strewn with weapons and ammunition; at the edge of the paddocks the old schoolhouse was a charred shell; Pucara aircraft in various states of damage and destruction littered the main gallops, which also serve as the grass airstrip. The community of Goose Green had taken a battering during their confinement for a month in the village hall, a month punctuated by fierce low-level attacks by the British Harrier aircraft. By Christmas 1982 the tidying-up operation had begun, though one of the Pucara was left on the airstrip. It is still there today, but it is the only sign of the Argentine occupation in the settlement except for the faint traces of the white letters 'POW' across the black roofs of the shearing sheds which the Argentine prisoners had hurriedly painted to ward off air attackers. At one end of the settlement, where the Argentine anti-aircraft battery had been sited, a smart two-storey wooden building with a green roof seemed all but complete. It is the replacement for the old school built for about £60,000, one-third the cost of one of the Brewster houses in Port Stanley, and about five times the size.

The new schoolhouse has been designed by Countryman Homes of Oxford who claim that they can make dwelling houses for the Falklands for £50,000 each, which would include the shipping of materials and construction in the Islands. The timber-framed designs appear more simple than the Brewster houses, but several are likely now to be ordered for settlements in camp, and possibly Stanley itself, where a further £1.5 million has been allocated for a new housing programme, under a quarter of the final bill for the Brewster houses. At Goose Green the FIC is likely to order two of the simpler designs to replace a pair of cottages which burnt down in early April 1984, killing a shepherd who was on a visit from Teal Inlet.

I was welcomed on my return to Goose Green by Dave Hewitt, the foreman now, whose family had lived in the back of the community hall throughout the occupation. He told me in his quiet voice that things seemed to be going pretty well. 'We've had over 100,000 sheep shorn this year, though the clip was pretty light,' he said. The store in the settlement is managed by Bob and Janet MacLeod, who had done so much for the community in May 1982, she with the team of cooks and he in keeping in touch with the outside world by amateur radio – until his equipment was taken and wrecked. The day the Argentines surrendered in the settlement, the manager, Eric Goss, took me to the store. It was covered with glass and overturned food tins and sweet-jars, and papers and rubbish were strewn across the floor; shelves were broken and splintered and thrown across the room as the young Argentines had their last fling before being herded to the surrender ceremony and thence to confinement in the sheep-pens. Today everything is as orderly and neatly laid out as it was chaotic then. Janet and Bob seemed a little subdued, possibly because the other journalists of our party attacked them with ballpoint and notebook scarcely had the formalities of introduction been completed.

'Well, I think things are improving,' said Bob to one of his interlocutors, who said he had already made up the headline for his feature article for the second anniversary of the Argentine invasion ('Was it all worth it?'). 'I think we're going to have a brighter commercial future and open up the Islands a bit,' said Bob, 'because of the new airport. It's bound to help bring business here and help get our exports out.'

The new airport at Mount Pleasant, which is due to open for military traffic in April 1985, is a big symbol of hope for the Islanders. But most realise it is for military as much as commercial use. The presence of the British Forces Falkland Islands (BFFI) is the most visible change since 1982. Try as they might, the soldiers, sailors and airmen cannot help being obtrusive. Talking to Islanders two years on from the conflict it was hard to discern whether it was the present prominence or the future impermanence of the garrison that worried them most.

# Chapter 11

# The Military Presence

'Fortress Falklands is a particularly bad description of what we're doing here,' was the bluntly stated view of the man in charge of defence policy in the Falklands from June 1983 to the middle of 1984, Major-General Keith Spacie. 'A fortress implies to me,' he went on, somewhat pedantically, 'a feature of point defence which should be wellnigh impregnable. Given the long coastline of the Falklands, plus the commitment to the whole area, which is roughly the size of Wales, this is clearly not on. Our main task is reconnaissance, to deter aggression and, should it occur, react effectively until reinforcements arrive.'

To help him in his task the Commander of the British Forces Falkland Islands has a battalion of infantry, a squadron of surface ships, extensive ground-based radar, batteries of air defence missiles, and a squadron and a half of Phantom and Harrier aircraft. Immediately after the conflict with Argentina in 1982 this involved a garrison of up to 5000 men. In the two years since General Menendez' surrender, the British garrison on the Islands has fluctuated from 4000 to 2500. With acute manpower shortages in the British army affecting its activities in Germany, Northern Ireland, Belize and Hong Kong, numbers of troops in the Falklands have been reduced quietly and steadily.

The first garrison battalion was from the Queen's Own Highlanders, who sailed from Britain in the summer of 1982 with orders to prepare to fight for the recapture of West Falkland. Instead, they had to stay for nearly six months to help clear up the mess in Port Stanley and the settlements the Argentines had occupied in camp. The Highlanders had an 'enhanced' battalion, which is military jargon meaning that they had an extra fighting company and were supported by a battery or two of artillery and a Royal Engineers squadron. Since the Highlanders went home the garrison battalions appearing for four-month tours of duty in the Falklands and South Georgia have been getting progressively slimmer. There are fewer companies in the battalions, the engineers come under separate command – they too have been steadily reduced as more construction work has been handed over to civilian contractors –

217

and in the southern autumn of 1984 the last battery of guns to be attached to the garrison force went home from Port San Carlos. Despite the leaner look to the garrison force, the cost of the commitment to defend the Islands since June 1982 has been enormous. By June 1987 the bill will reach the round figure of £3 billion, £1.4 billion for the first two years to June 1984, and about £1.7 billion for the remaining three years.

Two years after that evening in June 1982 when General Jeremy Moore toured Stanley to tell as many of its citizens as he could find in the dark that the Argentines had surrendered, the little port has come hardly to look like a garrison town. Some feared that it would become a miniature Catterick, and doubtless some of the military staff stationed in the Falklands would have preferred it so. Most of the soldiers and airmen based round Stanley live well away from the town, in the Portakabin pre-fabricated huts on the road to the old airport at 'Look Out' Camp or the crowded quarters of the coastels. Only sixty-seven troops were billeted in the town itself by April 1984. Some of the townspeople regretted that there were not more, particularly the families without children at home. Others clearly resented what signs remained of the military presence; for them the soldiers and their high standard of living were taken, however rightly or wrongly, as an indication that the civilians were second-class citizens and the military really ran the show. At first civilians resented being termed 'Bennies' – after one of the less intellectually endowed characters in the Independent Television serial *Crossroads*. Soon resentment turned to defiance; bumper stickers were produced by the local printer declaiming, 'Outnumbered but not outsmarted.'

On the hill above Government House stands one of the great follies of public expenditure in the Falklands in recent years, the hostel building for schoolchildren from camp. The estimate for the building was originally £250,000. The construction work was undertaken by a subsidiary of the FIC, Trans Ocean Trading Construction, set up for the purpose. The subsequent head of the FIC, Coalite's chairman, Ted Needham, calls the episode a 'shambles', as the finished product cost nearly five times the estimate, well over £1 million, and was condemned for use as a children's hostel within weeks of completion. The construction technique was 'experimental' according to Mr Needham, 'a kind of Meccano frame with concrete thrown at it'. The roof leaked and had not been strengthened to the correct specifications due to a miscalculation by the Property Services Agency. It was feared that it might collapse altogether if any heavy weight was put on it, such as a winter snowfall. However, further public embarrassment was saved by the Argentine invasion. General Menendez used the hostel as his military headquarters and a light anti-aircraft battery was successfully positioned on the roof.

The roof was still holding two years after the Argentines first took up residence, though the anti-aircraft battery has been removed. The ceilings leak from time to time and fire precautions have been less than perfect. Taking their cue from General Menendez, the British are using the rambling building, with its eccentric maze of corridors and poky little rooms, as their military headquarters. The offices, map rooms and security check-points would fit in perfectly with any of a hundred barracks and garrison buildings up and down the British Isles. Since the hostel fiasco Trans Ocean Trading Construction has not undertaken any other major projects in the Falklands, experimental or otherwise.

In the town itself the army has very few offices or establishments. This is in accordance with the policy of maintaining 'a suitable degree of separation' between the civilian and military populations. The garrison battalion's support unit, the rear echelon, used to maintain a sergeants' mess at Waverley House, but this fell victim to the separation policy. The bar resembled nothing so much as a 'snug' in one of Aldershot's less fashionable hostelries. Members of the mess used to invite guests from the town, itinerant journalists and the like, for evening 'socials'. In turn the rear echelon used to help out with the British Forces Broadcasting Service (BFBS) programmes, which were taped and transmitted from the Falkland Islands Broadcasting Service studios, a glorified shed in Davis Street.

Broadcasting to the garrison and the Islanders is run as a joint civilian-military project; but under General Spacie's command there was an attempt to separate the two into quite distinct services. Similarly, the hospital was run as a joint facility but relations between the army and civilian staff became as bad as any between service personnel and civilian colleagues in the Islands. The jointly run medical facility came to a sudden and terrible end when the old hospital burnt down in April 1984, and separate temporary hospitals were established at opposite ends of the town a month later.

One military office is destined to remain in the centre of Stanley for as long as there is a British garrison in the Islands. Opposite the Town Hall a sign identifies the EOD Headquarters, where bomb- and mine-disposal men, the Explosives and Ordnance Disposal team, from all three armed services have their base, cheek by jowl with the civilian and military police force. Few things in daily life remind the Falklanders of the conflict in 1982 more than the miles of rusty barbed-wire fencing marking the minefields on the hills and beaches around Stanley and the settlements occupied by the Argentines. Only more intrusive, perhaps, is the thunderous roar of the Phantom and Harrier jets as they take off across Stanley Harbour for their regular patrols to the west of the Islands.

Two years after the Argentines went home the mines appear to be as big a menace as ever. In March 1984 the officer in charge of the EOD unit, Major John Wyatt, told me that explosive material was being handed in at the rate of 1000 items a day, anything from rifle or pistol bullets to anti-tank rockets or mortar bombs; since June 1982 more than 2.5 million such items have been dealt with by his men. Two of his predecessors had their feet blown off searching ground they believed had been cleared already. Some areas, like the battlefield at Wireless Ridge, from where the 2nd Battalion the Parachute Regiment marched to be the first British infantry unit into Stanley in June 1982, have been combed more than half a dozen times for live ordnance. The bomb-disposal men say they have to use the dangerous and haphazard technique of the 'duck shoot', moving across the field in a line like the beaters and guns on a country shoot. Major Wyatt explained to me that the minefield warning maps distributed to every householder in the Islands were revised constantly and that fresh indications were displayed in public offices like the police station and the secretariat building. New editions of the minefield and firing-range maps have been printed every two or three months. In March 1984, according to Major Wyatt, there were still 142 minefields in the Islands, of which 111 were around Port Stanley alone. Since the fighting ended, he said, more than 40,000 acres had been cleared of mines and live ammunition.

The minefields will still take years to clear, but the Major was convinced that techniques will be developed eventually to tackle all the mines left by the Argentines. The main difficulties arise from the inaccuracy of the maps of minefields given to the British forces by the Argentines in 1982, and from the plastic anti-personnel mines that proved undetectable by conventional mine-disposal equipment. The heavy metal anti-tank mines might be sown in the same fields as the smaller plastic mines, which were mostly of an Italian or Argentine design. The anti-personnel mines have caused a lot of damage to livestock, killing and maiming sheep and cattle. The members of the EOD squads have found this aspect of their work particularly distressing, as they frequently have had to traverse known minefields to shoot badly injured animals. The day before I met Major Wyatt five heifers and a bull had strayed onto a minefield at Port Harriet, south of Port Stanley, and had blown themselves up, and with that most of the farmer's herd and the settlement's milk supply had gone. Though the weight of a cow is more than sufficient to trigger the anti-personnel mines, that of a penguin is not. For some months the bomb-disposal teams noticed that the penguins were navigating the minefields closest to the beaches with ease to get to their rookeries. In order to help them, the soldiers and airmen removed the lower of the regulation two strands of barbed wire which marked the minefields.

Most of the heavier ammunition found had been dug up from trenches and observation posts filled in quickly after the conflict ended. As the positions the Argentines held round Port Stanley were re-excavated crates of mortar bombs and 66-mm rockets were unearthed, many in a highly unstable condition. Major Wyatt was full of unfeigned praise for the attitude of the Islanders to the risks from live ammunition and minefields. He and his predecessors arranged for older boys and girls from the school to watch his men working in the field, awarding them certificates and badges as honorary bomb squad officers afterwards. 'The Islanders are terrific,' he concluded. 'Most of them know about live ammunition and how to handle it. They're always bringing the smaller items in here. No, it's not the civilians who worry me. It's the soldiers who are so bloody irresponsible about it at times.'

There has been controversy about the number of weapons in civilian hands, however, and the Falkland Islands government has been constantly urged to take in the Argentine weapons scattered throughout the Islands. Regulations were tightened up after a suicide in West Falkland in which an Argentine gun was used.

As living quarters and port facilities have been built to the west of Port Stanley, fewer servicemen are seen on the streets of the town itself. Sailors come ashore from the frigates and destroyers and their support vessels to hunt for souvenirs or make phone calls home from the Cable and Wireless offices. These afford a better service than you would get locally in London; since a satellite ground station was built shortly after the conflict the quality of phone calls has been superb. Men who were in the Falklands during the campaign or immediately afterwards visit the families they stayed or became acquainted with during those chaotic times. They are welcomed as lost sons and entertained royally each time they turn up. Falklanders, like many mountain and island people, are excellent correspondents and the links made in 1982 are maintained by frequent exchange of letters. The older people in Stanley regret the policy of separation between civilians and military and their regret is shared by the servicemen who knew the place and the people in 1982. An engineer officer I knew then told me two years later of his horror at the official frostiness between the military command of early 1984 and the people of the town. He ruminated gloomily, 'It is as if the army that came in with General Jeremy Moore was completely different from the

221

one in Stanley today; almost as if they belonged to completely different countries.'

The attitude of the soldiers and officers in Stanley stemmed partly from the policy adopted by Major-General Spacie. It could hardly be deemed a cheap canard to suggest that he is not one of nature's extrovert diplomats, nor a born front man. A son of the Parachute Regiment, he was promoted Major-General in 1983 at the age of forty-seven, after acquiring a reputation as one of the most successful brigade commanders in the British army. He arrived at the Falklands command almost by accident, because the man first chosen for the job unexpectedly failed his medical test. This was Major-General John Walter, a large and friendly man who first landed in the Falklands in 1982 as General Moore's deputy commander, and soon became a popular figure with the Islanders.

General Spacie lists his hobbies as 'cross-country running, athletics, walking, battlefield touring, and Victorian painting'. Frequently he was seen padding round the town in his tracksuit, and on organised cross-country runs he could still beat men twenty years younger. 'I like to get out as often as I can,' he told me. 'When I am running round the town I find I have time to myself to think.' In his presence one always felt the loneliness of the long-distance soldier, for General Spacie has the reputation in his regiment of carrying military professionalism to its heights. Once, when granted four days' leave in Northern Ireland, he joined a parachute battalion in Derry; rather than spend the time going back to England, he observed the paras first-hand on foot patrol and road blocks in the old walled city of the Foyle.

Natural shyness in the General led to almost undue sensitivity about criticism in the press. His antipathy to some public figures in the Stanley civilian community, such as the broadcasting officer Patrick Watts, became well known and personal irritation often appeared to affect the execution of details of policy. When he briefed new personnel from British Forces Broadcasting Service, General Spacie plainly stated his wish for separate studios and transmitters for the Islanders' own services and for a local forces radio station; this plan was only thwarted by the huge expense involved. Initially the General appears to have pressed as hard as anyone on the military side of the fence for a totally separate hospital for the services to be built as part of the barrack facilities at the new airport site on Mount Pleasant. At times his policy appeared to the civilians of Stanley as one not so much of 'a suitable degree of separation' between the two communities but one of total divorce.

General Spacie had a tough act to follow in succeeding two highly popular and extrovert Military Commissioners, General Sir Jeremy Moore and Major-General Sir David Thorne. General Thorne earned himself the nickname 'Jumping Bean' for his energy and his habit of travelling the length and breadth of the Islands to visit civilians and soldiers alike. Legend has it that he loved to wander about with no badges of rank on his uniform. One evening he strolled into one of the hangars down at the airport where he came upon an RAF technician servicing a piece of machinery from one of the fighters. He asked the General to hand him up a spanner, which he duly did while continuing his casual chat to the mechanic. Suddenly the phone rang at the end of the shed. The RAF man answered it and returned to his work, admonishing Thorne, 'If I were you, mate, I'd sod off. There's some bloody general prowling about the place.' With that the General departed without letting on about his identity.

Unfortunately, General Spacie's style of command had one particularly bad effect on his staff and senior officers. A journalist going anywhere near BFFI headquarters or the Cable and Wireless office just below it ran the risk of being stopped, like Coleridge's wedding guest, by at least one in three staff officers to be given a lecture about the strengths and deficiencies of Falklands society. The lectures always had the same refrain, that the farmers and shepherds in the country were all right, but that mischief-makers and ne'er-do-wells infested Stanley and made life very difficult. They had developed their own form of stockade sociology, painting the plight of the garrison in Stanley in rich and melancholy colours and luridly portraying the reckless and unreliable ways of the supposedly friendly 'Indians' outside. As surely as hot air rises, the higher the rank of the proponent the more elaborate this theorem. As a result of such attitudes, the civil and military communities came to mix less and less. One evening I was invited to a party given by Royal Engineers; there were no more than a handful of civilians, and no women. In April 1984 the new civilian-military liaison officer, a dashing major from the Signals, Craig Treebee, complained bitterly, 'I've been to three cocktail parties this week, and met the same people at all three. They were either from the Staff or senior members of government posted here by the Foreign Office. How do I meet real Islanders in Stanley?'

However, General Spacie himself did go to considerable lengths to meet Islanders outside Stanley. Frequently he would drop in at remote farms in East and West Falkland and stay for several hours talking to the farmers and shepherds. His easy access to helicopter transport irritated some members of the civilian administration who had to pay for a seat on one of the local air service's Islander aircraft if they wanted to get to anywhere in camp in a hurry. General Spacie tried to ensure that every serving man in the Islands managed at least one night away from Stanley, so that they would appreciate what life was like out on the farms. With a garrison force of several thousand throughout the summer, this proved impossible, but some units were very popular with farmers in the north of East Falkland and the remoter settlements of West Falkland. Most glamorous of the visitors were the Phantom pilots, who have tended to be adopted by one or two settlements on East and West Falkland. The farmers and their families guarded jealously their relationship with such glamorous guests. The pilots and their crews would arrive laden with gifts for two or three days' fishing or helping on the farms. A great favourite with the RAF men has been Tony Pole-Evans, the veteran manager at Saunders Island, one of the most beautiful, if dilapidated, settlements in West Falkland. A pilot and his navigator arriving on a thirty-six-hour leave pass took with them a large bottle of Scotch, only to be told by Tony that they would have to drink it between them if they wanted a container for the milk he would give them to take back to Stanley. As a gesture of thanks the Phantom crews would put on wonderful and illicit displays of aerobatics above the settlements of their hosts.

One of General Spacie's favourite haunts was the group of farms on the North Camp of East Falkland, known as Green Patch. Green Patch was an FIC farm that fell into decay in the mid-seventies; this led to its sale for subdivision into smaller farms of between 15,000 and 20,000 acres each, the first major experiment in subdivision of a large company farm in the Falklands. Some of the new farms have been very successful: Horseshoe Bay run by Peter and Margie Goss is now arguably the most efficient agricultural unit in the Falklands. If the subdivision of land proposed by the Shackleton Report is to have a chance of success, it will have to be based on the methods and approach of the Green Patch farmers. At one stage in his tour of duty General Spacie used to visit the farms at Green Patch and Horseshoe every fortnight or so. Sitting in on the debates of the Executive and Legislative he knew that the reorganisation of the farms proposed by Lord Shackleton was crucial. It was a measure of his seriousness and thoroughness that he spent so much care and trouble talking to the sorts of men and women who were likely to make a go of the new forms of holding in the Islands.

Education was another of General Spacie's particular interests. At a meeting of the Joint Councils, out of fourteen people present only he and one other, Councillor John Cheek, chairman of the Education Committee, spoke up for the need to spend more money on educational facilities. The record on schooling in the Islands, practically since the colony was born, has been little short of lamentable and even today money is spent on schools and teachers with the utmost reluctance.

General Spacie believed that if improvements were to be made in farming methods and services in Port Stanley, higher standards of education were essential; in particular, considerable improvement in technical education was required quickly.

The Commander BFFI also serves as Military Commissioner, which involves him in the civil administration of the colony. Often he has to work closely with the Civil Commissioner, an office held from June 1983 to 1985, by the former Governor, Rex Hunt. Sir Rex, as he became in the South Atlantic Honours List of October 1982, is very different in character from General Spacie. He is as ebullient and outgoing as the General is reserved, so much so that he seems like the Mayor in the children's radio serial of the fifties, *Larry the Lamb and Toytown,* a similarity not lost on some of his civil servants, who referred to him – somewhat inexplicably – as 'Larry'.

In his executive duties General Spacie endeavoured to follow the rather Byzantine formula laid down by the Order in Council of 18 June 1982. This states that most of the powers of the Governor of the Falklands will now belong to the Civil Commissioner, who is now responsible for government in the Islands. The Military Commissioner is responsible for the Islands' defence and internal security, except police matters. The crucial paragraph in the document is subsection 2 of Section 2:

> The Civil Commissioner shall consult with the Military Commissioner before exercising any function which appears to the Civil Commissioner to relate to defence or internal security (with the exception of the police) and shall act in accordance with the advice which the Military Commissioner then tenders to him; and he shall likewise act in accordance with the advice of the Military Commissioner on any matter on which the Military Commissioner considers it necessary in the interests of his responsibilities under this Order to give advice to the Civil Commissioner: Provided that the question whether the Civil Commissioner has on any matter consulted with the Military Commissioner or acted in accordance with his advice shall not be enquired into in any court.

Thus the Order gives to the Civil Commissioner most of the power in the Falklands, provided he consults with his Executive Council. But the Military Commissioner does have a wide area of autonomy; he can insist on his civilian counterpart taking his advice where anything remotely related to defence and security is concerned. The Order further confers on the General the right to take part in the Legislative Council and the Executive Council of the Falklands, though he may not, in fact, vote in either.

The military Command and the civilian government have held regular meetings between heads of department in the Liaison Committee, which has looked after matters of housekeeping in the administration of both communities. Somewhat bizarrely, a report in *The Sunday Times* on the second anniversary of the Argentine invasion suggested that the Liaison Committee was dominated by military representatives, who ruled the Falklands as a 'junta'. Much of the discussions of the Committee seem like the rows between Napoleon and his fellow exiles on St Helena about who ruled the cow. Small matters on the Falklands take on similar complexity. One deal, which took several meetings between civilian and military administrators, involved the loan of Portakabin accommodation on Crown land to the garrison, provided the military kitchen on the same site would supply food for the civilian contractors living in the rest of the huts there. The garrison does have a large administration – necessarily so, as it has to serve a garrison potentially two and a half times the size of the Islands' civilian population. Military units have always had a different method of accounting and budgeting to colonial administrations. For the Royal Engineers building the first installations for the RAF station at the old airport on Cape Pembroke, west of Stanley, the first requirement was to get the job done quickly; expense came second.

It is hard to gauge how much extra expenditure the military presence has incurred for the Treasury in Whitehall. Much of the money would have had to be spent on military facilities for British forces somewhere in the world anyway. The money for the forces on the Falklands has been provided by four different votes – accommodation, equipment, manpower and infrastructure – and it is difficult for the outsider to work out precisely what facilities and projects are being paid from what vote. The outlay on the military presence is huge – £3 billion by 1987 – particularly compared to the £50 million voted for the compensation and rehabilitation funds for the Islanders and the Shackleton development plan.

Because of the high running costs of many of the projects, the MoD and the local Command administration in the Falklands have discouraged co-operation with the civilian administration. In April 1984 the floating port and storage facility, Falklands Intermediate Port and Storage System (FIPASS), began operation. It is a wonderful piece of technology, and fascinating to anyone brought up on Meccano and Lego. The quays of the port rest on six North Sea oil barges, each ninety-six metres long. The storage sheds are built onto the quays to make handling of containers and loose cargo quicker and cleaner. The flotation of the dock complex and the storage inventories are computer-controlled. The whole project cost £27 million and is the most complex military dock built by British forces since they set up with the Americans the Mulberry Harbour pontoons off the Normandy coast in 1944. FIPASS will make considerable savings in running costs as the charter of vessels lying in Stanley Harbour and Port William acting as container store ships was costing between £10,000 and £20,000 a day. Some of the store space is being leased to the civilian administration, but once the garrison moves from Stanley to Mount Pleasant the FIPASS harbour will go. Ironically, the Shackleton development plan suggested that up to £7 million should be spent on a deep-water jetty for Port Stanley. Now that the military have built one, there is little chance of it being adapted eventually for civilian use. Apparently it would be very hard to maintain as there is so much computer technology involved. After three years the barges will have to be beached and scraped, and if the sheds on the quays were abandoned entirely by the army there would be far more storage space than the Islands could ever need. The likelihood is that the harbour will either be towed round to East Cove after three years to serve the Mount Pleasant airfield and garrison complex or sold to Middle East oil contractors serving drilling rigs in the Gulf. The Islanders will still be without their deep-water jetty.

The building of roads, accommodation blocks, and hut encampments round the FIPASS floating port to most Islanders is the outward sign of the difference in expenditure on military installations and on civilian improvement. The port and three coastels are sited near the Canache, a narrow piece of land connecting the airfield with the fields and open land to the east of Stanley. Two years after the Argentine soldiers dumped their arms by the side of the road leading to the airport from the town, the landscape has been transformed radically. The Royal Engineers have laid a completely new road along the shore to the airport. Huts, sheds and Portakabin prefabs seem to have popped up across the hillside like mushrooms overnight. The conspicuous expenditure amazes Islanders, and sometimes its smaller manifestations disgust them. Ration packs rejected by RAF personnel have been washed up on the shores round the harbours and the North Camp, the north-eastern part of East Falkland. Some of the luncheon boxes contained oranges in good condition, items of unimaginable luxury for the Kelpers who find it almost impossible to get hold of fresh fruit of any kind.

The lavish expenditure on installations evidently worries some of the soldiers as well. One Royal Engineer wrote to his MP about it, as he is entitled to, but his superiors became greatly alarmed when it was pointed out that the soldier's constituency was Finchley North, and his MP was

227

Mrs Thatcher. In the two southern summers since the conflict of 1982, the Royal Engineers have put more than 1200 of their men to work at a time. The accommodation facilities they have installed have cost well over £300 million. More than 800 Portakabin huts have been erected at a cost of more than £23,000 each. Accommodation for radar teams operating the two stations on two mountain sites in West Falkland have been disproportionately large; the insulated cabins have cost £45,000 each. Plant, tractors, bulldozers and trucks, have cost between £12 and £15 million, and provided a hidden bonus for Islanders.

Many of the vehicles with military markings found in Stanley now belong to Islanders. Plant is usually written off by the army over a fifteen-year period with the amount budgeted for repair and maintenance being reduced steadily each year. At first the army dumped equipment it no longer required. Then wily Kelpers began offering slightly above the budgeted figure for maintenance for choice items such as tractors, trucks and Land-Rovers. Bulldozers have been acquired for a few hundred pounds, either to be used on the farm or stripped. Valuable components like the hydraulic rams and parts of the engine are sent back to Britain to be sold at a fair profit. The army held auctions of old vehicles at the Moody Brook Camp, where the Royal Marines used to have their base and which was comprehensively rocketed by the invading Argentines on 2 April 1982. General Spacie encouraged the sales and said he was staggered at the mechanical ingenuity of the Kelpers.

Halfway between Moody Brook and Stanley is the municipal dump and, since the forces started using it, the site of a local recreation. When word goes round that the army is about to dump another interesting consignment there, Islanders young and old begin hovering like vultures. The pickings have been both exotic and practical. An almost new suspension for a Land-Rover has been picked up, and parts of tractors have turned up with comforting regularity. Some of the items seem to have been discarded quite casually. One farm mechanic picked up a manual on how to assemble a Rapier missile battery and put it in working order. It was marked 'Restricted', dated from 1978 and seemed fairly straightforward. He handed the book back to the Command Headquarters.

For all the expenditure on accommodation and installations, the garrison does not live in luxury. The thousand or so men living in the floating coastels have a warm building, with access to squash courts, a small swimming pool, a laundry, bars and mess rooms. Their sleeping quarters are tiny, however, and sometimes four men will live for four months in a space smaller than a sleeping cabin on a cross-Channel ferry.

Rooms in the Portakabin huts are shared by up to six men, and in the winter there is always the promise of a leaking roof or swollen door from the damp and the gales. Several of the accommodation huts have had their roofs ripped off by the wind and all need continual repair.

Apart from the port, most of the facilities round the Canache are devoted to the RAF base, the maintenance of the Phantoms and Harriers, the Hercules transport and reconnaissance planes, and the helicopters. About fifteen fighters – a squadron of Phantoms and at least five Harriers – are available at any time. They are the front-line response to any threat of incursion into the Falkland Islands Protection Zone (FIPZ). The Phantom pilots often invite visitors up from the town to see the planes, painted a dull slug-like grey for the southern skies. Each plane is armed with cannon, Sky Flash anti-radar missiles and the AM-9L Sidewinder, which proved the most effective single weapon system in the 1982 campaign. The Phantom is an old, powerful and reliable aircraft. One mechanic at Stanley airfield reckoned that only ten per cent of the original machine remained in the aircraft that he was servicing. Twelve second-hand Phantoms have been purchased from America to augment the planes in the Falklands, and the aircraft serving there will stay, only returning to Britain as scrap. They run regular patrols to the west of the Falklands where the pilots say they encounter some of the best flying conditions they have ever experienced: they can see for hundreds of miles in the pure, unpolluted air. Sometimes they stage mock air battles with the Harriers and conduct joint training exercises with the army and the surface ships of the Navy. Their role is fully operational, and each time they take off, their planes are armed for combat. The two-man crews of the Phantoms can expect to serve in the Falklands several times in a two-year period. In fact, it is planned that every Phantom pilot and navigator in the RAF serves there at least once.

Less glamorous are the conditions in which the soldiers of the garrison battalion serve. Their headquarters have been based for some time at Goose Green, though they are likely to be moved from time to time to Kelly's Garden, a piece of high ground above San Carlos settlement. The soldiers live in Portakabin huts about half a mile away from the Goose Green settlement. Some of the soldiers are sorry not to have closer contact with the local population and the Kelpers are sad not to see more of the soldiers. At Goose Green the farmers were genuinely upset when the battalion commander banned further visits by his men to the social club following a brawl there. The men were in the habit of coming into the settlement in twos or threes by invitation. On this occasion, a Kelper told me he was particularly aggrieved because the fight was between soldiers and did not involve locals at all.

Relations between the locals and the garrison troops have varied but have been nowhere near as bad as they might have been or as they have been painted by the local press and the rumour machine in Stanley. In the months following the conflict a corporal clerk was loaned by the Queen's Own Highlanders to teach the local children who would otherwise have been without regular schooling. One family says there has never been as good a teacher in the settlement before or since.

There have been some pockets of hostility: the manager in Port Howard made his antipathy to soldiery of whatever nationality plain fairly soon after the conflict and no unit has been based permanently there; at other settlements on West Falkland there has been the occasional incident when Land-Rovers and tractors have been damaged after dances and socials, one event at Fox Bay receiving exaggerated publicity in early 1984.

When the Royal Scots came to West Falkland they were given a rare chance to get to know the local community. Within three weeks of their arrival one of the companies was set to organise a training camp for the Falkland Islands Defence Force (FIDF), the first for nearly forty years. On a flat piece of boggy moor flanked by mountain and sea, a scene which could have been from the soldiers' native Scotland, they set about training the Falkland volunteers in tactics and target shooting, at which the Kelpers have traditionally excelled. Relations between them seemed excellent; a Scots sergeant told me that they were learning from the Islanders, first hand, things that they might never have discovered otherwise. On the morning of shooting practice with the sub-machine-guns, Sir Rex Hunt paid a visit; it had a certain viceregal quality about it. After watching the shooting and a few minutes' polite chat to the soldiers and volunteers he and his party repaired to a small tent for a lunch of hot stew with two choices of wine. 'You know, they wouldn't put that tent up for anyone else,' Sharon Halford, the assistant registrar for the Islands and the only woman volunteer present, told me afterwards. 'He should have seen the conditions we had to camp in.'

Some of the conditions of the living quarters for the garrison troops in camp have been primitive, to say the least. Just before Christmas 1982 I came across a platoon of the Royal Hampshire Regiment bivouacked in Burntside House, which had been riddled with bullets by 'A' company of 2nd Battalion the Parachute Regiment as they opened the battle for Goose Green and Darwin on 28 May 1982. The soldiers were cooking their Sunday lunch, a revolting pile of fried bread, dripping, cheese and spam. They were trying to repair the house, or at least to keep the wind and rain out. A corporal with a longing expression told me of his dream of a night out: 'A quiet walk down to Goose Green for a hot shower.'

Many of the soldiers have taken up rural pursuits in the Falklands with enthusiasm. Fishing, bird-watching and photography are favourite hobbies in the brief summer. Most of the battalions have provided small sailing dinghies and wind-surfers for recreation at San Carlos and Goose Green. Some men have tried pony-trekking and shooting rabbits and hares in the hills. But the life is spartan, and the daily round in rough weather exhausting. Boredom threatens every idle moment, and so the schedule is crammed with training exercises, night exercises, navigational exercises, cross-country marches and live firing exercises at battalion strength with support from the Navy and the Phantoms and Harriers of the RAF.

Flying across East Falkland to San Carlos over Mount Kent one might believe the whole of central East Falkland to be one huge bombing and ground fighting range. There are two big ranges, on East and West Falkland, several thousand acres in size, and many smaller ones on the two larger islands. Helicopter and aircraft weapons are tested continually with live ammunition, and small arms, mortar and artillery are tested at specialised sites. New types of ammunition and weapon improvements following the campaign of 1982 have been put through rigorous trials. Some of the local population have expressed alarm at the amount of land now being used for live firing. Before Christmas 1982 a party of school-children on an organised hike inadvertently strayed onto a range in West Falkland during a major live firing exercise. Tussock islands have been bombed and set alight and some shepherds' huts have received rough treatment – shot up by troops on exercise.

Many of the exercises are conducted to learn the military lessons of the 1982 conflict. The soldiers often feel the shadow of the campaign, whose incidents have now achieved exaggerated, even apocryphal, proportions. Equally exaggerated is the importance of some of the exercises designed subsequently. Commanding officers talk obsessively of the walking, the 'yomping' and 'tabbing' campaign and the need for the infantry soldier to attain ever greater standards of fitness. On arriving in the Falklands the 2nd battalion the Royal Regiment of Fusiliers were ordered to march seventy miles across country to their base at Goose Green, so they would appreciate the need for fitness and be able to 'yomp', they were told by their commanding officer. No battalion or commando in the conflict marched more than thirty or forty miles without two or three days' break.

Great play is now made of improvements to clothing and equipment since June 1982, such as the new boot with its high ankle support and the sleeping-bag. The boots, according to many of the soldiers, leak as much as ever and are, if anything, more uncomfortable than the old ones. Few sleeping-bags can match the Royal Marines' arctic bag filled with genuine down.

The most difficult and tedious work routine for the services has fallen to the Royal Navy. The Task Group to police the Protection Zone for a radius of 150 miles round the Islands is made up of two destroyers (usually Type 42s, the sister ships of the *Coventry* and *Sheffield*), an older frigate (of either the 'Leander' or 'Rothesay' class) and a modern frigate (Type 21, a sister ship of *Ardent* and *Antelope*). They are supported by a fleet tanker and a supply ship, both carrying helicopters for anti-submarine surveillance. An unspecified number of nuclear hunter-killer submarines is deployed. In Port Stanley are based three former oil-rig protection vessels led by HMS *Protector*; they will have an increasing role as the number of larger ships on patrol is reduced.

Ships patrolling west of the Falklands have to be on constant alert. Men are kept at defence watches, kitted in anti-flash masks and gloves, and ready to move to action stations with loaded weapons at a moment's notice. The commanders say that maintaining such vigilance day after day produces great strains on the ships' companies, particularly as there is little chance of action ensuing. Serving men with the Navy are now on their second, third or fourth tour in the Falklands, a deployment which now ties up almost a third of Britain's total frigate and destroyer force. On occasion there can be four ships deployed there, four on passage to or from the United Kingdom and four undergoing training in British waters. Therefore, four ships are retained with the fleet from the Reserve Squadron to make up Britain's NATO commitments in home waters.

As a relief from the rigours of the patrols the ships put into small harbours and settlements round the coasts of West Falkland, and North Arm and San Carlos in East Falkland. Relations with the Kelpers are said to be warm and hospitable and at Christmas the ships have thrown parties for the entire populations of some island and farm communities. Modifications to ships of the line since the conflict have made such visits more difficult, however. To fit more anti-aircraft guns ships' boats have been removed from their hoists and davits on the upper decks. A Type 42 destroyer has six 30-mm and 20-mm guns now and on operational duties has dispensed with at least two of its cutters and launches. Commanders are reluctant to offer hospitality to the smaller settlements when it means that the farmer will have to provide the boats and the crew. At shearing time the loss of manpower and boats to transport the sheep can mean big delays for the farmers and the shearing gangs.

The modifications made after the campaign were immediately apparent on a short visit to one of the ships of the Falklands Task Group.

On a blustery sunny day in March 1984 I visited the Type 42 destroyer HMS *Liverpool* as she lay alongside the maintenance ship RFA *Bar Protector* in San Carlos Water. *Bar Protector* was a maintenance ship for North Sea oil platforms and had proved so successful as a floating maintenance depot during the campaign that the MoD decided to buy her. The ship can maintain several vessels at a time, keeping her position in the water with pinpoint accuracy by rudders and bow propellers controlled by computers. The day I went aboard *Liverpool, Bar Protector* also had the 'Leander'-class frigate HMS *Penelope* alongside; the decks of all three ships were alive with maintenance workers, ship-wrights and mechanics in a scene of studied activity worthy of the gipsy encampment in *Il Trovatore*. On *Liverpool*'s upper decks 20- and 30-calibre anti-aircraft guns filled the gaps vacated by the cutters abandoned in England. Below decks the passageways were punctuated every ten yards or so with heavy anti-smoke curtains, a result of the experience aboard HMS *Sheffield* when she was hit and smoke spread rapidly throughout the ship. At strategic points throughout HMS *Liverpool* breathing-masks with bottles of air or oxygen hung from strips of plastic with large pockets sewn into them. Each mat contained about eight masks which would give a man several minutes' breathing time to search areas filled with poisonous gases and smoke.

The main improvement to the *Liverpool* over *Sheffield* and *Coventry*, I was told by her Captain, Pat Rowe, was in the modifications to the radar. With the installations on the high ground of East and West Falkland aided by the radar of the Task Group ships and the Phantom aircraft the forces on the Falklands have an infinitely greater surveillance capacity west of the Falklands than during the campaign. Rowe was the image of the gallant and genial naval officer, a modern Hornblower, and with his white silk choker round his neck he gave the impression that he had either come straight from the polo field or the shower.

He explained simply and precisely his main concerns as Task Group Commander. A great problem was fighting boredom for the men at their long defensive watches. They have to be alert, he said, as the main threat was a hit-and-run raid by the Argentine air force, which, after the battering it took over East and West Falkland two years before, was well up to strength and probably stronger than in 1982. He said cryptically that things would change in about the middle of 1984, when patrolling to the west of the Falklands would be less rigorous and more inshore work would be undertaken by the *Bar Protector*; this might release one or two of the frigates and destroyers of the Task Group for deployment in British waters.

One of the hazards of constant patrolling through the middle of the year was the weather. When I saw Rowe in Port Stanley at the beginning of April he related an amazing incident, worthy of Shackleton's journey with the *James Caird* from Elephant Island to South Georgia. He had been exercising round the outer islands of the Falklands with his main Task Group; turning to windward from the shelter of one of the smaller islands he was confronted suddenly by a huge wall of green water higher than *Liverpool*'s superstructure; from the bridge all he could see was a mass of water which, for seconds, blotted out the light from the sky. This was evidently a southerly cousin of the 'greybeards', the fifty- to hundred-foot waves that roll across the world's oceans, now unimpeded by land in the latitudes of Drake Passage. Rowe said he had never encountered sea conditions like this in twenty-seven years in the Navy.

Captain Rowe's assumptions about the change in the deployment of the Task Group round the Falklands in the middle of 1984 appeared to be based on three things, two of which have come to pass, one has not. The first assumption was that the new radar installations on East and West Falkland would be fully operational. These can 'look down' across the sea to well beyond the 150-mile limit of the Falkland Islands Protection Zone, and so take on some of the surveillance role of the surface ships patrolling to the west of the Islands. The second assumption was that the development of the airfield and base at Mount Pleasant would mean a smaller, more mobile, garrison force by early 1985; this would imply a steady reduction of the naval presence, which might begin about the middle of 1984. The third assumption was the likelihood of some interim agreement with Argentina leading to a declaration of the cessation of hostilities by Buenos Aires and the lifting of the Protection Zone by the British. The failure of Anglo-Argentine talks in Berne in July 1984 reduced the possibility of this happening until well after the strategic airfield at Mount Pleasant becomes fully operational.

The failure to reach understanding on ending hostilities has meant that the Navy has continued to patrol Falklands waters with its former vigilance. Added to the difficulties of maintaining ships' companies at defence watches for long periods were headaches about maintenance schedules for machinery, particularly the helicopters. The day I went aboard HMS *Liverpool* with a small press party, Captain Rowe talked openly of his worries about the drastic reduction in flying hours for the Task Group's Lynx and Sea King surveillance helicopters. The ship's Lynx had just been put on peacetime maintenance schedules allowing only thirty to thirty-five hours' flying a month, whereas it had been flown well over seventy hours a month on patrol in the South Atlantic. My reporting those concerns among the Task Group brought a remonstration from the Secretary of State for Defence, Michael Heseltine, about 'undermining the credibility of the Task Group', but doubtless the leak had its desired effect and more generous flying schedules were restored to the helicopter pilots.

Not that there is anything secret about the role and strategic intentions of the defence forces in the Falklands. They are laid out plainly in a document presented by Heseltine to the House of Commons in October 1983 entitled 'The Future Defence of the Falkland Islands' and based on recommendations from the House of Commons Select Committee on Defence. It notes concern about the continuing expense of the forces in the Falklands but also that 'it will be necessary to maintain an appropriate garrison to defend the Islands against the military threat posed by Argentina'. To minimise the detriment to NATO forces, as the paper puts it, extra Phantoms, Rapier missile batteries and other equipment have been ordered and the four ships due for the Reserve Squadron kept with the fleet. The key to future defence plans is the rapid development of the new strategic and civil airfield at Mount Pleasant, where, says the paper, the runway was expected to be operational by April 1985 and the full facility working the following year. In paragraph 8 the Minister accepts the defence committee's warning that the spending on defence projects should 'not be taken as a commitment to the establishment of a permanent military presence, which would have implications for our future diplomatic position'. It continues with a crucial passage outlining the defence secretary's and the Conservative government's position:

> The decision to build the airfield demonstrates our commitment to safeguarding the Islanders' future. The Government hopes the Argentines will draw the proper conclusions and that this will result in a policy characterised by peaceable intentions rather than belligerence and threats.

The Argentine government has taken quite the opposite attitude, and asked for the airport project to be stopped as it was a sign of Britain's continuing belligerence.

The paper makes some interesting observations about co-operation between the civilian and military administrations in the Falklands. It says discussion on joint projects between the military and civilian authorities must not cause delay to their being started; the road to the new airport will have to go ahead before it is decided what contribution should be made by the ODA, for example. In some areas co-operation is particularly desirable, such as the deep-water jetty and in improving the hospital. Since the paper was issued the military authorities have built their own port facility with FIPASS, and the old hospital has burnt down, bringing all but the sketchiest collaboration between civilian and military medical staff to an end.

The character of each military staff and formation is bound to be affected by the personality and outlook of the commander, particularly so in the isolation of the Falklands. General Spacie was succeeded in June 1984 by Major-General Peter de la Bilière, former director of the SAS and Britain's most decorated senior officer. From the first he has adopted a more relaxed style than his predecessor, which has been appreciated warmly by the citizens of Stanley. 'He looks like a typical SAS man, who could melt away easily in a crowd. He looks like a good man, and very uncomfortable in a suit,' was one verdict. It will be interesting to see if the General's quiet enthusiasm will overcome the natural boredom and bewilderment of the garrison.

Few of the servicemen serving in the Falklands have much interest for or understanding of their role. One only has to witness the euphoria of the majority of the service passengers aboard each Hercules transport as it takes off from RAF Stanley for Ascension. Many of the serving men find the natural environment hostile and the Islanders difficult to communicate with. Some, however, would like to know more about the place, the people and the policy. They are confused about whether the garrison is there to defend a principle, a strategic position or the place and its people. If there is to be any thriving community of people by the end of the decade in which Britain unexpectedly went to battle, it will depend largely on the success of the programme to develop and diversify the Falklands economy and bring new blood to the Islands.

Port Stanley street scene: the roads and contractor's lorry tell the familiar story

*Endurance* at anchor in the inner harbour, Port Stanley

*Above* and *right* The war cemetery at San Carlos. It stands just above Blue Beach, where the marines landed on 21 May 1982

Housing folly: Ross Road West and, behind it (black roofs), the Brewster houses, which cost £7.2 million. After nearly two years they were still being completed

Sir Rex Hunt talks to members of the Falkland Islands Defence Force on exercise near Doctor's Creek, West Falkland

Pat and Isobel Short in the kitchen at San Carlos farmhouse. After managing the most famous farm on the Falklands, they have now bought two sections of it

The author with *Endurance* being pulled off the rock. Orleans Strait is in the background

# Chapter 12

# Developing
# the Cool Desert

## The Developers Move In

'This place is a cool desert. It is a lot drier than you might think at first. Thank God the ground is like a sponge – otherwise the soil would just blow away,' said Dr John Ferguson, who headed the Islands' agricultural research unit from 1979 to 1984 (August). Following the conflict of 1982 this Scot, a graduate of Edinburgh University whose wit is weighted with a heavy edge of irony, served the Falkland Islands government as Agricultural Officer, advising on the subdivision of farms owned by absentee landlords and the loans for those wanting to work and own the new subdivisions. From 1975 to 1979 he worked in Colombia on agricultural aid projects, paid for by the ODA, and following his service in the Falklands took up a similar post in Bolivia. 'One shouldn't be encouraged to work in this kind of environment for too long,' was his counsel for fellow expatriate advisers in Port Stanley.

The unit John Ferguson headed has had three changes of title in almost as many years, indulging the Falkland Islands government's passion for bureaucratic upheaval and acronyms and initials. First the unit was the Grasslands Trials Unit, and throughout the Islands most farmers still refer to it as the GTU despite the rebaptisms proposed by the administration in Stanley. Following the conflict, in which laboratories and equipment were appropriated or smashed by the Argentines, the unit was expanded and renamed the Falkland Islands Agricultural Research and Development Centre (FIARDC), a title which lasted barely two years before it was redesignated the Agricultural Research Centre (ARC).

The unit, whatever it is called, is important to the future of the Falklands economy and the livelihood of its community, for it researches the raw statistics of farming and provides advice on its development. Despite attempts to develop small local industries and launch fishery projects, the economy of the Falklands in the mid-1980s is almost wholly reliant on farming, on the production of wool in particular. As this is unlikely to change in the next five or ten years, the fate of the Falklands community is largely dependent on whether new vigour and diversification can be found within the agricultural industry itself.

The 'cool desert' is almost unique in the world for the way peat is formed in it in spite of very low rainfall. Surprisingly, although the Islands have a reputation as a forlorn and soggy spot, average rainfall is lower than in most of Great Britain. The annual rainfall recorded in Stanley, the wettest part of the Islands, is between twenty-three and twenty-six inches. The soil is acid and lacks common plant nutrients, except potassium. The landscape consists of rocky upland, rolling downland of springy mosses and grasses, and the occasional pasture. Commonest of the naturally grown grasses are white grass and diddle-dee. Most of the sheep fodder comes from white grass, which has a characteristically Falkland awkwardness: if it is grazed intensively and neglected it suffers a condition known as 'dieback' and the leaf slowly turns a dark brown as it dies back towards the stem. The open and rugged terrain is suited to two forms of production above all others, the ranching of sheep for wool or a few head of cattle for meat.

In the early days of the Falklands colony cattle were almost as important as sheep. In 1834 Darwin recorded with wonder the wild spotted cattle with enormous spreading horns when he rode from Port Louis across East Falkland to the isthmus which now bears his name. The cattle were hunted and killed and eventually disappeared, and the sheep of the new settlers took their place. To the south of Darwin's isthmus lies the flat, open peninsula known as Lafonia, today an endless patchwork of mottled green grasses and glinting open water.

Lafonia is named after Samuel Fisher Lafone of Montevideo, who purchased the land for ranching in 1846. Later, his company was incorporated by Royal Charter to become in 1851 the Royal Falkland Land, Cattle, Seal and Whale Fishery Company. The gauchos first imported by Lafone wrought havoc on the herds of wild horses and cattle, and were regarded by the English settlers with disgust. The Falkland Islands Company benefited from generous legislation for shipping immigrants from Britain at low cost, and acquired within decades a reputation as a tough employer and for driving a hard bargain, a reputation it has not lived down to this day. Trading conditions from the first were far from easy, and several years in the nineteenth century saw no dividends distributed to shareholders. Samuel Fisher Lafone never visited the Falklands, and so became the first great absentee landlord of the colony's history.

Today the FIC owns forty-three per cent of the land, and in 1980–1 forty-six per cent of all sheep shorn on the Islands came from the company's farms. The biggest single farm is at North Arm in Lafonia; in the 1982–3 season it ran over 70,000 sheep. The biggest combined holding is the FIC's farms at Darwin and Walker Creek, with over 112,000 sheep, 390 horses, 1066 cattle, 109 dogs and 460 poultry between them. Darwin and North Arm together possess over a quarter of the Falklands' total sheep population, recorded at 669,144 in 1983. In recent years the company has undergone several changes of ownership and profits from wool declined sharply throughout the seventies. For some time the FIC was a subsidiary of the Slater Walker Group and was purchased next by the Charrington Fuel and Transport Group, which in turn was acquired by the Coalite Company of Bolsover, Derbyshire, in 1979. The FIC has often seemed part of government in many parts of the Islands because it has long supplied a vital part of the local infra-structure. For well over a century it has provided shipping within the Islands themselves and freight and insurance facilities for the shipment of wool from the Islands to Bradford in Yorkshire, where it had a stake in the principal wool-buyer for the Falklands, David Smith and Company. When David Smith went out of business the FIC set up its own company for buying wool from its own farms. Despite falling wool prices and profits on the FIC farm accounts, the trading and shipping side of the company's operations has shown a profit in recent years of between fifteen and twenty-five per cent on turnover, a remarkably high margin for such activities in modern times.

Three months after the conflict with Argentina ended the FIC was but the first and greatest of the overseas-based owners of Falklands land. At that time thirteen other overseas companies owned nearly forty-four per cent of the sheep shorn on the Islands, with the remaining twenty-three small farmers owning just over thirteen per cent. Since these figures were recorded, for the second Shackleton Report of 1982, one big overseas-owned farm, belonging to Packe Brothers on West Falkland, has been purchased by the Falkland Islands government, subdivided and sold to small farmers. Another estate at San Carlos settlement has undergone the process of subdivision and sale in October 1984, though amid much dispute between the vendor and the Falkland Islands government over land valuation and the loans for prospective buyers.

Few parts of the Falklands are suitable for any form of agricultural production other than ranching. In the crude definition ranching is acres to the sheep, rather than sheep to the acre. Some offer a more refined version of the maxim, describing ranching as the best use of natural resources with the minimum investment. In these terms Falklands sheep-ranching has been very efficient over the years, using between ten and fifteen per cent of the terrain for grazing sheep and cattle with low invest-

nt in labour, housing and fencing. Part of the attraction of the settlements is their sense of a pioneering way of life. Each has its manager's
house, sometimes a grand affair in stone built in the last century, sheep
corrals, shearing sheds, store, bunkhouse or cookhouse, windmill pump
and a small clump of trees, conifers or thick hedge. They strongly
resemble the first settlements in Patagonia, to which they were linked by
trade and blood ties. Many of the early farming families, like the Blakes
of Hill Cove on West Falkland, moved freely between Patagonia and the
Falklands. The Blakes acquired land in Patagonia and traded in breeding
stock bought there. Many of the Patagonian farmers today have Scots
and Welsh, and Falkland, blood.

In the late nineteenth century several families left East and West
Falkland to acquire land in Patagonia, and the story of one of these, the
Hallidays, is told in *From the Falklands to Patagonia* by Michael
Mainwaring, which was published in 1983. The author is a frequent
visitor to South America and on one of his visits he met the surviving
daughter of William Halliday, who left Port Stanley with his seven
children in 1885 to settle on a 30,000-acre farm in South America. The
story has a contemporary ring; Halliday left the Falklands to escape 'the
shackles of the Falkland Islands Company', as Mainwaring puts it, as he
was bound by contract to the Company as a second manager on one of
the farms. In the 1880s sheep-farming in the Falklands was going
through some dog days. An officer of the Royal Navy's South America
Squadron foresaw for the citizens of Port Stanley as gloomy a future as
that of 'the surviving innkeepers of coaching days'.

Some ninety years after the naval officer made his caustic appraisal of
the prospects for the people of Stanley, a sense of impending crisis was
growing once more in the Falklands community. In 1976 the Labour
government in Britain asked a committee under Lord Shackleton, the
sometime leader of the party in the House of Lords and the son of Sir
Ernest Shackleton, to report on the economy of the Islands and how it
might be revived. A team of experts travelled to the Falklands and
visited all of the thirty-seven main farms and settlements, and some went
to South Georgia with *Endurance*. The resulting Report ran to two thick
volumes, a fascinating social history, unique of its kind, which concluded with a schedule of proposals to stem the flow of people and profits
from the Falkland Islands. In his introduction, Lord Shackleton noted
that £5 million had left the Falklands in company profits in the twenty
years prior to 1976, at a considerable gain to the British Exchequer. His
Report warned of the possible collapse of the local economy if the drift of
potential investment funds from the colony continued and people continued to leave the Islands to seek a living overseas. The 1976 Report

recommended the subdivision of farms to attract more local families, the purchase of farms from absentee landlords to raise the level of investment in agriculture, the development of secondary industries such as fishing and the strengthening of the infrastructure, with better roads and air transport. The development plan would involve the investment of £12 to £13 million in capital projects.

Very little of the Report was acted on. One of the FIC farms, Green Patch on the North Camp of East Falkland, was sold. At the time the farm was said to be in a rundown condition and the FIC willing to sell only because of its inability to attract labour there. The runway at the Cape Pembroke airfield to the east of Port Stanley was extended and strengthened at a cost to the British Treasury of about £1.7 million. Otherwise little was achieved.

But in 1982 the earlier Report formed the basis of Lord Shackleton's second Falkland Islands economic study, which now provides the blueprint for development in the Islands following the conflict with Argentina. It is far shorter than the first and differs in several important respects. It proposes the compulsory purchase by government or a Falklands development agency of all farms owned by overseas companies or absentee landlords, the subdivision of such farms for sale to Falkland Islanders or suitable immigrants; the development agency should be headed by a new Chief Executive, and the machinery of government in Port Stanley should be strengthened by advisers from London, among them a Development Officer and a Political Adviser, who should also serve as Deputy Civil Commissioner when the Civil Commissioner is absent; the work of the GTU should be extended and funds provided for extra staff; encouragement and finance should be provided for salmon-ranching, inshore and offshore fisheries, and a wool mill; there should be increased investment in power and water utilities, roads and jetties, including a deep-water jetty for Port Stanley; and a new airport should be built for medium and long-haul traffic. The Thatcher government accepted the Report and nearly every one of its recommendations. In December 1982 the Foreign Secretary, Francis Pym, told Parliament that £31 million was to be allocated to the development of the Falklands over the next five years. The new airport project, already under way by then, was to be funded separately by the MoD at a cost of £213 million.

The first Report is more leisurely and elegantly phrased than the second. Unlike its successor, it looks at educational and social services in the Islands and broadcasting and telephone facilities. It also examines the possibilities of hydrocarbons being exploited in the Malvina Basin beween the Islands and Patagonia. In the late seventies the Argentine petrochemical combine YPF issued three licences for the exploration of the Patagonian side of the Basin, and BP carried out a survey closer to the Falklands in 1979. In fact, the prospects of closer links with Argentina in a communications agreement of 1971 may have been the spur for the 1976 Shackleton Report. The Report concludes that further exploration of the Basin could only take place with the full co-operation of Argentina since the operation would have to be based in Patagonia. The 1982 Report excludes the possibility of development of the Basin in the climate of Anglo-Argentine relations following the 1982 fighting. Presumably, one of the assumptions of the first Shackleton study was that Britain would need to have a viable Falklands society and economy in order to participate in offshore commercial activities, particularly in the Malvina Basin, on terms of equal partnership with Argentina.

The first Report is at its best in describing the structure of Falklands society, which it says can be a brake on economic development. It notes the hard-working and resourceful nature of many of the farmers and shepherds, but it also underlines the class system, which can mean undue dependence on owners, managers and company bosses. Even today few communities as small as the Falklands have such a highly developed sense of snobbery. The Report remarks on the division between native-born 'Kelpers' and immigrants, between the people of Port Stanley and those living in camp, and between managers and owners and hired hands. On page 74 it describes the qualities of the Kelpers:

> They include honesty, versatility, physical hardiness, and a capacity for sustained effort. Yet there appear to be other less encouraging features, such as a lack of confidence and enterprise at the individual and community level, and a degree of acceptance of their situation which verges on apathy.

In a later paragraph the effects of these qualities are described:

> More specifically, these features seem to show in the reluctance to undertake the several small commercial projects which appear feasible in the Islands. There is also a tendency to leave social action (e.g. in welfare and leisure associations) to non-local people. Politically, too, there seems to be a degree of inertia. Such attempts as there have been to rally opinion on local issues have not had much popular response. We heard a strong if resigned comment on the disbandment some years ago of Stanley Town Council, one of the very few potential counterweights to government, yet at the time of its abolition, there seems to have been little local resistance

. . . In recent memory no farm worker appears to have sat on the Legislative or Executive Councils.

The lack of incentive for young settlers and Kelpers to invest in their own small enterprises and the failure of the bigger farms to put money back into their businesses is largely responsible for the decline in population, according to the Report. The population had reached its peak in 1931, when the census recorded 2392 people living in the Islands, 1213 of them in Port Stanley alone. By 1970 the overall population had fallen to 1957 with 1079 of these inhabiting the town. The Report repeatedly emphasises the lack of cohesion and sense of identity in the community and points to the high divorce rate and low numbers of young marriageable women as symptoms and causes of social stress. Another symptom is the high incidence of alcoholism: 'It was said for example that a good deal of drunkenness occurs at dances,' runs the Report (page 83), 'and that it is customary for unattached men in camp cookhouses to spend much of their weekends drinking, largely for lack of other things to do. The pattern described is unfortunately common in comparable communities elsewhere, and it is doubtful if the situation is any worse than in some Scottish islands.' While critical of social services and provisions of support for the poorest families, the Report suggested that the medical services of the doctors and hospital were adequate and that sums spent on the health of the community were comparable to those spent in Shetland and Orkney. However, the section on medical services concludes with a peculiarly ominous sentence, in view of the controversy that developed after the hospital burnt down in April 1984: 'There is scope for improvement,' the conclusion of Chapter 14 runs, 'in relation to facilities available to the camp population, the irregular and erratic spending on replacement and repairs, and the present system of charging. . .'

The second Report is nothing like as good a read as the first and gives every impression of being hastily put together, which it was. It has several other defects besides: for example, no member of the team went back to the Falklands to revise the first Report and only people in Britain at the time were interviewed. It is shorter and blunter than its predecessor, but for all the vehemence with which it makes its recommendations, it is contradictory in its conclusions on subjects as various as the division of farms, salmon-ranching and offshore fishing. Many of the costings of capital projects, particularly on road-building and maintenance, have turned out to be wildly undercalculated. Despite these drawbacks, the document has become an almost inflexible model for development in the Falklands, an excuse for inaction on expenditure on welfare and education. In Port Stanley the £31 million voted by the Westminster Parliament for development projects is known as 'Shackleton money', and with the local administration the Report itself has taken on the quality of a Holy Writ. Lord Shackleton is mildly shocked to find that the document is being used in this way, and has said that he would have preferred it to be used as a basis for discussing further detailed planning tailored to changing circumstances in the Islands.

Today one of the characteristics of small island communities is that they seem fated to be bombarded by advice, in quantity if not in quality. One of Lord Shackleton's team serving with the Highlands and Islands Development Board described an island there as 'a piece of land entirely surrounded by advice'. In the six years between the two Shackleton Reports the Falklands suffered no fewer than seven separate studies of fiscal policy and reform, banking and wool production (by the New Zealand Wool Board), two on fishery (by the ODA and the White Fish Authority), one on krill (by the Food and Agriculture Organisation of the United Nations (FAO)), plus a report on salmon-ranching, commissioned as a result of Lord Shackleton's first proposals in 1976. Despite all the studies and analysis the 1982 Shackleton Report revealed an alarming deterioration in the Falklands economy and community between 1976 and 1981.

The population in that period had declined by a further three per cent and wool prices between 1976, a good year, and 1980, a very bad one, went down by twenty per cent, leading to a twenty-five-per-cent fall in Gross Domestic Product over the same period. Gross National Product decreased by four per cent, due to earnings from stamps and grants from London. Only one of the farms owned by overseas companies had been sold and divided, and that was the FIC farm at Green Patch, where the number of sheep had increased but the weight of the fleece decreased. Unfortunately, the Report did not go into the circumstances of the sale and division of the flock, which were peculiar to say the least. In the view of the Report, the level of expenditure on farm improvements throughout the Islands had been very poor, though it added that the FIC's investment record had been better than that of most of the overseas companies, and it noted that little had been done to diversify production both on and off farms. Lord Shackleton's own introduction contains a paragraph explaining why he recommended doubling expenditure proposed in 1976 to £30–35 million: 'The need to spend this larger sum is caused by the further deterioration of the economy of the Islands, which . . . is in danger of eventual collapse if urgent action is not carried out.' The section devoted to conclusions and recommendations is even more forthright in its warning: 'The internal economy of the Falklands is in grave danger of collapsing in the next five years or so without continued support and/or development.' In August 1984, two years after the second Shackleton Report was drafted, it was far from clear whether this strategy would be sufficient to avert a sudden crisis or the inexorable decline in the Falklands community.

The biggest development project in the Islands since the conflict of 1982 is the building of the new airfield at Mount Pleasant; it is most probably the largest single piece of construction ever likely to be undertaken there. Flying from Stanley to Darwin over the southern slopes of Mount Challenger and Mount Usborne, the huts and the tracks of the construction camp stand out like white lice on a carpet of green and rust brown. The project was already well begun by the time Francis Pym announced the Thatcher government's acceptance of the main proposals of the Shackleton Report in December 1982, and the building of the settlement at the airfield, the twenty miles of feed roads to the quarries and the airstrip itself, has proceeded apace. When I visited the site in March 1984 the runway was eleven weeks ahead of schedule, and it seemed that everything would be ready to receive the first aircraft from Ascension in April 1985. The full barracks complex for the garrison was planned for occupation by the troops and ground crews by April the following year. The airfield itself has been designated primarily a military project, costing the MoD about £220 million; and the barrack facilities could come to at least half, or possibly even the same, again. The airfield itself does not seem wildly expensive considering the remoteness of the site and the inadequacy of local material.

The headquarters of the building camp is in a ship, the *Merchant Providence,* tied permanently to the shore at Mare Harbour, one of the many creeks and inlets of the Fitzroy River estuary. She is known as the head vessel, and supply ships tie up alongside, using her as a wharf. A broad ramp from the ship to the beach is a runway for jeeps, tractors and catering vehicles. Inside, the ship is a sophisticated command post, with direct telex links to the headquarters of the construction consortium Laing, Mowlem, Amey Roadstone (LMA), in London. Stocks of materials and machinery are checked and recorded by computer. Six female clerks and secretaries live on board, in what must be as complete a state of sexual segregation as anywhere south of Buenos Aires. They were all volunteers, they told me, and were hardly allowed off the ship for the few months they were in the Falklands, nor were they allowed to talk to the press – for the record that is.

The *Resource* arrived at Mare Harbour in hardly the most auspicious circumstances: there was a full-blooded gale and it took days to moor the ship firmly; the first teams of construction workers had to leave the ship by raft; a bulldozer was landed to build up the shore banks. In the evening, the men returned to sleep on the floors of the cabins and assembly rooms, and many were seasick in the rough weather. Once established on land, however, conditions were hardly better, and men were sleeping up to eight to a room in the huts constructed in rows along the shore, close to the head vessel.

Across the lower slopes of March Ridge and Mount Pleasant crawled tall lorries, bulldozers and scrapers, a wandering tribe of metallic dinosaurs outlined against the grey wintry sky. More than twenty miles of roads have been laid for the heavy lorries to haul rocks from the quarries, spoil from the runway site and material and stores from the ships in the bay. Frequently the smaller vehicles have their tyres punctured by the sharp stones, and the big trucks have rolled off the track as the banking crumbled. More than £20 million worth of mobile plant has worked at the site, and much of it will stay and be written off.

We were welcomed at the helicopter landing-pad on the ship by a jovial West Countryman, Maurice Channings, the regional director of PSA, and Wynn Kenrick, the inside works director for LMA. By the time our little party of journalists arrived these two were seasoned hands at the guided tour of Mount Pleasant. Both were dedicated engineers, drawn by the challenge of the job itself. Maurice Channings was invited to take charge by PSA in August 1982 and had very little time to make up his mind. Both have had to leave their families for long periods, a common experience in their working lives. They told us that about 700 men were working on the site at the beginning of the Falklands winter of 1984, and the greatest number working on the airfield at any one time would be about 1500. Not surprisingly, both played down reports of widespread disaffection and large numbers of workers breaking their contracts to return home, and they denied that discipline had been a major difficulty. They calculated between about four and seven per cent would go home early, which was the average for construction projects in unpleasant overseas climates. Security and supervision were strict. Drunkenness at work or a punch thrown in anger would result in immediate repatriation and a considerable financial loss. Rates of pay, however, do not appear to have been enormous, construction workers getting a little over £10,000 a year tax free, plus passage and a fifteen-per-cent bonus on completion of their contract, which would run for up to fourteen months including leave in the United Kingdom. A skilled plant operator might have been paid up to £12,500.

In reputation and lifestyle the construction teams appear to have much in common with railway construction gangs in North and South America in the last century – rough life in the shanty, plenty of booze and very few women. Conditions at the outset were poor; accommodation huts were not built on schedule and there was a lack of good cooked food, particularly at midday. Later, a second camp was built near the airstrip itself, seven miles north of East Cove, where the *Resource* lay fixed to the shore. In the new huts the men lived two to a room. Officially, the site was called Pioneer Camp, but at the approaches a large hand-painted sign said, 'Welcome to HM Prison, the Maze'.

The teams arrived at East Cove by ship from South Africa, after ten days at sea. Those coming from Britain arrived by plane at Durban where they spent a few hours before setting sail, time enough for one or two to contract unsocial diseases. The enforced idleness of the voyage seems to have given the organisers, and the workers, more than a few headaches. A technical officer wanting to travel home from the Falklands via South Africa was told that he was welcome to return with the supply ship from East Cove to South Africa, but in no circumstances would they take his fiancée, and that that was in her best interest.

Towards Mount Pleasant itself the land rose dull velvet green from the moss, mottled with the rust and burnt brown of the soil. The small mountains and rocks stood grey and purple in the distance. Along the ribbon of the main haul road from the *Merchant Providence* and the base camp, heavy trucks and earthmovers were converging on the advanced camp settlement in greater numbers. Here the airstrip was being laid out in an increasing tempo of mechanical and human activity. The main runway is to be supplemented by another of 5000 feet, running at right angles. Initially this was a matter of some debate among the designers, but it was deemed necessary for emergency landings and to allow fighter air-craft, like the Harriers, to take off and land when wind conditions made this difficult on the main airstrip. When I was at the site in March 1984 the bosses were delighted that the work on the airfield, as opposed to the accommodation blocks, was eleven weeks ahead of schedule. Across the grassland lay a wide open trench several hundred feet across, as if a giant carpet of turf nearly 10,000 feet long had been rolled up. This was to be the main runway. At the side of the trench a mechanical excavator shovel had exposed the various layers of soil; at the top was the black mud of the peat, while below was the light fawn of the topsoil, and below that again the steely blue-grey of the clay at the bottom. In this part of the cool desert of the Falklands the topsoil is a foot deep or less at some points, while at others it is still found more than twelve feet beneath the surface. In the middle of the trench rose a hump of rock which was about to be broken by pneumatic drills. The broken rock was to be used as foundation for the runway, if suitable. Much of the local stone is not suitable as a building material and over a dozen quarries have been dug along the southern ridge of East Falkland in the search for hard rock. Most of the stone is tillite, which fractures easily and has a very limited use for foundation, and it is not thought stable or solid enough for runway foundations. Far better is the local quartzite, but this has not been found in sufficient quantity. In June 1984 LMA announced that it would have to ship 6600 tons of aggregate from Britain for the runway foundations. This has added about £3 million to the construction bill, but was not an unexpected development.

Head of the quarries at Mount Pleasant was Joe Shepherd, a philosopher of stone. As the diggers snatched away at one of the tillite quarries, Joe described the operation. He had forty-two men, he said, and he expected about half to go home early. Most had not been trained for what they had to do on March Ridge and he had to organise instruction for them as they worked. 'Quarrying is quarrying the world over,' Joe remarked casually, watching the heavy bulldozers coping with the thick mud thrown up by the previous week's rains. 'You've got rock to blow and load out and crush. Apart from the different varieties of rock, quarrying's quarrying wherever you are. No, the Falklands wouldn't be the top of the list of the places I'd prefer to work, no, not quite. The amenities are pretty frugal, but I don't mind it – put it that way. Compared with some of the places I've worked, like the Yemen for instance, it's far better, yes far, far better than the Yemen.'

The construction camps at March Ridge and Mount Pleasant have provided the rumour mills of Port Stanley with a munificent supply of material for gossip and fanciful stories. Local journalists have reported gang-fights around the site, conforming to the traditional images of 'B' movies of the North American railroad construction, the Californian gold-rush and the opening of the West. One of the best rumours was that boatloads of Argentine cement were being used for the main runway – the cargoes were shipped through Punta Arenas in Chile, so the story ran. Alas, the 'Great Argy Cement Scandal' did not stand up to close scrutiny because no one had seen the boats of cement either at Punta or East Cove.

In the short term the airfield's prime use will be military – for reinforcing and changing the garrison forces and supplying the air force contingents with urgently needed crews and equipment. The RAF has purchased half a dozen TriStar wide-bodied airliners from British Airways specifically for the route from Brize Norton in Oxfordshire for the Falklands via Dakar or Ascension. The TriStars will cut the journey south from Ascension by almost a half, making it in seven or eight hours rather than thirteen or fourteen by Hercules Transport.

There is little mystery about the military function of the Mount Pleasant airfield, but there are puzzling aspects about present plans for its commercial use. Few commercial airlines have expressed interest in running sporadic services via Ascension, and it would be very difficult to make such an operation profitable; there is unlikely to be sufficient payload in passengers and freight to justify more than one or two flights a month. The second Shackleton Report makes it quite plain that the commercial services are far more likely to succeed if they work from Montevideo in Uruguay or Punta Arenas in Chile. But both have commercial disadvantages: Montevideo is poorly connected to the main international air routes in South America, and Punta would be a mere staging-post in a long flight to Santiago to pick up regular intercontinental services. There is an outside possibility of a link to Rio de Janeiro but this might prove costly, with little chance of turning a profit. The previous commercial air operation to South America was that of the Argentine airline, LADE, from Stanley to Comodoro Rivadavia, which ran from 1972 to 1982. The best possible route from a practical and commercial point of view would still be via Comodoro, or, even better, to Buenos Aires, but obviously, this is politically impossible in the foreseeable future. Cynics have said that commercially the Mount Pleasant airport could rapidly prove a white elephant; others in the United Kingdom have gone further in suggesting that the airport will serve to enhance the value of the Falklands in an eventual deal with Argentina. The Argentine government, however, has seen nothing attractive about the construction of the airfield and has asked Britain to desist from the project, described as 'a needlessly provocative and aggressive' act.

One aspect of the airfield project at Mount Pleasant which raised a few eyebrows in Port Stanley is the amount paid to the FIC for the acquisition of the site. On 10 April 1984, Lord Trefgarne, a junior minister at the MoD, told the House of Lords how the sum had been calculated: 'The price paid for the 8300 acres was £55,000. In addition the normal severance compensation has been paid and was assessed to be £100,000. The construction of the airfield necessitates the resiting of Mount Pleasant House and other farm facilities and services to enable farming operations to continue, the cost of which is £83,877.'

Ted Needham, chairman of the FIC, has said that the contract was worked out by lawyers working for the MoD and the London firm of Slaughter and May, who were working on behalf of the FIC. The Mount Pleasant site was originally part of the FIC's farm at Fitzroy, the smallest of the Company's farms on East Falkland. In the 1982–3 season the farm ran 26,103 sheep, of which 25,287 were shorn; in the same year the

Walker Creek and Darwin farm, one of the biggest sheep ranches in the southern hemisphere, ran 112,669 sheep of which 105,659 were shorn, and at the third FIC farm in East Falkland, North Arm, 64,872 sheep were shorn out of a total of 70,823 (SOA Falkland Islands Farming Statistics 1982–3). The airfield project has cut a swathe out of the Fitzroy Farm from East Cove, across Mare Harbour and to Mount Pleasant, March Ridge, where a chunk of land of about 8000 acres was taken. The land is said to be good pasture by Falklands standards, though not necessarily the best in the Islands. Needham said he and his manager at Fitzroy, Councillor Ron Binney, felt that the farm would be so disrupted by the building of the airport, and its operations after it opened that they offered the whole of it to the MoD; but the Ministry refused, as it did not want to get involved in running a Falklands farm. Mount Pleasant House has been used as a shepherd's refuge, with sleeping-bags and equipment for anyone seeking shelter in an emergency; it was also a base for seasonal work. The price for the land is high in comparison with the sums paid for the different sections on the Packe Brothers' estate on West Falkland in 1983; the quality of the land there is variable but some of it is reported to be good pasture. Farm buildings and houses have frequently been resited in the settlements. One of the farming families who acquired a section in the subdivision of the former FIC farm at Green Patch, Peter and Margie Goss, dragged a house three miles overland from the Green Patch settlement to their homestead at Horseshoe Bay; it is doubtful whether the exercise cost them anywhere like £83,877.

Some of the land, at least, had been part of a Crown Grant of 1903, during Edward VII's reign. The difficulty of land transactions in the Islands arises in part from the fact that so little was surveyed properly before the first settlers started to carve out the farms. The agreement of the Crown Grant of 1903 allows the public authorities to take back up to one twentieth of the land for utilities such as roads and bridges, except in areas where buildings and gardens have been erected. Because, un-surprisingly, the word airfield is not mentioned, the lawyers decided not to invoke this clause. A later clause mentions that compensation could be paid where, 'any damage is sustained by reason of severance of the land acquired affecting the arnings of the claimant at the time of appropri-ation'. According to a law officer in Stanley, the Crown could have resorted to a compulsory purchase, but preferred to work on a basis of mutual agreement between the parties. Two important points in the final settlement were that a business at Fitzroy Farm had been damaged con-siderably and the fact that the airfield had to be prepared quickly. None the less the sum agreed by the MoD has put a high price, by local farming standards, on a piece of Falklands pasture and this has affected the prices demanded subsequently for land in the Islands.

Though the airport is the biggest single new project on the Islands, the most important aspect of the current development plans is that concerning the land, landowning and farming. The aim is to give small farms to as many Islanders as want them, to improve and diversify agriculture and secondary industries, such as the production of woollen garments and hides. A new Falkland Islands Development Corporation (FIDC) has been formed under a Chief Executive, assisted by a full-time General Manager and Farm Management Officer to oversee the land programme. This is the crucial part of the development plans for the Islands, proposed by Lord Shackleton and adopted by Mrs Thatcher's government in December 1982. The success of land reform has a symbolic as much as practical significance as a test of the viability of the Falklands' economy and community.

# The New Farming

Since Lord Shackleton's team visited the Islands in the mid-seventies only three of the thirty-seven holdings and estates they saw first-hand have been bought from overseas landowners and subdivided. Each of the three was bought by the Falklands government, who provided mortgages and loans for twenty purchasers of the subdivisions, sections of about 14–20,000 acres each. In early 1984 the directors of by now the most famous farm on the Falklands, at San Carlos, where the British paratroops and Royal Marines landed on 21 May 1982, agreed to sell. The Falkland Islands government did not purchase the farm outright as they had in the three previous cases but have provided partial loans and mortgages for some of the Islanders who have said they would like to own a section of San Carlos. The vendors have valued the property at £518,000, whereas the ODA and the Falkland Islands government put its value at £360,000, and the latter refused loans altogether to several of the applicants. The Falkland Islands government has also been in dispute with the six section-holders at Roy Cove over the distribution of the first year's profits. Roy Cove was sold in 1980 for about £190,000, and the section-holders were due to take up their small farms on 2 April 1982, the day of the Argentine invasion. The Falkland Islands government proposed that the whole of Roy Cove should be farmed together for the first year, but the late arrival of two of the new purchasers led to the dispute over profits.

The land-reform programme has not got off to a good start. At the first farm to be sold, at Green Patch in East Falkland, the section-holders, who took up their land in 1980, were left to fend for themselves. At the second estate to be sold, Roy Cove on West Falkland, as we have seen, the Falkland Islands government has been in dispute with its mortgagees. The third farm, the Packe Brothers' three holdings on West Falkland, was sold to the government for a round sum of £500,000, though the Islands' own agricultural research unit had recommended a valuation of £400,000, which the ODA later raised to £450,000. The government later raised the price to £500,000, for the development potential of Fox Bay East which they said would become a new village settlement. Most of the new section-holders of the Packe's estate moved onto their land in September 1983. Ten months later most had not seen a contract and had little idea of how long they had to repay their mortgage and at what rate. One unfortunate farmer revealed to a government official that he did not understand what a mortgage was. He thought he had received a loan from the government at simple interest, which would involve one payment of eleven per cent.

Following the sale of the Packe's farms, only one other big sale of land has been in prospect, that of San Carlos, which has involved vendors and government in acrimonious exchanges. The agent for the vendors in the sale has been Mr Colin Smith of the Wool Agency, J. G. Field of Bradford, who sell wool from many of the independent Falklands farms. He is an ardent supporter of the Shackleton land-reform programme. Like Ted Needham, Mr Smith takes a great, and sometimes quixotic, interest in the Falklands, which extends beyond the mere making of money. Both men provide possibly the most stimulating conversation on the commercial and social future of the place to be had, and are often better informed than government officials, either local or in Whitehall.

Colin Smith has asked for £518,000 for the buildings, 102,000 acres and 28,500 sheep of San Carlos. A parcel of land has been given to the Commonwealth War Graves Commission and the graveyard of Colonel 'H' Jones, VC, and his colleagues stands there today. The Falkland Islands government and, latterly, the Development Corporation have offered loans up to a value of £360,000, but Smith has said that the company will make loans to applicants up to the price he has put on the property. This price is based on several factors, principally the sum the Falklands government was prepared to pay for the Packe Brothers' estate. The holdings of Packe's on West Falkland covered considerably more ground than San Carlos but only 1750 more sheep were being offered. Recent figures show San Carlos to have declared a far greater profit to shareholders than Packe's; however, in 1980 Packe's recorded a pretax profit of £5576.98, and in 1982 San Carlos declared a pretax profit £40,813.59. (Some caution has to be taken with these figures for different years, because, as already explained in discussion of the second Shackleton Report, 1980 was a bad year for wool prices.) Smith has also argued that if a value-added element has been put in both the price the Falklands government paid for the Packe's estate and the compensation paid for the Mount Pleasant airfield for development potential, then a similar allowance must be made in the valuation of San Carlos. San Carlos, after all, has a deep-water anchorage capable of taking the *Canberra,* the *Norland* and the *Fearless*. Both the Falklands Development Corporation and Colin Smith have offered generous terms to the new farmers initially, setting interest on the mortgage loans at two per cent below bank rate at least. However, many of the new section-holders have very limited working capital, and undercapitalisation is likely to be a continuing problem for the smaller farmers despite the generous improvement grants announced by the FIDC. Some of the overseas-owned farms have hardly returned a profit at all in some years recently, and they have no mortgages or outstanding loan debts. Some of the new farmers, on the other hand, will be spending between a third and half of their gross income from wool on mortgage repayments for the next twenty to twenty-five years.

Two years after the Argentines went away, the land-reform programme has had several tangles to resolve. The method of valuation and prices has seemed confused, and so initially was the way the Falklands government treated the new owner-occupiers of the land. Far from being the programme of comprehensive purchase of land from absentee landowners, the subdivision of the farms has been partial, to say the least.

One of those most closely interested in the division of the land has been Bill Luxton, the biggest private owner-occupier on West Falkland. His family came to Chartres in the 1860s, and the fine farmhouse there is proof of the settlement's vintage. Bill, his wife, Patricia, and their son, Stephen, are ardent British Falklanders. All three were deeply affected by their enforced deportation by the head of the occupying Argentine military police, Major Patricio Dowling, at the end of April 1982. In gratitude to the British forces for liberating the Islands, Bill leased thousands of acres of his farm for training ranges at the nominal rent of £1, and Colin Smith did likewise at San Carlos.

Bill Luxton has the reputation of being a good, tough landlord and farmer, and he is one of the most forthright men on the Islands. Since 1981 he has been a nominated member of the Executive Council. Though a hereditary landowner, he is fanatically in favour of the subdivision of land and the policy of giving as many Falklanders as possible the opportunity to farm their own piece of land. At the time of the sale Bill was both chairman of the board of directors and a shareholder of Packe Brothers' estates. He told me he had to declare his interest in the deliberations of the Executive Council, but then was consulted by the councillors about the position of the vendors. 'He was in and out of the room like a yo-yo,' one of his friends said. Bill's own conversation is spattered with colourful expletives and hyperbole, and he quite clearly loves an argument with anyone he considers 'simpatico'. When I spoke to him in April 1984 he said he was concerned about the way the land division programme was going. 'Very, very worried indeed,' was how he put it with characteristic vehemence. 'The major emphasis now should be on land,' he went on, 'but it looks very much as if it is receiving the least emphasis at the moment. After the sale of Packe's and San Carlos it looks like the dead end. In the interest of the Islands the people who farm the land should own it and live on it. A farmer has got to be interested in the land, and it's not a big company business now.'

Strangely, the biggest farmer on East Falkland, Robin Pitaluga, chairman of the SOA, takes an opposite view. He considers much of the Falklands can only be farmed profitably in big units, and the subdivision programme must unfold slowly if overall profitability of agriculture is not to be impaired. Pitaluga's family also arrived in the mid-nineteenth century, originating from Gibraltar where they are still a prominent clan, and his farm at Salvador in East Falkland, appropriately, is called Gibraltar Station. His conversation is as easy and relaxed as Luxton's is vehement. He too has a high reputation as a farmer and landlord, and is generally reckoned by the experts to run the best large owner-occupied farm in East Falkland. Also like Luxton, he took a close interest in the sale of the Packe Brothers' farms, and led the committee granting government loans to the new farmers.

But what of the men seeking the loans and the prize of farming their own section of land in the Falklands? On a cool but fine April morning I paid a return visit to the manager's house at San Carlos to see Pat Short, whom I had first met in May 1982. I arrived in style, for Captain Colin MacGregor had generously given me passage from Port Stanley in *Endurance,* which was to pick up a team who had been surveying Port San Carlos. As we neared the opening to San Carlos Water, the sea fog filled the loch stretching from the mountains on either side like a huge, white bed bolster. Passing Fanning Head the ship was trailed by a school of pilot whales. The last time I had passed that way I had stood on the roof of the bridge of the ferry MV *Norland* with Colonel 'H' Jones, Major Chris Keeble and my colleague David Norris of the *Daily Mail,* looking through a night telescope for Argentine camp-fires. Once *Endurance* came to anchor I was whisked to the grass airstrip of San Carlos by helicopter. Pat Short was there to meet me, but his wife Isobel said she had given up waiting because she thought it must be somebody else in the gaily painted machine, like an exotic hornet with its red stripes.

Inside the farmhouse Pat told me of the sale of San Carlos and how he expected to buy two sections, 17,000 acres, 7200 sheep and the manager's house, for £134,000. He said he hoped to put down ten per cent and borrow the rest at eleven per cent over twenty years from the government. I replied that this seemed to incur a very large amount of repayment if he was to make at least as much money as he was getting as manager. 'Yes,' he said, 'eleven per cent is far too much, I think. There's not going to be very much at all by the time I've paid the freight, the shearing gang, and the mortgage. In 1983–4 there has been a very good wool clip, earning well over a £100,000 gross. Yes, it is going to be a very tight margin.' 'So why are you going ahead?' I asked.

Pat then replied with a statement which should be burned into the brains of anyone interested in any future for the Falklands, whether governor, councillor, administrator, bureaucrat or legislator in Whitehall or Westminster, or simply an interested observer. With the slow and almost lilting delivery of the Kelper, Pat said: 'I've been here [at San Carlos] now for four years. I've done a bit of shifting around in my time, and I feel I want to settle down and would like a piece of the land. There's better land that could come up, but only if I wait. There's supposed to be a gradual approach to cutting up land, but I can't wait too much longer. I am forty-four now, so it'll be fifteen years more of my working life . . . I hope my son will get an interest and take over from me.'

Because of the dispute over the valuation of San Carlos Pat Short was given a loan of £60,359 on one section only. The balance of the price for that section was lent by the vendors' agent Colin Smith, a sum of £36,141, as well as the entire price of the second smaller section, which was sold for £37,500. Colin Smith and his company have lent his one-time employees and others buying the sections of the San Carlos estate about £250,000, half the selling price in mortgage terms. Interest has been set for the first year at 8.5 per cent and repayment of principal at five per cent. This means that Pat Short will be repaying Colin Smith's company £9,941.54 in his first year as owner of the two sections of San Carlos at Salt Point. The Development Corporation has delayed payments of interest and principal for the first year, and after that interest will be at two per cent below base rate.

In his second year Pat Short could be laying out £18,000 in mortgage repayments, over half the calculated income from the two sections in the 1983–4 season, just before the San Carlos subdivision. In addition he will have fuel and freight bills for his wool and the cost of hiring casual labour to help with shearing. This allows a narrow margin for profit and investment, though he will benefit from improvement grants of up to fifty per cent offered by the Development Corporation for breeding stock, fences, buildings and seed.

Everyone who knew him spoke of Pat's qualities as a farmer and how deserving he was of getting the manager's house and the central block of the San Carlos land, though these are by no means the best sections of the farm. Pat Short's record of success or failure should be made the acid test of the credibility and record of the Falklands Development Council in its main task, the redistribution and increased productivity of the land.

After our conversation in the kitchen of the main farmhouse Pat and I walked down to the cemetery. After a few minutes we heard the Falkland Island Air Service's Islander aircraft and soon it appeared, a bright-red speck against the hillside where the marines had dug their defences and the positions for the Rapier missile batteries.

The Islander's next destination was Port Howard on West Falkland, a place I had seen only under distant puffs of smoke from artillery fire in May 1982. Flying across Falkland Sound my eye was confused by the strings of small islands and sandbanks below, yellow, green and brown with the heavy kelp beds which surrounded them like coils of rusty barbed wire. It was hard to work out where the line of the Sound itself parted the two big islands of East and West Falkland. It was here that HMS *Ardent* fought to her last, many of her crew just boys in their teens, the glow of the blue ball of flame as she blew up in the dark still a vivid local memory. HMS *Antelope*, her sister ship, was mortally hit in the same waters, and other ships were struck as they covered the men struggling to build defences and conceal their positions in the all too open landscape of the rolling moor on the eastern shore. In these waters the brave pilots of the Fuerza Area of Argentina came time and again and some fell to their deaths ambushed by patrols of Harriers or the machine-guns and missiles on the land. Very little remains to recall those strange days of late May and early June 1982. On the headland a small cross commemorates HMS *Ardent,* and a solitary buoy in San Carlos Water indicates where the wreck of HMS *Antelope* lies.

Port Howard is one of the most attractive Falkland settlements. The white houses with red roofs sit in a glen, huddling under a tall bluff of rock. The airstrip is a gently rising field beyond the houses. We were met by a gaggle of men, women, children and dogs. I had come to see Jimmy and Ginny Forster, who had bought a section of the Packe's land on the other side of the creek. Port Howard itself is the property of the Waldron family interest, owners who scarcely conform to the image of a negligent absentee landlord. The Waldron family and their heirs, apparently, believe in the estate being farmed in the best interest of the families working there, and take almost no profit at all away from the place. The managers have for some years been the Lee family, and in recent times the post has alternated between brothers, Robin and Rodney Lee. The whole settlement, from the individual houses to the store and the school, radiate well-being. As we passed through the settlement in the Land-Rover a man and a young woman were mending posts and rails over a low bridge; the pond, the bridge, the houses on the hill beyond could as well have been a village deep in rural England, fit for the front cover of *Country Life*.

I was taken first to the home of Bill Pole-Evans, Jimmy Forster's brother-in-law. Bill has two brothers and three sisters and his father is the manager of Saunders Island, which is owned by Hamilton Brothers, a Jersey-based company whose beneficiaries live in Argentina. Pole-Evans would like to take over Saunders in partnership with his niece, Norma, and her husband, Roger Edwards, a commander in the Royal Navy. Negotiations for the island and the other part of the Hamilton estate in West Falkland, Weddell Island, have proved embarrassingly tricky. At first the Falkland Islands government considered compulsory purchase, but the trustees and the main heirs of the estate, the family of Penelope Hamilton, who live in Buenos Aires, refused. Next, a ninety-nine-year lease was offered by the government and this too has been refused. The record of investment in the farms on Weddell and Saunders has been lamentable, according to the Pole-Evans family. Tony Pole-Evans was given a new tractor recently, though he did not want one; he needed instead many other improvements to the buildings and fences. He was told he had to take the tractor because they had bought one for Weddell as well. The FIDC will have to continue to unravel the problem of the West Falkland estate owned by an heiress in Argentina; it is likely to be the most complicated of all the thorny land deals they have to handle.

The Pole-Evans family are acknowledged for prowess in one field above others; they are wizards with short-wave wireless. Tony Pole-Evans has built up contacts halfway round the world since the thirties. He used to know most of the English-speaking radio hams in Patagonia, who, he said, would tell him what a dismal regime had taken over

Argentina with the military junta. Bill Pole-Evans helped build the two-metre band radio repeater on the hill above Port Howard. Following the conflict the Amateur Radio Association of Great Britain offered to fund three more radio masts to enhance communication within the Falklands and to the world beyond. As part of the Shackleton development package it was proposed to spend up to £1 million on improving telephones and radio communication throughout the Islands. A feasibility study was commissioned from British Telecom for £25,000; two affable engineers spent a few weeks touring the Islands and studying the manual phone exchange in Stanley. They came to the conclusion fairly rapidly that the settlements in camp had got the most economical system with the two-metre band radios, and all £1 million would buy was an automatic telephone system for Stanley, which would involve considerable re-curring expenses for maintenance. I was told all this behind the back of the hand as the two-metre system is not legal; the official radio net for camp is a high-frequency radio which has poor reception in many areas. Not surprisingly, the Falkland Islands government has shelved plans for investing £1 million in a new telephone service. Much of the credit for the communications on West Falkland at least must go to Bill Pole-Evans, his father and brothers. 'The trouble with Bill,' said a friend in Port Howard, 'is he's a bloody genius, but he's just got no ambition.'

As we drove round to Packe's Port Howard farm, Jimmy Forster explained why he had decided to buy the section there, 14,650 acres, 3000 sheep, a settlement house and paddocks, for £60,000. The Land-Rover skirted the inlet, which resembled a small Highland loch, separating the section from the main settlement farm of Port Howard. At the house, hardly in the first flush of youth and the best of repair, were the rest of the family, his wife Ginny, their three children and Ginny's sister, always known in the family as Biffo, who was on a visit from Pebble Island. Biffo, in her heavy black sweater, had more than a passing resemblance to the heroic bear of the comic cartoon in *The Beano* from which she took her nickname. Her husband, Raymond, was about to take over as manager of Pebble Island from his father, Grif Evans. Raymond had just been to New Zealand to study farming there; un-fortunately, he had to pay for himself and travel on a tourist visa, for it seems that no one in the Falklands public administration, nor the Foreign Office, could obtain for him even the most temporary work permit.

In the sitting-room of the farmhouse, still undergoing radical over-haul, Jimmy and Ginny explained that they had taken up residence the previous September. The house was little more than a shack and the buildings were in need of maintenance and repair, and still were after six months of occupation. Jimmy had come to the Islands seventeen years before as a contract labourer from Stockport in Cheshire where he had been made redundant as a steelworker. Four years ago he became the section manager at the Dunnose Head farm of the Packe's estate. Their reasons for taking the new land were remarkably similar to those given by Pat Short: 'We felt we had to take the chance when it came,' said Jimmy. 'If we didn't take it now there was no way we would have done it in the future, because the prices are going to rise anyway. As a business proposition I wouldn't say it was all that attractive, and the interest repayment does knock rather a big hole in the wool cheque at the end of the year.'

The terms originally offered by the Falkland Islands government loans committee were a mortgage of £54,000 at eleven per cent, repayable over twenty years. At least that is what the Forsters think the deal was, for they had no detailed confirmation in writing, no contract from the government and no copy of the deeds. Many of the farmers on the Packe's sections went nine months without any confirmation of how they were to repay their mortgages. One family at Dunnose Head told me, 'They treat us as yokels out here. Since we moved in September 1983 no one has come to see us and find out how we were getting on and proposed to pay the mortgage. We fear that at least one of the new farmers will give up or go under in less than three years' time. My husband was told he could come in to Stanley [in July 1983] and decide which way he wanted to repay his mortgage. The Attorney-General's office said they had devised two methods for repayment, but when my husband said he could come to town and would like an appointment, they said they hadn't quite decided what the two methods were yet.'

Since I met Jimmy and Ginny at Packe's Port Howard South in April 1984, the FIDC, guided by David Taylor and Simon Armstrong, the General Manager, have brought in very generous mortgage repayment terms. Fifty-per-cent grants for stock, seed and equipment and buildings have been announced, and these could rise to sixty per cent where two or more farmers agreed to buy machines and buildings and jetties as a co-operative. The scheme devised by Taylor and Armstrong, which is very similar to the grants given to marginal land farmers in Britain, apparently did not find favour with the Executive Council in Stanley or the Overseas Development Administration, who wanted loans and not subsidies. The Forsters' neighbour, Tim Miller at Many Branch Farm, has calculated that the new grants will allow him to split his land into six big fields, or 'camps' as they are known, in little over a year, whereas with no financial help it might have taken him several seasons to complete.

Even with the generous loan terms and the revolutionary policy of improvement grants introduced by the FIDC, families like the Forsters will hardly be living in luxury and creaming fat profits from their new holdings. Initially their income from wool would be about £16,000 a year. The main outgoings would be freight, fuel, insurance, and contract labour for shearing. The biggest overhead is likely to be fencing and repair for buildings and machinery. Traditional fencing costs £2500 a mile at least in the Falklands, and electric fencing with glass fibre posts, which is not suitable for all terrain, can cost as little as £800 or £900 a mile. In the first few years Jimmy Forster has to replace several miles of fences for his paddocks and camps and this will cost over £1000 a mile even with improvement grants. In the first few months at least, Jimmy said he often wondered if he might have been better off in his old job as section manager at Dunnose Head.

The conversation in the room was suddenly drowned by the roaring of a jet overhead. As we ran out of the house, we could see the black smoke trails and the slug-grey fuselage of a Phantom as it climbed over the hills to the north. In a few minutes it returned, making a low pass down the valley, which the pilot, apparently a friend of the Forsters, repeated several times. It was hard to work out whether he was photographing the creek or just showing off. Low flying over settlements is not allowed, but families, the children especially, love such air displays. The sheep and cattle did not seem to mind much either, but I was terrified that on the last of the passes, little more than thirty or forty feet from the ground, the plane was about to take the roof off the barn and the henhouse and end up in pieces amongst the audience. But the pilot pulled the nose up just in time, and with a roar of the afterburners and a victory roll over the steep green hillside it was away across Falkland Sound, homeward bound for Port Stanley.

After the aerobatic interlude, Ginny Forster explained why she had wanted to live near Port Howard. Ginny has a radiant face like a rising moon, a slow smile to go with her speech, which has the Falklands characteristic of rising at the end of each sentence. She said the main attraction was to be near a settlement and for the possibility of her two older daughters going to the school there. In this she was disappointed, as the school at Port Howard was full and she had to do most of the teaching herself at home; a travelling teacher arrived for a few days every six weeks, and most of these were unqualified. Ginny is a partner in the farm and seems to do two days' work in one, inside the house and on the land. She described how she had spent the day before my visit in April 1984:

*Opposite* New airport site, Mount Pleasant, East Falkland

The Argentine war cemetery, East Falkland

*Left* Kelp goose and upland goose, Horseshoe Bay, East Falkland. Six upland geese can eat as much grass as one sheep. *Right* June Goodwin stacking peat at Horseshoe Bay, one of the Green Patch farms. Across the water, Teal Inlet and the mountains above San Carlos

FIPASS, the new military flexible port and storage system at Port Stanley

Autumn sunlight on the roofs of Port Stanley, March 1984

267

Port Stanley looking west towards Mount Kent and Two Sisters

The Falkland Islands Company jetty and offices, Port Stanley, the centre of internal and external trade for most Islanders and farms

Port Stanley, looking east towards the town hall

HMS *Penelope* and HMS *Liverpool* alongside *Bar Protector* for maintenance,
San Carlos Water

Putting out the last of the fire on 10 April 1984 at the King Edward Memorial Hospital, Port Stanley, in which eight people died

The remains of the Hospital after the fire. Only the Churchill Wing, built in the fifties, was left standing

The new schoolhouse, Goose Green; at £60,000 it cost just over a third of the price of one of the new Brewster houses in Stanley

Phantom aircraft making a low pass at Packe's Port Howard, West Falkland

San Carlos Cemetery where men who died in May and June 1982 are buried. It was designed by the Commonwealth War Graves Commission and is tended by the local community

272

'We got up and I made a hot drink. Then we went out to milk the cow. We came in and I made the breakfast before settling down to one and a half to two hours' homework. This involves writing the diary and we do at least two pages of maths. We also do some English and history. We're writing an essay on the Stone Age at the moment. We always do a few pages' reading each morning, too. The teacher comes every six weeks and we get postal courses from Stanley. After we tidied the dishes, we washed the clothes and did some cooking, because the cake and bread tins were looking pretty empty. By then it was lunchtime.

'In the afternoon we went out carting peat. We thought we were doing pretty well so we decided to stop for tea. But after tea we got too greedy; we overloaded the Unimog[the truck] and it got bogged. We didn't get home till nearly dark, about six-thirty. We had fish for supper, and tea-berries and cream, and then it was time for washing and our baths.

'We don't have video; we have to save our pennies. In the evenings we play a game or read. The other night we played hare and tortoise. Quite often we repair the house after the children have gone to bed.'

All this activity is a working day in the slack season of the farming year. Ginny spent nearly a year in England after she got married. She said she liked England but felt lonely and missed the attraction of the Falklands, which she described as, 'just a good life, a very good life for us. It's so peaceful and everyone here is friendly. If we're in difficulty we can always call on help from our friends or the family. Everybody's friends here.' Strangely, West Falkland appears to be a friendlier community than East Falkland; it has a much smaller and more scattered population, with none of the tensions and complexities of Stanley.

The loans and grants for farmers like the Forsters and Pat Short are now administered by the Development Corporation, which opened for business in June 1984. The FIDC was one of the major institutional proposals of the Shackleton plan and is firmly modelled on the Highlands and Islands Development Board in Scotland, though how much it has been adapted to the peculiar circumstances of the Falklands today is not immediately clear. The Corporation is headed by the Chief Executive, another office devised by Lord Shackleton's team, who has some of the functions of the old Chief Secretary of the Islands' administration. The Secretary's responsibilities have been split, part going to the Chief Executive and part, the control of the different government departments, going to an FO civil servant appointed from London. The Chief Executive has three main roles: member of the Falklands government; director of development outside the Development Corporation; and head of the Development Corporation itself.

The man chosen for the new post, at a salary of £35,000 a year plus allowances, was David Taylor, a former colonial civil servant whose most recent job was head of a subsidiary of the Booker McConnell combine with responsibilities in East Africa, Malawi, the West Indies, Guyana and Zambia, though most of his work, he says, was London-based. At the age of fifty he was 'head-hunted' for the Falklands job, and was evidently flattered but daunted by the prospect. 'The Falklands responsibility has now become enormously complicated in relation to its size,' he told me. He added that he decided to take the job for three years to see how it worked out, and there would be an option of going on for a further two, if the Shackleton proposals for the role of Chief Executive are adhered to.

Taylor is a difficult subject to interview, even by the extravagant standards of circumlocution and reticence of the Falklands. His natural shyness makes him wary of the microphone or the reporter's notebook. On our first encounter we spent much of the time discussing the pros and cons of accepting the new post and the difficulties in getting to know the Island community well. In his discourse he has the businessman's ability to set a scale of priorities and will give precise figures of costings of the various development projects under his direction. I have only met him twice, in Stanley in March 1984 and in July at the London office of the Falkland Islands government. At the second interview he merely up-dated and elaborated the schedule of expenditure for development in the Islands, on which the £31 million of the Shackleton money is to be spent, which he had described at our first meeting.

A large proportion of the Shackleton money, as he described the plan, is to go on infrastructure: a new power station and water system for Port Stanley, and funding for roads and the deep-water jetty. In July 1984 £3.5 million had been allocated for the much-needed power station; the foundations had been laid and new generator sets were on their way from England. Progress had not been so rapid for the new water system, which had been delayed because of lack of manpower in the winter in the Royal Engineers contingent. The water-supply would first be needed for the Royal Navy and for merchant ships replenishing their tanks. Plans for the new jetty were still 'up in the air', according to David Taylor in July 1984, as the project could well cost three times the original Shackleton projection of £3–5 million, and for the time being civilians could use the army's Lego-style wharf at FIPASS at the Canache. The proposal to spend £1 million on improvements in telephone and radio communications had been temporarily shelved, too. £2.6 million is to be spent on expanding FIARDC and £1.25 million on improving and expanding the school hostel, which will mean as many children from camp as need to can attend the secondary school in Port Stanley. £3.5 million has been allocated for salary supplements and allowances for OSAS workers and to pay their fares to and from England. In July it was thought that about forty such officers would be working in the Islands. £1.5 million is to be devoted to a 'rolling' housing scheme, where houses are built for £50,000 each, for sale to Islanders and immigrants. £1 million has been put aside for land purchase, though quite how this will be used is not clear as there are no further sales in prospect following the break-up of San Carlos. Working capital of £4.6 million has been allocated for the Development Corporation over five years, though there will be separate funds for specialised fishery projects.

The two inshore fishery schemes are to be based at Fox Bay East, where it is hoped to start a new village, a project unique for the Falklands as it will not be dependent on one single farm estate, which hitherto has been the pattern for camp settlements. £908,000 has been put forward for two years to fund an inshore fishery by a new Falklands venture called Fortoser, which will employ five or six men and one boat brought by its owner, John Williams, from Humberside. The fishery will concentrate on shellfish, scallops and crabs. Salmon-ranching will also take place at Fox Bay or at Camilla Creek, where 2 Para hid in the grasslands the day before taking Port Darwin in May 1982. Stirling University has carried out a preliminary study for the scheme, which is likely to be chancy; the study suggests that it will be eight years before the runs yield any form of return. There is some debate about the most appropriate species for the Falklands creeks and streams, and BAS life scientists say that the wrong strategy could be damaging to the ecological balance of existing species and their food. None the less £500,000 has been allocated to the pilot project and David Taylor says that at least two commercial firms in America and Britain are showing real interest in the possibilities of Falklands salmon. With both shellfish and salmon, packaging and shipping to markets more than 8000 miles away is likely to prove a large obstacle to commercial viability, particularly as there is every indication that the North American and European demand for salmon seems more than adequately catered for.

The symbol of success for the new economic order Taylor and his colleagues hope is now about to dawn in the Falklands is to be the FIDC and all its works. The main role of the FIDC will be the direction of the subdivision of the big farms that come on the market. It will supervise those mortgages already granted for Green Patch, Roy Cove, Packe's and San Carlos and advise farmers on improvement and investment.

The FIDC's work is not entirely in the field of agriculture and fishery. It has advanced money for one or two small manufacturing enterprises.

£7000 has been granted for a new bakery established by an entrepreneur called Simon Powell who has made a name for himself for a successful fast-food business in Port Stanley specialising in muttonburgers. Simon comes from a family with strong army connections; both he and his wife, Sarah, have had relations in the Queen's Dragoon Guards. They both decided to try their luck on a short-term venture in the Falklands, and besides the fast-food and the bakery, Simon also hires motorbikes to soldiers in the garrison and Islanders who want to take off for the mountains for the weekend.

Simon looks like a character from a novel by Evelyn Waugh or Anthony Powell; a winsome smile and diffident manner of speech hide a sharp business acumen. He and Sarah managed the coup of the Stanley social calendar when they decided to get married there in March. Morning suits were shipped quickly from London via Hercules air transporter from Ascension. General Spacie gave the bride away and Sir Rex and Lady Hunt staged the reception at Government House, Sir Rex in full regalia, cocked hat with plume and red striped uniform.

Simon Powell has made it plain that he does not intend to stay for ever, but meanwhile his bakery is filling a big gap both for the people of Port Stanley and the garrison. The defence secretary's paper of October 1983 on the Falklands mentioned the need for the civilian population to help supply services like laundries, shoe repairs, a barber's shop, a butchery and even a dairy. This could have been a real short-term business opportunity for the Islanders and new immigrants, but there were no houses for the latter and the services have had to supply their own facilities, at considerable expense. The MoD is said to have offered to fund in part a new dairy to replace the one put out of business by the Argentines, whose mines blew up many of the cows and ruined the pastures of the old one. Two years after the end of the conflict there is still no new dairy, though the FIARDC is to put £160,000 into one. The main garrison bakery before Simon Powell started his business was used by Montgomery's Eighth Army in the Western Desert in 1943 and recalled for active duty in the Falklands from an army museum.

The most important manufacturing project funded by the FIDC is the wool mill at Fox Bay which will be run by Richard and Griselda Cockwell. They are two of the most attractive talkers in the Islands, pouring out verbal cascades of pure enthusiasm, fresh as a mountain stream. Richard was manager at Packe's for more than a dozen years and in 1980 decided he would like to create a small woollen and knitwear industry based at Fox Bay. He reasons that this would enormously enhance the value of wool exports from the Falklands. Instead of wool being exported raw at about £3 a kilo, it would be sold at £25 a kilo as manufactured knitwear. The FIDC has lent him £130,000 and he will employ two or three men at first. The launch of the project has been far from easy; first, the conflict intervened, and then finding the right machinery and product line took far longer than expected. Machines and knitwear designs have been prepared by the Scottish College of Textiles at Galashiels, and two tons of wool have been bought for the first run from Councillor Tony Blake, who bought the Packe's holding at Little Chartres. The machinery is second-hand and arrived a year behind schedule. Fox Bay has a reputation for erratic water-supply, which means that the mill can offer only limited facilities for scouring wool before it is exported to England (this reduces the weight of wool by washing out sand and dirt). In addition, the transport of the garments by air or sea to Britain and America could prove costly. The Cockwells will also suffer disadvantages in communicating with the outside world; to place an international phone call or have a conversation by telex they will have to take the plane to Port Stanley. The fledgling Development Corporation announced its terms for support of the Cockwells' wool mill in the latter part of 1984. Of the £130,000 of public finance for the project, £85,000 was provided by a soft loan and the balance took the form of an issue of 45,000 ordinary £1 shares. The Cockwells themselves raised additional working capital of £30,000 privately. Residents at Fox Bay chipped in funds for a co-operative to provide a village shop. After all the travails and delays in buying and shipping the machines for the wool plant, plans were laid to provide finished garments for the Falklands market by Christmas. In addition to the labour force of three working in the mill at Fox Bay, the Cockwells were given the help of two members of the Development Corporation to serve as directors giving advice in book-keeping, administration and marketing strategy.

Griselda Cockwell was one of the most realistic of all the people I met on West Falkland in March and April 1984. She said she realised that time was limited for development in the Falklands. Governments change quickly, she recognised, and with them whole policies. As she talked she displayed some beautiful scarves and sweaters, which had the natural fine quality of Falklands wool, on the kitchen table. Griselda certainly has confidence in the products but, she told me bluntly, 'there's going to be no future in the Falklands unless we make it in the next year or two.'

Over thirty years ago a similar development project to the wool mill was planned for a trade in frozen mutton from East Falkland. A slaughterhouse and refrigeration plant were built at Ajax Bay on San Carlos Water. The new plant operated for only two or three seasons before it was closed. Few farmers, it seems, were prepared to ship their stock to such a remote spot and the plant itself had defects: for example, the floors were level and therefore the blood of the slaughtered animals did not drain easily. Even today it is unlikely that a frozen meat or fat lamb trade could be established in the Islands. The Shackleton Reports claim it would be too expensive to bring slaughtering standards to levels required by the EEC, and the smallest freezer plant and cold storage available would be larger than required for the Falklands and too expensive. Breeding output from the national flock would have to increase by about thirty-three per cent to make such a trade feasible in a way which would not detract from breeding new stock for wool. A limited trade *could* be established with the garrison, and the master butcher in the catering corps selected some twenty-five beasts at Goose Green to be driven to slaughter in Stanley. The carcasses were reasonably good he said and only a quarter had to be rejected. However, the animals were very expensive, as the butcher wanted young stock and the army was made to pay what the farmer might have expected to get from the animals' fleeces in the years to come.

The plant at Ajax Bay stayed empty for thirty years, a white elephant, a monument to an attempt to diversify Falklands agriculture. It was the wrong plant for the wrong trade in the wrong place. However, in 1982 the long sheds and the solid concrete floor made it ideal for the field hospital set up by Commander Rick Jolly and Colonel Bill MacGregor. Hundreds of Argentine and British wounded were operated on and tended there and wonders of field surgery were performed; only two of the injured who were taken there died of their wounds.

The FIDC has two full-time officers besides the Chief Executive; these are the General Manager and Farm Management Officer. According to the projection in the Shackleton Report of 1982, the salaries and allowances for the three officers will total annually about £110,000, or twice what Jimmy Forster has borrowed to buy Packe's Port Howard and roughly the same sum Pat Short has been trying to borrow from the Falklands government to buy two sections of San Carlos. The elaborate apparatus of the Development Corporation is one of the most surprising aspects of public policy in the Falklands. Many Islanders are alarmed at the amount of duplication that appears to have taken place in the appointment of farming and development advisers, particularly as they now appear to have a much narrower policy and smaller role than envisaged in Lord Shackleton's recommendations of 1982. One highly qualified public official with more than thirty years' experience of colonial administration I met when I was in Port Stanley wondered whether in the present circumstances a Development Corporation was really required at all.

The policy of land reform and redistribution has been watered down dramatically since Lord Shackleton's 1982 Report. Far from being a radical plan to acquire as many as possible of the overseas-owned farms for sale to Islanders and immigrants the official policy is now one of 'gradualism'. Farms will only be taken for redistribution as they come on to the market; this was not how things were seen by Shackleton nor by the Islanders in 1982. David Taylor told me that there is no political will in the Island's Legislative Council for either nationalisation or wholesale redistribution of absentee-controlled land. A survey following the conflict of 1982 indicated that up to sixty Islanders wanted to buy their own pieces of land. But Taylor says that many of the replies were very specific, and Islanders often stated they would want to buy one particular piece of land in one place if it came up, and did not want any piece of land that became available. However, not all councillors appear to have been pleased at the change in emphasis of the land-reform programme from a bold radical plan put forward by Shackleton to the softer gradualist approach now being adopted by the government in the Falklands and the ODA. John Cheek, who represents Port Stanley, told the Legislative Council in July 1983 that he resented the Foreign Office's inference that the Council unanimously favoured the gradualist approach following a debate on the Shackleton Report in December 1982. Cheek argued that the questionnaire on land reform had not in fact reached all Islanders but, none the less, replies to it showed that ten per cent of the population would like their own land if they had the opportunity. He continued, 'It is now obvious that gradualism, the purchase of land as it comes on the market and its redistribution, will not satisfy the demand for land.' One year after he made this speech a senior ODA official told me, 'The Falkland Islands government has enough on its plate already. It is now time to consolidate on the present position.'

The FIDC will administer loans and give advice on only four farms purchased from absentee landlords since 1976, and the public authorities have been in dispute with the section-holders or would-be purchasers of sections on two of those farms, Roy Cove and San Carlos. The one area where there has been no slowdown or gradualist approach is in the creation of advisers and administrators. In September 1984 the Falklands government has its own Agricultural Officer and Development Officer, and of course the FIDC has its General Manager. The new farmers should be able to obtain advice in agronomy, ecology, grassland culture and veterinary and animal husbandry from the twelve experts of the newly expanded FIARDC. Despite the reduction of the land-reform programme, the following advertisement appeared in the *Economist* of 28 July 1984 for a Farm Management Adviser, Falkland Islands Development Corporation:

Duties: To advise the Falkland Islands government on all economic and agricultural matters relating to land subdivision; to service loans and improve the productivity of new farms; to provide advice and assistance to farmers; to monitor the performance of subdivisions in terms of farm income, flock structures and technical matters and to maintain a set of farm management data; in collaboration with Falkland Islands Agricultural Research and Development Centre [FIARDC, now ARC] team members advise on the agricultural, economic and farm management aspects of their work with a view to facilitating appropriate shifts in the balance and direction of the research programme; to organise reciprocal visits by FIARDC scientists and farmers to the experimental sites and individual holdings. Qualifications: Applicants preferably 25-40 years, should be British citizen with a degree in agriculture, postgraduate training in farm business management and knowledge of extensive sheep farming systems.

The patronising tone of the advertisement is reminiscent of an Islander writing in the *Falkland Magazine* in 1897: 'We are ruled as if we are a colony of illiterate blacks.' The 1982 Shackleton Report takes half the space of the advertisement to describe the function of the Farm Management Adviser, which should be that of 'advising newly created small farms on farm business management', and 'the administration of agricultural grants and loans', of which the advertisement makes no mention. The newly appointed officer will be working alongside the General Manager and Chief Executive in the Development Corporation, a Development Officer for the Islands and a Government Agricultural Officer. In addition there will be the dozen or so officers of the Agricultural Research Centre offering their advice to the farmers. In all, seventeen advisers, administrators and scientists could be offering counsel to some twenty-seven small farmers whose mortgages are funded wholly or partly by public money.

Taylor was delighted with the appointment of the new General Manager, Simon Armstrong, who had been recruited from the Highlands and Islands Development Board. He had helped Lord Shackleton in preparing his recommendations, though had not been a member of the Committee on the 1982 Report. In July 1984 Taylor said that Armstrong would be using a computer he had set up for the Highlands and Islands to identify investment strategies for the new farmers. I asked Taylor what the Development Officer, created as part of the Shackleton recommendations, would be doing since there would now be a General Manager and a Farm Management Adviser at the FIDC, a Government

Agricultural Officer and the experts and advice of the ARC to help the farmers. I was told that the present Development Officer, John Reid, had a year of his contract to run, and he would be travelling round the farms thinking up new ideas for the things they might do.

Selection for the board of the Development Corporation has had an accent on youth. An Executive Councillor, Terry Peck, was appointed with Terry Betts of the GEU, Stuart Wallace who works for Cable and Wireless, Alastair Cameron the new London representative, the former acting London representative of the Falkland Islands government and heir to the Port San Carlos estate. When he was working in David Taylor's office early in 1984 Cameron had the inspiration to prepare a straightforward and clear questionnaire for those already on Packe's estate land applying for loans for San Carlos; in this questionnaire they would declare their assets and state how they intended to service their mortgages. For some it must have seemed like locking the stable door after the horse has bolted, as six of the Packe's farmers had already been on their holdings for six months. So far, only one Falklands farmer has been appointed to the FIDC, which besides the Chief Secretary has the Civil Commissioner and the Financial Secretary as ex-officio members. The only man with direct experience of farming in the Falklands in the early stages of the FIDC, at least, will be Neal Watson, who is the owner-occupier of Long Island, one of the subdivisions of Green Patch.

In early 1981 Anglia Television broadcast a documentary on the Falklands community in which farmers were shown dipping sheep at Green Patch. Sitting on a wooden fence by the sheep-pens they looked the young pioneers with a new vision of frontier life in the Falklands. They all said they expected a bright future and hoped the Islands would remain British. It must have been only the first or second season they dipped and sheared the sheep since taking over the land. Within a year of the film being screened on television the Islands, albeit temporarily, were no longer British. In the week the Argentines invaded some of the farmers were still putting up new buildings, repairing fences long broken, and one family moved a house several miles overland from the Green Patch settlement to their farmstead. That was the family of Peter Goss, one of the most dynamic farmers in Falkland history. Today he and his wife, Margie, are owners of the Horseshoe Bay and Bacon and Ham sections of the original Green Patch Farm. In 1977 they began negotiations to buy 13,800 acres and 3200 sheep for £32,080, and borrowed £12,000 from the government at seven per cent. Such terms have led to much muttering among the traditional landowners about 'soft loans devaluing the land', and one hereditary landlord publicly declared that all the new farmers must learn to stand on their own two feet.

The Green Patch farmers have not had the easiest time in developing their businesses. The division of the lots at Green Patch was chaotic, according to the new farmers, and resulted in a very unbalanced share-out of the sheep. Some farmers found they had an imbalance of full-mouthed, mature sheep, and others that they had far too much young stock. Some have had heavy yields from comparatively small numbers of sheep. Peter Goss has doubled the number of stock carried by his land to 7200 in 1984, the highest rate in the Falklands, just over two acres to the sheep, his gross income from wool topping £40,000 for the 1983–4 season. His methods have been carefully scrutinised by other farmers and by the ARC.

I was met by Margie Goss at the airstrip one bright day in early April 1984. She gave me a breezy hello as if she had only seen me the Sunday before, but this was our first meeting. Driving up the track to Horseshoe she told me what she would do for the farm if she had the opportunity. She said she would really branch out if the track to Stanley was improved, for at present it took four hours to get into town by truck. She would run a small dairy, do some market gardening and would even have a go at fattening a few lambs for a quality meat trade. As it was, she was providing special wools for hand-weaving and knitting.

At the house we met Peter Goss, a blond, barn-door of a man. In his views on sheep-rearing in the Falklands, he is completely self-confident; agricultural experts are locked in friendly rivalry as they scrutinise and check his methods and results. But he is adamant about his way of sheep-farming. He told me that the key to his size of holding was fencing pasture properly and grazing intensively, as this 'knocked the bog into shape'. He thought he might be able to raise the number of stock even higher. Part of his success lay in the fact that he and Margie checked the sheep and the fences daily and they looked after or 'hefted' the young stock carefully to bring them on for first shearing. 'Hefting' seems about the right word for Peter's beefy frame. Thousands of sheep are lost in each Falklands winter, however, dying in ditches and bogs and some-times falling into the sea. In some years up to ten per cent of the national flock has been lost, and anyway up to 20,000 old animals have to be culled each year.

Peter Goss has a wonderful Falklandism in his vocabulary when describing how he started at Horseshoe. For him the past definite of 'arrive' is 'arrove'. 'When we arrove here,' he told me, 'the place was dreadfully run down. The paddock fences were in a bad state and some had been rolled up and thrown in a ditch. There was a small powerhouse, a house about a hundred years old, a twelve-foot by twenty cook-house and two cowsheds and that was about all.' He added there was no secret to the way he was managing to increase the number of stock. Half the farm was subdivided with animals rotated round the paddocks. 'All you need to do is go in for subdividing, rotate-feeding, keep an eye on the sheep, making sure they're not settling along the fences and getting too thin.' On the larger farms shepherds sometimes do not see their flocks for days, hence the tendency of the sheep to wander and get into difficulties.

Peter said he could pay off his mortgage tomorrow, and his independent style and independent means cause some feelings of envy among other Falklands farmers. A few years after school he began one of the first contract shearing gangs in the Falklands, a very profitable business if you are young and fit. One season Margie came along with the gang to carry the fleece from the shearing boards, and together they went into partnership buying sheep for rough grazing on the mountains round Mount Kent. After a few years they married and decided to look for land. Peter has been the winner of the 'Golden Shears' award for the fastest and most efficient shearer on the islands and has recently competed in international contests at the Bath and West Show in Britain. Peter's independent attitude has coloured strongly his views on the future of farming development in the Falklands.

For some time he has enjoyed the sense of rivalry with the ARC, the Research Centre which he, like most Falklands farmers, insists on calling the GTU. 'Hopefully,' he told me, 'they will come up with a package of proposals for improving farming, but personally I can't see this happening. It will either be the bionic sheep or improving the ground to perfection.' He gave me a suitably embellished account of how one of the 'GTU' experts had been examining the grass in one of his fields and could not explain why it was so healthy. The soil did not appear particularly good or the brand of grass very exciting. Peter said he had to explain that the grassland had been fenced well and grazed intensively, and it was in sheltered ground away from the prevailing wind blowing in from the sea. He said the number of overseas advisers now working in the Falklands bothered him, as did the kind of deals being offered the new farmers at Packe's on West Falkland. He said by 'doing quick figures' on his calculator he thought the interest being paid for Packe's farms and San Carlos 'ridiculously high'. This was when eleven per cent was being asked but, as it is, the Packe's farmers are likely to pay about ten per cent and those with private loans at San Carlos could be paying at equal rates. 'I just don't see how the guys starting off can think of making a living out of it,' he concluded. He was equally sceptical about the appointment of a Farm Management Adviser from Britain. 'It would be far better if we can get a Farm Management Officer who was recruited locally, who knows the system here, rather than this idea of getting one from overseas who will know a very limited amount about the country. In particular, people here need to receive help on how to run proper accounts for their farms; and this is sadly lacking now.'

I asked Peter why he did not stand for office in the Islands' Legislative Council. He said he was too tied up to get involved, and the Council's performance worried him: 'Some points don't get to the Council that should, and even so those that do aren't dealt with satisfactorily.'

But both Peter and Margie thought there was a good future for them at Horseshoe, despite uncertainty about relations with Argentina. They said they lived one day to the next and would worry about tomorrow only when it came. They would go to New Zealand if Argentina took over. In the meantime, Margie was dreaming of a little homestead surrounded by white posts and rails and a horseshoe arch at the gate, just like the Ewings' 'South Fork' in *Dallas*. She took me outside to see her Jacob sheep which she took from the 'Noah's Ark' of animals shipped to the Islands from Britain after the conflict. They were pets she said, but provided fine black wool for the home weavers and irritated the traditionalists of the Sheep Owners' Association. Apparently there has been a taboo against black-faced sheep and black wool in the Islands, where the strains are predominantly a mix of Merino, Romney, Corriedale and Polwarth.

The Goss family were the first husband-and-wife team of the new farmers to join the SOA, which, though a bastion of the Falklands establishment, has been trying to provide services specially tailored to the smaller section-holders. I visited the secretary, Jim Clement, early one morning. He and another stalwart of the Falklands farming scene, Sidney Miller, were drawing names from a hat for the finals of the sheep-dog trials due to be held at Port Howard. There were to be horse-races and a lottery worth £1500, and it promised to be a great 'Two Nighter', a settlement dance and sports event which went on for at least two days and nights. Jim Clement and Robin Pitaluga, the SOA president, recognise that the bulk of their membership will come from smaller farms, and Colin Smith has helped found a Small Farmers' Union which has already produced an attractive label for selling Falklands knitting wool and yarn across the world; the Japanese in particular are showing great interest. The small farmers can belong to both organisations, which provide different services, and many do already. Jim said he hoped the SOA would provide a group buying system for purchasing goods and tools at cost, rather as the National Farmers' Union has operated a similar scheme in Britain. The SOA is also considering funding a travelling farm secretary service to help draw up accounts and make tax returns, a more modest but very likely more necessary service than that being offered by the Farm Management Adviser. I asked Jim what he thought the one improvement most needed for the Falklands economy was. 'Ah,' he said wistfully, 'we need a proper road system, something that should have been done in the last century.'

After my visit to Horseshoe Margie Goss took me over to Green Patch. As we left the farm buildings her cousin, June Goodwin, was stacking peat for the winter, silhouetted against the distant hills across the Bay, above San Carlos and the Sound. Green Patch itself clings rather desperately to the side of the moorland and winds from Antarctica and South Georgia hit the houses head-on, gusting from the open sea. In one of the woolsheds I found Neal and Glenda Watson pressing the last few bales of their wool clip. The young farmers of the Falklands could hardly have a better representative and spokesman in the Development Council than Neal, an open-faced man with blond hair and fair complexion. He talks coolly and even-temperedly about the future but, like Peter and Margie Goss, he has more than a few worries about it. He told me that output was improving slowly on his farm, Long Island, but he could not expect the spectacular results that Peter Goss was achieving, as the quality of soil and the layout of his holding were not so good. Neal had borrowed £19,000 at seven per cent for 15,000 acres, including an island of 800 acres, and 3100 sheep. He had worked previously for the FIC in their shipping office and later helped with arranging flights out of the Falklands via Argentina. Besides being a newly appointed member of the Development Corporation he had been one of the Loans Committee giving mortgages for the Packe's subdivisions. He was very critical of the kind of loans and interest rates that had been contemplated. He said: 'I wouldn't be rushing in to buy, not having done the sums. The margins left for development are pretty small.' He elaborated this into a general criticism of the development programme. 'Prices on the farms are too high – that's the major factor now. It's not beneficial to the colony as a whole for revenue, and profits will be smaller than old-style ranching.' He agreed with Peter Goss about the style of government: 'It's very hard to get anybody to come up with a firm decision if you go to the administration with a firm question. Everything is muddling along.'

As we had been talking Neal's youngest son, Ben, was circling round the shed on his bicycle. Glenda Watson said the education of young children in camp was a major problem. There were too few teachers, who could only spend about ten days in six weeks with the child, and that might embrace two weekends, which they would have as days off.

Most of them were unqualified, she said, and too much was left for the mother, hardly the ideal tutor for young children. However difficult the immediate future looked both said they would not consider leaving the Islands, unless the Argentines took over.

The fount of scientific wisdom about Falklands farming is the ARC. It was set up in 1975 to study the improvement of pasturing sheep and animal husbandry. A grasslands specialist, Tom Davies, had looked at what such a unit might do on a six-month study visit to the Islands in 1969–70. Tom succeeded Dr John Ferguson as the head of the GTU/ARC in August 1984. He is a jolly Welshman, popular with farmers and citizens of Stanley. His wife, Gwen, teaches in the junior school and has done a great deal for the Falklands Foundation, a form of heritage trust for the study of Falklands traditions and history. The GTU has been the butt of many jokes in its short history. The sceptics cannot see how it will come up with a miracle package of proposals that will lead to increases of output of wool of twenty-five per cent. The favourite joke is about 'the goose man', the ecologist who has been study-ing the impact of upland, Brent and kelp geese on pasture. They can be devastating, destroying up to twenty per cent of prime paddock in a season. Not that this is a revelation of any newfangled science, for in the 1870s Robert Blake of Hill Cove stated the problem quite simply: 'They say that seven of those birds,' he wrote in his journal, 'eat as much as one sheep. So we have to keep them down.' The question today is how to keep them down. If they are shot, the environmentalists and wildlife pressure groups protest and the geese only go away for a short respite and often return in greater numbers. The 'goose men' have found the socioecological equation hard to balance.

Dr Ferguson, the former head of the GTU, described its role in quite straightforward terms. Its first job was to provide raw statistics and data about Falklands farming. Records in the past have been poor and many of the first settlers went onto land that was never surveyed. The ARC intends to come up with a package of proposals for farm improvement which will involve management, grasslands improvement, and recommendations on animal husbandry; there will have to be a strong veterinary element, as any change in regime for animals produces disease according to Dr Ferguson. The Grasslands Trials themselves will be a programme with a longer perspective, relating to similar studies on marginal peaty land in other parts of the world.

The Unit was dealt a severe set-back by the Argentine invasion in April 1982. Argentine forces wrecked the laboratory hut, smashed equipment and shipped some back to Argentina, and they festooned the area with barbed wire and minefields. Minefields also flanked the trials plot at Camber, a spit of land immediately across the water from Port Stanley. Records and archives were burnt and destroyed. With a £2.6 million grant from the FIDC and the new strength of twelve scientists and technical officers, the GTU has managed to relaunch its programmes under the guidance of John Ferguson and Tom Davies.

One Sunday morning Davies and Ferguson gave me a guided tour of the trial plots at Camber. Strips a few metres wide were laid out with different grasses, and the pattern was repeated in different locations where different quantities of seed and different fertilisers were applied. Each plot was cropped four times a year by a small tractor and mowing machine. Traditional white grasses grew alongside Yorkshire fog, long a favourite import with Falkland farmers, fescues, rye-grasses and cocksfoot, trefoil and a few other legumes. Turnips did not seem to be doing too well. Davies's discourse, based on more than thirty years of scientific experience, baffled me, but he emphasised the peculiarities of the Falklands terrain, the poor acid soil and the high winds. His trials at Camber would be repeated on a more generous scale at Fitzroy, and Brooke Hardcastle, the FIC's camp manager, had a large reseeding experiment at Darwin. Robin Pitaluga's farm had similar plots at Salvador, but Davies said it was hard to blend pure scientific research with commercial farming.

As we wandered round the plots we were observed from a Rapier battery on the point. 'At least it isn't a dummy made of cardboard,' said one of the scientists – many of the farmers suggested some of the batteries out on the hills were. As we walked back towards Moody Brook groups of blue-eyed shags took up our close observation. Both scientists said that they realised that no farmer would indulge in a reseeding programme if it proved costly and involved repeated applications of seeds and fertilisers year after year. They hoped to improve the quality of home pasture in the paddocks to increase the survival rate of the young stock. 'It's really a question of keeping the little brutes alive until we can get them to the shearing boards,' was John Ferguson's summing-up of the short-term programme.

The GTU has had one outstanding achievement to date in the veterinary field. Steve Whitley was for years the vet in the Unit and he set about reducing the traditional sheep disease ked. His greatest success, however, was with a disorder called hydatids, which comes from a parasite that passes through the sheep's digestive system. From an incidence of nearly fifty per cent Steve managed in several years to reduce hydatids in the Falklands flock to under one per cent, a record only matched by Ireland. Hydatids is dangerous to humans when the parasite has also been passed through a dog's digestion and then taken up in the sheep's carcass. The parasite gets into the blood and can attack a number of organs in the human body; it has peculiarly dreadful effects when it reaches the brain. Steve visited every farm several times a year to push forward his eradication policy, and today no dogs are allowed in Stanley. Steve was one of the most popular figures with Island farmers. He volunteered to stay on during the conflict and his first wife, Sue, was in fact killed in the last British bombardments of Port Stanley. He had a brilliant reputation as a veterinary scientist but could also readily turn his hand to the cultivation of trees on the Islands. In 1984 he left the Islands and for the time being, at least, has abandoned veterinary practice.

Among Steve's greatest admirers are Cecil and Kitty Bertrand who owned and farmed Carcass Island in West Falkland for twenty years to 1974. Cecil and Kitty are first cousins who married, and are legends in the Falklands today. They possess a fund of wisdom about Falklands agriculture which the Farm Management Adviser might envy. Today they are retired and live in Stanley as Cecil is crippled with arthritis. But he can still recall the day when he went for his first farming job in Patagonia, taking his saddle with him as his entry fine for the post, and the four years of whaling from South Georgia in the thirties. More sharply he puts forward his views on the improvement of sheep-farming. He told me that in the past not enough attention had been paid to winter feed for sheep. When he had his schooner at Carcass he used to see the sheep come down to the sea in winter – they were so weak that they would get trapped by the high banks of the shore as the tide came in and they could not climb to safety. He said New Zealanders had great success using local seaweed as fertiliser, and he and Kitty had raised bumper crops of vegetables after applying a mixture of beach sand and crushed shells. They also had to thank one of the first settlers on Carcass, Jason Hanson, for the cultivation of the native tussock which provided superb winter break for the sheep. Sadly the Tussock Islands are in decline now, and one or two have been burnt by both Argentine and British forces using them for aerial bombardment in exercises. Kitty and Cecil recall planting 40,000 tussock shoots in the deep winter, dibbing them in like potatoes.

Any one of a dozen farmers now retired and living in Stanley could provide from their experience advice on practical and inexpensive improvements to traditional Falklands husbandry. One wonders how much they will be heeded by the cohorts of new technical and advisory officers associated with the ARC and the Development Corporation.

In fairness the achievements of the new FIDC have been little short of miraculous, particularly when compared to the lack of advice and input in the farming community by the Falklands administration previously. Much of the credit must be given to the imagination and energy of the Chief Executive, David Taylor, and the General Manager, Simon Armstrong, who stated forcefully his intention of taking the first plane or boat back to Scotland if plans for the success of the FIDC were thwarted. Within a few weeks of his arrival in Stanley he had visited nearly every new farmer already in residence in the small farms on East and West Falkland. With his computer and economic models constructed from his previous experience with the Highlands and Islands Development Board he analysed each of the new section-holders' finances, from expected income each year from wool to outgoings on mortgages and other recurrent expenses. On 25 September he called in each prospective buyer of the San Carlos sections to discuss their prospects. He and David Taylor were dismayed to find that one prospective purchaser would have had a net annual income of £900 on the private mortgage terms he was offered originally.

The FIDC moved quickly to relax the terms of their mortgages to two per cent below base rate, with a moratorium on all repayments for the first year. Farmers with 5000 sheep or under could qualify for the fifty-per-cent grants for machines, seed, breeding rams, buildings and landing jetties; and these could rise to sixty per cent for co-operatives.

From a distance, Armstrong's activity gives the impression of an agronomic whirling dervish. He had drawn up a syllabus of simple training programmes for the new farmers and businessmen almost before he got off the plane from Ascension to Stanley. He has written a postal course on simple book-keeping specially for the Falklanders and will be offering a short course entitled 'Start Your Own Business' on marketing, production and finance for anyone intending to set up a business or new farm in the Islands. The FIDC is also proposing a purchasing co-operative for independent farmers so they can buy goods, spare parts, and food supplies in bulk in Britain and ship them on their own terms. This might circumvent one of the most lucrative trading activities of the Falkland Islands Company.

For all the bustle and activity of the Development Corporation, the programme of purchase of overseas-owned land in the Islands is very much smaller than that envisaged by the 1982 Shackleton Report. By the end of the decade, when the FIDC has completed its first five years, and very probably to the end of the century, the FIC will still own over forty per cent of Falklands land and about forty to fifty per cent of all livestock. For the immediate future the Company will still control much of the sea transport to and from the Islands and within them. The FIDC has done all that could be expected to bring success to most of the new farmers, the wool mill, inshore fishery, the new butchery and the Stanley Dairy, but its funding of £4.6 million from the Shackleton funds will not seem generous after three or four years. In late 1984 there is little prospect of further purchases of absentee-owned estates, though David Taylor has reaffirmed his intention to pursue negotiations to buy the Hamilton estate on West Falkland. The subsidy and grant scheme is likely to involve heavy recurrent expenditure. Ironically the restriction on holdings of 5000 sheep rules out the two most prominent figures in the small farming world of East Falkland, Peter Goss and Pat Short, who own more than 7000 sheep each. Two of the Packe's subdivisions at Fox Bay were sold with only a five-year lease on houses in the settlement, as these might be needed for the new village development. The farmers could then need help to build or buy new homes.

The new brief from the FIDC to its Farm Management Adviser is to 'act as the prime source of advice to all small farmers'. Rather than the best endeavours of his computer or calculator, the most useful assistance he might often be required to provide is from the bending of his back and the sweat of his hands. Most of the new small farms are run entirely by husband-and-wife teams. If one partner is struck by illness for more than a few weeks, the whole enterprise is in jeopardy, and the wisdom of postgraduate agronomy will not be capable of saving it.

For its part the FIC has proposed alternatives to subdivision as a way of bringing more people onto the land. The Company has proposed selling fifty-acre plots along the Darwin Road at £1000 each, but quite what for has not been made clear. The entire Island economy would only require produce from two well-run market gardens on such acreages, and the size of the plots is hardly suitable for smallholdings. The FIC has also proposed share-farming schemes. But one drawn up for the Great Island/Swan Island Group just before the conflict in 1982 would hardly look out of place as a contract of *métayage* in pre-Napoleonic France. The agreement says that profits will be shared at twenty-five per cent for the Company and seventy-five per cent for the farmer, but the farmer must provide the farm vehicles and a boat for the island; he must repair and maintain the house; he must hire labour, whose liability would be entirely his; he would have to insure himself against sickness and accident. Furthermore he would have to accept directions from the Company's managers, to whom he would have to give access at all times. The farmer can only indulge in outside business activity with express written permission from the Company. Boat fuel, radios and travel to and from the islands must be paid for by the farmer. Goods for the farm have to be imported through the Company and, of course, the wool clip and other commercial produce are to be exported via the Company.

There are no provisions for the farmer's subsistence in lean years, when profit might be negligible or non-existent, and there appears almost no incentive to take managerial decisions. In many respects the contract treats the share-farmer like a Company employee.

However, such agreements are not part of the responsibilities of the Falkland Islands government nor the FIDC. Their interest is primarily in the land for which they have provided government mortgages and loans, where the new farmers will now have a platoon of advisers, scientists and consultants to lend them their counsel and the service of their calculators and computer. The way the new farms fare will be an important pointer to whether the internal economy of the Islands can be reinvigorated, or, as Lord Shackleton has hinted, they decay and collapse by the end of the century. Another important clue to the durability of the Falklands community is the way in which important public amenities not considered by the second Shackleton Report are treated, particularly education and health care. Proof of the Islands' government and Councillors' attitude to such questions is likely to be given by what they do to provide the community with a new hospital and accommodation for old people.

# Chapter 13

# The Fire in
# the Hospital

A hard west wind was blowing that night, 10 April 1984, trying to whip itself into a miniature gale. At about five o'clock in the morning the sirens wailed over Port Stanley; within minutes I could see one or two blue lights flashing against the ceiling of the bedroom as a couple of jeeps roared through the empty streets. They were followed by heavier vehicles. Finally I was shaken completely from sleep by a knock on the door. Mrs King, the owner of the Upland Goose, said with characteristic thoughtfulness, and directness, 'We thought we should wake you. The hospital is on fire. Anna [the Kings' younger daughter] managed to escape through a window. It's still burning and we thought you should go down there.'

By the time I arrived at the King Edward Memorial Hospital most of its roof had fallen in. Flames were shooting above the trees, licking the sky in which the first streaks of dawn were appearing. The tongues of blue and orange were bending with the trees and seemed as if they might set the wooden houses behind the hospital on fire as well. RAF fire-tenders were parked right up against the part of the hospital still standing, the yellow-helmeted crew moving into the wrecked building with professional briskness. Islanders helped the town firemen train hoses onto the flames and roasted wreckage of the old hospital wing, which had been made largely of wood. Some of the rescued stood on a low wall, shivering in the bright-blue blankets wrapped round their shoulders.

Two tugs had moved closer into shore, their lights brightly shining as their crew prepared to pump water to the fire-tenders. General Spacie had ordered them to move as close to the shore as possible as soon as he recognised that the fire was still out of control. The General himself moved quietly among the servicemen, prominent but not obtrusive, a cool figure of authority, decisive but not stubborn. Equally characteristic was the role played by Sir Rex Hunt, a bustling figure in a blue anorak and furry hat. He was helping the local firemen and hospital staff, by being among them. He had been one of the first on the scene and had helped rescue some of the first patients to escape from the burning building, and then hauled in the hoses from the fire-tenders. Outside the nurses' home opposite the hospital Dr Alison Bleaney, still in a baby-blue tracksuit, was helping comfort the bereaved and burnt. I asked what I could do. 'Get us some tea, that's the best thing for us at the moment,' she said.

It was a scene of grief and confusion slowly shaking itself into a semblance of order. Within an hour of the fire breaking out, most of the old hospital was in ashes, as was the prefabricated cabin forming the new military wing. This had cost about £500,000, and possibly double once all the equipment had been installed inside it. It had been opened officially by Mrs Valerie Spacie a month before; but when the fire caught it, it had burnt to the ground in a few minutes.

At first no one was quite sure if everybody had been rescued from the old building, the surgical and maternity wards and a makeshift old people's home. I found my friend Tony Chater, who runs a souvenir and bookshop in Stanley, helping the local firemen. He said he thought five or six people had died in the smoke and fumes; most had managed to jump from the windows – Land-Rovers had been driven close to the building and the patients had jumped onto their canvas roofs.

It took most of the morning to establish that eight people had died inside the hospital. All the patients in the military wing had been rescued quickly. Topsy MacPhee, wife of the Fire Superintendent, Pat MacPhee, who was leading the town fire-fighters outside, died in the smoke and fumes. Teresa MacGill, who had given birth to a baby daughter, Karen, a few days before, also died. So too did the civilian nurse on duty, Barbara Chick from Bristol. Four of the old people, Gladys Fleuret, Mary Smith, Mabel Nielsen and Fred Colman, who was confined to his wheelchair, perished. Some of their bodies were found close to the doors; they had nearly succeeded in making their escape. One of the last to be rescued was the Catholic priest, Monsignor Daniel Spraggon. He had managed to get his head to a window so he could breathe fresh air, and though his lungs were affected, his head was midway between the heavy smoke clinging to the ceiling and the poisonous fumes rising from the floor.

As the flames whipped through the outhouses, the old paint shop exploded, throwing sparks and a fireball into the dawn sky. Minutes later the wind dropped suddenly and the firemen began hosing down the smouldering ruins and putting out the last few flames in the twisted wrecks of beds, furniture and surgical equipment. Two houses nearest the hospital had been scorched and the printer had to dump his machinery and books outside on the street, only to find some of them soaked by the water from the pumps.

Tony Chater, one of the first to arrive after the sirens had sounded, described the scene as the fire began to grip the whole building. 'The hospital appeared to be burning in the middle, more or less on the east end. The military chaps got here very quickly; the civilian fire-fighting force were here very quickly as well, but they had a lot of trouble with their water pumps, and it took a long time before we could really get things rolling and it was a long time before the casualties started coming out. Some people were coming out of the window, but most were coming out of the west-end door, and I think five dead were taken out on stretchers.

'The military equipment got working quickly up at the east end, but the one hose taken into the west door, that took a long time to get going. There were men with no lights and oxygen masks, but they could not do anything because the fire was going in front of them. Sir Rex Hunt was carrying dead out on stretchers and hauling hoses. He was leading from the front, and working very hard. The General was here too. There were a lot of people, but nobody really knew what was going on. At that stage of the morning it was pitch-dark and with faulty equipment, there was a lot of confusion. Here we are at half past seven in the morning and half the hospital is gone; we're going to need a new hospital now.'

As Navy helicopters flew overhead bringing emergency first-aid equipment from the garrison quarters near the airfield, Jeremy Smith, one of the Stanley Fire Brigade, described what the fire looked like at its height, when he and the local fire teams arrived on the scene: 'Just the whole wing was alight. Big flames. This whole wing was tinder dry . . . It was mainly wood – very, very dry. I suppose it just went up in ten minutes; then the whole lot was gone. We reeled the hoses out as quickly as we could and got to work. The military came down very, very quickly, too. I think everybody thought about this for years, but never thought it would happen quite like this.'

Much of the old part of the hospital had been made of wood, and the solarium on the northern side had a wooden frame. The old wing had been completed in 1914 and opened on 8 December that year to receive casualties from the engagement between Admiral Sturdee's squadron and that of Graf Von Spee at the battle of the Falklands. A second wing was built in 1953, called the Churchill Wing. This had been left standing by the fire, though the walls were badly cracked. The grey cement outside had been daubed with huge red crosses, painted during the Argentine occupation. The hospital had served as a refuge for civilians then, as the Argentines used the aircraft hangar to the west of the town as their military dressing station.

294

The hospital had long been in a poor state of repair, and badly in need at least of a major overhaul and at best complete replacement. The matter had been debated and discussed well before the Argentine occupation. The fact that the building had to be shared between civilian and military medical teams for eighteen months following the conflict merely added greater strain on the already creaking facilities. Even by the time the military doctors and nurses had set up their wards and equipment in the new Wyseplan hut adjoining, there was no prospect of a major overhaul to the old hospital in sight, let alone its replacement with a new hospital and separate old people's home. Future medical provisions for the Island community and the garrison had been debated endlessly in the Falklands and in Whitehall since June 1982, an item of contention bounced endlessly between the ODA, the MoD, the Falklands Command and the Falklands government like a ball round a tennis court. This is why the fire at the hospital must be seen as something more than the terrible domestic tragedy it was for the Island community. The way welfare and health-care policy have been handled has been a symptom of the disjointed, and sometimes casual, manner in which much public administration of the Islands has been conducted for years.

Many of the fire-fighters must have felt badly let down by the poor state of the equipment as they tried to prevent the fire from getting out of control. Two of the fire pumps on the tenders did not work at first, and pressure in one of the hydrants was too low: this was confirmed subsequently by the Commission of Inquiry. Inside the hospital, a set of fire doors had not been fixed in the old wing, and fire hose reels had not been connected. A few days before I had visited the old building, which always had a tired aspect despite valiant efforts to tart the fittings up with the odd lick of paint. Wires trailed in festoons from power sockets in the main staff rest-room. By chance, on the way out I noticed labels with red print on the fire hose reels, saying they should not be used as they were not connected to the water main. This is no self-regarding boast, for I know other visitors had noticed the same thing.

In the previous months half a dozen electrical fires had broken out in Stanley. The week before the hospital burnt down, a peat fire had raged on Golding Island and civilian and military volunteers had to be flown out from Port Stanley. The weekend before, a cottage had burnt down at Goose Green, killing Henry Smith, a shepherd visiting from Teal Inlet. In the space of four days nine lives had been lost in fires. In 1983 the number of births had exceeded the number of deaths in the Islands for the first time in years; the population had increased by nine. In the seventy-four days of the Argentine occupation and fighting three civilians had died; now three times as many lives had been lost in four days.

After a brief conversation with Sir Rex Hunt about when the news of the fire might be broadcast, after the next of kin had been informed, I wandered down to the Town Hall where the military medical teams were establishing a temporary ward for the survivors of the fire. I had been the only outside journalist present at the fire and hoped to gather as much first-hand information on the state of those who had been rescued from Dr Alison Bleaney, the Senior Medical Officer for the Falkland Islands, and, perhaps, her military counterparts. On my way I was informed by no fewer than two staff officers and one civilian press officer for the military force that I was to go to supper with the General and his wife.

At the Town Hall I found the General's wife preparing tea and biscuits for the patients and helpers. I thanked Mrs Spacie for her invitation and went to seek information from the new ward. I was met by a colonel who appeared to be in charge. 'Who are you? And what are you doing here?' he asked. By this time I had been joined by the Islands' broadcaster, Pat Watts. I explained that it was usual in times of accident for journalists to find out as accurately as possible what the state of the injured was – my job demanded it. The colonel seemed unimpressed, so I explained further that the General knew who I was and what I was doing. By this time this senior person was goggling at us through his rimless spectacles, his neck and head stretched and taut like an angry tortoise. 'But does the General know you are here?' he shouted. I said if the General did not his wife certainly did as we had just had an amiable conversation in the adjoining room.

Relations between the press and the armed forces have traced a fairly winding course since the end of the conflict in June 1982. Later that year the House of Commons Defence Committee reported on press coverage during the campaign, but did not come up with any startling revelations or conclusions, and much of the taking of evidence was patchy. Not much heed was paid to the two of us primarily engaged in radio coverage, and we were not called to give evidence, despite the fact that radio proved the quickest and most reliable means of getting dispatches back and that newspapers frequently relied on the radio reports for their copy.

The Navy decided it was best to try to remain the silent service despite the fact that every other ship in the merchant fleet and the Royal Fleet Auxiliaries now have Marisat telephone and telex facilities. The army, mindful of the experiences of Northern Ireland as much as the Falklands, has continuously tested and examined its policy on press relations. The dynamic head of Army public relations at the time of the conflict, now Major-General David Ramsbotham, organised an exercise for fifty journalists to take part in the regular autumn manoeuvres of the British Army of the Rhine, codenamed in October 1983 'Exercise Eternal Triangle'. The sight of journalists driving between columns of tanks and armoured troop carriers in the autumn gold of the German plain close to the banks of the Weser had something almost theatrically absurd about it, their progress reminiscent of the procession of the carriages of the Duchess of Richmond and her guests from Brussels to observe the Battle of Waterloo. David Ramsbotham believed the soldiers had to establish a basis of trust with the reporters and photographers working with them in the field. The study produced by General Sir Hugh Beach which came out a few weeks later also suggested this was how matters should be conducted and the censorship policy should be established between the men at the top, the editors and the defence chiefs and commanders. Things seemed to work best in the field when a certain amount of mutual trust and cordial respect could be established with those at the front. On the morning of 10 April in Port Stanley there was little mutual trust or cordiality between the military and the press in the Town Hall.

I met Dr Bleaney downstairs at the Town Hall and she told me that Monsignor Spraggon was not very well. Another patient had burns, she said, and two more had been sent home. Fifteen beds had been set up in the Town Hall, and the military had done 'a fantastic job'. The old people had been taken to the home of Councillor Tim Blake and his wife, Sally, who had opened their house to them. At the time I spoke to Dr Bleaney it was not clear what kind of temporary hospital would be provided for the winter. I asked her to describe the old hospital. She replied: 'It was old, and it needed, part of it, rewiring; it needed a lot doing to it, I don't think it is going to get done now.'

The old hospital had been designed to take twenty-seven patients. After June 1982, the military presence had meant more than forty patients might by staying overnight. At times relations between the civilian staff and the military medical team had become tense; at best the atmosphere had been coolly cordial, at worst distinctly acid. Very possibly the military doctors and nurses found the free-wheeling and slightly anarchic ways of Falklands social commerce hard to take, as the senior men at least were used to deference from their juniors in rank and qualifications. Many were brilliant specialists of consultant level and above. The Islands' doctors on the other hand felt they were being treated as junior housemen or ordinary GPs with a small role in the specialist work of modern hospital life. The Islands' doctors generally have to have a specialist qualification before they are accepted; Dr

Bleaney, for example, was first taken on at the hospital as a generalist and anaesthetist.

Disagreement between the civilians and the military doctors had led to a curious clash of wills at Christmas 1983. Dr Bleaney's team felt it was necessary to get a supply of a drug called Anti-D quickly as a mother just delivered of her baby in the hospital was in urgent need of it. Anti-D is administered to a mother with a Rhesus-negative factor and whose baby is Rhesus-positive, as a precaution against a future occurrence of what is known as the 'blue baby syndrome'. Stocks of the drug had disappeared from the hospital dispensary, which was administered by the military medical teams. No one could say how or when the drug had been removed. The military doctors are not involved in obstetrics and they did not feel an urgent need to get fresh stocks of Anti-D on the occasion in question. The argument was carried to the highest level with Sir Rex Hunt, the Civil Commissioner, insisting that General Spacie, the Military Commissioner, do something quickly to get the drug to Stanley. Shortly before Christmas a Hercules aircraft was dispatched to Ascension to fetch fresh stocks. The civilian doctors and the local administration were irritated by the implication that the needs of an Islander were second to those of a serviceman.

Shortly after noon Sir Rex said he believed that all the next of kin of victims of the fire had been informed and that a broadcast could be made to the BBC. During the day the PWD had moved in with bulldozers to clear the wreckage of the old wing of the hospital. I was told this was to look for any remaining bodies; heavy tracked machines with loaders seemed odd instruments for such a task.

In the evening I called at the General's residence. The supper was a pleasant if somewhat strained occasion with just the three of us, the General, Mrs Spacie and myself. As we were having coffee afterwards the General advised me to take the next Hercules transport plane for Ascension, which would leave the following day, Wednesday. 'There's nothing more in this for you,' he said. I replied that the BBC would expect coverage of the funerals; the last would be held at the weekend. I made my professional excuses, I suppose, thanked the General for the supper and stayed for four days.

The following day the town's community was beginning to feel the full impact of the shock. Many were silent and subdued, others angry. Such disasters can have quite violent effects in very small villages and towns. In the earthquake in Friuli in northern Italy in May 1976, I recall talking to a woman steadily doing her laundry by a pump. I asked her about her family, and she seemed to have difficulty recalling whether she had four or five children. Next I asked about her neighbours. Both families had been wiped out: behind us her house was still standing and the two houses which adjoined it on either side were heaps of rubble. She was in a state of extreme trauma. Some people I knew well in Stanley turned their anger on me, an outsider they felt should not be there. Pat Watts was angry that I did not listen to his stories of the Military Police keeping townspeople from helping in the rescue. I said I had not seen this and it was usual for police to keep bystanders away from professional fire-fighters in big disasters. 'Why didn't the BBC report they tried to stop us helping with the rescue, why didn't you do that, mate?' he raged, jigging in the street as if he had St Vitus's dance. Dr Bleaney told him to pipe down. But for the military teams, she added, the fire might not have been put out at all. Later, the genial Tom Davies of the GTU shouted across the street, 'Are you still here then?' Kitty Bertrand remonstrated, 'You should not have made that broadcast. That was the way the girl's mother found out she had died.' And she had touched her mark.

In the afternoon we helped Dr Bleaney and her team fetch the bodies in order to prepare them for burial. The Falkland Islands have no full-time undertaker and this function is normally carried out by the PWD. The military medical team were typically quiet and thorough as they helped to prepare the bodies so that the doctor and nurse could lay them out for their coffins.

The first funeral was for Topsy MacPhee. On the Friday the four old people were buried after a funeral service in Stanley Cathedral at which Sir Rex Hunt gave the oration, opening with a short quotation from John Donne:

'Over twice as long ago as the first British settlers came here to Stanley, John Donne wrote the following lines: "Any person's death diminishes me because I am involved in mankind. Therefore never send to know for whom the bell tolls. It tolls for thee."

'In the early hours of Tuesday morning 10 April 1984 eight of our close-knit community perished in a fire in the old wing of the King Edward Memorial Hospital in Stanley. They could have been anyone of us here today. Since the old wing was opened on 8 December 1914, battle day, many of you and your parents before you were patients or served as staff there. So why 10 April 1984? And why these unfortunate eight? Mortal man has no answer to these questions. All we can do is join together, and united in tragedy, console those who are still torturing themselves for not having done more at the time. It is too easy to say after the event "if only. . ."; but that way madness lies. Instead of tearing ourselves apart for what we might have done, we must accept what has happened, and share the grief and sorrow of the bereaved in lamenting for those that have gone.

'We knew them all, except, of course, for the new-born babe, Teresa, Topsy, Mabel, Mary, Gladys, Fred, Barbara. We shall remember them and may their souls rest in peace.'

Mortal man may have had no answer as to why the disaster had happened that week in April but he would have some important questions about it for the public inquiry held a month later. And he still should be asking questions about the state of the old hospital and fractured policy over finding a replacement, today.

The four old people were buried together in the Port Stanley cemetery. The following day was the last of the funerals of the Islanders. A requiem mass was held in the little wooden Catholic church close to the Town Hall. The service was taken by the chaplain, Father Augustine Monaghan, who had worked hard all week comforting the distressed and injured, among them Monsignor Spraggon, who watched the mourners assemble from the makeshift ward in the building opposite the church. Over a hundred Islanders, friends and well-wishers crowded outside as the aisles and organ gallery were packed. The order of service was plain and unadorned. There was no homily nor encomium; but outside the weather trumpeted and roared its valediction. As the service was about to begin a bright-blue sky turned to driving hail, then snow and squalls rushing in from the mountains to the west. By the time the coffin was carried to the helicopters, the sky had cleared again, and they took off for Fitzroy where the mother and her child were to be buried.

Teresa had been a member of the Defence Force, and had worked at the hospital as a laboratory assistant. Her friends and colleagues in the Defence Force had gathered by the graveside, which was on a steep bank of moor overlooking a bend in the Fitzroy River; many had driven four and five hours overland that morning to get there. Beside the grave was a mound of dozens upon dozens of bunches of flowers, wreaths and bouquets, nosegays and sprays, an almost incongruous flash of colour against the rust and green of the landscape. There was a short rite of committal; family, friends and colleagues filed past the coffin laid in the earth as a piper from the Royal Scots played 'The Flowers of the Forest'. The wind got up again and we sat in the Land-Rovers waiting for the helicopters to return. The wind and the rain and the hail came blasting in from the west.

I left the Falklands that afternoon, and have not returned since.

At the end of May the Commission of Inquiry into the hospital fire held three days of public hearings in Port Stanley, and took evidence from forty-seven witnesses. The chairman was a prominent Queen's Counsel, David Calcutt, and the other members were a senior naval officer,

Captain Fretwell, RN, a Falklands farmer, Eric Goss, the FIC manager at North Arm, and Mrs Jan Cheek, a schoolteacher. The report was published in July 1984.

The Commission had been asked to look into six aspects of the disaster: the cause of the fire, the way it was fought, fire risk at the hospital and on the Islands as a whole, fire precautions at the hospital, and whether there was adequate financial provision for such measures and whether they were carried out. The sixth area of investigation was defined as 'such other matters as the Commission may consider to be relevant in their inquiry into the matters set out above'.

The report is a thin green booklet of some twenty-five pages of widely spaced print, with six chapters reaching eight simple conclusions. It concludes that the fire-fighting was carried out bravely and well, within the constraints of the circumstances. It praises the courage of the town fire-fighters and has particularly warm commendation for the efficiency, speed and skill of the RAF fire-fighters from the airfield at Stanley. Two of the town's fire pumps did not work properly and water-pressure was low at one of the hydrants used. There was about ten minutes' delay in sounding the fire sirens because of an antiquated procedure at the telephone exchange, which has now been remedied. The work of Lance-Corporal Shorters, on duty in the hospital that night, is given prominence for the manner in which he raised the alarm, sent for help and rescued patients. Other military personnel, however, did not seem to have been made fully aware of fire-drill procedures.

The fire appeared to have started in a storeroom containing mattresses, next to a bathroom in the old wing, at the south-west corner of that part of the building. There was no firm conclusion on how it had been started. Wisps of smoke were seen coming from that direction when Nurse Chick and Lance-Corporal Shorters first suspected fire. Expert evidence from a Home Office Fire Inspector ruled out an electrical fault, and there is some indication that the bathroom and the adjoining rooms had been used by staff as rest-rooms for a smoke. Spontaneous combustion in the mattresses was ruled out.

The report's most severe criticism is reserved for the Public Works Department for not ensuring that the fire hoses were connected and for securing fire doors in the body of the old wing. The report says of the evidence given by the PWD director, George Webster: 'Whilst entirely accepting the facts to be as stated by Mr Webster, we are quite unable to agree that they constitute a reasonable explanation for the failure to connect the internal hospital hose reels to the water-supply.' It then criticises the whole way the Department had been run. In his evidence Mr Webster had said that he had only seven craftsmen to work on and maintain all public buildings and there were eight vacancies for craftsmen in the PWD. (This, despite the fact that up to six supervisory posts had been filled at any one time, including two surveyors.) Work schedules were monitored in an unsatisfactory way, from week to week according to the report. Since the fire and before publication of the Commission's findings, George Webster resigned from his post.

The report refers to an assessment of fire risks in the hospital in a document entitled, 'Report on the Fire Fighting Services in the Falkland Islands', drawn up by a Mr D.T. Davis, Assistant Divisional Officer of the Cheshire Fire Brigade. On the hospital Mr Davis wrote: 'The means of escape are not to a satisfactory standard. There is no internal separation either horizontally or vertically of fire-resisting construction. The construction of the older section (i.e. the Old Wing) presents a considerable risk to patients and staff in that a fire could occur, be undetected for a considerable period of time, and subsequently show itself when it was at an advanced stage.' The 1984 Commission states Mr Davis's 'general assessment of the risk at the KEMH [King Edward Memorial Hospital] would still appear to have held true at the date of the fire'.

In its summing-up the Commission suggests that the 1977 Davis Report, seven years after it was presented, should be updated and used as a programme to ensure improved fire safety measures. Other recommendations are improvement in the fire siren system, the water-supply for fire-fighting and repairs to the fire pumps on the civilian tenders. Clearer fire instruction and division of responsibilities for fire drills there would be necessary in any new civilian-military hospital. Windows should be better constructed for escape in such a building, the report continues, and there should be an urgent review of methods of monitoring and setting priorities in the work schedule of the PWD.

The body of the report had referred to complaints made in November 1982 by Mr Webster's predecessor as director of the PWD, Mr John Brodrick, about amendments and additions made to the hospital wiring by the Royal Engineers for the military medical units: 'The indiscriminate amendment . . . without reference to PWD has escalated the danger to the lives of patients and staff alike.' The army later rectified the wiring, and the upstairs part was rewired. But before leaving his post on the Islands Mr Brodrick gave quite specific warning: 'The hospital has in the past been the subject of much debate regarding fire risk and a report from a visiting Crown Agent expert put the fire resistance of the building under an uncontrolled fire as no more than three minutes.' Mr Brodrick went further: 'The KEMH can, for very little longer, accept the strain of overloaded services and utilities. Furthermore, the fire risk is appalling with a 27-bed hospital of ancient vintage catering for 50 beds.' He was not called by the Commission in 1984. Nor were the victims represented, though Mr John Laws, Counsel to the Commission, agreed to act in their interest. However there is no Legal Aid in the Islands and most of the next of kin probably could not have afforded to brief Counsel, particularly if it meant lawyers coming from London.

Following the hearings of the Enquiry there was a statement by the head of the military hospital, Colonel Michael Templer, RAMC. The Commission had specifically excluded examination and discussion of reports about the construction of a new hospital in the Islands, long debated but never finalised, though part of the brief had been 'to inquire into . . . such other matters as the Commission may consider to be relevant to their inquiry into the matters set out above.' Examination of the reports and investigations of the need for a new hospital would have been highly revealing, for nearly every expert who looked into the matter expressed deep concern about the parlous condition of the King Edward Memorial Hospital. Despite the restrictions imposed by the Commission, Colonel Templer decided to go public with his views in an interview with BBC Radio which was broadcast on the *Today* programme of 5 June 1984.

If there was to be a new hospital, said Colonel Templer, it should be built where the military garrison would be barracked at Mount Pleasant airfield. 'If you build a hospital for 5000–6000 people, you are then left with the recurrent expenditure which, if the military do leave, the Falkland Islands government will have great difficulty in meeting. It costs a lot of money to run a hospital: it costs a lot of money to heat and light it and clean it, even before you put people in it. We do not want to leave the citizens of Stanley with a white elephant they cannot afford.

'There's been grandiose talk about a fifty-bed hospital. In fact in the National Health Service one doctor's panel is 2000–2500 people. The population of the Falkland Islands only rates one doctor by NHS standards. They have to have more than that to provide for leave and distances, but fifty-bed hospitals for 1800 citizens is not economic.'

Colonel Templer was asked if he thought suggestions that the British government should pay for a hospital to be built in Stanley were a mistake. The Colonel went on: 'Well, I would see it as a mistake from the point of view of the servicemen for whom the hospital is partly – or largely – being built, since they are going to be in the majority. The servicemen would then be in the absurd position of being sent down to Stanley to see their own military specialists, only to be sent back to Mount Pleasant to be aeromedded back to the United Kingdom. The distance involved would be fairly small in the presence of a proper road.

303

None the less if the military are providing the medical services, then the patients, or rather the military doctors, need to be where the patients are.'

What about the project of having a joint civilian-military hospital? 'This is not in keeping with normal British practice, where general practitioners refer patients to specialists who deal with them in hospital and then refer them back to the care of their general practitioner. And this is the system I would like to see operating in the Falkland Islands. As it was before the hospital fire, we were finding that patients were having too many doctors. They were having both military and civilian doctors, both looking after the patients and not necessarily agreeing with what each other was doing.'

The interviewer suggested that opinion seemed quite strongly in favour of a hospital in Stanley and he was asked what he thought about the prospect.

'If the political will is thus, then so be it. But I think it would be wrong and I think it would be a waste of money, and it may well, as I say, leave the civilian population caring for a white elephant that they cannot afford. Since the lifespan of a hospital, a modern hospital, is not very long these days it would be better that a military hospital was built away from Stanley and if necessary abandoned when it is of no further use to the military and presumably then lines of communication would be re-established with the Argentine.'

The timing of the public utterance took even the local command by surprise and the fluttering in the BFFI dovecot could almost be heard 8000 miles away in London. David Taylor went on the local Falklands Radio with a statement that he had been reassured by the General that the view put forward by Colonel Templer was strictly personal, and that it was still intended to go ahead with plans for a joint civilian-military hospital in Stanley. However, despite Mr Taylor's reassurances it had been known that the local command had favoured an entirely separate hospital at Mount Pleasant and very senior officers had been advocates of the proposal.

The analogy between the Falkland Islands Medical Service and the National Health Service are scarcely germane. The Falkland Islands doctors have to run a community service and each of the three has specialist skills. They have to run a flying doctor service, which means visiting outlying communities on a regular basis to check medical supplies and stores, to confer with those in charge of the medical supplies and to get to know the people to whom they will have to give prescriptions and directions for medical care over the radio. Unlike the garrison doctors they have to provide midwifery, obstetrics and geriatric services. They are also responsible for environmental health and public hygiene in Stanley and the settlements. They frequently board the trawlers of the fishing fleet in harbour to inspect conditions and examine crew for infectious diseases before they land. Doctors also have to supervise social services and administer the welfare fund. In the past, surgical and natal complications would be referred to Comodoro Rivadavia in Argentina, but now much more surgery will have to be done in the Falklands. The hospital will have to give increasing help to the old, because the Falklands population is steadily ageing; it is hoped that proper sheltered accommodation for the old and infirm will form part of a new hospital set-up. Nor does the numbers game work out quite as Colonel Templer implied. Nearly all the briefs for the Falklands medical service state quite categorically that it is responsible for helping the international fishing fleet in an emergency and this can number now up to 5000 men. A week after the old hospital burnt down a Polish fisherman was brought ashore in Stanley with serious head injuries and an emergency neurosurgical operation had to be carried out in the temporary hospital in the Town Hall. If the main hospital is at Mount Pleasant it will mean that Islanders from Stanley will have to make a fifty- or sixty-mile round trip, on a track which will be something less than the M1 if the recent difficulties in Falklands road building are anything to go by, and if they are not employed by the ODA or the FO they will not have subsidised fuel bills.

Colonel Templer left the Islands a month or so after his broadcast. But something of his views appeared to have hung on in the official thinking of the military and civilian administration. During the Falklands winter of 1984 the doctor hired for the Mount Pleasant construction camp died of a heart attack. A military GP was assigned to cover his responsibilities, and then it was said that he could not be spared. At this time there were only two civilian doctors on the Islands, as Dr Bleaney had gone on leave to Britain. One was ordered to Mount Pleasant, leaving one to look after the hospital in Stanley, the old people, the flying doctor service, the morning consultations by radio with the outlying settlements. One of the doctors, David Edwardes-Moss, had been told by a very senior military officer at BFFI that he did not know how the Islands' doctors found enough to do all day. At the time, when the Islands' doctors were discovering their resources so badly stretched, the army apparently had four doctors who could undertake GP responsibilities for the garrison – one was on his way by boat to the small garrison at South Georgia. Unlike the military doctors, who care for physically fit young servicemen, the civilian doctors have to deal with the old and infirm, the sick and the pregnant and, besides covering the health needs of the 1800 Islanders, the fishing fleet of up to 5000 Poles, Russians,

Bulgarians and Spaniards, the two doctors in the Islands medical team were looking after a team of possibly 800–1400 construction men doing dangerous work in the Falklands winter, and that on a project paid for by the MoD and primarily for use by servicemen.

By the time the report into the Hospital Fire was published in July 1984 it was far from understood what facility was to replace the old one, where and when, or who would pay for it. A temporary ward system had been set up in the accommodation cabins for the workers on the Brewster houses; medical staff say that the fire doors and precautions for the building cost over £20,000 and the whole safety installation about £200,000 to build.

On 30 August 1982, two and a half months after General Menendez surrendered his forces in the Islands, the Executive Council meeting in Port Stanley resolved 'that the idea of a new joint hospital, serving both civilian and military needs should be pursued by both the Foreign and Commonwealth Office and the Ministry of Defence.' For two years this declaration has remained pious hope rather than physical reality. In 1983 alone no fewer than three important studies were undertaken by experts for the ODA into the King Edward Memorial Hospital, what could be done to repair it and bring it up to date, or, better still, replace it. A further study of a similar nature was undertaken by Major Roger Thayne for the MoD, and two senior officers visited the old hospital in the course of the year, a Colonel D. MacPhie and the head of the Royal Army Medical Corps, Lieutenant-General Sir Alan Rey. Throughout the year medical staff at the hospital warned about the state of repair, and the lack of essential fire precautions. The question of the hoses not being connected to the hospital's water main was last raised on 9 April, the eve of the fire itself, at a joint civilian-military hospital committee meeting at which Fire Officers were present. Some precautions, such as the installation of smoke-detectors, were taken.

The ODA reports of 1983 were not considered by the Commission of Inquiry into the fire, presumably because they dealt with the construction of a new hospital, and this was specifically excluded by the Inquiry committee from their brief. But all three reports by the ODA experts have pertinent and specific remarks about the state of the King Edward Memorial Hospital as they saw it. These precise descriptions of the general state of repair of the place receive no mention at all in the final report of the enquiry team as presented in July 1984. The three reports were by an architect, John Shelley, a doctor, Dr Penelope Key, and a nursing expert, June Allen, and a specialist in hospital administration, Mr John MacBride. It is worth, perhaps, giving a brief summary of what these four people had to say.

John Shelley visited the Islands from 19 to 26 March 1983. His summary of the position was terse: in Recommendation 3.02 he stated that 'the original timber wing be regarded as both a fire hazard and having reached the end of its economic life, and scheduled for replacement and demolition in the medium term of 2–4 years.' Mr Shelley says that overcrowding in the hospital which he found in March 1983 seemed likely to impede important repair and renovation work; this was relieved subsequently by the military Wyseplan accommodation being opened up on the last day of February 1984. On the old timber part of the hospital Mr Shelley concluded, 'It is my considered view that the original timber wing, built in 1914, is reaching the end of its useful life and is a very real fire hazard, particularly under its current occupancy pressures. It is not worth spending on it the sort of money necessary to bring it up to present-day standards of hygiene/safety.'

The architectural expert's report on the hospital goes into detail about what new accommodation might be built and where. At one point, in discussing the problem of making repairs in the current conditions, Mr Shelley says: 'All that can be done under present circumstances is patch and mend as required, and hope that the boilers hold out.' In Falklands public administration jargon 'patch and mend' seems to mean '*mañana*'.

The medical experts, Dr Penelope Key and June Allen, had studied the hospital. Dr Key stated that 'the actual safety of the building is now open to question.' She and Miss Allen proposed a nine-point plan for immediate repairs, relieving of overcrowding in the wards, reorganisation of the wards and operating theatre, establishment of a separate out-patient clinic, an improved switchboard, new laundry and new electric autoclave. Their tenth point of recommendation ran, 'It should be recognised that the above are interim patching measures, making the best of a difficult situation [for] both working and caring for patients in far from satisfactory conditions.' The next recommendation said, 'In the long term we recommend the construction of a new civilian hospital . . . There is a strong case now to commence identifying funds.'

John MacBride, the administration expert, visited the Islands in June 1983 and informed the Chief Secretary, Dick Baker, that the ODA architect's view was that 'the military wing is past its useful life and the Churchill Wing was functionally obsolete'. He suggested that in the immediate future the choice was between a major refurbishment programme or a 'patch and mend' job. He registered a request to return to Port Stanley in January and February 1984.

By July 1983 it was known, or putting it more pedantically, it could have been known or should have been known, at the highest level in the ODA in Whitehall of the grave misgivings of three sets of experts about the state of repair and conditions in the hospital in Stanley. Three experts, Mr Shelley, Dr Key and June Allen, had said plainly that safety standards were clearly at risk in the old building. But by the week of the fire in April 1984 no concrete plans had been drawn up for a replacement to the obsolete hospital, nor had funds been identified for the major repair programme advocated for the civilian medical facilities in Port Stanley. In the very week of the fire another ODA architect was due to go to Port Stanley to see what plans might be suitable for refurbishing the old hospital buildings, but not replacing them.

In the northern summer of 1984 a new hospital administrator for the Islands was appointed by the ODA; the civilian doctors had been badly in need of one practically since the conflict of 1982. The new administrator was Major Roger Thayne, who had worked out the schedule of priorities and functions for a joint civilian-military hospital with Dr Bleaney in August 1983. Meanwhile the ODA in London had begun to calculate the cost of a new joint civilian-military hospital which one expert, on a rough estimate, put at between £15 and £18 million. On a proportional basis in relation to the size of patient population on the Islands at any one time this would involve the civilian administration in a capital expenditure of between £4 and £6 million. The PWD director made a similar calculation of from £5 to £10 million. The Islands' Hospital Committee were concerned that quite apart from the outlay of £4 million initially for the new facility, there would be the likelihood of much higher contribution to recurrent running costs, which would require careful consideration by the Falkland Islands government. It would be very difficult for them to find funds, particularly as the hospital and health services were excluded from the programme to which the £31 million was to be devoted under Lord Shackleton's proposals.

The second Shackleton Report shows medical services for the Islands required an expenditure of about £270,000 for the year 1981–2. The debate about the new hospital is coloured by the tiny margin of expenditure that the Falklands government has in its annual budget of about £3,250,000. In November 1983, Sir Rex Hunt asked the Director of Public Works to work out the cost of rewiring the hospital to a safe and efficient level; he hoped to get the MoD to pay the bill of some £50,000. Well before the King Edward Memorial Hospital burnt down the project for new hospital facilities and old people's accommodation had become a football between the ODA, MoD, Falklands government and local Command at BFFI.

The day after the fire, Timothy Raison, the Minister for Overseas Development, responsible for the ODA, told the House of Commons: 'Looking ahead, we stand ready to help the Falkland Islands government in the urgent task of building a new hospital as soon as possible. A hospital architect will travel to the Falkland Islands within a few days. We shall provide the Falkland Islands government with financial and other assistance in the construction of a new hospital.'

Four months after that statement was made there was little indication of what funds would be available for such a project. The architect from the ODA, Brian Hitchcox, travelled to the Islands as promised, and drew up a report. This will be the fourth feasibility study commissioned by the ODA in eighteen months. A senior civil servant at the ODA told me in July 1984 that the plan will now have to be scrutinised by the Falkland Islands government. Earlier, he had hinted that it was possible that the capital sum for the civilian contribution to the new hospital might have to come from the £31 million 'Shackleton money'. He also told me that the Islands' administration still had to decide what they really wanted from a hospital. An ODA official had previously suggested to one of the Islands' medical staff that the Falklands administration had to decide if they could afford a hospital at all, in particular the recurrent running costs of a modern facility.

This view is shared by some Islanders. One Falklands official in London put it to me that the Islands perhaps would have to find a way of doing without a hospital if they could not afford one.

In the days immediately after the fire I asked Sir Rex Hunt if there should not be an appeal specifically for medical facilities for the Islanders themselves. He declined the suggestion on a number of counts, though the Bahamas-based philanthropist 'Union' Jack Hayward had already pledged £1 million for a new hospital. Sir Rex feared that such generous donations might be absorbed by the ODA and subtracted from the budget they had already allocated for the Islands. Shortly after the conflict the people of Guernsey offered £250,000 for old people's accommodation; this sum has been reduced to £100,000 as nothing was done immediately with the original offer.

Alastair Cameron, now London representative of the Falkland Islands government, told me that 'there had been enough appeals for the Falklands already'. Indeed one newspaper columnist referred to the Islanders as 'scroungers' after the fire. However, there might still be grounds for money being raised by appeal if it was realised how very little public money has been spent on the Islanders themselves as opposed to defence installations, the subsidies and salaries of administrators, bureaucrats, functionaries and advisers, their allowances and their air fares to and from Britain.

The fear expressed by senior members of government and the community in Stanley is that heavy capital expenditure by the Island administration will take it into such heavy debt that the Falklands will have to be run on grant-in-aid and so effectively controlled by ODA and FO officials in Whitehall and that this would mark the beginnings of the end of the community of the Falklands.

At the end of October 1984 Brian Hitchcox returned to Stanley with plans for a new hospital to be shared between the military and civilian doctors and nurses, and to be constructed on the site of the old one at a cost of £6.4 million. Throughout the English summer and autumn the MoD and ODA had wrangled about sharing the cost, and some military opinion favoured continuing with separate facilities either in Stanley or at Mount Pleasant: a further £1 million was already being spent on military operating theatres and other services at the coastel accommodation near RAF Stanley. The plans produced by ODA for the new, smaller, twenty-five-bed hospital were to be approved by the Islands' Joint Councils. The initial cost for the civilian side of the facility was to be put up by the British government through the ODA, and it would be separate from the £31 million Shackleton funds. Islanders, however, continued to be concerned about the prospects of high recurrent annual expenditure which the new hospital complex might involve. Recurrent expenditure on public facilities, as well as the undercapitalisation of new farming enterprises and development projects, seem to present the most serious doubts about the future of Islands' economy. Initial estimates were that the hospital staff would cost the Falklands Treasury £300,000 annually. The administration was being asked for a similar sum to maintain the road between Mount Pleasant airfield and Stanley each year.

Before the architect had flown to Stanley at the end of October 1984 it was being made clear that the Islanders' representatives would only agree to what they thought they could afford to maintain, and the facilities being proposed from London might have to be trimmed back considerably. The new plans did not cover sheltered accommodation for old people. The most damaging effect of the bickering about who was prepared to pay for what in a new hospital in Stanley, and who was prepared to pay for a new full facility at all, was that few of the public and private arguments of the case seemed to consider the provision of adequate care for the elderly and sick as a fundamental of any civilised society. A society that cannot achieve this or places a low priority on it, is surely one incapable of supporting itself, and in danger of imploding.

# Chapter 14

# Beyond
the Falklands

In the bright days of early April the fishing fleet rode at anchor in
Berkeley Sound. Most of the trawlers were Polish, but at different times
they have been joined by Russians, Poles, Spaniards, West Germans,
Japanese and even a Bulgarian vessel. Neal Watson said some mornings
he would wake up to see three large factory freezer ships tending the
fleet, from the windows of his farmhouse at Long Island.

Beyond the Falklands lies one of the richest fishing grounds in the
southern hemisphere. Since the conflict of 1982 the pattern of fishing
there has altered radically, for these used to be almost exclusively the
preserves of the Argentine fleets. But since June 1982 only one or two
trawlers from the Patagonian coast have attempted to run the gauntlet of
the Royal Navy's patrols. In place of the Argentines, the Russians and
Poles came to start taking fish in greater numbers than before. In 1983
the ships paid £250,000 in harbour dues to the Falklands, and in a three-
month period from September to December, Les Halliday, the harbour-
master, calculated that the Poles alone caught 110,669 tonnes of fish in
Falklands waters. Conservation experts reckon the fleets of the Eastern
bloc have been taking at least half a million tonnes of fish a year from
grounds within 200 miles of the Islands' shores.

Lord Shackleton recommended that the British government consider
declaring a 200-mile fishing limit, following a practice adopted by many
countries, including Britain. The fishing limit has become the great
dream for a Falklands bonanza; for the Islanders it is the way their
community can win the football pools or the Irish Sweep, as it were.
However, Mrs Thatcher's administration has steadfastly refused to heed
their request for the unilateral declaration of a fishery zone, which Lord
Shackleton calculated would net the Islands' Treasury at least £3 million
a year, and almost double its fiscal revenue overnight. On her visit to the
Islands in early 1984, Baroness Young, the FO Minister responsible for

the Falklands, suggested that any move to declare a fishing limit would be diplomatically inopportune while Her Majesty's Government was trying to 'normalise' relations with Argentina. Besides, a fishery zone would involve the Navy in further patrolling commitments beyond the Islands' coasts.

Plans have been laid by the FIC in partnership with the Japanese fisheries combine Taiyo to develop a deep-water fishery based in the Falklands. The scheme has been embraced with enthusiasm by Ted Needham. £200,000 of the Shackleton development fund has been allocated for placing two observers with Taiyo ships for two fishing seasons round the Falklands; but once more what Sir Rex Hunt refers to as 'that strange combination of Murphy's Law and the Falklands Factor' intervened. In 1983 the Taiyo ships sailed without the funds being available for the observers. Protests from the FIC at the delay reached as far as Downing Street. The replies from Port Stanley had the logic of the chicken and egg argument: it was hardly worth considering the development of offshore fishery until a limit was declared, so with no limit there would be no Falklands offshore fishery. But two observers were scheduled to work with the Taiyo ships from January 1985.

The waters beyond the Falklands are the home of more than twenty species of fish; few of the varieties are household names. Most numerous are hake, blue whiting and a species still most commonly known by its Latin name, *Notothenia rossii marmorata,* which is frequently found close to South Georgia. The biggest harvest is expected to be from krill according to the 1982 Shackleton Report, though its estimation of a potential annual haul of 75–150 million tonnes now appears wildly exaggerated. It is also apparent that some of the expectations from the catching of fin fish may have been too optimistic. A study by the White Fish Authority, cited by Shackleton, observed that many of the blue whiting caught offshore from the Falklands were infected with parasites, making them suitable only for the fishmeal and animal feed trade. The Falkland Islands Foundation, one of the best organised of Falklands pressure groups, which is affiliated to the World Wildlife Fund, has warned that fish stocks are now being seriously depleted by the activities of the Russian, Polish and Japanese fleets. Harbour officials at Port Stanley say they noticed a high proportion of immature fish in the catches they had seen aboard the Eastern European trawlers. BAS life scientists say they suspect the breeding stock of fin fish across the Antarctic Convergence between South Georgia and the Falklands are in danger of being fished out. Some years ago breeding stock of fin fish round the French dependency of the Îles Kerguelen were all but wiped out in a matter of a few seasons. The Falkland Islands Foundation has argued that a fishery limit round the Falklands has been needed as much for reasons of conservation as commercial exploitation.

Despite investment in small bakeries and wool mills and the like from the FIDC, the second greatest revenue earner in the Falklands, as with so many curious corners of late European colonialism, has been trade in postage stamps. Before the conflict of 1982 stamps brought in a revenue to the Falklands Treasury of about £600,000 a year, and the Shackleton Report calculated that this could be increased to about £1 million or more a year. However, Lord Shackleton and his team said they did not welcome the prospect of an island community defended by 3000 soldiers which was dependent on stamps for a large part of its external revenue.

In the *annus mirabilis* of 1983 the income from stamps did very nearly top the £1 million mark. A handsome issue commemorating the 150th anniversary of the Colony sold in their hundreds to collectors across the world. Many of the designs had the bold colours and heavy naive quality of simple woodcuts, and they were adapted successfully for a series of postcards and calendars. Other sets commemorating the campaign and liberation from the Argentines sold well to the troops, though revenue from philatelic services fell in 1983 to about £600,000 again. The Dependencies' stamps make about £100,000 profit a year which goes to the administration of South Georgia, and the British Antarctic Territories' issues clear about £250,000, which, to the chagrin of the Falklands administration, goes to BAS.

Since 1976 a small set of rooms hidden at the back of the Port Stanley Town Hall has carried the grandiose title of 'The Philatelic Bureau'. It has been in the charge of Lewis Clifton, a Falkland Islander who served several years in Antarctica with BAS. Since the stamp boom after June 1982 Lewis has had to move his desk to the back section of the Magistrates' Court Room, where it is fenced in by piles of cartons, envelopes and packaging materials. Lewis looks at the mountain of cardboard and envelopes with a resigned air, as if it is about to engulf him. He was one of the few Islanders who told me he was thinking of going away from the Falklands, not for fear of any political deal with Argentina, but to find a new career. Recently the distribution and sale of Falklands stamps has been taken over by the Crown Agents with two representatives marketing them in Britain and Europe, and North America. Lewis said his job could become fraught with controversy, particularly in his role on the committee which chooses the design for new issues and covers. Some sets had been designed by professionals in Britain and overseas, some by local artists like the author and painter Ian Strange. Members of the committee or the Stanley establishment were almost never unanimous in their appreciation of new issues and discussions over the designs of the 150th Anniversary of the Falklands series had been outstanding for their acrimony, Lewis suggested. The designs of the campaign and liberation covers and issues had a comic-strip aspect: planes, soldiers, ships in martial bustle and busyness like the overcrowded scene of the plaque on the Port Stanley memorial to the conflict. Some collectors have complained that too many Falkland stamps have been produced since June 1982, and this has affected their value with professional dealers.

Another growth activity beyond the Falklands, and because of them, has been in pressure groups and part-time advisers in Britain. First in the field was the Falkland Islands Association, which grew up at the suggestion of four Executive Councillors in 1968 when they feared a Labour government sell-out of the Islands to Argentina. The leading light has been E.W. Hunter Christie, whose quixotic and acerbic book *The Antarctic Problem* is an excellent guide to the tangled diplomatic history of Antarctica and the South Atlantic up to the 1940s and is still used as a standard reference text by the Foreign Office. The Association and its parliamentary lobby offshoot, the Falkland Islands Committee, had a success quite disproportionate to its size in blocking the lease-back or condominium proposals tentatively put forward by Nicholas Ridley to the House of Commons in December 1980. A second success was the establishment of a permanent Falkland Islands government representative in London, for whom the Association provided offices. At first the post was held unofficially by Councillor John Cheek during the months of the Argentine occupation of the Islands from April to June 1982; John Cheek had been due to return to the Falklands after completing a management course for his employers, Cable and Wireless, being held in Surrey on the day the first Argentine marines moved into Port Stanley. The first official Falklands Representative was Adrian Monk, a staunch member of the Kelper farming community, who worked in London for eighteen months for no salary.

The Falklands Association for a number of years held a reception each June at Lincoln's Inn. The gathering in June 1984 was noticeably smaller than in the previous year, and Hunter Christie announced he was retiring from running the organisation.

Best organised and best funded of the pressure groups is the Falkland Islands Foundation, 'For the Conservation of Wildlife, Wrecks and Places of Historic Interest', which is chaired by Sir Peter Scott, with a former Falklands Governor, Jim Parker, as the vice-chairman. The Foundation places heavy stress on the Islands' natural history, and has printed a handsome colour poster for the garrison troops. It shows where the main colonies of seals, birds and penguins are to be found and enjoins

314

the soldiers to look after them. The Foundation also promotes the conservation of wrecks which litter the Falklands coasts by the dozen, giving
a complete archaeological catalogue of the navigation and commerce of
the waters of Patagonia and the Horn: Breton whalers, Spanish cargo
vessels, Norwegian sealers, British, French and American men-of-war,
and early steamships. John Smith, the proprietor of Sparrow Hawk
House, the Stanley guesthouse, is an enthusiastic archivist of the wrecks;
he has drawn several maps marking where each of nearly 100 ships
foundered round the Falklands over the past three centuries. He believes
the wrecks almost as much as the wildlife and fishing of salmon trout in
the Falklands streams could be attraction for a small quality tourist trade
to the Islands. In the name of conservation of fishing stocks, as we have
seen, the Falkland Islands Foundation has become a powerful lobby for
the creation of a 200-mile fishing limit round the Islands.

Rather less public in their activities is the South Atlantic Council
which draws members from both the Labour and Conservative back-
benchers, such as Charles Townshend (Tory) and George Foulkes
(Labour). The Council is guided by two academics, Dr Walter Little of
Liverpool University and Dr Chris Mitchell of the City University,
London. The organisation does not publish regular policy documents,
but is known to favour a diplomatic solution to the Falklands dispute as
soon as possible. In June 1984 Council members visited Argentina and
there were suggestions that Britain and Argentina should agree to run
jointly a fishing zone off Patagonia and round the Falklands. This has
faint echoes of Lord Shackleton's original proposals in 1976 of co-
operation between Britain and Argentina for the exploitation of hydrocarbon resources in the Malvina Basin, where British technology and
investment would combine with Argentine enterprises working from
Patagonia, Comodoro Rivadavia, Rio Grande or Rio Gallegos. There is
no doubt that many Falklanders still dream that oil will bring the big
pay-off at the end of the rainbow. In the middle of 1984 Sir Rex Hunt's
office announced that exploration licences had been granted to drill for
oil at Douglas Station on East Falkland, the property of Harry Camm,
an old friend of the FIC chairman, Ted Needham.

Perhaps the most picaresque and colourful of the groups interested in
helping the Falklands from Britain, though possibly the most intermittent and irregular in its business, is the South West Atlantic Group,
SWAG. Led by Lord Shackleton and Lord Buxton, chairman of Anglia
Television, SWAG tries to find projects and ideas that will boost the
Falklands economy, and encourage a diplomatic settlement of the
dispute with Argentina on the right terms. But all such groups suffer
from the difficulty of access to the Falklands and the lack of a regular

flow of accurate information from there. Eighteen months after the conflict discussion of whether charges of war crimes could be brought against some Argentine officers was still on the minutes, and one of SWAG's more frequent attendants was still seriously considering trying to persuade a consortium from the City of London to sink £100 million worth of investment in the Islands. Rather more modestly, some SWAG members have been trying to promote an enterprise called Pebble Island Projects, the production and sale of souvenirs, such as polished pebble paperweights from Pebble Island, costume jewellery of similar origin, 'herbal sachets' with Falklands herbs and grasses, and a 'reproduction scrimshaw' like those made by South Georgia whalers.

In the middle of Port Stanley is a house painted an aggressive salmon pink and bearing the unsurprising legend above the door, 'The Pink Shop'. It is owned and run by Tony and Annie Chater who provide a quality souvenir trade in knitwear, books, calendars and pictures, etchings and prints. They are settlers who have invested their lives in the Falklands, though their names will scarcely dance upon the conversation at Government House or in the deliberations of the FIDC. Unlike the other small enterprises they are not working on a development grant or loan and yet they are providing a quality trade as the traffic of soldiers and visitors about to return to England through their front door proves. Tony studied as a graphic artist and sells his own prints of penguins and birds. His posters of the diving birds and the penguins are among the most popular wall decorations in the South Atlantic. Lately he has been selling attractive print reproductions of James Cook's map of his course from Cape Horn to South Georgia. Tony arrived from England – 'pure south London, Croydon, mate' – to work a few seasons as a farm hand or navvy; he married Annie, the estranged wife of a manager, who hails originally from the north of England, and this offended the Byzantine complexities of West Falkland social propriety. Two years after the conflict they say they intend to stay and that the Falklands are their living – so much so that in order to build up the business Tony gave up the chance to go back to his friends and relations in England in the summer of 1984 and Annie and their two boys went alone.

Annie told me she also planned to work for the business, having now resigned as the supervisor of education in camp. Her skill as a teacher is admired throughout the Falklands but education has now lost her services. As camp supervisor she pioneered teaching by radio in the more remote settlements. She also insisted on better conditions and qualifications for the travelling teachers, but received little positive response. Until recently, most of the camp teachers were unqualified, lived out of suitcases and had to pay their fare back to England. They did not enjoy full OSAS supplements like the teachers from Britain working at the school in Stanley, as they were paid locally. Annie recommended that each camp teacher should have a base, a room in a house in one settlement, to which they could come home after a week or so of travel. The lack of education for the children under ten in several settlements, as I heard from Ginny Forster, Glenda Watson, Rosemary Wilkinson, Margie Goss, has been little short of scandalous. Since Annie's resignation there have been some improvements: the local administration has agreed to pay fares to and from Britain for camp teachers and to provide a base for them in the settlements. Though she found the state of camp teaching frustrating, it was not the sole reason for her resignation.

When the post of Supervisor of Education became vacant in 1983, Annie and a teacher at the Stanley Senior School, Peter Felton, applied. The advertisement said that applicants required a degree and a teaching qualification, and that they should have been head of a department or school with experience of administration and keeping accounts. The job paid a salary of £7120 and an OSAS supplement of £7800 tax free if the successful applicant came from Britain, plus a bonus of fifteen per cent on completion of the contract. Both applicants from Port Stanley were rejected without being extended the courtesy of an interview, which reflects the casual approach and lack of public disclosure that pervades so much of Falklands public administration. After some months Annie received a personal letter from Sir Rex Hunt, which suggested that she did not have the experience required by the advertisement (this despite her taking responsibility for the running of the camp education department) and that 'the right person needed to be identified' for the post from the United Kingdom. For whatever reason, which was never fully made public, an experienced teacher and department head with direct knowledge of the Islands and schooling there and one who would live in her own house on a local salary was rejected for a person who 'still needed to be identified'. That person, if he or she came from Britain, would be paid a salary supplement funded by the British taxpayer and he would require his own house, doubtless among the smart new residences in Jeremy Moore Avenue, the Virginia Water of Stanley.

The new Supervisor of Education will find a department in need of a few running repairs and in some areas a thorough overhaul. But a remedial policy is likely to be one of the Falklands' 'patch and mend'. There is to be a recruiting drive for camp teachers. However, even if the authorities in Stanley do manage to recruit the full quota of camp teachers, the first time they will have succeeded in this for some years, their qualifications are still likely to be considerably lower than those of their more qualified colleagues in Stanley, employed by the ODA and rewarded with OSAS supplements. But where camp settlements have their own schools, conditions can be difficult.

A teacher hired by the FIC to run their school at Goose Green explained to me that while his class of a dozen or so may appear to be small, he has to teach in one room children whose ages can range from three or four to ten and eleven. The Falkland Islands government has pledged to spend £1.2 million on expanding hostel buildings in Port Stanley so all children from camp who want to can attend the secondary school in Port Stanley.

The secondary school is a great barn of a building that looks well worn in its years, and conditions for teaching the wide range of talents and interests are hardly ideal. A misfortune for the Islands is that the brightest children tend to go abroad, as the school does not run many A-level GCE courses. The British Council awards Falklanders bursaries to the Thomas Peacocke School at Rye in Sussex. Of Falklanders completing degree and diploma courses in universities and colleges in Britain and overseas, a high proportion remain abroad; though numerically small this drain of native talent has had its effect on the Falklands community.

An import awaited in the Islands with mixed emotions has been the long-anticipated new constitution. It will change the face of the public administration by encouraging more disclosure and it will favour a more open style of government. Hitherto the Legislative Council has been the Islands' main debating forum with six elected representatives taking part, together with senior government officers such as the Civil Commissioner (or in the years before June 1982, the Governor), the Chief Secretary (or his modern equivalent, the Chief Executive) and the Financial Secretary. But administrative measures and decisions of government have been taken in the Executive Council, which consists of two Legislative and two Executive Councillors nominated by the Governor or Civil Commissioner, who is the presiding officer. He is joined by the Chief Secretary and the Financial Secretary and, since 1982, the Military Commissioner (though the rules prevent him from voting). The Executive Council carries out all its discussions in secret, and only its final decisions are summarised and announced publicly. Outsiders may put forward matters to be deliberated but they may never know the substance of the debate, the arguments for or against the executive decision. The reason Ex. Co. (as the Council is always called in the Islands) members give for maintaining such secrecy is that they feel it would be unfitting and counter-productive in such a small community to air in public the business and family affairs of individuals and local companies. However this has earned Ex. Co. a reputation for eccentric and even arbitrary action, and some Islanders think its authority is too narrowly based. Since the 1982 conflict, for long periods, only one Executive Councillor has been nominated (Bill Luxton of Chartres on West Falkland) instead of two. One elected Councillor, Terry Peck, has resigned for personal and political reasons. The new constitution proposes only one elected council of eight members with both legislative and executive functions. With so much public attention and money now concentrated from Britain on the Falklands the demand has grown for greater public accountability in their administration. Critics of the old system would like secrecy in the discussions leading to executive action to be the exception rather than the norm.

If this had been the case in the recent past there would be some explanation of how the Ex. Co. could take a decision in August 1982 to demand a new hospital and yet pursue this with such laggard resolve. There might be some indication of why the gradualist approach to the Shackleton recommendations came to be adopted in the Islands, explanations of the intricacies of educational policy which have eluded people like Annie Chater, and clarification of exactly how the price and manner of purchase of pieces of land like the Packe's were arrived at and the policy of loans and assistance to the new farmers of San Carlos was evolved.

At the end of 1986 the Development Corporation will review its activities. By that time it will have revealed its strategy for disposing of the £4.6 million of its allocation from Shackleton funds, in addition to the £1 million allocated for farm purchases under current development plans. However, it is likely that the Falklands economy will reach a crisis, a real turning-point, well before the deadline David Taylor has given for review of the FIDC's progress. A dip in wool prices could put a number of the new farmers in financial straits. An official with direct administrative experience in both the military and civilian sectors in the Islands, a rare enough qualification, has told me of his fears that 'there could be the makings of a disaster', in 1985, if civilian-military relations are not resolved over matters such as the new hospital and health-care facilities for the Islanders and servicemen. Already, two years after the Argentine surrender, it has been suggested to me by Sir Rex Hunt himself that the £31 million 'Shackleton money' will not be sufficient for the development of the Islands' economy to the end of the decade and a further similar amount will be needed when the five-year period of the Shackleton programme comes to an end in 1988. It seems hardly likely that any government in Westminster or Whitehall department, such as the ODA, will welcome such a prediction, particularly in the light of the rising bills for

Britain's other commitments overseas in the late eighties. St Helena, for instance, has begun to demand similar development aid to the Falklands; the population, at 6000, is three times that of the Kelpers and nine out of ten St Helenians are dependent on government for employment or social security. Defence commitments outside NATO to Belize, to reinforcing Gibraltar, and providing aid and forces in the Gulf and Red Sea areas are beginning to prove more substantial than projected two or three years ago.

As the sea of advice round the Falklands threatens to become an ocean, and as the cohorts of advisers, consultants, and general experts staggering off the Hercules flight from Ascension grow to a legion, one must hesitate in recommending yet another public review or inquiry into the administration and development of the Falklands. Yet many, including some connected with the drawing up and execution of Lord Shackleton's recommendations, think that such an inquiry should be considered urgently. Lord Shackleton himself told me he thought somebody should study how his recommendations were being carried out, from the perspective of the Islanders themselves.

Access to public information in the Falklands by interested people in Britain is not as easy as it seems. Journalists can pay over £2000 for the round air-trip with the RAF, but they have to be cleared for entry to the Islands by the immigration authorities in the Islands or by the FO. They find themselves shepherded about military installations by the MoD press officers; they have to charter their own tickets on the Islands' efficient but not very cheap air service if they want to visit settlements outside Port Stanley. Incidentally the Falkland Islands Government Air Service is a model of how a development enterprise could work in the Falklands. It has four pilots, three local men and one on OSAS, and runs two Islander aircraft and a De Havilland Beaver. At the end of his contract the OSAS man will be replaced by a local man. The airline offers a thoroughly reliable and flexible communication service between the islands of the Falkland group five days a week. It is subsidised, and it charges visitors a fifteen-per-cent surcharge, but it shows every prospect of working to budget with an entirely local staff. The snag is that it will only run at weekends in an emergency because of overtime costs.

The expense of travelling to and within the Islands has prevented first-hand study by more than a handful of Britain's MPs and MEPs. Overseas travel funds for the House of Commons Select Committees are restricted, but it is likely that there will be a growing demand in Westminster for a rigorous review of current Falklands policy either by Select Committee or government itself.

A prime reason for such a review is that first-hand evidence for Lord Shackleton's Reports was taken over eight years ago in 1976, and the economy and community have changed greatly since then. A second reason is that his original proposals for development in the Islands, put forward in 1982, have been watered down considerably, submitted to an approach of gradualism; in some areas, current development plans resemble the original recommendations only in shadowy outline. Since the conflict the land purchase programme has involved loans for only one and a half estates owned by overseas companies and landlords; programmes on immigration and housing have been subject to delay and bureaucratic muddle; and there is confusion over development of higher education and provision of hospital services for the civilian population. On the other hand, most, if not all, of Shackleton's proposals for the creation of new government posts or development officers have been carried out.

Judging by the speed with which both of Lord Shackleton's committees worked, investigators for such a review need spend only a month to six weeks in the Islands and prepare their findings in three to four months. It need not be a long or elaborate procedure and it could confine itself to six main topics, which are interlocking:

1. Land reform; the viability of the land purchase scheme as executed so far; and the assistance given to the new farmers. Suspicion that many of the new subdivisions are undercapitalised should be examined, as should the long-term funding of grants and subsidies to Falklands farmers. In addition, tenancy and share-farming arrangements should be looked at, where appropriate, to ensure adequate guarantees of welfare and social security are given to the share-farmers should they run into difficulty and profit margins be inadequate.

2. The structure of the Development Corporation, its manpower and the funding of the programme now being undertaken.

3. Housing and immigration. Following the expenditure of £7.2 million, due to bureaucratic muddle and delays in dispatch, on fifty-two Brewster houses, £1.5 million has been allocated for a 'rolling housing' programme. Houses will be built and sold, the revenue being used to build further homes. This has meant a moratorium in an immigration programme for the Falklands. Few settler families have gone to the Falklands to seek a permanent livelihood there in the two years from June 1982. Shackleton's main brief was to devise a programme to arrest the decline in population and develop the Falklands economy. How long a delay in an immigration programme can be expected?

4. Subjects specifically excluded from the second Shackleton Report: education, medical and hospital services.

5. Public administration; the Falkland Islands government.

6. Civilian-military relations; the impact of the garrison on the community in general and on civil administration in particular.

Most if not all of these subjects have been discussed in detail or outline in the essay which forms the second part of this book, but before I conclude I would like to make one or two further comments. Any discussion of the future role of government in the Islands and of constitutional reform should look at the office of Civil Commissioner. It has almost too many functions to be vested in one person. The Civil Commissioner is the Head of the Falklands government, the Representative of the Crown, the appointee and servant of the Foreign Office. He is a local executive, a diplomat, a negotiator with a speaker's role, who represents London to Stanley and Stanley to London, and much of his time is taken up with bilateral relations, bargaining, begging and borrowing from the Military Command in the Islands.

This is not to imply personal criticism of Sir Rex Hunt who has worked with the energy of men many years his junior. Unlike some more recent appointments to the Falklands administration he has always been accessible to journalists and open about policies and actions of the government there; he and Lady Hunt have been hospitable beyond the call of duty to itinerants like myself.

But the role of Sir Rex's successor should be made less complex, as it has become increasingly difficult to be accountable to both the government of the Islands and the FO in Whitehall. One solution would be for a chairman to be elected to head the new eight-man council and this chairman would have to be an Islander. London would appoint a governor who would have authority over both the civilian administration and the Military Command, in all but purely tactical matters.

There are some grounds for questioning whether the kind of person recruited by the FO today is well suited for service in a remote rural community like the Falklands. The graduate with ambitions for an ambassadorial career looks peculiarly out of place among the Kelpers, farmers, sheep-men. You can spot them a mile off at Stanley airport or in the roads with their soft shoes, striped shirts and expensive windcheaters, a desperate if practical gesture to dress for the climate. Similarly it is questionable whether a background in the commerce of the City of London or an imposing array of degrees and doctorates in agriculture are entirely sufficient for those who are to pilot the development programme and advise the new farmers. They say they feel more at home with people who know a bit about 'dog and stick' farming, someone used to living with mud on his boots.

The test of the success of any policy towards the Islands themselves must lie in the development programme, particularly in its agricultural aspects, the improvement of husbandry on the farms, the appropriation and subdivision of large estates and related industries like the Fox Bay Woollen Mill. Without a thriving farming community the garrison and their defences form a hollow ring of hardware and sentinels. At the time of writing there seems to be a measure of indecision about whether the land development programme and the subdivision of big farms should be run on purely economic lines or on a social and political basis to encourage more people to own their own land and work it and to bring more settlers to the Islands. John Ferguson, the former head of the ARC and Agricultural Officer for the Islands government, told me that on balance much of the programme had to be run on social and political lines. If purely commercial criteria are to be applied to the small farmers' operations, as they appear to have been at San Carlos, there is evidence that many are badly undercapitalised and with rising costs of fuel and fencing and fluctuating wool prices (between 1970 and 1973 wool prices fluctuated nearly 250 per cent according to the first Shackleton Report), then they risk failing before the decade is out. There are already signs that one or two farmers who bought land in the earlier subdivisions before the sale of Packe's estate are on the point of giving up. If the land programme, meagre though it is compared to Lord Shackleton's original intentions, fails then farmers will leave derelict land, which could return to cool and windswept desert. Despite the boomings of hereditary landowners resident in the Islands about the new men and women on the land 'learning to stand on their own two feet', the small farmers will have to be given a helping hand with generous loan terms and a scale of subsidies comparable to those available to the hill farmers and cultivators of marginal land in the Highlands and Islands of Scotland, and it is the intention of David Taylor and Simon Armstrong that this should be done. Terry Betts, chairman of the GEU, painted me a pungent and depressing scene if the current plans to develop farms, fishing and light industry fail. 'At the moment,' he told me at the end of our second interview, 'fishing has been buggered up politically. Us little "ches" [che, as in Che Guevara, a term of affection used in the South Atlantic, even more so since the Argentine presence in the Falklands in 1982] will get the blame for not pushing hard enough, if development does not succeed. At the end of the day what we'll find is that by 1987 we'll be back where we were in 1977. The thing most people don't realise is that most of the money is being spent here to go straight back to the UK.'

The biggest social and political change in the Falklands since the colony began in 1833 has been the British military presence in the Islands from 21 May 1982, the day of the San Carlos landings. During the Second World War a garrison of about 2000 men was stationed in the Falklands, but they had nothing like the impact of the present garrison as they were under strict wartime security conditions and many were connected with naval deployments well away from the Islands themselves. Despite the policies of the local BFFI Command for the separation of the civilian and service populations, the garrison has had an irreversible political and social impact on the Falklands community. Successive Military Commissioners have tried to ensure that the garrison did not engulf the local community, particularly in Port Stanley: 'We want them to feel we are just down the road,' was the characteristically elegant formulation General David Thorne gave the policy. General Keith Spacie summed it up more bluntly: 'We don't want them [the civilians] to look on us as a crutch.' But the Military Commissioner is involved in the councils and decision-making of the civilian community. He has a large administrative staff working in the middle of Port Stanley. The superior spending power of the individual servicemen is conspicuous in the handful of cafés, shops and pubs in the little town. The superior spending power of the MoD, too, is apparent in their approach to the few joint civilian-military projects they are involved in, such as the plans for a new hospital. The fact that they have more money to spend on manpower has made them try to control the pace and direction of policy, and in the case of the hospital dictate what is 'good' for the Islanders. In such areas, even by UK standards, let alone Falkland, the military have lavish powers of expenditure. The annual budget for salaries and allowances for army doctors is put conservatively at about £1,250,000, and this leaves out the expenditure on Royal Navy and RAF doctors; the total expenditure by the Falklands government on medical services for 1981–2 was £270,000 according to the Shackleton Report.

The military presence can have an indirect impact, too. Kevin and Diane Kilmartin farm 30,000 acres at Bluff Cove Farm, shearing 2650 sheep out of a flock of 4500 on mountain and pasture grazing. They are settlers from Britain who have sunk their lives' hopes and investments in a future in the Falklands as much as have the Chaters, the Gosses, the Watsons, the Shorts, the Forsters and the Cockwells. Kevin qualified as a barrister in England but chose the quiet life of sheep-farming in the Falklands. Diane was a nurse at the King Edward Memorial

Hospital when they met. In the short campaign of 1982 they gave help and assistance to the British soldiers moving across their land for the final march on Stanley, ferrying ammunition by tractor to the troops dug in along their eastern boundary fence and giving the whole of 2 Para a hot meal. The Kilmartins are held in very warm affection still by the battalion commanders in 1982, Colonel David Chaundler, and the now Lieutenant-Colonel Chris Keeble. But since June 1982 the military presence has been with the community of Bluff Cove continuously, in more or less obtrusive fashion. Soldiers walk across their land to visit penguin colonies on the shore, which the Kilmartins do not mind provided their permission is asked beforehand. Phantoms have carried low-level runs along their fence lines and the fences are now to be taken down to make way for the road to the new airfield at Mount Pleasant, only a few miles away. The couple who came to the Falklands for a pastoral life where they willingly chose tranquillity rather than financial reward will have a strategic airport on their doorstep and the farming day from sunrise to sunset will be marked by the roar of regular fighter patrols taking off and landing.

Kevin is a man who keeps his own counsel, his mood and thoughts hard to discern on a face covered by the rug of blond Viking beard. In a quiet moment of conversation in the farmhouse kitchen, one of the tidiest and lightest in the Falklands, he told me how he thought the military presence had changed expectations in the Islands. He said that his total profit from the farm was the equivalent of a sergeant's pay, without all the hidden allowances a serviceman expects to receive. This was roughly the same as what the matron who was also acting as hospital administrator would earn at the King Edward Memorial Hospital in Stanley. He said the gross earnings of the farm were about comparable to a major's pay. Such considerations were bound to affect the outlook and expectations of farmers and workers in the Falklands, he suggested.

A friend of Kevin and Diane with direct experience of both civilian and military administration in Port Stanley, has suggested to me an immediate remedy to improve civilian-military relations: 'It is a lesson we have had to learn again and again from the Malayan Emergency on,' he said. 'You really have to have one man in charge, a supremo with the clout and weight to tell both the civilian and military sides of the fence what to do,' and he suggested a man of the ability and standing of Sir Gerald Templer in Malaya or Hugh Foot, later Lord Caradon, in Cyprus.

The military presence will only diminish in numbers when the new airport is opened and diplomatic relations are restored with Argentina; and at the time of writing the first now looks likely to take place well before the second. Relations with Argentina now haunt the thoughts of

325

most Islanders though they are infrequently a topic of conversation. After the shock of the fire at the hospital, the two civilian doctors, Alison Bleaney and David Edwardes-Moss, both noticed that Islanders were talking a lot more about the conflict than before, and they reminisced about 'the war', as they call it, rather than discuss the fire.

In the image the Falklanders have of themselves and their own community and the image they present to the outside world there is paradox. The Islanders feel British, and yet they are of the southern hemisphere with cultural similarities and sometimes direct blood ties with the families of Scottish, Welsh, Irish and English extraction in Patagonia and mainland South America. Following the conflict there has been, naturally, more emphasis on the British identity than on the South Atlantic one, though sometimes the Kelpers have found precious little in common with Britons who have come among them since 1982. In a way, the Kelpers are a group of *colons,* to use Franz Fanon's formulation, like the *pieds-noirs* of Algeria, in a place where there are no *colonisés.*

Lord Shackleton noted in his first Report that despite its small size the Falklands community was divided – between native Kelpers and settlers and expatriates; between the people of East Falkland and those of the West; and between the people of camp and the citizens of Stanley. There has been small sense of a coherent national identity. This lies at the heart of the paradox of the external relations of the Falkland Islands, and in particular the dispute between Britain and Argentina over their sovereignty. For the power that claims the Islands in the name of national self-determination, Argentina, has adopted in practice a far more imperialist stance than Britain, the actual imperial power running the colony. Britain, for her part, is trying to cultivate an attitude of independence and national self-determination among the people of the Islands themselves.

Sovereignty is likely to be the sticking-point of any negotiations between Buenos Aires and London for the foreseeable future. The claim to the Falklands, the Islands of the 'Andean Loop', of the Scotia Sea and the Antarctic Peninsula form part of the 'machismo' of Argentine nationalism, the virile image of a youthful and increasingly powerful South American state. In the recent past British diplomats appeared to have underestimated this aspect of the Falklands dispute. The former Argentine foreign minister Nicanor Costa Méndez is reported to have said that whenever he met his British counterpart in the corridors of the UN it was if the Falklands question was item number 271 on his list of priorities, always destined to stay somewhere near the bottom of his 'in' tray. When negotiators from the British and Argentine foreign ministries met in New York at the end of February 1982 the British thought they had effectively postponed discussion of the sovereignty question, but the tactic was one of the links in the train of events leading up to the outbreak of hostilities just over a month later.

Similarly, the British negotiating team endeavoured to have the sovereignty issue put to one side when a meeting was held in Berne in July 1984 between senior diplomats to discuss the possibility of restoring normal diplomatic relations. The meeting had been prepared carefully for months through the good offices of the Swiss and the Brazilians. The British hoped that the Argentines would raise the sovereignty question at the beginning of the talks, the claim would be minuted and then discussion would move to more practical matters. These would have involved the British lifting the Protection Zone round the Islands and the Argentines making a formal declaration of the cessation of hostilities. Both sides would then discuss the joint management of a fishery protection zone round the Falklands. However, even this was too much for some diehard Kelpers, like the London Representative Adrian Monk who said, 'Why give away the title-deeds to your property if you don't have to?' The talks were aborted almost before they were begun. On the first morning of what was to be a two-day gathering, it was announced from Buenos Aires that the foreign minister, Señor Dante Caputo, would make an announcement that afternoon, local time. His message in simple language was 'no talks about sovereignty, no deal on normal relations'.

The British team returned to London quite perceptibly shaken. In the words of one of them, they realised finally that President Alfonsín's government intended to stick to the principle of what the American professional diplomats inelegantly refer to as 'linkage'; in other words, any deal over the future of the Falklands would be tied to serious discussion of the transfer of sovereignty over the Islands from London to Buenos Aires. This left the Falkland Islands and the Kelpers isolated from the nearest piece of South American mainland. It also left the diplomats who look after their destiny in London with furrowed brows. One told me that he feared that 'the heavies might now be beginning to feel their oats', referring to President Alfonsín's softer line towards the military hierarchy in Argentina. General Spacie himself has said that there is still a real military threat to the Falklands from Argentina, as the air force in particular is now stronger and better equipped than it was in early 1982. Few at BFFI in Port Stanley anticipate another all-out amphibious assault but they say there is some possibility of an aerial attack.

President Alfonsín's government appears to have adopted a principle of linkage not only in the way it presents the claim to sovereignty but also in the nature of the claim. During his visit to Spain and France in the summer of 1984 the President himself stated plainly that the claim to the Falklands was part of that to South Georgia, the islands of the Scotia Sea and Antarctica. Britain, too, under Mrs Thatcher's administration, in a typically British pragmatic manner seems to have forged a similar form of linkage. For Mrs Thatcher's policies of offering extra funds to BAS, the extension of the period of service of HMS *Endurance*, if not the length of her intermittent patrols in Antarctica, and maintaining the British military presence and the principle of British sovereignty in the Falklands have become inextricably interwoven, not least in the mind of Mrs Thatcher herself.

Following the conflict of 1982 one body of opinion in Britain suggested that there might be ways of uncoupling the different parts of British policy in the South Atlantic and Antarctica. Lord Carrington, the former foreign secretary, was said to be interested in the possibility of South Georgia becoming part of the Antarctic Treaty, drawing the Treaty boundary at the natural barrier of the Antarctic Convergence in the South Atlantic rather than at 60°S. The counter-argument was that this would entitle both Russia and America to build bases on the island, and that they would continue to maintain them if the Antarctic Treaty collapsed. As I have suggested in the first part of this book, the conundrum of the aftermath of the South Atlantic conflict of 1982 and the policy of Fortress Falklands could become part of a wider drama of the southern oceans and Antarctica.

If current policy over the Falklands fails, the whole of Britain's stance on Antarctica and the Southern Ocean could be threatened. Until recently, Britain's presence in Antarctica was under the noonday shadow of Empire and imperialist aspiration. But today the British presence is maintained largely by the scientists and assistants of BAS who are there primarily for the sake of 'doing science', though lately both the British government and corporations like BP have shown interest in the long-term commercial prospects for the Antarctic region. Since 1982 the Falklands have come to hold a pivotal position in policy towards the Antarctic continent and the Southern Ocean; previously, the Islands were peripheral in such considerations, except in both World Wars. Because of this central role, little official mention has been made either by the British government or the principal party of opposition about compensation for Falklanders for abandoning the Islands to settle elsewhere. Nor do the architects of Britain's policy in the Southern Ocean appear to contemplate seriously giving up the Falklands to Argentina, and use instead South Georgia as Britain's 'gateway to Antarctica', in Sir Ernest Shackleton's words. Such a policy would entail digging in with a substantial garrison on Stromness and Cumberland Bay, building a naval port and airstrip, and so giving rise to a 'Fortress South Georgia' policy.

Since April 1982 the Islands have absorbed enormous feelings of interest, pride, dismay and rage from a wide spectrum of the British population; continuing policy towards the colony and reaction to that policy make an interesting commentary on Britain herself in the eighties. The Falklands in a way are the recessive gene in British colonial history, the sport or throwback at the end of the line. It is surely something of a paradox that nearly £3.5 billion will have been spent on the defence of 2000 people by a medium-sized industrial power 8000 miles away, which also has to cope with a declining economy and three million unemployed.

When he reached 71°10'S on 30 January 1774, James Cook saw a brilliant glow in the southern sky above the pack ice. His is one of the best descriptions of a phenomenon known as iceblink, a reflection in the sky which indicates distant expanses of ice. Cook speculated that the ice might run as far south as to the Pole itself.

Today something of the political or historical equivalent of iceblink can now be seen in the future of Antarctica and the Southern Ocean. As more countries seek direct access to the enormous frozen continent and the oceans round it and more claim rights to its riches through the UN and the non-aligned movement a new political, scientific, and commercial era in Antarctic history is unfolding. Britain's policy and interest in Antarctica, the tradition founded by James Cook, is now linked to her interest and policies in the Falklands and the Scotia Sea. The Antarctic Treaty is unique for the way it embraces thirty-one nations, including America and Russia. It also holds inactive a treaty in which three powers, Argentina, Chile and Britain, claim the same piece of land in the Graham Land and Palmer Peninsula.

One could liken this territorial dispute to a fossil, a piece of diplomatic palaeontology like the skeleton of a delicate fern or the giant penguin found in the Antarctic ice-cap. But it is more like the unpredictable volcano of Deception Island; it could become active again and erupt should the Antarctic Treaty collapse under the pressure of individual nations and corporations making a grab for commercial gain from the natural resources of the continent and its Ocean.

At the end of a visit to the headquarters of BAS in Cambridge, the director, Dr Richard Laws, turned and said, almost as an afterthought, 'It's a pity it took a war to make people realise that there is something beyond the Falklands.'

# Bibliography

**ANTARCTICA AND THE SOUTHERN OCEAN** (OP = out of print)

Honnywill, E. *The Challenge of Antarctica* (A. Nelson, ne, 1984).

King, H. G. R. *The Antarctic* (Blandford, 1969, OP).

**NAVIGATION, ICE, THE OCEANS AND WEATHER**

The Royal Navy *The Mariner's Handbook* (Hydrographer of the Navy, Taunton, Somerset, 1979, in conjunction with Supplement No. 2, 1983).

The Royal Navy *The Antarctic Pilot* (Hydrographer of the Navy, Taunton, Somerset, 4th ed. 1974, in conjunction with Supplement No. 6, 1983).

**THE HISTORY, GEOGRAPHY, POLITICS AND ECOLOGY OF ANTARCTICA**

Brewster, B./Friends of the Earth *Antarctica: Wilderness at Risk* (A. H. Reed: G. Philip, 1982).

Cherry-Garrard, A. *The Worst Journey in the World* (Scott's last expedition) (Penguin, 1983).

Christie, E. W. H. *The Antarctic Problem: an historical and political study* (Allen and Unwin, 1951, OP)

Cook, F. A. *Through the First Antarctic Night* (1898–9 *Belgica* Expedition) (Heinemann, 1900, OP).

Cook, Capt. James *Voyages of Discovery* (Dent, Everyman Library, 1906, reissued 1976)

Darlington, J. *My Antarctic Honeymoon* (the Ronne 1947 Expedition) (Muller, 1957, OP).

Fuchs, Sir V., and Hillary, Sir E. *The Crossing of Antarctica: Trans-Antarctic Expedition 1957/58* (Cassell, 1958, OP).

Fuchs, Sir V. *Of Ice and Men* (a history of the FIDS and BAS) (A. Nelson, 1982).

Headland, R. K. *The Island of South Georgia* (CUP, 1984).

Huntford, R. *Scott and Amundsen* (Pan, ne, 1983).

Lansing, A. *Endurance* (Hodder, 1959, OP).

Mitchell, B. *Frozen Stakes* (International Institute for Environment and Development, 1983).

Orrego Vicuna, F. (ed.) *Antarctic Resources Policy* (CUP, 1983).

Scott, R. F. *Scott's Last Expedition: the Journals* (Methuen, 1983).

Shackleton, Sir E. *South* (Century, 1983).

Worsley, F. A. *The Great Antarctic Rescue* (Times Books, 1977, OP; Sphere, 1979, OP).

*The Antarctic Treaty Handbook 1983* (from affiliated members of the Treaty).

## THE FALKLANDS AND THEIR HISTORY
Cawkell, M. *The Falkland Story 1592–1982* (A. Nelson, 1983).

Chatwin, B. *In Patagonia* (Cape, 1977; Picador, 1980).

Mainwaring, M. *From the Falklands to Patagonia: a record of pioneer settlement* (Allison and Busby, 1983).

Smith, J. *Seventy-four Days* (a settler's view of the 1982 conflict) (Century, 1984).

Trehearne, M. *Falkland Heritage: a record of pioneer settlement* (A. H. Stockwell, Ilfracombe, 1978).

## OFFICIAL PUBLICATIONS FROM HMSO
Franks, Lord *Falkland Islands Review: report of a committee of Privy counsellors* (Cmnd 8787) (1983).

House of Commons Defence Committee *The Handling of Press and Public Information during the Falklands Conflict*, 2 vols (1982).

Shackleton, Rt Hon. the Lord *Economic Survey of the Falkland Islands* (1976).

Shackleton, Rt Hon. the Lord *Falkland Islands Economic Study, 1982* (Cmnd 8653) (1982).

*From the Falkland Islands government on the authority of HE the Civil Commissioner:* Report of the Commission of Inquiry into the fire at the King Edward Memorial Hospital, Stanley, on 10 April 1984.


*Post-1982 books useful for background to subsequent Falklands policy:*

Barnett, A. *Iron Britannia* (Allison and Busby, 1982).

Harris, R. *Gotcha: media, the government and the Falklands crisis* (Faber, 1983).

Hastings, M., and Jenkins, S. *Battle for the Falklands* (Pan, 1983).

Pearce, J., and Honeywell, M. *Falklands/Malvinas: whose crisis?* (Latin American Bureau, 1982)

Strange, Ian J. *The Falkland Islands* (David & Charles, 3rd ed., 1983)

# Index